THE BOOK OF THE
GERMAN SHEPHERD DOG

Title page: 1971 Grand Victor Champion Mannix of Fran-Jo, ROM. Owned by Joan and Fran Ford.

THE BOOK OF THE
GERMAN SHEPHERD DOG

by Anna Katherine Nicholas
with special sections by Helen Miller Fisher
and Dr. Joseph P. Sayres

Dedication

To "Derby" and to "Lady" who, back in the early 1920's, taught me to love the breed and also taught me that some Shepherds really do consider themselves to be lap dogs!

Distributed in the UNITED STATES by T.F.H. Publications, Inc., 211 West Sylvania Avenue, Neptune City, NJ 07753; in CANADA by H & L Pet Supplies Inc., 27 Kingston Crescent, Kitchener, Ontario N2B 2T6; Rolf C. Hagen Ltd., 3225 Sartelon Street, Montreal 382 Quebec; in ENGLAND by T.F.H. (Great Britain) Ltd., 11 Ormside Way, Holmethorpe Industrial Estate, Redhill, Surrey RH1 2PX; in AUSTRALIA AND THE SOUTH PACIFIC by T.F.H. (Australia) Pty. Ltd., Box 149, Brookvale 2100 N.S.W., Australia; in NEW ZEALAND by Ross Haines & Son, Ltd., 18 Monmouth Street, Grey Lynn, Auckland 2 New Zealand; in SINGAPORE AND MALAYSIA by MPH Distributors Pte., 71-77 Stamford Road, Singapore 0617; in the PHILIPPINES by Bio-Research, 5 Lippay Street, San Lorenzo Village, Makati, Rizal; in SOUTH AFRICA by Multipet Pty. Ltd., 30 Turners Avenue, Durban 4001. Published by T.F.H. Publications Inc., Ltd., the British Crown Colony of Hong Kong.

Contents

A head-study of Ch. Cuno von der Teufelslache, SchH III, FH, ROM, owned by Helen Miller Fisher, Lake Elmo, Minnesota.

In Appreciation

A good number of prominent and dedicated German Shepherd Dog fanciers have helped to make this book of interest and value to our readers, for which the author is grateful. The assistance I have received has been far beyond my expectations; thus I am especially happy that it has turned out so well, and I hope that all who have participated in making it a valuable book will share my pleasure.

Helen Miller Fisher, that knowledgeable, dedicated, talented lady who is one of America's leading judges of Working Dogs, has written for us an excellent chapter on judging, along with providing some priceless photographs and helpful information.

Mary Schuetzler has provided invaluable additions to our wide collection of photographs of famous German Shepherd Dogs. This is the lady, owner of Schutzenhaus German Shepherds, who with her late husband, Art, originated the idea of putting together a collection of photographs of all of the American Grand Victors and Grand Victrixes, arranging the collection on cards in a beautiful display and exhibiting these cards for the pleasure and education of current fanciers at each of the German Shepherd Dog Club of America National Specialties—an inestimable service to the breed and one which we do not believe is equalled by fanciers of any other breed. Mrs. Schuetzler's devotion to Shepherds by no means stops with this project; she is ever ready to assist in whatever effort she feels will prove beneficial to these dogs, and our

readers and I owe her a deep vote of thanks for her help in the photographic material we've been able to assemble.

Cappy Pottle is another person who really pitched in with very worthwhile assistance; she permitted me to borrow her German Shepherd Dog Club of America Registry of Merit *Yearbooks* of the past ten years—invaluable in looking up the great producers and their progeny! They were tremendously informative and her permission to use whatever I wished of the material was most gratefully received.

Connie Beckhardt provided many names and addresses of people to contact. Helen Hess and Joan Ford went all out going through their kennel records for us, as did Mary Roberts.

Then we have Dr. Joseph Sayres' always outstanding "Veterinarian's Corner" geared especially toward German Shepherd Dogs.

Our most heartfelt thanks to Marcia Foy for proofreading and doing other helpful "odd jobs" in connection with the book; to each and every person who has loaned us even a single valuable picture; and to those who have answered questions and expressed opinions when requested to do so, which includes the Ken Rayner family, various members of the Board of the German Shepherd Dog Club of America, and countless others. We couldn't have done it without you, and we hope you will find the results of our effort not only worthy but also outstanding.

Anna Katherine Nicholas

The author as a little girl in the 1920's with her parents and the family German Shepherd Dog, Derby.

About the Author

Since early childhood, Anna Katherine Nicholas has been involved with dogs. Her first pets were a Boston Terrier, an Airedale, and a German Shepherd Dog. Then, in 1925, came the first Pekingese, a gift from a family friend who raised them. Now her home is shared with a Miniature Poodle and a dozen or so Beagles, including her noted Best in Show and National Specialty winner, Champion Rockaplenty's Wild Oats, an internationally famous Beagle sire, who as a show dog was top Beagle in the nation in 1973. She also owns Champion Foyscroft True Blue Lou, Foyscroft Aces Are Wild, and, in co-ownership with Marcia Foy who lives with her, Champion Foyscroft Triple Mitey Migit.

Miss Nicholas is best known in the Dog Fancy as a writer and as a judge. Her first magazine articles were about Pekingese, published in *Dog News* magazine about 1930. This was followed by a widely acclaimed breed column, "Peeking at the Pekingese," which appeared continuously for at least two decades, originally in *Dogdom* and, when that magazine ceased to exist, in *Popular Dogs*.

During the 1940's she was Boxer columnist for the American Kennel Club *Gazette* and for *Boxer Briefs*. More recently, many of her articles of general interest to the Dog Fancy have appeared in *Popular Dogs, Pure-Bred Dogs, American Kennel Gazette*, and *Show Dogs*. She is presently a featured columnist for *Dog World, Canine Chronicle*, and *Kennel Review* in the United States and *The Dog Fancier* in Canada. Her *Dog World* column, "Here, There and Everywhere," was the Dog Writers Association of America selection for Best Series in a dog magazine which was awarded her for 1979. And for 1981 her feature article, "Faster Is Not Better" published in *Canine Chronicle* was one of four nominated for the Best Feature Article Award from the Dog

Writers Association. She also has been a columnist for *Poodle Showcase, Dogs in Canada,* and *World of the Working Dog*.

It was during the 1930's that Miss Nicholas' first book, *The Pekingese*, was published by the Judy Publishing Company. This book completely sold out two editions and is now an eagerly sought-after collector's item, as is her *The Skye Terrier Book*, published through the Skye Terrier Club of America during the early 1960's.

Miss Nicholas won the Dog Writers Association of America award in 1970 for the Best Technical Book of the Year with her *Nicholas Guide to Dog Judging*. Then in 1979 the revision of this book again won the Dog Writers Association of America Best Technical Book Award, the first time ever that a revision has been so honored by this association.

In the early 1970's Miss Nicholas co-authored with Joan Brearley five breed books for T.F.H. Publications. These were *This is the Bichon Frise, The Wonderful World of Beagles and Beagling, The Book of the Pekingese, This is the Skye Terrier,* and *The Book of the Boxer. The Wonderful World of Beagles and Beagling* won a Dog Writers Association of America Honorable Mention Award the year that it was published.

In addition to her four Dog Writers Association of America awards, Miss Nicholas received in the late 1970's and again in 1982, the Gaines "Fido" as Dog Writer of the Year and she has two "Winkies" from *Kennel Review* as Dog Journalist of the Year on separate occasions.

All of Miss Nicholas' recent releases from T.F.H. have been received with enthusiasm and acclaim; these include *Successful Dog Show Exhibiting, The Book of the Rottweiler, The Book of the Poodle, The Book of the Labrador Retriever, The Book of the English Springer Spaniel,* and *The Book of the Golden Retriever*.

Can. Grand Victor, Am. and Can. Ch. Ulk Wikingerblut, SchH III, FH. CACIB, ROM, Select, sired by Holland Sieger, U.S. Victor Ch. Troll v. Richterbach, SchH III, ex Natja Wikingerblut, SchH I, and whelped November 26th 1956. Breeder, Erich Sander, Bad Essen, Germany. Here receiving congratulations from David Upright, President of the Harbor Cities Kennel Club, upon winning the Best in Show award over 2,530 entries, America's largest outdoor show that year, 1961. Mary Roberts is the happy handler of this magnificent dog co-owned with her husband, Ralph.

CHAPTER ONE

History and Development in Germany

The noted artist Ward Binks made this 1935 portrait of the magnificent imported Ch. Giralda's Dewet von der Starrenburg, a son of German Seiger Odin v. Stolzenfels, one of the foundation dogs of Giralda Shepherds. A Best in Show winner, he was owned by Mrs. M. Hartley Dodge of Giralda Farm, Madison, New Jersey.

The magnificent present-day German Shepherd Dog is, as one assumes from the name of the breed, a product of Germany—a quite modern product in the world of purebred dog history. Although the breed has roots which reach back in time to the ancient Persian Sheepdogs and the early herding dogs who guarded the shepherds' flocks so capably, German Shepherd Dogs actually were perfected and brought to the stage with which we are acquainted almost entirely during the twentieth century. His progenitors were an assorted collection of several different types of canines, each best fitted for the conditions and area where his services were performed. The mutual characteristics of these dogs were strength, intelligence, soundness, and stamina, all of which equipped the dog for the greatest, most complete efficiency as he worked. Appearance was of little or no consequence and therefore varied widely.

The passage of time and the growth of civilization brought with them an increased interest in the herding dogs as individuals. People able to travel about more freely visited in areas other than their own, making new friends and learning

about life there. Those involved with animals paid heed to one another's herding dogs, which resulted in a new recognition and admiration for the qualities of intelligence and performance setting some of the dogs ahead of others in the efficient handling of their task. The desire to breed one's own dogs to those with superior qualities naturally followed, and the offspring of these litters were highly valued.

As awareness increased, so did a desire to learn more about the dogs. This resulted in the formation of small groups of people sharing a mutual interest and a desire to increase their knowledge by the exchange of opinions and ideas. This is, of course, similar to the motivation for joining a present-day specialty club, of which these groups were very likely forerunners. This action led to the keeping of breeding records and to the sort of planning which brought about a gradual uniformity of type not previously noted.

It was early in the 1890's that the first German Shepherd Dog Club was formed in Germany, dedicated to the best interests of the native German shepherds' dogs. This was an ill-fated attempt at organization as it turned out, since this

11

group, called the Phylax Society, survived only briefly. Its short existence was not entirely without result, however, as it did succeed in arousing a greater consciousness of the potential of the herding dogs, the importance of selective breeding, and more awareness of type along with efficiency.

The Foundation of the Breed

It was at the turn of the century, on April 3rd 1899 to be exact, when two gentlemen attended one of the earliest dog shows for all breeds ever held in Germany, at Karlsruhe, and came away not only with a dog but also with an idea for a club for the breed. These men were Rittmeister Max von Stephanitz and his friend Herr Artur Meyer, and they had come to the event to see what Shepherds might be present as their interest in these breeds had been quite strongly drawn by some outstanding herding performances they had just previously seen in Thuringia, Saxony, and Württemberg. They were not to be disappointed at this show, for almost immediately their attention focused on a medium-sized wolf-like yellow dog, never dreaming at the time, we are sure, that this would go down in history as the foundation of the German

Ch. Giralda's Teuthilde v. Hagenschiess, SchH II, imported for her Giralda German Shepherds by Mrs. M. Hartley Dodge.

Ch. Afra v. Kollerskitten of Giralda, another foundation import for the Giralda Shepherds owned by Mrs. M. Hartley Dodge at Giralda Farm. This portrait made in 1936 by Ward Binks.

Shepherd Dog as the breed would become. Noting with satisfaction the behavior and splendid appearance of this animal, they made inquiries of the handler, and a closer scrutiny of the dog, which only confirmed their first impression. The dog was not a show dog, the handler explained, but a true working Shepherd used for the herding of sheep. Then and there von Stephanitz purchased this dog (whom we understand had previously passed through several ownerships) and in his excitement and dreams for the future, on that very same day von Stephanitz, and Herr Meyer, decided to form the *Verein für Deutsche Schäferhunde, S.V.*, naming von Stephanitz the organization's first President. His new purchase, with the name changed from Hektor Linksrhein to Horand von Grafrath, received the designation S.Z.1, the first German Shepherd Dog to be registered with the new Verein. Horand became the foundation of von Stephanitz's Grafrath Kennels and of the new era for the breed. The Verein grew to become a tremendous power in the canine world and the largest specialty club, its individual membership eventually exceeding fifty thousand persons and its affiliated clubs numbering more than six hundred. The Verein was a charter member of the *Deutschen Kartell für Hundewesen*, and von Stephanitz's influence in the canine world was inestimable.

The Verein immediately started to keep a stud book for the breed and early on began to circulate a semi-monthly publication, *The Gazette*, among its members. It initiated its own Sieger shows, at which one dog and one bitch annually were selected Sieger and Siegerin. The first of these winners, in 1899, were Jorg von der Krone and Lisie von Schwenningen, respectively.

The Verein, and von Stephanitz through his interest therein, held a tight rein over all German Shepherd Dog breeding throughout Germany. The von Stephanitz motto of "utility and intelligence" was closely adhered to, with the Verein holding jurisdiction over which dogs and bitches could be used for breeding purposes; which dogs and which bitches were suitable for breeding to one another; the number of and which puppies could be kept, and raised, from each litter; and what the breeding age limitations were to be on dogs and bitches. In fact, the German breeder was merely a tool in the hands of the Verein (and thus of von Stephanitz). Breeders accepted this situation because this type of authority was in keeping with living conditions in Germany at the time, and the system could never be said to have been less than successful, as one contemplates the results which took place within a comparatively short time in the breeding of German Shepherds.

While herding had been the Shepherd's traditional occupation, progress was making it of less importance as time passed. It was von Stephanitz who recognized the necessity of involving

Ch. Falko von der Diederichsenstiftung, Sch III, FH, C.D., C.D.X., U.D.T., the Top Working Dog of Europe in 1951 with his American owner, Helen Miller Fisher.

This beautiful German import, Mike von der Wienerau, owned by Gerlinde Hockla, was never shown in the United States but was a valuable asset to her kennel.

these dogs in other fields of usefulness, and he persuaded the government to accept some of them for police work. It took a bit of doing, as the authorities were at first inclined to view the suggestion with amusement; but von Stephanitz, with his persistence, finally won out. The results speak for themselves, as the success of the venture is well known around the world, and German Shepherds have distinguished themselves in many forms of service, both in times of war and in peace.

Other of von Stephanitz's efforts on behalf of his beloved breed include the writing of a most impressive book, *The German Shepherd Dog in Word and Picture*, which was translated and widely sold around the world during the 1920's. Now a collector's item, this book belongs in the library of every Shepherd fancier. It was in some ways a controversial book, and parts of it are now outdated; but it is, nonetheless, a worthwhile book which contains useful, valuable information for the reader.

Von Stephanitz was a prolific writer, having had published hundreds of articles dealing with Shepherd-related subjects. His lifework and dearest ambition was to see perfected a sound, reliable, able, and intelligent working German Shepherd which could reproduce itself through judicious breeding. His tight breeding program and indomitable determination served him and

This is the lovely bitch, Debora von Weimar, who in 1920 came from Germany to Mr. Peter A. B. Widener, Jr.'s Joselle Kennels (in the United States) along with the notable dog German and Austrian Sieger, later Am. Ch. Dolf von Dustern-brook, the two having been purchased as a package deal for the sum of ten thousand dollars! This kennel was noted for the excellence of its bitches, of which Debora is a prime example. Photo courtesy of Janet Churchill.

his breed well: It can be said, I am certain without fear of contradiction, that by the time of his death, in April 1936, his goals had been attained.

The dog, Horand von Grafrath, like the man, von Stephanitz, was destined to become a dominating influence in the shaping of this breed. Horand's son, Hektor von Schwaben, was the second German Shepherd Sieger, in 1900, repeating the honor in 1901. Like his sire, Hektor became a stud force with which to reckon, his sons including Beowulf, Pilot III, and Heinz von Starkenburg. The first two were brothers, from Thekla 1 von der Krone, a Horand daughter; this breeding was typical of von Stephanitz's belief in close inbreeding or line-breeding as the means of perfecting the qualities he considered essential. It must be noted that von Stephanitz and his friends were continuously alert for bitches deemed appropriate for Horand, the criteria being sufficient similarity to this dog to assure reproduction of his type. The discovery of a bitch fulfilling the requirements could lead to several repetitions of the breeding, depending on the success of the initial venture and the quality of each ensuing litter. Freya von Grafrath, S.Z.7, was such a bitch, with her total litters by Horand numbering four.

Horand's son, Beowulf, distinguished himself particularly well through the quality of his daughters. Through him came the line to Geri von Oberklamm, to Cito Bergerslust, and to Attila Argus. Another Horand son, Pilot III, was the grandsire of Graf Eberhard von Hohen-Esp, foundation of the Kriminalpolizei and von Boll lines, which led out to Eichenpark and Reidekenburg, Mohr Secretainerie, and Harras von der Juch. But it was the third Horand son, Heinz von Starkenburg, whose impact was the most notable as we study the development of the breed.

It was a litter from Heinz and a bitch named Bella von Starkenburg, born in November 1903, that included a black dog puppy later named Roland von Starkenburg. So vast a genetical improvement was noted in this Horand grandson that eventually he was used as the model for the breed. His influence on the breed was so extensive that it is almost impossible, if one traces back sufficiently far, not to find him in the background of a vast majority of our current famous Shepherds.

His son Hettel Uckermark was generally considered to be the finest of the Shepherds sired by Roland. The Sieger of 1909, he became the sire

Ch. Argus v. Schlosskessflsweiher of Giralda, an early importation of the 1920's-1930's brought to start the German Shepherd breeding program at Mrs. M. Hartley Dodge's Giralda Farm in New Jersey. Portrait by Ward Binks.

of Alex von Westfalenheim (from Bella von der Leine) who became the sire of the renowned 1920 Sieger and National Grand Champion Erich von Grafenwerth (from Bianka von Riedekenburg). Erich's veins thus carried the blood of Hettel, Dewet, Krone, and Roland lines; and he was a dog from whom an imposing number of greats descended. He was a double grandson of Hettel Uckermark and a grandson of that most highly praised bitch, Flora Berkemeyer. He came to the United States to join the Hamilton Farm Kennels, where his influence as a producer was inestimable.

The great bitch Flora Berkemeyer whose influence on future generations of German Shepherds, both in Germany and in the United States, was inestimable.

Gerlinde Hockla brought this dog, Dargo Blitzgreiger, with her from Germany in 1959.

Above: Ch. Cito v.d. Markfeste of Giralda, an early importation used in the founding of the Giralda German Shepherds by Mrs. M. Hartley Dodge, Madison, New Jersey. From the late 1920's- early 1930's period. **Below:** Ch. Barda v. Hagenschiess of Giralda, imported foundation Shepherd at Giralda Farm, Mrs. M. Hartley Dodge.

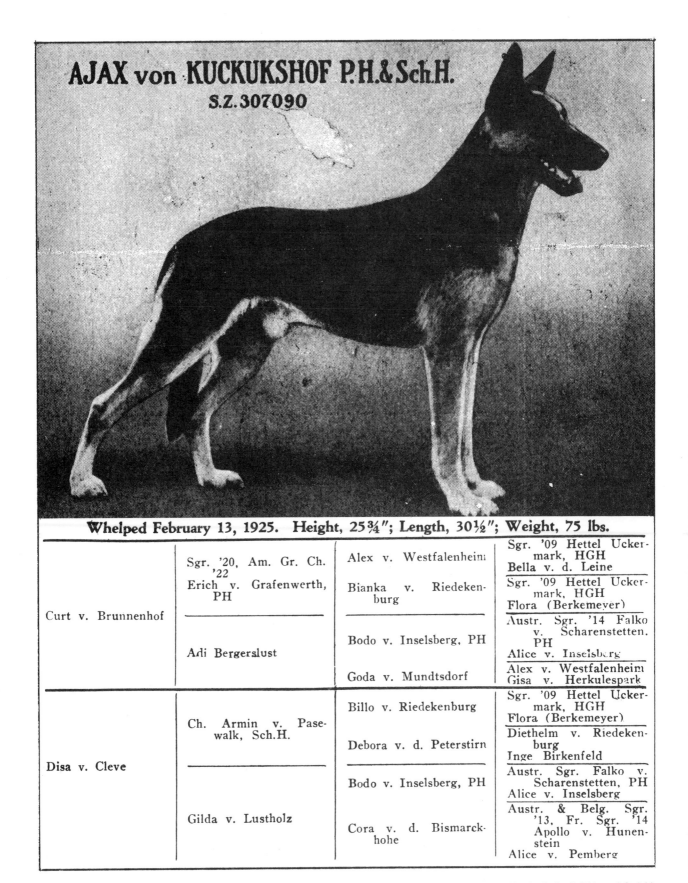

AJAX von KUCKUKSHOF P.H.& Sch.H.
S.Z. 307090

Whelped February 13, 1925. Height, 25¾″; Length, 30½″; Weight, 75 lbs.

Curt v. Brunnenhof	Sgr. '20, Am. Gr. Ch. '22 Erich v. Grafenwerth, PH	Alex v. Westfalenheim	Sgr. '09 Hettel Uckermark, HGH Bella v. d. Leine
		Bianka v. Riedekenburg	Sgr. '09 Hettel Uckermark, HGH Flora (Berkemeyer)
	Adi Bergerslust	Bodo v. Inselsberg, PH	Austr. Sgr. '14 Falko v. Scharenstetten, PH Alice v. Inselsberg
		Goda v. Mundtsdorf	Alex v. Westfalenheim Gisa v. Herkulespark
Disa v. Cleve	Ch. Armin v. Pasewalk, Sch.H.	Billo v. Riedekenburg	Sgr. '09 Hettel Uckermark, HGH Flora (Berkemeyer)
		Debora v. d. Peterstirn	Diethelm v. Riedekenburg Inge Birkenfeld
	Gilda v. Lustholz	Bodo v. Inselsberg, PH	Austr. Sgr. Falko v. Scharenstetten, PH Alice v. Inselsberg
		Cora v. d. Bismarckhohe	Austr. & Belg. Sgr. '13, Fr. Sgr. '14 Apollo v. Hunenstein Alice v. Pemberg

Photograph and pedigree of an importation from Germany during the 1920's. Ajax von Kuckukshof, PH and SchH, SZ 307090, was Germany's 1926 Youth Class Sensational Winner, who came to this country under the ownership of Louis H. Storz, Omaha, Nebraska. Courtesy of Janet Churchill.

German Youth Seiger Klodo aus der Eremitenklause with his son Ch. Volker vom Schaeferleben, sire of Blanka and Biene v. Finsternwald owned by Gerlinde Hockla.

German Working Dog Degrees and Ratings

As you read the pages of this book, you will find many abbreviations of German Working Dog degrees and ratings following the names of German Shepherds who were raised or are owned in Germany. For your better understanding of them, we give the following information.

The most frequently seen abbreviation is SchH, SchH I, SchH II, or SchH III. These indicate that the dog has passed one or all of the tests for which each schutzhund degree is awarded. These tests, or trials, are somewhat like obedience trials in the United States, although the two differ in many ways and the schutzhund tests are more stringent. At various levels, the dogs are tested for general obedience, tracking or trailing, and protection; and each degree indicates that the dog has gone one step higher until Schutzhund III has been attained.

Other Working Dog ratings used in Germany (and what they indicate) are as follows:

BIH—a guide dog for a blind person, or *Blindenfuhrer Hund.*
DH—a service dog, or *Diensthund.*
FH—a trailing dog, or *Fahrtenhund.*
GrH—a border patrol dog, or *Grenzenhund.*
HGH—a herding dog, or *Herdengrebrauchshund.*
KrH—a war dog, or *Kriegshund.*
LawH—an avalanche dog, or *Lawinenhund.*
MH—an army dog, or *Militathund.*
PH—a dog trained for police work, or a *Polizeihund.*
SH—a Red Cross dog, or *Sanitätshund.*
ZPr—a dog recommended for breeding (having successfully passed Breed Survey), or *Zucht prufung.*

18

Ch. Odin von Busecker-Schloss, ROM, owned by Mr. and Mrs. Sydney F. Heckert, Hope Ranch, Santa Barbara, California. This half-brother to Sieger and Grand Victor Ch. Pfeffer von Bern, ROM, was by Dachs von Bern ex a Klodo von Boxberg granddaughter and was imported by the Heckerts in 1938. An important winner and a dominant stud dog, he was one of the early greats in the United States.

The Sieger and Siegerin titles, of course, are those accorded the dog and bitch chosen as outstanding in his and her sex at the annual Sieger show for the breed. This occasion is a true dog show spectacular in every sense of the word—a three-day event attended by literally thousands of German Shepherd fanciers from all over the world who have brought their dogs to compete or who have come just to see and study the proceedings.

The classification, divided by sex, consists of the Youth Class in which Shepherds competing are between twelve and eighteen months of age; the Young Dog Class, entered by Shepherds from eighteen to twenty-four months of age; and, most competitive of all, the Utility Class, for which Shepherds must be more than twenty-four months of age, must have previously attained at least one working degree, and must have received a rating of "SG" (*Sehr Gut*, or very good) or "V" (*Vorzüglich*, or excellent) at a

Landesgruppen (local club) or previous Sieger event. Puppies under twelve weeks of age are ineligible for the Sieger shows; they are judged at regional events specifically for this purpose.

Each dog is individually judged at the Sieger event. In order to become eligible to compete for a Select rating, and thus compete for the title of Sieger or Siegerin, a German Shepherd must have an "a" (accredited hips) stamp; a Schutzhund II degree or a Schutzhund III degree (unless this is their first year in the Excellent Select Class); a grade of "V" (*Vorzüglich*) or "VA" (*Vorzüglich Auslese*, or excellent select) on its performance and a passing grade in a test for courage conducted in an adjoining ring; a complete set of perfect teeth; and unless under three-and-a-half years of age, a *Körklasse* (Breeding Survey Class) rating of *Körklasse* 1 (the highest recommendation for breeding). Before selecting the Sieger and Siegerin, a pedigree study is often conducted, breed wardens' opinions are sought, and, in dogs several years or more of age, producing records also enter into consideration. Following all this the dog awarded VA-1 and the bitch awarded VA-1 are crowned Sieger and Siegerin, respectively.

German Siegers and Siegerins

The first Sieger and Siegerin in this breed gained the honor in 1899, the year in which the *Verein fur Deutsche Schaferhunde* (S.V.) came into being. The first Sieger was Jorg von der Krone, and his female counterpart was Lisie von Schwenningen. The dog was sired by a dog from the Sparwasser strain ex Nelly, and the bitch was by Basko Wachsmuth ex Schafermadchen von Hanau. Since that time, through 1937, a single Sieger and Siegerin were selected from a class. Then the feeling developed that perhaps doing it in this manner was overemphasizing the breeding behind that single dog and single bitch, and so in 1938 a new system was inaugurated: a group of dogs deemed especially suitable for breeding was chosen, and these became known as the select group, or the *Auslese*. This system was used until 1955, when the Sieger and Siegerin titles again became effective. All dogs chosen for the Excellent Select (*Vorzuglich Auslese*) group are rated, and the dog and the bitch who receive the VA-1 rating from the judge of their respective classes (the President of the S.V. is the judge of the males while the club's second-in-command judges the females) are crowned Sieger and Siegerin of that year. These titles were not awarded from 1974 through 1977; but in 1978, they were once again restored and they continue to be used at the present time.

For the benefit of historians, we include a list of the Siegers and Siegerins of Germany from 1900 through 1981. (In all cases the Sieger is listed first.)

1900—Hektor v. Schwaben
      Canna
1901—Hektor v. Schwaben
      Elsa v. Schwaben
1902—Peter v. Pritschen, KrH
      Hella v. Memmingen
1903—Roland v. Park
      Hella v. Memmingen

1904—Arlbert v. Grafrath
      Regina v. Schwaben
1905—Beowulf v. Nahegau
      Vefi v. Niedersachsen
1906—Roland v. Starkenburg
      Gretel Uckermark
1907—Roland v. Starkenburg
      Hulda v. Siegestor, PH
1908—Luchs v. Kalsmunt-Wetzlar
      Flora v.d. Warte, PH
1909—Hettel Uckermark, HGH
      Ella v. Erlenbrunnen
1910—Tell v.d. Kriminalpolizei
      Flora v.d. Kriminalpolizei
1911—Norbert v. Kohlwald, PH
      Hella v.d. Kriminalpolizei
1912—Norbert v. Kohlwald, PH
      Hella v.d. Kriminalpolizei

Ch. Alarich von Ermsleben, by Gotz v. Meisterrecht ex Amsel v. Ermsleben, was whelped in February 1948. He was brought to the United States from Germany and finished in 1950 and 1951. Owned by J. L. Sinykin, La Salle Kennels, and handled by Helen Miller Fisher.

Ch. Volker vom Schaeferleben, German import brought over by Ernest Loeb and owned by Rene Bennett, was handled by Gerlinde Hockla to a good win at the German Shepherd Dog Club of Maryland in 1966.

1913—Arno v.d. Eichenburg
    Frigga v. Scharenstatten

1914-1918—No awards were given during
    World War I.

1919—Dolf v. Dusternbrook, PH
    Anni v. Humboldtpark

1920—Erich v. Grafenwerth, PH
    Anni v. Humboldtpark

1921—Harras v.d. Juch, PH
    Nanthild v. Riedekenburg, PH

1922—Cito Bergerslust, SchH
    Asta v.d. Kaltenweide, SchH

1923—Cito v. Bergerslust, SchH
    Asta v.d. Kaltenweide, SchH

1924—Donar v. Overstolzen, SchH
    Asta v.d. Kaltenweide, SchH

1925—Klodo v. Boxberg, SchH
    Seffe v. Blasienberg, SchH

1926—Erich v. Glockenbrink, SchH
    Arna v.d. Ehrenzelle, SchH

1927—Arko v. Sadowaberg, SchH
    Elly v. Fuerstensteg, ZPr

1928—Erich v. Glockenbrink, SchH
    Katja v. Blasienberg, ZPr

1929—Utz v. Haus Schutting, ZPr
    Katja v. Blasienberg, ZPr

1930—Herold a.d. Niederlausitz, SchH
    Bella v. Klosterbrunn, ZPr

Pfeffer von Bern came to the U.S. in 1936, where he became Grand Victor twice, a ROM sire, and an important all-breed show winner. By Dachs von Bern ex Clara von Bern, he was strong in the Utz von Shutting line. John Gans, Pfeffer's owner, took him to Germany in 1937, where he won the Sieger title and Best in Show, thus defeating all the Siegers of every breed entered.

1931—Herold v.d. Niederlausitz, SchH
      Illa v. Helmholtz, ZPr

1932—Hussan v. Haus Schutting, ZPr
      Birke v. Blasienberg, ZPr

1933—Odin v. Stolzenfels, ZPr
      Jamba v. Haus Schutting, ZPr

1934—Cuno v. Georgentor, ZPr
      Grete a.d. Raumanskaule, SchH

1935—Jalk v. Pagensgrub, ZPr
      Stella v. Haus Schutting, SchH

1936—Arras a.d. Stadt-Velbert, ZPr
      Stella v. Haus Schutting, SchH

1937—Pfeffer v. Bern, ZPr, MH 1
      Traute v. Bern, ZPr

1938-1954—No Sieger or Siegerin was elected.

1955—Alf v. Nordfelsen
      Muschka v. Tempelblick

1956—Hardt v. Stuveschacht
      Lore v. Tempelblick

1957—Arno v. Haus Gersie
      Wilma v. Richterbach

1958—Condor v. Hohenstamm
      Mascha v. Stuhri-Gau

1959—Volker v. Zollgrenzschutz-Haus
      Assja v. Geigerklause

1960—Volker v. Zollgrenzschutz-Haus
      Inka Grubenstolz

1961—Veus v. Starrenburg
      Assie v. Hexengolk

1962—Mutz a.d. Kuckstrasse
      Rike v. Colonia Agrippina

1963—Ajax v. Haus Dexel
Maja v. Stolperland

1964—Zibu v. Haus Schutting
Blanka v. Kisskamp

1965—Hanko v. Herschmuhle
Landa v.d. Wienerau

1966—Basko v.d. Kahler Heide
Cita v. Gruchental

1967—Bodo v. Lierberg
Betty v. Glockenland

1968—Dido v.d. Werther Konigsalle
Rommy v. Driland

1969—Heiko v. Oranien Nassau
Connie v. Klosterbogen, SchH II

1970—Heiko v. Oranien Nassau
Diane v.d. Firnskuppe

1971—Arras v. Haus Helma
Kathia v.d. Rheinliese

1972—Marko v. Cellerland
Kathinka v.d. Netten Ecke

1973—Dick v. Adeloga
Erka v. Fiemereck

1974-1977—No Sieger or Siegerin title awarded.

1978—Canto v. Arminias
Ute v. Trienzbachtal

1979—Eros v.d. Malvenburg
Ute v. Trienzbachtal

1980—Axel v.d. Hainsterbach
Dixi v. Nato Platz

1981—Natan v.d. Pelztierfarm
Anusch v. Trienzbachtal

Ch. Bar v. Weiherturchen, ROM, won twelve Bests in Show, forty-six Group firsts, and 107 Bests of Breed. Owned by John and Barbara Schermerhorn, imported by Ernest Loeb, and handled by Denise Kodner. This was the famous "Bear Dog" who swept the boards so consistently during his show career.

The judge pictured here is of particular interest as he is the late Lloyd Brackett of Long Worth Kennels (Virginia McCoy, also active in Long Worth Kennels and a famous judge is his daughter); he is known as the "father of the German Shepherd Dog in the United States" and the author of an outstanding book on Shepherds. This occasion was the German Shepherd Dog Club of Wisconsin Specialty in 1959, where he is awarding honors to Mrs. Helen Fisher Miller with her Ch. Meadowmill's Appolo, a grandson of Ch. Cuno von der Teufelslache, SchH III, FH, ROM, a sire of tremendous importance to the breed in the United States.

CHAPTER TWO

Ch. Nero Affalter, PH, was a popular stud dog in the United States in the period immediately preceding the 1920's. Owned by the Elmview Kennels of Mr. Benjamin H. Throop, he was a dog upon whom opinion was sharply divided; some admired him for his great size while others considered him common. Nonetheless he was consistently used at stud.

Arrival and Development in the United States

Otto Gross, a widely known authority on dogs, is credited with having brought the first member of the German Shepherd breed, a bitch named Mira of Dalmore (or Mira of Offingen, as she had been known abroad), to the shores of the United States. Mira was whelped in 1905, sired by Beowulf ex Hella von Schwaben, and bred by P. Stetter. H.A. Dalrymple's Dalmore Kennels, in Pennsylvania, exhibited Mira a few times in the Miscellaneous Class (where on one occasion she turned up as a Belgian Sheepdog), and she won blue ribbons at Newcastle and Philadelphia. Correctly entered as a German Shepherd at New York in 1908, she met competition from another German Shepherd, Queen (or Queen of Switzerland), by whom she was defeated. Mira was never registered with the American Kennel Club, and she finally returned to Germany, taken back there by Mr. Gross.

Queen of Switzerland, under the ownership of Adolph Vogt, became the first German Shepherd officially registered by the American Kennel Club.

Early Activity

Activity in the German Shepherd world really started taking shape in 1912 when two fanciers, Benjamin H. Throop of Scranton, Pennsylvania, and Miss Anne Tracy of Highland Falls, New York, each registered some dogs and immediately set about the business of organizing the German Shepherd Dog Club of America, which in 1913 was on its way with twenty-six charter members. The club was incorporated in 1916 in the state of New York, and the charter members included Anne Tracy, Margaret C. Throop, Edith Mae Schiley, Vernon Castle, John Volkman, Paul Hulon, and R.B. Ruggles. Mrs. C. Halstead Yates was President (her husband was estate superintendent for Thomas Fortune Ryan), F. Empkin was Vice-President, and Mr. Throop was Secretary. The club's first Specialty show took place on June 11th in Greenwich, Connecticut, and was judged by Miss Tracy. Forty German Shepherds (resulting in a four-point major) turned out for the occasion. Miss Tracy also judged the second Specialty, which this time took place in New York City the following year, where the then impressive total of ninety-six assembled! Interestingly, the point ratings system had been revised in the interim, so this second Specialty also accorded just four points.

1913 saw the recording of the first two German Shepherd Dog champions in the United States. They were Lux (or Luchs) belonging to Miss Tracy and Herta von Ehrangrund owned by L.I. De Winter at Winterview Kennels.

It was in 1914 that the first really noteworthy German importation arrived in the United States to join Mr. Throop's kennel. This was Apollo von Hunenstein, a leading winner in Europe who had earned Austrian and Belgian championships in 1913 and French and German championships in 1914 prior to his departure for the United States. His American championship followed with ease. Apollo was born in February 1912. Before leaving his homeland he was bred to the great and influential bitch Flora Berkemeyer, from which came the Riedekenburg "D" litter including Danko, Diethelm, Dorte, Drusos, and Dulo von Riedekenburg.

We understand that despite all his winning in Europe, German judges were inclined to be somewhat critical of Apollo, claiming him too feminine in type. Be that as it may, history credits this dog with having brought to America refinement, quality, and length of body—virtues

Grand Victor Ch. Apollo v. Hunenstein, PH, was the second American Grand Victor German Shepherd Dog, having attained the honor in 1919, and was one of the early great winners and sires imported to the United States. Photo courtesy of Mary Schuetzler.

Ch. Gero v. Rinklingen was the winning Shepherd in New York in 1914. Baron Rochester imported and owned this dog. Photo courtesy of Mary Schuetzler.

unfortunately not too fully recognized by many at the time.

Apollo's owner, Mr. Throop, who had contributed so tremendously to early Shepherd progress, passed away during 1923. After Mr. Throop's death, Apollo, then eleven years old, joined the Joselle Kennels of Mr. Widener, where he happily lived out his life with the good care he deserved. Upon his death, Apollo's mounted body was placed on display (along with numerous other dogs who had been selected to represent their breeds as outstanding examples of correct type and beauty) at the Peabody Museum at Yale University. This was considered a tremendous honor in those days when the collection was being assembled, with fanciers competitive among themselves over whose dogs might be chosen. I am not quite certain whether these dogs still are on display there, as I heard some years ago that several of them had been privately purchased by fanciers of individual breeds for their own collections.

Following World War I, Mr. Widener's Joselle Kennels brought over a grandson of Apollo who became an international champion and was a popular stud dog in the United States. He was Dolf von Dusternbrook, by Luchs von Uckermark ex Dorte von Riedekenburg, she from Flora Berkemeyer's Apollo litter. Dolf had been the 1919 German Sieger and the 1920 Austrian Sieger. He was well received in the United States, becoming almost invincible in the

Ch. Afra von Hoheluft, sired by the great import Ch. Pfeffer v. Bern, ROM, U.S. Grand Victor in 1937 and 1938. Another fine representative of John Gans' Hoheluft Kennels.

show ring and bringing home many a Best in Show trophy for Mr. Widener's collection. At the same time as Dolf, Mr. Widener also brought over a bitch, Debora von Weimar, at a rumored total price of $10,000. Still another of Mr. Widener's important Shepherds was the first jet black of the breed exhibited in the United States, Champion Freia of Humboldtpark.

Quite a busy little group of German Shepherd fanciers had become prominent in the United States prior to World War I. In addition to those already mentioned, their numbers included Thomas Fortune Ryan, Mrs. Alvin Untermeyer, Mrs. Elliott Dexter, and, the most lasting of all, that dedicated, long-time, highly respected importer, breeder, and exhibitor, John Gans of Hoheluft Kennels, Staten Island, New York, who weathered two World Wars in the Shepherd Fancy and whose name is synonymous with true

1924 and 1925 Grand Victrix Ch. Irma von Donerhof was an early importation of John Gans, coming to the United States shortly after placing second at the big Sieger Show in Hamburg.

A rare and very interesting picture taken in the mid-1920's and loaned to us by Mary E. Schuetzler. This most impressive line-up of German Shepherd greats includes, from left to right, Ch. Dolf von Duestenbrook, Ch. Eric von Graffenwerth, Ch. Annie von Humboldt Park, Ch. Cito Berganslust, Ch. Debora von Weimar, Ch. Schatz von Hohentann, Ch. Irma von Donerhof, Ch. Iso von Donerhof, Ch. Freia von Humboldt Park, and the young American-bred Ch. Dolf of Joselle.

greatness where dogs of this breed are concerned. The dogs with which John Gans was associated could fill an entire chapter, for their influence on the breed was enormous.

It was thanks to Mr. Gans that a magnificent father and son team came from Germany. They were International Champion Geri von Oberklamm, an Austrian Grand Champion whelped in August 1917 and purchased in partnership with Reginald Cleveland (owner of the famous Rexden Kennels), and a son of Geri, Grand Victor Champion Cito von Bergerslust, SchH, who was Grand Victor in the United States in 1924 and 1925. These dogs, like some of the best earlier imports, were strong in the Flora Berkemeyer bloodline, and both of them had striking impact on German Shepherds in the United States. Because Geri took unkindly to kennel life and failed to prosper under this confinement, he went to live with an important California Shepherd lady, Mrs. Elliott Dexter, where he ruled the roost as house dog and dearly loved companion and at the same time contributed his share as a stud dog, passing on many desirable traits to West Coast Shepherds. Cito, sired by Geri, was born in 1920 from Goda von Munsdorf. The 1922 German Sieger, he continued his winning ways in the United States, amassing a splendid record in several years of competition.

Hoheluft Kennels also became the American home of Champion Attilla Argus, Siegerin and United States Champion Traute von Bern, and, perhaps the most notable of them all, the superlative Sieger and Grand Victor Champion Pfeffer von Bern, ZPr, MH, ROM, who was Grand Victor in the United States in 1937 and 1938—memorable dogs, each and every one!

The Thomas Fortune Ryan kennel, Oak Ridge, was founded in 1913. This was a short-lived involvement with the breed, and before long the Oak Ridge Shepherds had been presented to Mr. Ryan's estate manager and his wife, Mr. and Mrs. Yates, previously mentioned as early admirers of German Shepherds and Mrs. Yates as the first President of the German Shepherd Dog Club of America. One cannot help but wonder if perhaps it was not Mr. and Mrs. Yates who persuaded Mr. Ryan in the beginning to acquire some Shepherds; their interest seems to have preceded and certainly to have outlasted his own. The Yates, in turn, sold Mr. Ryan's leading import, Alarich von der Alpenluft, to the California fancier Mrs. Alvin Untermeyer, who used him to the breed's advantage on the Pacific Coast.

With the entry of the United States into World War I in 1917, the growing popularity which had been underway in German Shepherds in the United States came to an abrupt halt. Feeling was strong against anything German at that point, and due to that fact, these lovely dogs temporarily slipped into oblivion except with a handful of devoted owners.

In an attempt to stem the tide of unpopularity, the American Kennel Club changed the breed's official name from "German Sheepdogs," as they had been known, to "Shepherd Dogs," with no named country of origin. This actually did very little to reverse the trend.

Post-WWI Rise in Popularity

When American soldiers returned home to the U.S. following the Armistice in 1918, they brought with them some almost unbelievable accounts of the intelligence, nobility, and loyal bravery of the German Shepherds with which they had become acquainted overseas. The public looked at these dogs again with respect as tales were told of their work with the Red Cross, at the front, for police, and on guard duty—just a few of their many contributions to the war effort. Some of the returning servicemen brought members of the breed back with them, and suddenly just as quickly as the pendulum had swung against the breed at the beginning of the war, German Shepherd Dogs were again being regarded not only with approval but also with new admiration.

Adding impetus to the rise in popularity were those two beloved silent film stars, Rin Tin Tin and Strongheart, both of which were Shepherds and both of which immediately won the hearts of the American public. Without a doubt these dogs became two of history's most admired canines, and along with their popularity came a desire on everyone's part to own a dog just like these heroes!

The original Rin Tin Tin was brought when still a puppy to the United States from France by one of the returning soldiers, Lee Duncan. Rin Tin Tin was born in 1919 and lived to be thirteen years of age. He was later followed by several other Shepherds who were given the same name. Probably no pre-talking movie star was ever more important to the public than was the original Rin Tin Tin. He was credited with almost human talents in the portrayal of his roles and had an incredible number of fans. Captain Bryant is listed as Rin Tin Tin's breeder, his sire and dam having been inauspiciously named "Fritz" and "Betty." His dam, if not both parents, almost certainly were involved in active duty during the war.

More is known regarding Strongheart's background, as he had been a fully trained German Police Dog. Born in 1917, Strongheart was in real life Etzel von Oeringen and he was brought

Back in 1929 this very typical-of-her-day German Shepherd bitch won Best in Show at the Snohomish event in Washington. She was Rosel von der Johannaslust, owner-handled by Mrs. L. Zingler. The judge was George Pearson. Picture courtesy of Mary E. Schuetzler.

This is Strongheart, the famous silent movie star, proudly overseeing his puppies and their dam. Strongheart's real name was Etzel von Oeringen, and he was a German import. Whelped in 1917, this splendid Shepherd had been fully trained for police service from which it was necessary to un-train him for his fabulous movie career.

to America by Bruno Hoffman of White Plains, New York, owned by actress-writer Jane Murfin, and trained for his movie career (after being untrained for police work) by Larry Trimble. I recall Strongheart as a very handsome animal who made friends by the thousands for his breed. It is interesting that Strongheart's sire was purchased and brought to America, undoubtedly on the strength of Strongheart's fame, by Lawrence H. Armour of Green Bay Kennels, Lake Forest, Illinois. He was Nores von der Kriminalpolizei, born in March 1915, who, in addition to having sired Strongheart also numbered among his progeny the 1921 German Grand Champion Harras von der Juch along with some other dogs less well-known than these two. Obviously, everyone who admired Strongheart could hardly wait to breed to his sire, for what could be more fun than to own a sister or brother to one's favorite movie star? Unfortunately, we understand that Nores' popularity

as a sire proved to be somewhat less than beneficial to the breed.

Hamilton Farm Kennels have been prominently associated over the years with several different breeds of dog, the first of which was the German Shepherd. The granddaughter of the original owners, Mrs. Ailsa Crawford is, at the present time, a very active breeder of Jack Russell Terriers, maintaining a large kennel of them at Hamilton Farm and keeping the official club registry for the breed. In between the ownership of J.C. Brady, who had the Shepherds, and Mrs. Crawford were Mr. and Mrs. Cushing (she was formerly Mrs. Brady), who were pioneer breeders of Lhasa Terriers (which started out in the Terrier Group in the United States), now officially recognized as Lhasa Apsos (now a breed in the Non-Sporting group)—a truly dog-oriented family, this one! Mrs. Crawford talks with enthusiasm of her grandparents' German Shepherds, although she personally has not been active with that breed.

The outstanding Shepherd Dog at Hamilton Farm was Sieger and Grand Victor Champion Erich von Grafenwerth, the United States Grand Victor of 1922. The leading Shepherd

One of the handsome German Shepherd Dogs owned by Mr. and Mrs. J. C. Brady, Hamilton Farm Kennels, Gladstone, New Jersey. This photo from the 1920's courtesy of Mrs. Ailsa Crawford.

German Police Dog Ch. Falko v. Isarwinkel, owned by Mrs. James C. Brady, Hamilton Farm Kennels, was one of the outstanding early Shepherds whom Otto Gross brought to the United States.

Hamilton Iris, a typical and lovely bitch from the 1920's, owned by Mr. and Mrs. James C. Brady, Hamilton Farm Kennels.

bitch there was Anni von Humboldtpark, the 1919 and 1921 German Siegerin and Holland's female champion for 1919. It was Otto Gross, who had brought the first Shepherd to the United States some years earlier (see the beginning of this chapter), who made the selection of these dogs and brought them to Hamilton Farm where his selection was met with approval. Erich was considered by breeders of his day to be the outstanding sire of the time. He was a son of Alex von Westfalenheim ex Bianca von Riedekenburg, she a daughter of that widely admired bitch Flora Berkemeyer. Erich's stud fee was $200 when most of his contemporaries were offered in the $50 price range; and I gather he was well worth it, passing on balance, temperament, and general excellence to his progeny. In his later years, Erich was sold by Hamilton Farm to Mrs. M. Hartley Dodge of Giralda Farm, where he lived out the remainder of his life among admiring and loving friends— as befitting so memorable a dog.

Although it is not generally known, one of the earliest breeds I owned was the German Shepherd (two of them, a dog and a bitch), which made me especially aware of the breed and alert to those being shown when I started attending dog shows in the mid-1920's. Three ladies whom I grew to know and admire for their own knowledge of and devotion to the breed as well as for their dogs were Miss Marie Leary, owner of Cosalta Kennels in Greenwich, Connecticut; Mrs. M. Hartley Dodge of Giralda Farm Kennels at Madison, New Jersey; and Miss Adele S. Colgate of Hobby House Kennels at Tuxedo Park, New York.

Cosalta German Shepherds were started with French bloodlines, Miss Leary's first having been an importation from France named Hector, who came to the United States in 1923. This was her first show dog. Later her bloodlines were basically developed through those of three noted importations: Champion Giralda's Schatz von Hohentan, Champion Giralda's Iso von Doer-

Miss Adele S. Colgate, owner of Hobby House Kennels at Tuxedo Park, New York, was one of the leading Shepherd breeders of the 1930's-1950's.

nerhof, and, a bit later, Grand Victor Champion Utz von Haus Schutting, the latter by Sieger Klodo von Boxberg (that very important dog who was credited with bringing the "new type Shepherd" into existence during the mid-1920's).

Miss Leary was a strong advocate of obedience training and was a pioneer among American German Shepherd fanciers in this regard. She owned or bred a countless number of champions, both conformation- and obedience-titled dogs. It was not in the least unusual for her to put a dozen or more dogs on the benches at a single show (at Westminster in 1937 there were no less than eighteen German Shepherds owned or co-owned by her among the entries). She was an energetic, enthusiastic fancier who loved handling her own dogs, a true sporting lady, and a tremendous asset to the breed. Miss Leary imported few dogs herself but was quick to use on her bitches those imported by other breeders. Among the noted dogs one associates with her are Champion Kirk of San Miguel, whom she purchased from the California-based San Miguel Kennels; Champion Armin von Salon, SchH III, who gained a Tracking Dog degree in the United States; Champion Cosalta's Ace of

German Shepherd Dogs, or "German Police Dogs" as they were popularly, and erroneously, called at that time, from Mrs. Walter S. McCammon's Aimhi Kennels at Wayland, Massachusetts. Mrs. McCammon was a long time breeder-exhibitor and a highly respected judge. This 1920's photo courtesy of Janet Churchill.

Wyliwood, C.D.X., ROM; and a great many more, including the impressive Ch. Hugo of Cosalta, C.D.

It was Miss Leary who took positive action in her kennel when she noted the appearance of hip dysplasia, and she was one of the first German Shepherd breeders to start the custom of having her dogs x-rayed in an effort to control the spread of it. Working with her veterinarian, Dr. Harold Kopp of Greenwich, Connecticut, she succeeded in erasing it from her kennels in only two generations of careful, selective breeding. Dr. Kopp speaks with enthusiasm of her determination and success in this regard.

Cosalta Kennels remained active from 1923 into the early 1960's.

1923 seems to have been a magical year for German Shepherd progress in the United States, as it was then, too, that Mrs. M. Hartley Dodge (Geraldine Rockefeller Dodge, daughter of William Rockefeller, niece of John D.) acquired her first of the breed. Mrs. Dodge was a dedicated dog fancier, loving every aspect of our sport and maintaining extremely active kennels at Giralda Farm, her estate at Madison, New Jersey, over a period of more than four decades. Shepherds especially appealed to her, but her keen interest also included Bloodhounds, English Cocker Spaniels, Rottweilers, Pointers, Golden Retrievers, Beagles, and various other breeds as well. It was Mrs. Dodge who in 1927

These are Ch. Cotswold of Cosalta and Ann of San Miguel with owner Miss Brundred and judge Lew Starkey at a San Diego Dog Show during the 1940's.

decided that America should have a truly unique, spectacular, and memorable annual dog show and who created for us exactly that through her Morris and Essex Kennel Club events. One can close one's eyes nowadays and dream about the grandeur that was Morris and Essex—the close-cropped well-manicured lawns on which the dogs were judged; the great expanse of tenting provided so that the entire proceedings could go undercover should it rain (and stood idle when the weather was good); the spaciousness of every ring; the vast parking areas; the delicious catered hot luncheon from one of New York City's most famous restaurants, available not just to judges but to all who attended the show; the gorgeous sterling silver trophies and the number of them in competition; the always exciting judging panel; and, of course, the quality of competition all this attracted. Small wonder that the show grew in size to more than 4,000 dogs! Morris and Essex, although classified as an all-breed show, actually was not. Usually only about forty to fifty breeds were selected to be included there, based on their popularity and the size of the entries they were likely to draw. Many Specialty clubs sponsored these classes. The show was held annually except during the years of World War II, and the final event took place in 1959.

But we digress from the Shepherds! Mrs. Dodge provided a true service to the German Shepherd Fancy when she imported fabulous dogs of this breed from Germany's leading pro-

H. K. L. Castle, who drew so splendid an entry of German Shepherds when he officiated in the breed at Westminster in 1937, is pictured on his ranch, Kaneohe, in Honolulu with a guest, the famed novelist Fannie Hurst, and one of his German Shepherds. Photo courtesy of Janet Churchill.

ducing lines and then made them available, at very affordable stud fees, for use by breeders in the United States. Among her leading importations were the black dog, Champion Giralda's Iso von Doernerhof, sired by the Austrian Sieger Claus von der Furstenburg; the International Champion Schatz von Hohentann; and the handsome Best in Show winner, Champion Giralda's Dewat von der Starrenburg, SchH III (sired by the German Sieger Odin von Stolzenfels), a dog widely acclaimed in the American judging rings.

As do the majority of intelligent breeders, Mrs. Dodge recognized the importance of and placed particular emphasis on the quality of the *bitches*, and hers were a very noteworthy lot. Included among them were an outstanding half-sister of Iso (also sired by Claus), Champion Arna aus der Ehrenzelle, the 1926 German Siegerin; Pia von Haus Schutting, an Austrian

Siegerin; and Champion Giralda's Teuthilde von Hagenschloss. Grand Victrix Champion Giralda's Thora von Bern was another prominent import.

Mrs. Dodge used her foundation stock to the best possible advantage and produced many strikingly splendid homebred champions. They included the 1938 Grand Victrix Champion Giralda's Geisha and one of the last lovely Shepherds shown by Mrs. Dodge, the beautiful Champion Giralda's Pixie, who Giralda's good friend and kennel manager, Edwin A. Sayres, Jr., handled to a notable career.

We are excited about featuring a lovely collection of photos of Giralda Shepherds among our illustrations, loaned to us by Mr. Sayres. They point out the fact that Mrs. Dodge's homebreds never wandered too far in type from her "old-timers," particularly in head and expression, both of which were very outstanding.

The highly successful Ch. Giralda's Pixie, one of the last of the Giralda German Shepherds in the ring, brought some fine honors to her breeder-owner Mrs. M. Hartley Dodge, Giralda Farm, Madison, New Jersey, during the 1950's.

Ch. Western Candidate of Giralda, still another splendid result of the well-planned breeding program at Giralda German Shepherds, Mrs. M. Hartley Dodge.

Minka of Hobby House, owned by Mrs. Thomas Stetka, on July 5th 1959, at the German Shepherd Dog Club of Western New York Specialty. A lovely representative of Adele S. Colgate's Hobby House Shepherds from Tuxedo Park, New York.

When Mrs. Dodge passed away during the 1970's, animals lost a true friend. This lady was the founder of St. Hubert's Giralda, at Madison, New Jersey, a refuge establishment which does inestimable good work each year for the welfare of needy dogs, cats, and other animals. Unlike many fanciers of purebred dogs, Mrs. Dodge truly loved *all* dogs, having just as much heart for an unfortunate mongrel stray as for the most beautiful Best in Show winner. Warm, kindly, and sympathetic, she was a wonderful lady whose fantastic "eye" and intuition made her highly respected throughout the dog-show world.

Adele S. Colgate, at Hobby House, was a breeder-exhibitor and popular judge of German Shepherds over many years. Regretfully, I have been unable to locate records or photos of her dogs. Upon inquiry, I find that all of this material was sold at auction following her death, and the whereabouts of it is unknown to the several mutual friends who have attempted to locate it for me.

The late Major General Ira Hamilburg photographed during the mid-1930's with his German Shepherds. Photo courtesy of Janet Churchill.

Overview of the 1930's-1950's

In 1931, the *German* Shepherd Dog became the breed's official designation, approved by the American Kennel Club, just as the breed was rising on a new crest of popularity.

Where does one even begin to list all the people, and the dogs, who have figured in the progress and development of the German Shepherd Dog in the United States? There have been a great many of them, actually necessitating a mere tapping of the surface when one reviews past history.

The Ruthland Kennels owned by Paul Tishman was a busy Shepherd headquarters through the 1930's and 1940's, with some notably splendid dogs representing it. Mr. Tishman primarily used John Gans' Sieger and Grand Victor Champion Pfeffer von Bern, ZPr, MH, ROM, on his bitches. This dog sired for him, among others, Grand Victor Champion Noble of Ruthland, Grand Victor Champion Nox of Ruthland, ROM, Grand Victrix Champion Lady of Ruthland, ROM, and Grand Victrix Champion Olga of Ruthland.

San Miguel Kennels, belonging to Joan Michler and Zoie Brundred, were successful with dogs winning in both conformation and obedience. Used in the breeding program here one finds the names of the Champion Odin von Busecker-Schloss line and the names of Cham-

Baron von Vogel in 1937. Janet Churchill, owner.

Ch. San Miguel's Baron of Arbor, C.D., owned by Rancho San Miguel Kennels. This 1940's photo courtesy of Mary E. Schuetzler.

pion Chlodulf von Pelztierhof, Champion Utz von Haus Schutting, the Cosalta dogs, Canadian and United States Grand Victrix Leda von Liebestraum, and the dog Judo von Liebestraum, ROM.

Long Worth Kennels, located at Allegan, Michigan and owned by Lloyd C. Brackett, were among the most respected in breed history. Mr. Brackett was a truly great authority on the breed, the author of an outstanding book about it, and a gentleman who contributed inestimably to German Shepherd progress in the United States. His daughter, Mrs. Virginia McCoy, carries on the family interest in Shepherds and is a most popular judge.

Mr. Brackett's dogs were produced through a combination of the bloodlines of Champion Odin von Busecker-Schloss, Grand Victor Champion Pfeffer von Bern, Champion Marlo von Hoheluft, and Champion Garry of Benlore.

Ch. Uncus of Long Worth, bred and owned by Long Worth Kennels, taking Best of Breed at the German Shepherd Dog Club Motor City Specialty Show, November 1957. Handler, Dick Vaughn. Judge, Ernest Loeb. Photo courtesy of Mary E. Schuetzler.

One finds much mention of Dr. William Shearer's Shereston Shepherds as one researches through the 1930's period. Dr. Shearer won fame as owner of the 1934 Grand Victor Champion Erikund of Shereston. This kennel came to an abrupt close upon its owner's death.

Personal recollections of my own include Violet Baird back in the 1930's and Madeleina (Mrs. Charles W.G.) Baiter who was a German Shepherd lady and a fine Working breed judge. Both of these ladies eventually transferred their interests, at least in part, to Schipperkes. Violet Baird, too, was a popular judge.

Mr. and Mrs. Sidney Heckert, Jr., Villa Marina Kennels, Hope Ranch in Santa Barbara, California, were showing Shepherds in the 1930's. It was they who imported Odin von Busecker-Schloss in 1938 when he was four years old. Odin was a half-brother to the great Pfeffer von Bern, their sire having been Dachs von Bern. He won well and he was used widely at stud, to the benefit of the breed both on the West Coast and in the East. The Heckerts are the fanciers who made Santa Barbara Kennel Club's dog show so large and respected an event, just as Mrs. Dodge gave us Morris and Essex. Their Hope Ranch made an ideal setting, and those who have attended both clubs' events debate back and forth over which may have been the more huge, well run, and memorable. Santa Barbara, of course, continues, thanks largely to the interest and efforts of Mr. and Mrs. Tom

Mr. and Mrs. Sidney Heckert's great Best in Show-winning star of the early 1940's, Ch. Odin v. Scrimpenhauer, taking one of his numerous all-breed Bests in Show. Handled by Ben Brown. The judge here is Fred Hamm, a top Working breed authority of that period.

German Shepherds make devoted companions for children. This is Baron von Vogel. Photo courtesy of owner, Janet Churchill.

Stevenson and Mr. Frank Sabella. It is interesting that it was German Shepherd people who were so instrumental in the development of both of these magnificent shows.

On the East Coast, Mr. and Mrs. Charles J. Ketcham were showing in the 1940's. Blanche Beisswenger was already active in the breed. Dornwald was underway, Eleanor Cole a familiar figure in our rings as she most capably piloted many of her fine dogs to victory. Margaret Horn's Grafmar Kennels were making an enormous contribution to breed quality, the dogs from there making splendid records in conformation and obedience.

Robert F. Norton was an exhibitor of many Shepherds during the 1950's, bringing into the rings large numbers of entries from his Ralston Kennels at Sea Bright, New Jersey. Bernard Daku was doing well with the breed. Gustave Schindler, for whom Julius Due was handler, had an important dog in Champion Cito von der Herrmannschlense and an important bitch in the 1948 Grand Victrix Champion Duchess of Brownvale. Jeff-Lynne Kennels, Highland Park, Illinois, were also in the limelight.

An historic picture, courtesy of Peggy Lee. Ch. Fels von der Rottumbruke, on the right, taking Best of Breed as Ch. Hessian's Belle completes her title going Winners Bitch and Best of Opposite Sex. Belle was bred to Fels and produced a splendid litter, progeny from which in turn produced Ch. Jonlyn's Samantha, Jonlyn's Georgy Girl, and point-winning Jonlyn's Dustin of Bellemere. Fels belonged to Mr. and Mrs. James A. Cole's Dornwald Kennels, Belle to John J. Berry.

David McCahill's Am. and Can. Ch. Valiant of Da Ru Mar Hill, 1948 Grand Victor, noted winner of the late 1940's-early 1950's, taking Best in Show from Alva Rosenberg at Baltimore County Kennel Club, April 1950. Jane Forsyth handling.

Anton Korbel, California wine magnate, in 1936 imported a splendid dog, Chlodulf von Pelztierhof, who was a strong influence on the Pacific Coast dog fancy.

Grant E. Mann of Liebestraum Kennels is another gentleman who was a dedicated Shepherd person and a truly notable breeder. Founded in the late 1920's and located at Lamont, Iowa, this kennel was synonymous with quality, and Mr. Mann was a highly respected authority on the breed and took particular pleasure in training and showing his dogs himself.

It was in 1923 that Grant Mann purchased his first Shepherd, from which time on he was never without at least one member of the breed. His first big winner was Champion Luana von Liebestraum, who was co-owned with Marie Leary. Among the greats from this kennel were 1946 Grand Victrix American and Canadian Champion Leda von Liebestraum, ROM; 1947 American and Canadian Grand Victor Champion Jola von Liebestraum, ROM; 1951 Grand Victrix Champion Tawnee of Liebestraum; 1956 Grand Victor American and Canadian

Champion Bill vom Kleistweg, SchH I, ROM; Bill's son, Champion Rikter von Liebestraum; Champion Liedo von Stuveschacht; Champion Leu von Kahlgrund; Zaida von Liebestraum, ROM; Vonda von Liebestraum, ROM; Judo von Liebestraum, ROM; Champion Zarek von Liebestraum, ROM; Champion Elly von Liebestraum, C.D.X.; and Champion Electra von Liebestraum, C.D.

Under the auspices of the Roy Freuhauf Foundation, for several years during the 1950's, Grant Mann raised German Shepherds almost entirely for the Leader Dog League of Rochester, Michigan. At this time a small kennel was established for experimental purposes by him in Germany under the Mannstraum identification.

Mr. Mann's death, during the late 1970's, was a sad loss to the entire Shepherd Fancy.

Ch. Dux vom Sixtberg in an historic moment winning the German Shepherd Dog Club of Minneapolis and St. Paul Specialty in 1963. Handled by Helen Miller Fisher for owners Heinz Ritter and Charles Walton (pictured on the right). The judge is Ed L. Cocq of Edgetoun Kennels, owner-breeder of 1951 Grand Victor Ch. Jory of Edgetoun, C.D.X., ROM.

A Proud Mother and Her Children, Hamilton Farm

H. A. STROHMEYER

1923			MARCH		1923	
SUN.	MON.	TUE.	WED.	THU.	FRI.	SAT.
				1	2	3
4	5	6	7	8	9	10
11	12	13	14	15	16	17
18	19	20	21	22	23	24
25	26	27	28	29	30	31

This March 1923 calendar shows photos of a Hamilton Farm mother and babies, a head-study of one of the big winners, and a basketful of charming puppies. Owners, Mr. and Mrs. J. C. Brady of Gladstone, New Jersey.

The lovely Ch. Debora von Weimar, one of the fine bitches owned by Mr. and Mrs. James C. Brady, Hamilton Farm Kennels, Gladstone, New Jersey, during the 1920's. Photo courtesy of Mrs. Ailsa Crawford, granddaughter of the Bradys.

From Hamilton Farm Kennels, Mr. and Mrs. J. C. Brady, another stunning dog from the 1920's. All of these Hamilton Farm dogs pictured were well-known winners, but as so often is the case in historical research, the photos of several are unidentified.

A superb example of Hamilton Farm German Shepherds, this dog was among those representing the kennel back in the 1920's. Owned by Mr. and Mrs. James Brady. Photo courtesy of Mrs. Ailsa Crawford.

One of the beautiful Hamilton Farm bitches, typical of the finest of the 1920's, owned by Hamilton Farms Kennels, Mr. and Mrs. J. C. Brady. Photo courtesy of Mrs. Ailsa Crawford.

Above: This lovely German Shepherd bitch is Ch. Giralda's Geisha, C.D., from a 1936 portrait by Ward Binks. Geisha was the 1938 Grand Victrix and was bred and owned by Mrs. M. Hartley Dodge, Giralda Farm, Madison, New Jersey. **Below:** This painting by Ward Binks shows two very handsome creams, Ch. Giralda's Dawn and Day, from another strain developed by Mrs. M. Hartley Dodge at Giralda Farm, around 1940.

Above: A Ward Binks' painting of two fine examples of the black German Shepherd line at Giralda Farm. These are Ch. Giralda's Susan (1931-1939) and Ch. Giralda's Sarah (1931-1942), bred and owned by Mrs. M. Hartley Dodge.
Below: Ch. Giralda's Lola, a homebred of the 1930's-1940's period from Giralda German Shepherds belonging to Mrs. M. Hartley Dodge. Portrait by Ward Binks.

This excellent dog, Ch. Giralda's Falko, was another homebred belonging to Mrs. M. Hartley Dodge of Madison, New Jersey. Portrait by Ward Binks.

Ch. Giralda's Ulla, from the late 1930's, was a highly successful winner for Giralda Farm, Mrs. M. Hartley Dodge. A homebred by Giralda's Hettel, C.D.X., from Giralda's Now Then, Ulla was whelped in October 1937. She was an all-breed Best in Show winner.

The famous black dog, Ch. Giralda's Iso, who did his share for black German Shepherds. Owned by Mrs. M. Hartley Dodge of Madison, New Jersey. Portrait by Ward Binks.

Ch. Giralda's Chlodo, again from a Ward Binks' portrait, owned by Mrs. H. Hartley Dodge, Giralda Farm.

Ch. Giralda's Gelmar, a homebred from the late 1940's and early 1950's, bred and owned by Mrs. M. Hartley Dodge, Giralda Farm, Madison, New Jersey. This was one of the homebreds which Ed Sayres, Jr., handled with great success during that period.

The homebred Ch. Giralda's Playboy from the Giralda German Shepherds of Mrs. M. Hartley Dodge.

Ch. Gwinda's Ludwig, a son of Ch. Frigga v. Hoheluft, bred by John Gans in the 1940's. Photo courtesy of Bernard Daku.

Ch. Ingo of La Salle, by Park von Ronstadt ex Teckie of La Salle, Best of Breed at Minneapolis Kennel Club 1958 under Bob Waters. Handled by Helen Miller Fisher for owner Jack L. Sinykin, La Salle Kennels.

Ch. Rolf von Hoheluft, Canadian Grand Victor, was a very famous and important German Shepherd of the mid-1900's. Bred by John Gans, he was a son of Ch. Frigga Von Hoheluft, American Grand Victrix 1944. Photo courtesy of Bernard Daku.

Ch. Arno of San Miguel, owned by Rancho San Miguel Kennels, was an important dog of the early 1940's. Sired by Anton Korbel's imported Ch. Chloduff's Pelztierhof ex Ch. Ramona of Cosalta, he was born in January 1939.

Am. and Can. Ch. Von Darion's Cuno, line-bred on San Miguel bloodlines, was born in 1959 and was a great dog of true quality. Owner, Marion Darling. Photo courtesy of Denise Kodner.

Ch. Uncus of Long Worth, by Arry vom Burghalderring, ROM, ex Ch. Facsimile of Long Worth. Judge, Maureen Yentzen. Handler, Virginia McCoy. Club President, David Wiltfong, Motor City 1959.

The great Ch. Chimney Sweep of Long Worth; bred, owned, and handled by Virginia McCoy. Photo courtesy of Mary E. Schuetzler.

Ch. Rollingreen's Arco of Waldhorn, by Ch. Cuno von der Teufelslache, SchH III, FH, ROM, ex Waldhorn's Prima of Long Worth, taking Best of Breed at Lake Minnetonka K.C., June 1956. Owned by Bill Bliss, this was a prominent winner of the 1950's.

Opposite, above: At only seven months old, Meadowmill's Harras, by Grand Victor Ch. Troll vom Richterbach ex Meadowmill's Charmaine, winning the Bred-by-Exhibitor Class at the German Shepherd Dog Club of Minneapolis and St. Paul Specialty in 1959. Judge, Virginia McCoy, noted Shepherd breeder of Long Worth Kennels. Breeder-handler-owner, Helen Miller Fisher. This very handsome red, gold, and black puppy was typical of what Troll was producing. Note that in those days the handlers did not overstretch the hindquarters! **Below:** A very young Jane Forsyth winning with Ch. Storm of Deamair, C.D.X., at Ladies Dog Club in 1950. Owned by Mrs. Shipley Bayless. The judge is Mr. A. E. Van Court.

An excitingly historic picture of Ciro of Fieldstone, seventeen months old, by Ch. Cuno von der Teufelslache, SchH III, FH, ROM, ex Freia von der Weikau, taking Winners Dog at the 1957 San Joaquin Valley German Shepherd Specialty. The judge here is Jack Sinykin, owner of La Salle German Shepherds, who is of the Master Eye Foundation and still a judge at more than ninety years of age in 1982. Owner-handler of Ciro is Dr. R. M. Hansen of San Francisco.

Opposite, above: Ch. Carlo von der Hardtperle, by Klodo aus der Eremitenklause, 1960 Youth Sieger, ex Carin von der Abtsburg, a famous German import owned by Harlan K. Gibbs, Jr., York, Pennsylvania. Photo courtesy of Janet Churchill.
Below: Ch. Blitz vom Steverufer, by Grand Victor Troll vom Richterbach ex Cita vom der Malmannsheide, another splendid Shepherd from the 1960's owned by Harlan K. Gibbs, Jr., Kragspoint Kennels, York, Pennsylvania. Photo courtesy of Janet Churchill.

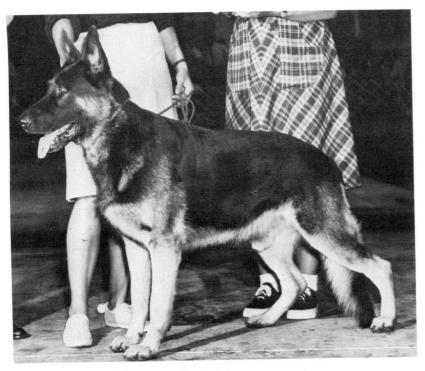

Henry Stoecker awarded Best in Show at Duluth Kennel Club, August 1967, to Ch. Bar v. Weiher-turchen, ROM, handled by Denise Kodner for Barbara and John Schermerhorn. Bar was imported by Ernest Loeb.

The famous Group-winning black German Shepherd, Ch. Den-Lea's By Jiminy, owned, bred, and handled by Denise Kodner, winning the Shore-line German Shepherd Dog Club Specialty in June 1960 judged by another great Shepherd expert, Mr. Anton Korbel.

At Catonsville Kennel Club in October 1966, Mrs. Augustus Riggs, IV, gave top honors in the Working Group to Ch. Fleetwood's Aristocrat. This dog was a homebred belonging to Fred and Iris Popick and handled by Jane Forsyth.

Ch. Jonvires Curt, owned by June Bruesseau and handled by Gerlinde Hockla, winning at the German Shepherd Dog Club of Long Island Specialty Show, May 1965. The judge was Dr. Christopher Rummel, President of the German Shepherd Dog Club of Germany at that time.

Ch. Heller of Mill Lake Farm, by Ch. Kondor vom Wickratherschloss ex Arda of Mill Lake Farm, winning at Motor City Kennel Club, 1960, under judge Gustave Schindler, left. Breeder, Stewart L. Bryant. Owners, Ralph and Mary Ellen Norwotny. Photo courtesy of Mary E. Schuetzler.

Opposite, above: The Group winning Ch. Quasar of Clover Acres, by Ch. Tannenwald's Igor ex Clover Acres Frolich, taking Best of Breed at the German Shepherd Dog Club of Greater Washington D.C. Specialty Show judged by Donald J. Ames. Owned by Sylvia Lazzarin; handled by Ken Rayner. **Below:** The noted Ch. Fels v.d. Rottumbrucks of Dornwald winning the German Shepherd Dog Club of Detroit Specialty, June 4th 1967. Dornwald Kennels (Mr. and Mrs. James A. Cole) owners. Lamar Kuhns, handler. Harold Sands, judge.

GERMAN SHEPHERD
CLUB OF DETROIT
JUNE 4, 1967

BEST OF BREED

JUDGE
MR H. E. SANDS

Select Ch. Gidget von Mur-Wood, handled by Luke Geraghty and owned by Bid-Scono Associates, taking Winners Bitch at the Detroit Specialty in 1966. This is the older full-sister to 1971 Grand Victrix Aloha von Bid-Scono.

Opposite, above: Ch. Den-Lea's Hi Jinks, one of the numerous fine German Shepherds owned by Denise Kodner, Highland Park, Illinois. **Below:** Meadowmill's Volt, a Cuno granddaughter whelped August 1958. Owner-handler, Helen Miller Fisher.

Blanka von Finsternwald, litter-sister to Biene, sired by Ch. Volker vom Schaeferleben, owner-handled by Gerlinde Hockla to Best Puppy in Sweepstakes at the German Shepherd Dog Club of Long Island in 1967, judged by Herr H. Flasspoehler.

Opposite, above: A noted Shepherd of the 1970's, Ch. Von Nassau's Sherpa, C.D., winning Best in Show at Cedar Rapids Kennel Club in 1974 under judge Henry Stoecker. Owned by Betty A. Radzevich and handled by Denise Kodner. **Below:** Ch. Harry Luftigan Hoe He, owned by Edward Legee and Alfred Espinosa, taking Best of Breed from the classes at the German Shepherd Dog Club of Greater Washington D.C. Specialty, August 1969, over close to a dozen specials. Gerlinde Hockla, handler.

BEST IN SHOW
CEDAR RAPIDS K.A.
JUNE 22, 1974
OLSON PHOTO

GERMAN SHEPHERD DOG CLUB
of
GREATER WASHINGTON DC

AUGUST 16 1969

BEST OF BREED

Von Nassau's Rustan, by Ch. Seahurst Count ex Alta von Nassau, handled by Helen Miller Fisher for John Collins at the German Shepherd Dog Club of Minneapolis and St. Paul Specialty in 1961. The late Dick Ayers is judging.

Ch. Waymarsh's Jamie, an example of beautiful breed type, by Fritzlund's Farmboy ex Ayrwood's Holly of Waymarsh, taking Best of Breed at Sussex Hills in 1979. Bred and owned by Marie Sagendorf. Sue Rayner, handler.

On the way to Best in Show, Ch. Kameraden's Crusader, bred and owned by William and Gisela Herr of Northport, N.Y., places first in the Working Group at Des Moines in September 1982 under Helen Miller Fisher. Ken Rayner, Jr., handles this famous current Best in Show dog.

Ch. Amber's Action, by Ch. Doppelt-Tay's Hawkeye, ROM, ex Amber's Nancy, shown to title by Fran Keyes for owner Penny Hughes. Here taking Best of Winners at Danville Kennel Club in 1981.

Am., Can., and Mex. Ch. Von Nassau's Grand Prix, by Am. and Can. Grand Victor Ch. Lakeside's Harrigan, ROM, owned by Dr. Zoltan and Helena Puskas and Ann and Bud Shaw.

Cobert's Whisper Jet at nine years of age. Connie Beckhardt of Tenafly, New Jersey, owner.

SHEPHERD DOG
OF AMERICA
V. 6, 1976
CCT DOG

ROBERTS
PHOTO BY
A. ABRAMSKY

Am. and Can. Ch. Val-Koa's Roon taking a first in the Working Group at Flatirons Kennel Club in 1971. This dog won a Quaker Oats Award for his co-owner Mary Roberts (who owned him with Dr. G. William Anderson).

Opposite, above: Am. and Can. Ch. Cobert's Reno of Lakeside, ROM, by Grand Victor Ch. Lance of Fran-Jo, ROM, ex Cobert's Melissa, ROM. Co-owned by Vito Moreno and Connie Beckhardt. **Below:** Ch. Covy's Starwars of Tucker Hill, by Ch. Amber's Gille of Will-Ve's ex Grand Victrix Ch. Covy's Rosemary of Tucker Hill, ROM. Bred by Cappy Pottle and Gloria Birch, who co-own with Nancy McCloud.

Select Ch. Chewing Gum von Tara Haus, owned by Shirley and David L. Panijan, Trenton, New Jersey.

Ch. Farmils Chantz, by Select Ch. Kismets Impulse von Bismark ex Farmils Abbey of Dolmar, taking Reserve Winners Dog at the German Shepherd Dog Club of Rhode Island Specialty Show. Eighteen months of age here, this dog, bred by Doris Farrell, is owned by Charles and Doris Farrell, Farmil Kennels, Roxbury, Connecticut.

Echo Knolls Sonic of Waymarsh, by Ch. Treffer of Clover Acres ex Gambit's Elanora v. Brode, bred by H. Broderson and owned by Marie Sagendorf. Ken Rayner handling at the National Capital Kennel Club, March 1977.

Ch. Farmils Chantz, Maturity Dog 1981, here at twenty months of age making a fine win at the Mid-Atlantic Futurity. Owned by Charles and Doris Farrell.

1980 Select Ch. Die Herzogin's J.J. winning Best of Breed at the German Shepherd Dog Club of Detroit, May 1981, B. Amidon judging. Owned by Shirley and David Panijan, Trenton, New Jersey.

GERMAN SHEPHERD DOG
CLUB OF DETROIT
MAY 31, 1981
JUDGE – B. AMIDON
BEST OF BREED

PHOTO – TOM MONAHAN

Ch. Dolmar's Rhyme taking Best of Breed at Glens Falls Kennel Club, August 1982. Judge, William Kendrick; handler, Henry Dancosse. A. E. Canna and Mrs. M. Dolan, owners. Rhyme went on to a third in Group that day under Gerhardt Plaga.

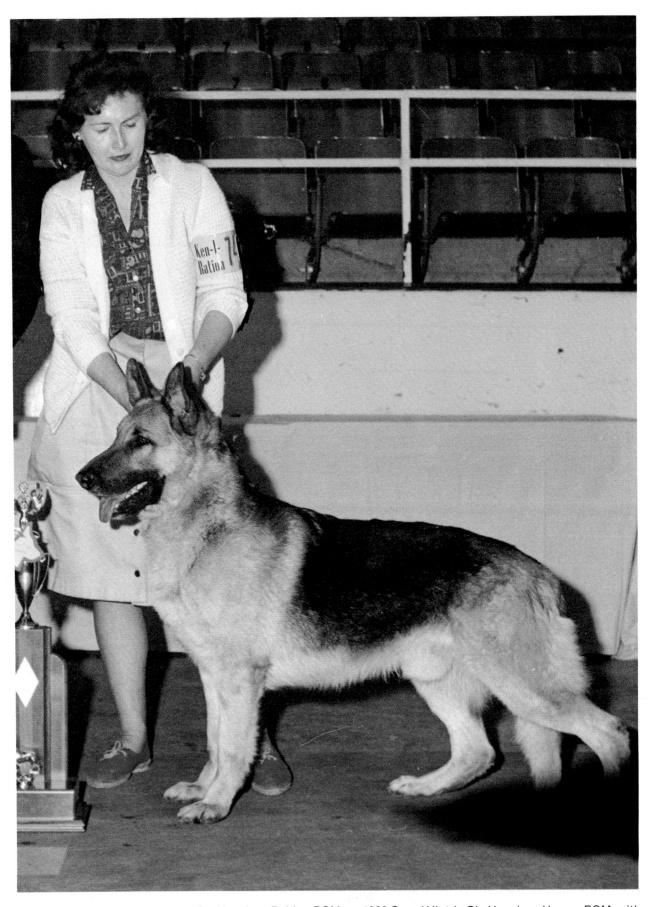

Ch. Hessians Exaktor, by Select Ch. Hessians Baldur, ROM, ex 1963 Grand Victrix Ch. Hessians Vogue, ROM, with her breeder-owner-handler Helen Hess, Hessian Kennels, Goshen, Ohio.

Billie of Ingomar, by Select Ch. Wellspring's Ironsides ex Select Ch. Nootka of Ingomar, bred and owned by Diana Riddle and Jerome Rozanski, Zelienople, Pennsylvania.

Kummervoll's Holly, pointed, the dam of Imp-Cen's Elsa and Imp-Cen's Golden Horizon, handled here by owner, Connie Halliday, to Best of Breed at Bald Eagle Kennel Club, 1980.

Leuchtag's Grok of Ingomar, by Ch. Lakeside's Gilligan's Island, ROM, ex Ch. Yasmin of Stahl Farm, bred by Diana Riddle and Sarah L. Leuchtag and owned by Diana Riddle and Russell Endean.

Opposite, above: Jonlyn's Kojak, by Jonlyn's Andy (Ch. Fels v.d. Rottumbrucke of Dornwald ex Ch. Hessian's Belle) from Ch. Jonlyn's Samantha, one of the excellent Shepherds from Mr. and Mrs. John J. Berry's Jonlyn Kennels at Atlantic City, New Jersey. Kojak here is winning Best of Breed at the Central New York Kennel Club, May 1977. **Below:** Select Ch. Nootka of Ingomar, by Grand Victor Ch. Scorpio of Shiloh Gardens, ROM, ex Leuchtag's Happy of Ingomar. Breeder, Diana Riddle. Owners, Diana Riddle and Jerome W. Rozanski.

A magnificent head-study of Ch. Kubistraums Kane, ROM, by Ch. Cobert's Reno of Lakeside, ROM, ex Falkora's Catalina, C.D., ROM. Number Four Producing Sire, 1981 Futurity-Maturity Tabulation and Number Three Living ROM Sire, 1981 ROM Tabulation. Bred and owned by Verna M. Kubik, St. Joseph, Wisconsin.

Fenton of Ingomar, by Kaleef's Kannon of Checkmates ex Ch. Winooska of Ingomar, bred and owned by Diana Riddle and Jerome Rozanski, Zelienople, Pennsylvania. Best Puppy at the German Shepherd Dog Club of Miami Valley, April 1981.

Fritzlund's Debutante, by Ch. Treffer of Clover Acres ex Brunhilda of Fritzlund (a daughter of Ch. Matmar's Pro of Clover Acres), bred and owned by Charles and Betty Fritz. Handled by Chips Rayner.

Ch. Ayrwoods Linus, the sire of Ch. Kamara den's Crusader. Bred by E. Ayres, sired by Schwenke's Farook of Mil-Mar ex Glenhart's Della of Ayrwood, and owned by W. and G. Herr. Photo courtesy of Ken Rayner.

CHAPTER THREE

Kennels in the Continental United States

Ch. Barithaus' Bryn von Varick, inbred to the great Grand Victor Ch. Lance of Fran-Jo, ROM, represents the splendid Shepherds owned by Ed and Rosemarie Barritt, Esperance, New York.

There is no better way to describe the progress of a breed than by telling you of the individual breeders and kennels that have contributed along the way. On the following pages we are proud to present summary descriptions of these breeders and their kennels and of many important German Shepherds and the background from which their success was attained. We tell you not only about the long-time breeders, many of whom are still active; but we also pay tribute to the comparative newcomers as well. Each has contributed to the well-being and development of these splendid dogs; and on the shoulders of the newcomers in particular, squarely rests the task of carrying on and preserving what has already been accomplished, and the responsibility for the future well-being of the breed. Study these pages well and you will come away with an increased knowledge of where the best German Shepherd Dogs have been bred, the care and forethought expended toward their progress and improvement generation after generation, and the exciting results of the efforts of these breeders.

Abadee

Abadee was a very famous German Shepherd Dog Kennel of the 1940's and 1950's, owned by Mr. and Mrs. Gustave Schindler of Port Washington, New York. Here the emphasis was placed on both brains and beauty; the Schindlers had top stars in both obedience and conformation competition.

One of their most famous dogs was the impressive Alf vom Kroppelberg, who had championship points to his credit and who was an absolute standout in obedience, having brought some very special honors to his owners. Alf came from Germany in 1953, bringing with him a V (excellent) rating from German dog shows. The Schindlers placed him in the capable hands of Mrs. Winifred Strickland (owner of Margelen's Chieftain, U.D.T., who won top obedience dog of 1951, followed by another of her own, Hussan vom Haus Kilmark, in 1952 and 1953). So well did Alf perform for Mrs. Strickland that he edged out Hussan for highest honors in 1954. Soon after his arrival in the United States, Alf made his obedience debut at Hartford, where he

One of the very youngest German Shepherd Dogs ever to complete his title, Ch. Abadee's Peter of Browvale here is winning in 1953 under noted German Shepherd Dog breeder and judge Mrs. Charles W. G. Baiter. Peter achieved the notable accomplishment of completing his championship when just over one year old. He was owned by Mr. and Mrs. Gustave Schindler, then of Port Washington, New York, whose Abadee Kennels were noted for outstanding show and obedience Shepherds.

scored a win of 199½ points. He followed this up on a later occasion by becoming the first dog in history, we understand, to make a double perfect score, 200 in both Open B and Utility, on the same day; and he finished all four working degrees in less than six months. He won his C.D. with an average score of 199 in four trials, his C.D.X. with an average of 199½ (with two perfect scores of 200), and his U.D. and tracking degrees with almost perfect scores as well. He won first fourteen times, on seven occasions was highest scoring dog in trial, and twice won the highest combined score. In between these ac-

complishments, he also was Winners Dog at Westchester for a three-point major. This truly was a dog in whom to take pride!

Another of the Schindlers' noted Shepherds was the 1948 Grand Victrix Champion Duchess of Browvale, a bitch of much quality. There also was the beautiful Champion Peter of Browvale.

Abadee was disbanded some years back when Mr. Schindler decided to concentrate more on judging than on showing dogs. The Schindlers now live in New York City. Even though they no longer own Shepherds, they still love the breed and take an interest in it.

Alf v. Kroppelberg, owned by the Abadee Kennels of Mr. and Mrs. Gustave Schindler, is pictured here with Mr. Schindler on the right, his daughter Nicole in the center (Nicole is now Mrs. George Jeffords, whose husband's mother, Mrs. Walter Jeffords, is a famous breeder of Pekingese), and on the left, Mrs. Winifred Strickland, who trained and handled Alf for the Schindlers. Alf, in the mid-1950's, became the first dog in all history to make a double perfect score: 200 in both Open B and Utility on the same day.

Ch. Barithaus' Gymi of Shadyhaven,
C.D., belongs to Barithaus Kennels, Ed
and Rosemarie Barritt, Esperance, New
York.

Barithaus' Dulcinea, dam of Barithaus Ramblin' Rose, ROM, is from the kennels owned by Ed and Rosemarie Barritt.

Barithaus

Barithaus Shepherds, at Esperance, New York, have been developed by Rosemarie and Ed Barritt through a carefully balanced breeding program founded on their first bitch, Hilltop's Brite Star. Brite's grandam, Champion Cobert's Ernestine, C.D., and her brother, Champion Falco of Thunder Rock, were to become the dominant lines in Barithaus' pedigrees.

A breeding to Champion Cobert's Reno of Lakeside, ROM, and eventually to his sire, Grand Victor Champion Lance of Fran-Jo, ROM, added new line-breeding through Lance. Barithaus' pedigrees at this stage were line-bred on Ernestine (and Falco) and Lance, with the resulting generations coming together through two different litters sired by Champion Eko-Lan's Paladen, ROM. Thus, at present the influence of three Shepherds dominates at Barithaus, namely Ernestine, Lance, and Paladen.

There is a daughter of Champion Barithaus' Bryn von Verick, sired by Champion Barithaus' Bonanza, C.D., who will be bred to Barithaus' Bete Noir du Noel, once again tightening the lines.

Ch. Barithaus' April of Heldhaus, shown at one year of age taking her first major reserve. Owned by Ed and Rosemarie Barritt, Esperance, New York.

Ch. Barithaus' Bonanza, C.D., taking his first major. Bonanza is the son of the foundation bitch at Barithaus Kennels, Hilltop's Brite Star. Ed and Rosemarie Barritt, owners.

Barithaus' Bete Noir du Noel, pictured at twenty months of age. Owned by Rosemarie and Ed Barritt.

Bel Vista

Bel Vista German Shepherds were started in the early 1960's by Joe and Charlotte Poepping of Lebanon, Illinois. Their original stock was from the Hessian Kennels, and they line-bred to many famous dogs including Grand Victor Yoncalla's Mike, ROM; Grand Victor Lance of Fran-Jo, ROM; Champion Eko Lans Shiloh, and Champion Marty von Bid-Scono, thus making their present-day stock a melting pot of the best in the United States.

The Poeppings have bred and owned numerous Select champions, including the 1970 Number Three Select Male, Champion Bel Vista's Hooligan, and the 1970 American Grand Victrix Champion Bel Vista's Solid Sender. Probably their most famous Shepherd is American and Canadian Select Champion Bel Vista's Joey Baby, ROM. This dog, first shown in the United States at the age of twelve months and one week, went Winners Dog at the Tulsa German Shepherd Dog Club Specialty. At thirteen and one-half months he was the youngest male German Shepherd Dog ever to become a United States champion. He was the Maturity winner and merited the title of ROM in Canada and the United States by the time he was seven years old. Recently he won the Veterans Class at the 1981 National Specialty. To quote his owner, "His vitality is as fantastic as his temperament."

Although less active now than formerly as breeders, Mr. and Mrs. Poepping still attend the shows as exhibitors and Mr. Poepping is a judge.

1970 U.S. Grand Victrix, Ch. Bel Vista's Solid Sender, owned by Bel Vista Shepherds, Mr. and Mrs. Joseph Poepping, Lebanon, Illinois.

Ch. Bel Vista's Joey Baby, ROM, was among the top multi-Best in Show winning German Shepherds of the mid-1970's and is among the current top producers. Here he is winning the Working Group at Rubber City Kennel Club under Helen Miller Fisher, handled by Terry Hower for Charlotte and Joe Poepping. Photo courtesy of Mrs. Fisher.

Bergluft

Bergluft Kennels, located at Sewickley, Pennsylvania, were established in 1962 by Mrs. Dorit S. Rogers who has bred, trained, and shown German Shepherd Dogs in conformation and obedience.

Mainly German and English bloodlines, based on working ability, were used. The most important ones were Champion Axel von Deininghauserheide, SchH III, DPH, FH.; Champion Hein vom Richterbach, SchH III, ROM.; 1961 Sieger Champion Veus von der Starrenburg, SchH III; Champion Donar von der Firnskuppe, SchH III, FH; and the famous Klodo aus der Eremitenklause, SchH III, ZPr, AD, ROM. The English lines were English and Canadian Champion Vikkas Chieftain of Deanthorpe and English Champion Moonraker of Monteray. Large, heavy-boned German Shepherds with excellent temperaments came from these lines.

Long-Haven's Friendship, C.D.X., was acquired at the age of three years. She was a granddaughter of the well-known Champion Bernd vom Kallengarten, SchH III, ROM. She was trained and shown to her titles by Mrs. Rogers, and in 1966 she became one of the Top Ten German Shepherds in obedience in the nation.

With the acquisition of her first Rottweiler in 1967, Mrs. Rogers terminated her breeding program of German Shepherds, and since then the Bergluft Rottweilers have been highly successful and become widely known and respected.

Above: The famous Victor Klodo a.d. Eremitenklause, SchH III, ROM, a German import. Photo courtesy of Mrs. Dorit Rogers. **Below:** Long-Haven's Friendship, C.D.X., in 1968. Owned by Mrs. Dorit Rogers, who comments: "Although long-haired, she had excellent conformation, tremendous bone, and beautiful gait."

From left to right: Ch. Danka vom Molzberg, Ch. Drossel vom Molzberg, and Ch. Kuhlwald's Little Iodine, C.D., all Rottweilers, with their friend Basko von Bergluft, C.D., German Shepherd, snapped in the summer of 1970 by Dorit S. Rogers, Bergluft Kennels.

Long-Haven's Friendship, C.D.X., was Number Seven in the United States in obedience competition for 1966. Dorit S. Rogers, owner, Bergluft Kennels, Sewickley, Pennsylvania.

Basko von Bergluft, C.D., by Klodo aus der Erimitenklause, ROM, ex Long-Haven's Friendship, C.D.X., at twenty months old. This May 1968 photo courtesy of Dorit S. Rogers.

Basko von Bergluft, C.D., High Scoring German Shepherd, First Novice B, May 1969 at Cumberland, Maryland. He is shown winning under Carlton Williams, a well-known and respected judge. The owner-handler is Mrs. Dorit S. Rogers.

Ch. Gailand's Magic of Fran-Jo, owned by Mr. and Mrs. Robert Slay, taking Best in Show at the German Shepherd Dog Club of Alabama Specialty, December 1969. The judge is noted Shepherd breeder, Grant Mann.

Bokann

Bokann German Shepherd Dogs were founded in the mid-1960's by Mr. and Mrs. Robert H. Slay (Candye and Bob) following Bob's reassignment to shore duty with Naval Intelligence in Charleston, South Carolina.

Bob Slay had grown up with dogs of the Working breeds and had especially grown to love the German Shepherds through one owned by his mother while he was a teenager. When he was in a position to become actively involved with dogs, and since his wife shared his enthusiasm for the breed, Shepherds were what they decided to own. Judy's Heidi joined the family, selected as a nice show-prospect by Bob. She finished her title with ease and proved her worth as a producer when she presented her owners with a highly successful male who became Champion Bokann's Gallant Gent, who won well at both Specialty and all-breed shows. A young handler just starting out at the time, Doug Crane, had charge of the Slays' dogs in the ring and piloted several of them, in addition to Heidi and Gallant Gent, to their championships.

While living in Charleston, Bob Slay was involved with the organization of the German

Above: Mr. and Mrs. Robert Slay's first German Shepherd to become a champion, Judy's Heidi. Bokann Kennels, Beech Island, South Carolina. **Below:** Bob Slay owner-handling his beautiful bitch Ch. Bokann's Charm to her title at the German Shepherd Dog Club of Orlando Specialty, June 1971.

Shepherd Dog Club of Charleston, for which he served as President and first Show Chairman. In 1970, he applied to the American Kennel Club for approval as a judge, doing several all-breed shows that year followed by his first Specialty assignment in 1971. Now he is approved for all

Ch. Bokann's Molly winning the German Shepherd Dog Club of Charleston Specialty Show, October 1974, under Dick Robshaw. Owned by Mr. and Mrs. Robert Slay.

Working breeds and Best in Show, and his breeding activities have been phased out considerably as judging takes more of his time.

The Slays continue to have several Shepherds which they "live with and enjoy" as family members. These include Bob's particular favorite, the eleven-year-old Champion Bokann's Molly, who became a champion in stiff competition over large entries. Interestingly, she is the fiftieth champion progeny of the greatest producing Shepherd of all time, Grand Victor Champion Lance of Fran-Jo, ROM.

The Slays are now located at Beech Island, South Carolina. Since moving there, both have become active in the kennel club in Augusta, Georgia, for which Bob now is Bench Show Chairman. He is also a member of the German Shepherd Dog Club of America.

A bitch from Mr. and Mrs. Robert Slay's most recent Shepherd litter, Ch. Bokann's Polly, winning a Group first owner-handled from the classes under Mr. Lou Harris—a particular honor as Mr. Harris is a Shepherd breeder and Polly is the first of the breed to whom he has ever awarded a Group.

Burgerland

Burgerland German Shepherd Dogs, of Downey, California, were started by the late Dr. Zoltan Puskas and his wife, Helena, after their home had been burglarized on numerous occasions, despite their alarm system (which seemed rather easy for the unwanted guests to disconnect). Each had owned dogs during childhood, a St. Bernard in Dr. Puskas' case while Helena and her family even then had German Shepherds. Although Dr. Puskas was a very busy surgeon with a schedule leaving little time for other activities, it was decided to purchase a male and a female German Shepherd and to attempt to train them. The dogs were of good bloodlines, but at this period Dr. and Mrs.

Dr. Zoltan Puskas, owner of Burgerland German Shepherds, with his special favorite, Gigi, U.D., whom he called "Old Faithful" because she never failed. Gigi was the foundation bitch at Burgerland German Shepherds and was sired by Ch. Juvenko's Cito, who represented the Ulk line.

Helena Puskas with her favorite, Princess Ila Von Burgerland, daughter of Gigi, U.D., winner of the *Dog World* Award. Von Burgerland German Shepherds, Downey, California.

Puskas were not thinking in terms of breeding and showing. They simply wanted efficient watchdogs.

Training the dogs proved to be an easy task and a relaxation for Dr. and Mrs. Puskas. After one year, by which time they were headed toward Utility Dog degrees with both Shepherds, their male suddenly refused to jump. Examination proved that he had hip dysplasia; the female had the same problem, although to a lesser extent, and she was able to continue to her U.D. degree.

After this sad experience, Dr. and Mrs. Puskas went "kennel hopping," determined to find one where they could purchase dogs free of hip problems. It seemed almost impossible at that period! However, they finally located their Gigi, a four-month-old female, and Dr. Puskas offered a high price for her provided she be x-rayed and found free of hip problems. She was, and she became

Select Ch. Matmar's Pro of Clover Acres, by Select Ch. Tannenrald's Igor, one of the many fine German Shepherds owned by Burgerland Kennels, Dr. and Mrs. Zoltan Puskas.

the foundation bitch for Burgerland Shepherds, giving them twenty-seven puppies in four litters. Most of these were clear of hip problems, and some were kept for breeding and for showing.

Now that they were involved with breeding Shepherds of their own, Dr. and Mrs. Puskas asked for permission to register the kennel name which had been used by Mrs. Puskas' father back in Virginia. Thus the Burgerland Shepherds were founded, based on Gigi's progeny.

Gigi, whom Dr. Puskas called "Old Faithful" because "she never failed," had forty-nine Registry of Merit points when she died at twelve years of age. She produced Champion Brunhilda Von Burgerland, C.D., and eleven other of her progeny earned points toward their championships. Additionally, Dr. and Mrs. Puskas acquired two famous males, American Select Champion Matmar's Pro of Clover Acres (an Igor son) and American, Canadian, and Mexican Champion Von Nassau's Grand Prix, a Grand Victor Harrigan son.

Dr. and Mrs. Puskas were instrumental in the formation of the German Shepherd Dog Club of San Gabriel Valley and of the German Shepherd Dog Club of Long Beach, holding offices in

Ch. Lakeside's Gilligan's Island making one of his Best in Show wins, at Spartanburg in 1971, for Daniel Dwier. Photo courtesy of Connie Beckhardt, Tenafly, New Jersey.

both. They belonged, as well, to the Obedience Club of Lynwood and to the Downey Obedience Club.

When he was sixty-nine years old, Dr. Puskas suffered a stroke which left him paralyzed. Gigi, at that time, had her second litter by Champion Iphis and would carry her puppies to her master's bedside to entertain him. Mrs. Puskas, who is a corrective therapist, says that "Gigi helped me to teach him to walk again, and the love that surrounded him aided in his recovery."

After this stroke, Dr. Puskas retired from his practice, spending his time with his family and their lovely dogs, which made him a happy man. Before he passed away, in January 1980, Mrs. Puskas promised him that she would follow in his footsteps with the dogs, promised to follow his concepts of the breed and "never to breed dogs with bad hips or open coats." Mrs. Puskas continues to carry out his wishes. Burgerland Shepherds are not only splendid in conformation but also have a high intelligence as well. Mrs. Puskas derives great pleasure from personally caring for the dogs and raising the puppies.

Cobert

Cobert German Shepherd Dogs, owned by Connie and Ted Beckhardt at Tenafly, New Jersey, are a small and very specialized operation dedicated to producing beauty of type and excellence of temperament. The Beckhardts are extremely conscientious in regard to the future of their puppies and greatly concerned about the homes to which they will be going. If necessary, they will sacrifice possible future show careers in favor of placing the puppies in the type of homes which will appreciate them, assuring the opportunity for each to live out healthy, happy lives. Every puppy whelped at Cobert is raised in the Beckhardts' home, with all the extra love and attention, the best of medical care, and the finest food to help them off to a good start; and their breeders make every effort to place each puppy where it will receive the same kind of care.

Despite the stringent requirements for those who will own members of their dog family, the Beckhardts have seen the dogs they have bred achieve fantastic success in the show ring. To

Ch. Brunhilda Von Burgerland, C.D., by Ch. Philberlyn's Iphis, ROM, ex Gigi Von Burgerland, owned by Burgerland German Shepherds, Dr. Zoltan and Helena Puskas, Downey, California.

94

date they have bred or co-bred twenty-seven champions (this as of October 1982) and ten Register of Merit Shepherds. With special pride they point to Cobert's Melissa, ROM-of whom they are the breeders and co-owners, who is the Top Producing Dam in the history of the breed! Her offspring include eight champions and six Register of Merit sons and daughters. She is the dam of the 1972 American and Canadian Grand Victor Champion Lakeside's Harrigan, ROM; of a top Group and Best in Show winning German Shepherd Dog, Champion Lakeside's Gilligan's Island, ROM; and of today's top living Register of Merit dog, Select American and Canadian Champion Cobert's Reno of Lakeside, ROM, who is the sire of fifty-three American champions and thirty Canadian champions. Reno, at twelve years of age, still thrills the German Shepherd Fancy when he appears in the Parade of Greats at the National Specialty show.

Much inbreeding and line-breeding have been done on the Cobert bloodlines, and using these lines has worked out very successfully for numerous breeders in the United States and Canada. It is hard to find a pedigree that does

Four times Select Ch. Cobert's Reno of Lakeside, ROM, is the highest living ROM sire. By Grand Victor Ch. Lance of Fran Jo, ROM, ex Cobert's Melissa, ROM, Reno is co-owned by Vita Moreno with Connie Beckhardt, Cobert Kennels, Tenafly, New Jersey.

The great producing bitch Cobert's Melissa, ROM, surrounded by photos of some of her noted progeny. Owned by Connie Beckhardt, Cobert Kennels.

Grand Victor Ch. Lakeside's Harrigan, ROM, here is taking Grand Victor at the National Specialty Show in 1972. Judge, Ralph Roberts. Connie Beckhardt, owner.

Select Ch. Cobert's Golly Gee of Lakeside, ROM, at the National Specialty in 1970, handled by Kim Knoblauch for Connie Beckhardt, Cobert Kennels. Golly Gee is one of the progeny from the famous Grand Victor Ch. Lance of Fran-Jo, ROM, ex Cobert's Melissa, ROM, breeding.

not have the Cobert's Melissa, ROM American and Canadian Grand Victor Champion Lance of Fran-Jo, ROM, combination in the background. Mrs. Beckhardt mentions especially an exciting line-breeding of the bitch Champion Cobert's Windsong, who is co-owned with Gail Sprock. Windsong was a daughter of Grand Victor Champion Scorpio of Shiloh Gardens out of the Beckhardts' Select bitch, Champion Cobert's Golly Gee of Lakeside, ROM. Bred back to her uncle, Reno (Golly's full brother), Windsong produced two champion bitches and a Register of Merit male in the first litter, and a repeat of the breeding produced two more champion bitches. The Beckhardts kept a bitch from the first litter for themselves; this bitch became Champion Cobert's Zephyr of Windigail, who has made the Register of Merit title, has earned the TT (has passed a temperament test), and is now going out to earn her obedience title—with time out for whelping a litter, of course.

Ch. Cobert's Zephyr of Windigail, ROM, taking Best of Breed under Richard Robshaw, handled by Sandra Dancosse for Connie and Ted Beckhardt, Tenafly, New Jersey.

The Beckhardts' young male, Champion Cobert's Trollstigen, is sired by Champion Doppelt-Tay's Hawkeye and out of Zephyr. He is just three years old and already has a champion daughter plus several other winning progeny with major points. His daughter, Champion Hy-Hope's Bernadette of Towaco, is out of a dam who was sired by Cobert's Whisper Jet, a brother to Windsong out of a Reno daughter. Once again very close breeding was done with great success.

The Beckhardts have done the principal share of their showing at Specialty shows and have never become involved with Group competition at all-breed shows, principally because German Shepherd handlers on the whole are not interested in waiting for the Group judging to begin when the breed judging has ended, sometimes a matter of at least several hours. The Beckhardts really feel that the German Shepherd Dog is a

Ch. Cobert's Trollstigen, by Ch. Doppelt-Tay's Hawkeye, ROM, ex Ch. Cobert's Zephyr of Windigail, ROM, taking Best of Breed at the New Jersey German Shepherd Dog Club Specialty under Sam Lawrence. Handled by Henry Dancosse for Connie Beckhardt.

very popular Group favorite with the spectators, and certainly Champion Lakeside's Gilligan's Island was much loved by fanciers of all breeds. Mrs. Beckhardt comments, "We are pleased to see that today we have more Shepherds appearing in the Groups and placing in them than has been the case for many years."

Connie Beckhardt has been a breeder, a lecturer, an exhibitor, and a judge of German Shepherd Dogs for many, many years. Ted Beckhardt has been actively involved in the Cobert breeding program, in obedience work, and in administration of the German Shepherd Dog Club of America as well as with their local German Shepherd Dog club. Both of the Beckhardts are as in love with their wonderful breed as they were the day they first became involved with it.

Ch. Hy-Hope's Bernadette of Towaco at twelve months of age. Line-bred heavily to the Cobert dogs, Bernadette is by Ch. Cobert's Trollstigen ex Hy-Hope's Jenny Wade of Towaco. Handled by James Moses for Connie Beckhardt, Tenafly, New Jersey.

Select Ch. Val-Koa's Kellee, ROM, sired by Select Ch. Ulk Wikingerblut, SchH III, FH, CACIB, ROM, ex Ray Mor's Vali. Whelped January 6th 1964. Breeder, Joseph Totora. Dam of ten champions, including a five-champion litter with four Best in Show winners and three Selects. Dam of Ch. Val-Koa's Roon, the all-time U.S. Shepherd winner. Owners, Mary Roberts and Joseph Totora.

Covina Knolls

Covina Knolls Shepherds were established in 1946, when Ralph S. and Mary C. Roberts of Covina, California, purchased their first of the breed, a granddaughter of Odin von Busecker-Schloss. Since that time their dogs have produced eighty champions, including many Best in Show, Select, and Register of Merit sires and dams.

During one period of time, they owned the Top Winning Shepherd *of all time*, the Highest Register of Merit Sire *of all time*, and the Highest Register of Merit Dam *of all time*. Of the three Shepherds to date in history to have won the Quaker Oats Award, Mr. and Mrs. Roberts have owned two: American and Canadian Champion Val-Koa's Roon and American and Canadian Champion Covy-Tucker Hill's Finnegan.

In this family team, Ralph plans the breeding program and makes the selection of animals for the show ring. He has been a judge since 1950

Ch. Frei v.d. Burg Kendenich, SchH I, sired by Bob vom Sultersberg, SchH III, ex Briska v.d. Burg Kendenich, SchH I. Whelped November 15th 1955. Breeder, Peter Langen, Bad Essen, Germany. Owners, Ralph and Mary Roberts, Covina, California.

and has judged the National Specialty several times.

Mary is responsible for the conditioning, training, and handling of the dogs. She first began handling dogs in obedience and thereafter in the conformation ring; and with her owner-handled Shepherds she has won 110 Bests in Show, 337 Working Groups, and 937 Bests of Breed, including sixty-five Specialty shows. Small wonder that she was the first person to be elected to the *Kennel Review* Hall of Fame with three consecutive wins as the Best Female Owner-Handler.

The Roberts continue their line-breeding program based upon the late Rolf Osnabruckerland, begun in 1958 with their first German import, Champion Frei von der Burg Kendenich, SchH I. Champion Frei, winner of sixteen Specialties, was line-bred upon Rolf 3-2.

Their next import came in 1960 with Canadian Grand Victor, American and Canadian Champion Ulk Wikingerblut, SchH III, FH, CACIB, ROM, twice Select, considered to be one of the most outstanding show dogs ever in the breed.

Ulk was imported from Bad Essen, Germany, in April 1960, at three and a half years of age. He was sired by the famous International Champion Troll vom Richterbach, who was the 1956 Holland Sieger and the 1957 United States Grand Victor. Ulk was line-bred upon Rolf 3-3, 4.

By the end of 1962, Ulk had become the *all-time* Top Winning Shepherd in the United States, a distinction he held for eight years. He continued to set records as a producer, with forty-eight champions to his credit. Additionally, Ulk became the Highest Register of Merit Sire *of all time*, succeeding his late sire, Troll. To the Roberts' knowledge, Ulk was the first Shepherd in history to hold simultaneously the all-time winning and producing records.

At the same time as Ulk, the Roberts imported Sascha Wikingerblut, also line-bred upon Rolf. Bred to Ulk, Sascha produced American and Canadian Champion Fant Wikingerblut, who became the Number One German Shepherd winner in the United States for 1963 and 1964, following his sire's top ranking for the previous three years. Sascha, with progeny sired only by Ulk, became the Highest Register of Merit Dam *of all-time*. She held this title until shortly following her death.

Following the showing of many of the champions sired by Ulk, including several Best in Show, Group, and Select winners, in February 1964 the Roberts imported another outstanding show dog and producer, Champion Vox Wikingerblut, ROM. Vox was again in the same breeding line so successfully utilized by the Roberts in the past, Rolf 5-3, 5, 5. Vox also was Rosel-Backer 5-5, giving him additional firm foundation for the Roberts' breeding program, particularly to Ulk daughters.

Vox became a leading German Shepherd winner in the United States from 1965 through 1967, winning twelve Bests in Show. Vox also gained his ROM title, producing nineteen champions, including a five-champion and four-champion litter and five Best in Show and four Select winners.

Vox's greatest success as a producer came from his matings to the Ulk daughter, Select Champion Val-Koa's Kellee, ROM, co-owned

with Joseph Totora. Their first litter produced five champions, including four Best in Show winners and three Select winners. Eventually these two produced ten champions in four matings.

Kellee, in her own right, was also a Best in Show winner, accomplishing this win from the Open Class while still on the way to her championship. Kellee became not only a Select winner but also earned a place on the Register of Merit. She remains ranked in the *all-time* Top Ten Register of Merit Dams.

From the second mating of Vox ex Kellee came the outstanding American and Canadian Champion Val-Koa's Roon, co-owned with Dr.

Am. and Can. Ch. Val-Koa's Roon, by Ch. Vox Wikingerblut, ROM, ex Select Ch. Val-Koa's Kellee, ROM. Whelped April 7th 1968. Breeders, Mary Roberts and Dr. G. Wm. Anderson. America's all-time Shepherd winner! Here winning a Best in Show under judge Ed Bracy with Mary Roberts handling.

Am. and Can. Ch. Vox Wikingerblut, ROM, 1962-1974. Winner of sixteen Bests in Show, sire of nineteen champions including a five-champion litter and a four-champion litter. Owners, Ralph S. and Mary C. Roberts, Covina, California.

Above: Select Ch. Linnloch Sundown von Freya, Number One Shepherd winner in the U.S. for 1980. Born in 1977. Owned by Mary Roberts and James Halferty. **Below:** Ch. Sregor's M.C., Best in Show-winning son of Am. and Can. Ch. Val-Koa's Roon, U.S. all-time Shepherd winner. Born in 1973. Owned by Ralph S. and Mary C. Roberts.

G. William Anderson. Roon was bred by Mary Roberts and Joseph Totora and was whelped in April 1968. This dog became the Number One Shepherd in the United States from 1972 through 1974 and was only the second German Shepherd in history to win the prestigious Quaker Oats Award.

Roon, as his grandsire before him, Champion Ulk Wikingerblut, went on to become the *all-time* Top Winning German Shepherd in the United States, a record which he continues to hold as this book is written; and, in the Best in Show tradition of his line, Roon also produced a Best in Show son, Champion Sregor's M.C.

In 1975, American and Canadian Champion Covy-Tucker Hill's Finnegan, ROM, was acquired from Covy-Tucker Hill Kennels owned by Gloria Birch and Cappy Pottle. Finnegan was whelped on April 4th 1974, sired by Covy's Oregano of Tucker Hill, ROM, ex Fate of Tucker Hill, ROM. As with Frei, Ulk, Vox, Roon, and M.C. before him, Finnegan has eight lines to Rolf.

For 1976, 1977, 1978, and 1979, Finnegan became the Number One German Shepherd in the United States. In 1976, he was also the Number One United States Working Dog and during the same year won the Quaker Oats Award. The Roberts are justifiably proud of being the owners of two of the three Shepherds who have earned this outstanding award.

Am. and Can. Ch. Covy-Tucker Hill's Finnegan, ROM, Best in Show during 1979 under Helen Fisher, handled by co-owner Mary Roberts. Finnegan was Number One U.S. Shepherd in 1976, 1977, 1978, and 1979; Number One U.S. Working Dog in 1977; winner of the Quaker Oats Award in 1977; and Number Two all-time Shepherd winner in the U.S. Ralph and Mary Edwards, owners, Covina, California.

Ch. T-Mar's Ticker Tape, a Best in Show son of Ch. Ulk. Mary C. Roberts and Harry Joyce, owners.

Finnegan is currently the Number Two German Shepherd winner *of all time*, standing behind his late kennel-mate, Roon. Finnegan has earned his Register of Merit title, having produced ten champions thus far, and he is still available at stud.

The standard bearer for 1980 for the Roberts was Select Champion Linnloch Sundown von Freya, co-owned with James Halferty. Sundown was whelped September 9th 1977 and has several lines to Rolf. He was awarded Select at two years of age, and in 1980 he became a Best in Show dog and ranked as the Number One Shepherd for that year.

Covina Knolls may well be the top winning German Shepherd kennel in breed history. Their dogs have been ranked either Number One or Number Two Shepherd in the United States for the past twenty-one consecutive years, with fourteen of those years as Number One—most certainly an awe-inspiring achievement. Remarkably, all of these Shepherds have been owner-handled by Mary Roberts, who a great many people in this sport consider very definitely to be the "first lady" of the German Shepherd world.

Covy-Tucker Hill

Since joining forces to establish Covy-Tucker Hill Kennels, Cappy Pottle and Gloria F. Birch, at Cotati, California, have created one of the most successful German Shepherd breeding and showing operations in the United States. Utilizing their well-known bitches, including the 1970 United States Maturity Victrix and Seven Times Select Champion Tucker Hill's Angelique, C.D., ROM, and Champion Kovaya's Contessa, C.D., ROM, and breeding them to prepotent studs of harmonious structure possessing sound hips and temperament, they have produced many outstanding dogs, including more than fif-

ty champions. Among these champions, particular pride is taken in Grand Victor Champion Lakeside's Harrigan, ROM, and Champion Lakeside's Gilligan's Island, ROM, of Cobert Kennels; and, of course, the noted "Spice" litter, by Grand Victor Champion Lakeside's Harrigan from Angelique, which included the 1976 U.S. Grand Victrix Champion Covy's Rosemary of Tucker Hill, ROM; twice Select U.S. Futurity Victrix Champion Covy's Tartar of Tucker Hill, ROM; twice Select Champion Covy's Tarragon of Tucker Hill; Covy's Oregano of Tucker Hill, ROM; and Champion Covy's Caraway of Tucker Hill.

Ch. Kovaya's Contessa, C.D., ROM, by Obernauf's Daemon ex Crickwood's Gillie, ROM. A famous producing bitch bred by Gloria Birch and Sally Holcombe and owned by Gloria Birch and Cappy Pottle.

1970 Maturity Victrix, world record seven times Select Ch. Tucker Hill's Angelique, C.D., ROM, dam of the famous "Spice" litter, is a daughter of Holland Sieger Gauss v. Stauderpark, SchH III, ex Jodi of Tucker Hill. Bred by Cappy Pottle and A.L. Gibson; owned by Cappy Pottle, Jean Stevens, and Gloria Birch, Cotati, California.

Grand Victrix Ch. Covy's Rosemary of Tucker Hill, ROM, by Grand Victor Ch. Lakeside's Harrigan, ROM, ex Ch. Tucker Hill's Angelique, C.D., ROM. Born February 1973. Owned by Cappy Pottle (co-breeder with Jean Stevens) and Gloria Birch.

Ch. Covy's Caraway of Tucker Hill, by Grand Victor Ch. Lakeside's Harrigan, ROM, ex Ch. Tucker Hill's Angelique, C.D., ROM, at nine years of age. Owned by Cappy Pottle and Gloria F. Birch, Covy-Tucker Hill Kennels.

Top Ten Sire, Covy's Oregano of Tucker Hill, ROM, by Grand Victor Ch. Lakeside's Harrigan, ROM, ex seven times Select Ch. Tucker Hill's Angelique, C.D., ROM, is another member of the famous "Spice" litter. Bred by Cappy Pottle and Jean Stevens; owned by Cappy Pottle and Gloria Birch.

Ch. Covy-Tucker Hill's Triumph, a very appropriately named bitch whose show career has, indeed, been a triumph! Her dam is the 1976 Grand Victrix Ch. Covy's Rosemary of Tucker Hill, most famous of the Harrigan/Angelique Spice litter, and her sire the outstanding producer, also from a multichampion litter, Cobert's Sirocco of Windigail, ROM. She is from the same litter that produced Ch. Covy's Mazarati and Select Ch. Covy's Mercedes of Tucker Hill. Bred and owned by Cappy Pottle and Gloria Birch, Covy-Tucker Hill Kennels, Cotati, California.

Special plaudits also go to the Top Winning U.S.A. Shepherd, 1976 through 1979, Champion Covy-Tucker Hill's Finnegan, ROM; the U.S. Maturity Victor, Select Champion Covy-Tucker Hill's Durango, ROM; Champion Covy's Felita of Tucker Hill, ROM; Covy-Tucker Hill's Zinfandel, ROM; and Covy-Tucker Hill's Carmelita, ROM.

1976 U.S. Grand Victrix Champion Covy's Rosemary of Tucker Hill, ROM, from the "Spice" litter, has herself made a splendid producing record. Among her progeny are Champion Covy's Mazarati of Tucker Hill, Select Champion Covy's Mercedes of Tucker Hill, Champion Covy-Tucker Hill's Triumph, Champion Covy's Starwars of Tucker Hill, and American and Canadian Champion Covy-Tucker Hill's Manhattan.

Another of the particularly successful producing bitches at this kennel is Champion Kovaya's Contessa; she is the dam of Champion Kovaya's Judd, ROM; Champion Kovaya's Jill, ROM; Champion Covy's Feuta of Tucker Hill, ROM; and Champion Kovaya's Lurch, C.D.

Covy-Tucker Hill has successfully incorporated Select American and Canadian Champion Cobert's Reno of Lakeside, ROM, and Select Champion Cobert's Golly Gee of Lakeside, ROM, with Grand Victrix Champion Covy's Rosemary of Tucker Hill to produce the previously mentioned multiple champion "car" litter. Covy's Bonita of Tucker Hill bred to Reno produced the 1978 Grand Victrix Champion Jo-San's Charisma.

While the list of champions and top producers goes on and on, the dogs at Covy-Tucker Hill never forget their "working dog" heritage. Littermates and offspring of these top winners can be found earning their keep at Guide Dogs for the Blind, police departments, and working ranches, as well as in loving families throughout the United States and other countries.

Am. and Can. Ch. Covy-Tucker Hill's Manhattan, by Covy's Flanigan of Tucker Hill (Select Ch. Lakeside's Gilligan's Island, ROM, ex Ch. Kovaya's Contessa, C.D., ROM) from Grand Victrix Ch. Covy's Rosemary of Tucker Hill, ROM (Grand Victor Ch. Lakeside's Harrigan, ROM, ex seven times Select Ch. Tucker Hill's Angelique, C.D., ROM). Owned by Shirley and David Z. Braunstein; bred by Cappy Pottle and Gloria Birch.

Ch. Covy-Tucker Hill's Charmalita, a 1981 champion and Group winner by Cobert's Sirocco of Windigail, ROM, ex Covy-Tucker Hill's Carmelita, ROM. Owned by Charles and Priscilla Countee and Morgan and Gloria Krumm of New Mexico; bred by the Krumms and Cappy Pottle and Gloria Birch.

Destino

Destino German Shepherds belong to Mrs. Mary Eischen Greene at Lithonia, Georgia, who is particularly proud of her current show star, Champion Destino's Serge, a homebred by Champion Aspen of Fran-Jo (grandson of Champion Eko-Lan's Paladen, ROM) from Champion Shadyhaven's Glory, C.D., a Paladen daughter.

Completing his championship at twenty months of age after only seven weeks of campaigning, Serge thus achieved quite an outstanding accomplishment in this breed. He is the 1980 Futurity Victor and Best of Opposite Sex in the 1981 Midwestern Regional Futurity. As of December 1982, he had acquired ten Best of Breed wins from both Specialty and all-breed shows.

Serge is line-bred on one of the top Register of Merit Sires alive today, Champion Eko-Lan's Paladen.

Champion Shadyhaven's Glory, C.D., Serge's dam, is Mrs. Greene's foundation bitch. She carries the Paladen and Champion Cobert's Reno of Lakeside, ROM, lines, so highly successful for breeders in all parts of the country.

Ch. Destino's Serge taking Best of Breed at the Shoreline German Shepherd Dog Club Specialty, June 13th 1981. By Grand Victor Ch. Aspen of Fran Jo ex Ch. Shadyhaven's Glory, C.D., this dog was the 1980 Futurity Victor. Owned by Mary Eischen Greene, Lithonia, Georgia.

1980 Select Ch. Die Herzogin's J. J. as a puppy at the Delaware Valley German Shepherd Dog Club in 1978. Shirley and David Panijan, owners, Trenton, New Jersey.

Die Herzogin

Die Herzogin German Shepherd Kennels are owned by Shirley and David Panijan and located at Trenton, New Jersey. The Panijans started their breeding program back in 1970, based on Igor and Clover Acres bloodlines.

In 1973, they purchased a lovely bitch, Chewing Gum von Tara Haus, who became a champion in about twelve shows and went on to take Select at the 1975 German Shepherd Dog Club of America National Specialty. Unfortunately, Chew died at an early age, a tremendous loss to the Panijans.

Fortunately, the Panijans had another excellent bitch, Von Nassau's Valta of Louron, by Champion Lakeside's Harrigan, ROM, ex Valta Rae of Louron. Breeding her to a well-known stud dog, from her litter came Die Herzogin's Hutch von Hensan who proved his worth as a stud dog by siring the 1980 Select Champion Die Herzogin's J.J. who has become a Top Winning Black German Shepherd Dog in the United

Die Herzogin Hutch v. Hensan, one of the fine Shepherds belonging to Shirley and David Panijan, Die Herzogin Kennels.

Above: Leypa's Kachena at the Mohawk Hudson Specialty in April 1981. Owned by Die Herzogin Kennels, Shirley and David Panijan, Trenton, New Jersey. **Below:** Best Puppy and Reserve Winners Dog for five points at the Tampa Bay German Shepherd Dog Club Specialty, Von Gruenwald Taurus, seven and a half months old. Owned by Shirley and David Panijan, Die Herzogin Kennels.

States. J.J. was shown only nine times, including Puppy Classes, en route to his championship. Best Puppy at ten months and Reserve Winners Dog in a four-point entry at thirteen months from the Novice Class, he gained his title with all majors except for a single point. Out as a Special, by November 1981 he had set a new record, his owners tell us, for a black Shepherd: shown nineteen times, gaining sixteen Bests of Breed and two Bests of Opposite Sex—a very handsome dog and a splendid representative of the breed.

Die Herzogin Kennels only breed about four litters each year and own an average of eight adult dogs.

Dolmar

Dolmar Shepherds belong to Mrs. Marge Dolan of Woodbridge, Connecticut, whose love of the breed started as a teenager while living in India. Two male Shepherds were owned by the family during this time, the second having been acquired as a replacement following the death of the first. There was little beyond schooling for a young girl to do in those days; and so, upon acquisition of the second Shepherd, Marge decided that she would see how well she could train him. She did that and more, as she found the dog to be willing to please and eager to work. Years later, as a married lady when she and her husband and children built their present home in Connecticut, Marge Dolan decided that the time had come to continue her association with German Shepherd Dogs, and so a telephone call was made to a breeder-friend regarding the purchase of another male. The friend could not find a male to fill Mrs. Dolan's standards, but she did suggest a bitch puppy who was available. Mrs. Dolan hesitated, as she had never previously owned a bitch, but went to see the puppy anyway and was immediately conquered by her per-

Eko-Lan's Rhyme winning the Novice Bitch Class at Elm City Kennel Club in July 1972. Rhyme is the foundation bitch of Mrs. Marge Dolan's Dolmar Kennels at Woodbridge, Connecticut, and is co-owned by Mrs. Dolan with Carol Lordo.

sonality and looks. Five years later Mrs. Dolan decided to breed this bitch, resulting in a litter of seven puppies. Mr. Dolan was convinced that they would find themselves "stuck" with eight dogs (mother and pups), but that was not the case at all; and he was pleasantly surprised when his wife sold the puppies, in the process meeting some wonderful people who "hooked" her into doing some more and serious breeding right then and there. When the original bitch died, Marge Dolan turned to *German Shepherd Dog Review* in which she read of a litter which interested her. This was when she became acquainted with Carol Lordo—the turning point in her life

as a breeder. Through Carol, Mrs. Dolan was able to acquire, late in 1971, co-ownership on a young bitch, Eko-Lan's Rhyme, and from then on it was all uphill! Carol made the excellent suggestion of breeding Rhyme to "an unknown young male" then just starting out, Cobert's Reno of Lakeside, who later went on to become an American and Canadian Champion, several times Select, and a Register of Merit Sire. Rhyme and Reno were bred on four occasions with excellent results in all four cases. Out of Reno's first three champions, two were Rhyme's, namely Dolmar's Cara of Spring Rock and her litter-brother, Concho. The second

Ch. Dolmar's Concho of Spring Rock, owned by Joan Peck and Carol Lordo, taking five points for Winners Dog at the German Shepherd Dog Club of Greater New Haven Specialty Show, October 1974. Judge, Mary Southcott. Handler, Fred Olsen. The second of the Dolmar-Shepherds to finish, just two months after his sister.

Ch. Dolmar's Eli of Spring Rock, bred by M. Dolan and C. Lordo and owned by Joan Traver. A full brother by a later litter to Cara and Concho, Eli finished in 1977.

repeat breeding produced yet another champion, Dolmar's Eli of Spring Rock and litter-sister Echo, who, when bred to Champion Zeto of Fran-Jo, produced the Dolan's fourth champion, Dolmar's Noel of Spring Rock. The Reno-Rhyme "click" not only produced champions but also good producing stock who in turn also were able to produce champions of their own.

Prior to the acquisition of Rhyme, Mrs. Dolan had lost, through no fault of her own, four bitches. Her husband had urged her to give up breeding, but she was determined to try just one more time by taking Rhyme. How glad she is that she did so, for with Carol Lordo's help and guidance she did make it this time, and the success she has attained speaks for itself! Mrs. Dolan comments, "Because of the help I received, I am very eager to be of assistance to any

novice breeder who wants to learn, hopefully trying to give them the same benefits I had. You might call it paying back society."

Mrs. Dolan and Carol Lordo together have bred four champions, and Mrs. Dolan has another which she co-bred with another dear friend, Andrea Washburn. This one is Champion Andiron's Ricochet of Dolmar, by Champion Langenau's Winchester ex Dolmar's Gala of Spring Rock (she from the third repeat Reno-Rhyme breeding). One of the accomplishments in which Mrs. Dolan takes special pride is the fact that Eko-Lan's Rhyme did achieve her Registry of Merit, a very coveted breeding title bestowed by the parent club; Mrs. Dolan adds, "I believe she is only the second bitch in the state of Connecticut to have gained this title over a period of about the past fifteen years [as of

Ch. Dolmar's Noel of Spring Rock, bred by M. Dolan and C. Lordo and owned by Joan Traver, taking Best of Opposite Sex at the Bay State German Shepherd Dog Club for a four-point major. Handler, James Moses.

1982].'' Another meaningful accomplishment is that Mrs. Dolan now has three German Shepherd "grandsons" who have earned their championship title; the first champion "grandson" was out of Dolmar's Gail of Spring Rock from the third Reno-Rhyme breeding, the second was out of her Champion Eli, and the third was from a bitch she co-bred who descends from the Reno-Rhyme combination several generations back. She also has other "grandchildren progeny" close to championship (probably finished by the time you are reading this). Seeing the descendants of her Shepherds doing so well gives Mrs. Dolan the good feeling that she has contributed her share to breed progress—which is what it is all about!

Dolmar dogs have been exhibited at the National Specialty since 1974, taking their share of placements at this event where one meets the "cream of the crop."

Mrs. Dolan's is a small kennel and usually keeps its number of dogs to six at a time. This

way each dog gets the important personal attention it needs and deserves, although it does make it more difficult to achieve one's goal statistically speaking when you are in competition with breeders who operate larger kennels. Dolmar averages only two litters a year (Mrs. Dolan had raised a total of 153 puppies, as of late 1981), but her feeling is that overall quality is of greater importance than quantity! She cares about each and every puppy born in her family and makes a special attempt to find the best possible homes for them, whether for show or as pets. As she says, "If I don't, who will?" This is the attitude that makes apparent why it is to one's advantage to purchase from a breeder than from other sources, as described elsewhere in this book.

Mrs. Dolan has a wise word for new breeders and those of the future. "A house is only as good as its foundation, and this applies also to a breeding program. Animals sound in mind and body are a 'must' with which to start out; otherwise you will have nothing except problems which may return to haunt you later on."

As a postscript to the above, Mrs. Dolan is basking in the fact that one of her "grandsons," American and Canadian Champion Elkovar's Jolly Roger, went Select Number Three at the 1982 National at Cleveland, Ohio, and two other young "grandsons" took placings in the classes.

Ch. Dolmar's Oncore, one of the beautiful and successful Shepherds from Marge Dolan's kennel in Woodbridge, Connecticut.

Dornwald

When Eleanor S. Cole (Mrs. James A. Cole) of Pound Ridge and New York City in New York passed away in the late 1970's, it brought to an end a very great and prestigious German Shepherd kennel, Dornwald, which the Coles had founded in the late 1930's.

During its first twenty years alone, Dornwald produced or owned fifty-seven German Shepherd champions. I do not have the exact total since that time, but I am certain that the number is extremely impressive.

Among the noted dogs at Dornwald were American and Canadian Champion Fels von der Rottumbruke, an importation who did a great deal of winning in keenest Eastern competition; Champion Marrilea's Vetter of Dornwald, C.D., ROM; Champion Lollie of Dornwald, ROM; Champion Firelei of Dornwald, ROM; Champion Marrilea's Rima of Dornwald, U.D.T.; Champion Ariel of Dornwald, C.D.X.; Champion Olympia of Dornwald, C.D.; Champion Farra of Dornwald, C.D.; Champion Kismet of Dornwald, C.D.; Canadian Grand Victor Champion Haakon of Dornwald; Champion Sappho of Dornwald, ROM; Champion Eroica of Dornwald, ROM; Champion Koldo of Stone Home, C.D.; American and Canadian Champion Croesus of Dornwald; and Champion Nox of Dornwald, who was the Shepherd Mrs. Cole was owner-handling with notable success when I first knew her in the 1940's. These dogs are just a sampling of the many great winners from Dornwald—there were dozens more!

Mrs. Eleanor Cole, owner of the Dornwald German Shepherds, was a highly respected Working Dog judge. Here she is making an award to a handsome dog handled by Denise Kodner at the Shoreline German Shepherd Dog Club in 1963.

Ender-Haus

Ender-Haus German Shepherds, at Mishicot, Wisconsin, came about when their owner William Endries, as a young man on patrol duty with the U.S. Army in 1953, spotted what appeared to be a German Shepherd running across the desert of New Mexico. After picking him up, our friend proceeded back to the base where the dog was introduced to his new master's fellow comrades who then treated him to one of "the Army's outstanding meals."

Two years later, in 1955, Mr. Endries purchased his first pedigreed German Shepherd Dog from Copper Canyon Kennels in Utah. Sadly, this Shepherd died at the young age of two years from an apparent heart attack.

More enthusiastic than ever over the breed, Mr. Endries started attending Specialty shows where he hoped to gain additional knowledge of the breed. During this period he purchased several bitches, but they turned out to be disappointments.

Visiting several of the big kennels, a wise decision was reached: to wait before the next purchase until the dog he really wanted appeared and then to try to become owner of that one. At

Margo von Bid-Scono, ROM, daughter of Eko-Lan's Paladen, ROM, winning Best in Maturity, Midwest, in 1974. Owned by William J. Endries, Mishicot, Wisconsin.

Margo von Bid-Scono, by Eko-Lan's Paladen, ROM, here is winning the Best in Futurity Award, Midwest, for her owner, William J. Endries, Ender-Haus Kennels.

the National Specialty in Detroit, Michigan, in 1971, Mr. Endries noticed from the ringside "an outstanding moving machine by the name of Aloha von Bid-Scono." Here was what he had been seeking, everything he wanted in a Shepherd! The following day she went Grand Victrix, and Mr. Endries succeeded in buying, from Luke Geraghty of Ohio, the owner, another of similar breeding, Margo von Bid-Scono, sired by the outstanding producer, Eko-Lan's Paladen, ROM, who belonged to Fred Migliore.

Margo fulfilled Mr. Endries' hopes for her when she went Best in Futurity, Midwest, in 1973 and Best in Maturity there in 1974. Her litter-sister, Mylanta von Bid-Scono, is a champion, as are two litter-brothers. Margo also is on her way to her ROM, having produced two champions: Champion Ender-Haus' Commotion, by the famous Lakeside's Reno, and Champion Krisselhof's Aliv Enderhaus, sired by Champion Nocturne's Hale of Krisselhof. There are several promising Margo puppies coming along and Mr. Endries hopes to complete their championships and their dam's ROM. Margo herself, at ten years age, is full of fine spirits and fire.

Farmil

Farmil German Shepherds, located at Roxbury, Connecticut, were established in 1975 by Charles and Doris Farrell following their pleasant experience of successfully taking two members of this breed through obedience. These were Schwartzwalds Ernestine, C.D.X., and Vel-Bren Harlow von Freya, C.D. As foundation for their breeding program, the Farrells selected a beautiful and well-bred bitch, Dolmars Ilise of Farmil, who was a daughter of Zeus of Fran-Jo, ROM, and a granddaughter of Champion Cobert's Reno of Lakeside, ROM, from Eko-Lan's Rhyme, a combination that had produced several champions.

Ilise was bred to Cobert's Whisper Jet, a breeding later repeated, and produced several Futurity winners, namely Farmils Abbey of Dolmar, Farmils Bonne of Dolmar, and Farmils Breene of Dolmar. Farmils Abbey of Dolmar, in turn, was bred to Select Champion Kismets Impulse von Bismarck and from this combination came the handsome young Champion Farmils Chantz, who was the top Teenage Dog at the Northeast Futurity in 1980 under Joan Ford and the Mid-Atlantic Maturity Victor for 1981.

Farmils Abbey of Dolmar, at seven months of age, the dam of Ch. Farmils Chantz, bred and owned by Doris Farrell, Farmil Shepherds, Roxbury, Connecticut.

Farmils Bonne of Dolmar, at eleven months of age, by Cobert's Whisper Jet ex Dolmars Ilise of Farmil. Bred by Doris Farrell; owned by Jean Sarnacki.

114

Ch. Farmils Chantz at eleven months of age. Owned by Doris Farrell.

Chantz gained his championship title in good order, with four majors in seven shows.

Currently (autumn 1982), Doris Farrell is campaigning the young Farmil Flintlock, co-owned by Ann Hickman in Louisiana, through the South. He is a promising youngster, so hopes are high for his success.

Farmils Flintlock, being campaigned in the South, is co-owned by Doris Farrell and Ann Hickman of Louisiana.

Fran-Jo

Fran-Jo German Shepherds, which have earned a position of very special recognition and respect throughout the dog show world, belong to Mr. and Mrs. Francis L. Ford, Sr. (Joan and Fran) of Grove City, Ohio. The Fords had always been great dog enthusiasts, with a special inclination toward the Working breeds, and had been owners of a few Boxers, some Danes, and a Cocker Spaniel when, in the early 1960's, Fran decided that he would enjoy becoming more deeply involved with the breeding and showing of dogs; he narrowed his choice of breeds to either Dobermans or German Shepherds. Joan cast the deciding vote between the two, as Shepherds were far and away her preference. Thus it was that the "die was cast" and the groundwork for what has become a dynasty in the German Shepherd world begun.

The Fords' first Shepherd, a show-prospect puppy, turned out to be extremely shy and had some teeth missing. It had come from a reputable kennel, however, and since it did not live up to expectations, the breeder replaced it with another. This time things worked out better and this second Shepherd gained an obedience C.D. plus some blue ribbons in the conformation classes. The Fords' interest and enthusiasm for

Joan and Fran Ford, owners of the Fran-Jo German Shepherds, snapped informally at the party in celebration of Grand Victor Ch. Aspen of Fran-Jo, ROM, in 1980.

1967 U.S. and Canadian Grand Victor, Am. and Can. Ch. Lance of Fran-Jo, ROM, bred and owned by Joan and Fran Ford, Fran-Jo Kennels, Grove City, Ohio, on his last appearance in the show ring, at about nine years of age, at the Parade of Greats, Atlanta, Georgia. This marvelous dog left a legacy of greatness in the German Shepherd world.

the breed grew steadily, causing them to move from Columbus, where they were living at the time, to their current location at Grove City, where what had started out as a house with pets soon grew to include a new three-run hobby kennel which over the years has increased in size to more than twenty runs.

The first Fran-Jo litter was born during the autumn of 1963 and consisted of four puppies who won some placements in Futurities—surely a nice way to start, but the Fords were not really happy with the quality of the litter. Even as novices they possessed the "eye" for what is correct in the breed, and they considered side movement to be especially important.

The second litter made up for any previous disappointment or dissatisfaction. This time they had leased a six-year-old bitch, Frohlich's Elsa von Grunestahl, ROM, whom they had admired. In search of advice about how best to breed this bitch, Joan went to Lucy Woodard, breeder-owner of the famous "F Arbywood" litter, which was by the famed International Champion Grand Victor Troll vom Richterbach, ROM, from Frigga of Silver Lane, ROM (owned by Lucy Woodard). To digress a moment, this "F Arbywood" litter was something of a phenomenon: six out of its eight puppies

became champions and three became Register of Merit Sires. On this lady's advice, Joan Ford bred Elsa to Champion Fortune of Arbywood, ROM, an outcross breeding which truly made history. Elsa was a double great-granddaughter of Hein vom Richterbach, ROM, and Fortune's sire, the mighty Troll, was by Axel von der Deininghauserheide. Elsa whelped her litter of seven puppies on February 27th 1964—a litter which contained that very memorable dog, American and Canadian Grand Victor, American and Canadian Champion Lance of Fran-Jo, ROM, and an outstanding bitch, Champion Lonie of Fran-Jo, ROM, Futurity Victrix.

Lance started his show career, at slightly over four months of age, at a match show with more than one hundred entries, which he won. By eleven and a half months of age he was winning consistently at the matches and, measuring twenty six and a half inches at the withers, appeared ready to start out in the Open Class at point shows. Just when everything was going so well, Lance was stricken with panosteitis, a disease often referred to as "long bone disease" since it is the long bones of the leg which are affected. The disease causes the bone to produce more marrow than is needed; this appeared on Lance's x-rays as a white shadow in the long bones of his legs. The disease moves from one leg to another, causing considerable pain to its victim. Lance's muscles atrophied, and his suffering as he limped was heartbreaking. The Fords were advised by the veterinarians to put Lance to sleep and after long deliberation, and unable to bear seeing him in such pain, Joan Ford agreed to have it done; she put Lance in the car and called her husband over to say good-bye. Then she simply could not go through with it. She returned Lance to his kennel, and, almost miraculously, the dearly loved dog started to improve. At fifteen months of age, Lance had the appearance of an awkward teenager: all legs, gawky, and somewhat uncoordinated. After going through all that he did while maturing, Lance grew into a remarkably handsome, well-balanced, superbly moving animal—a joy to watch and a trailblazer for the Shepherd as we know the breed today. No longer uncoordinated, Lance moved with a smooth, extra long and powerful, well-suspended gait and possessed elegance in the form of a masculine refinement which gained him hosts of admirers. The Shepherd Fancy speaks of him as having started a

Ch. Lonie of Fran-Jo, ROM, 1965 Futurity Grand Victrix and litter-sister to the great Grand Victor Ch. Lance of Fran-Jo, ROM, owned by Mr. and Mrs. Francis Ford, Sr. (Joan and Fran), Fran-Jo Kennels, Grove City, Ohio.

new era in the breed, which sounds to this writer like an accurate description of what has taken place.

Lance quickly stepped into the Winners circle at the dog shows, as did his sister, Lonie. These two gave the Fords many a thrilling day by coming away with *both* Winners Dog and Winners Bitch, and they both finished their championships on their second birthday, at the same dog show in Louisville, Kentucky. This was especially exciting for the Fords because, even though they were novices at the time, Fran Ford piloted Lance to his title (except for just two points), which is nice going in so highly competitive a breed as this one.

In addition to finishing Lance and Lonie during 1966, the Fords also had the fun of seeing Lance become the year's Maturity Victor and Select at the National Specialty. Lonie had been the 1965 Futurity Victrix while Lance was still recovering from his illness.

The Fords arranged to team Lance up with the talented young handler Jimmy Moses, with whom he made history despite being sparingly shown. He earned a total of thirty-six Bests of Breed, eight Group firsts, two all-breed Bests in Show, and nine Specialty Bests of Breed. In 1967, he became both American and Canadian Grand Victor.

Grand Victor Ch. Lance of Fran-Jo, putting in a busy evening as host of a party in his honor, is accepting a tasty morsel from his owner Joan Ford.

Ch. Zeto of Fran-Jo, ROM, an in-bred son of Grand Victor Ch. Lance of Fran-Jo, is from Ch. Misheim's Abbey, ROM. Owned by the Fords.

Lance's contribution to the future of German Shepherds has been inestimable. He has produced more United States and Canadian Grand Victors and Grand Victrixes than any other sire in the breed's history. He, a Grand Victor himself, is the sire of the 1969 Maturity Victor and 1971 Select American Grand Victor Champion Mannix of Fran-Jo, ROM, and through the latter is the grandsire of the 1972 American Grand Victor Champion Scorpio of Shiloh Gardens, the 1975 Grand Victor Champion Caesar von Carahaus, and the 1975 Grand Victrix Champion Langenau's Tango, for three generations of Grand Victors.

The list of sixty champions sired by Lance truly reads like a *Who's Who* in the world of German Shepherds. To name just a few, one thinks

1973 U.S. Grand Victor Ch. Scorpio of Shiloh Gardens, ROM, owned by Thomas L. and Carol McPheron, a son of the 1971 U.S. Grand Victor Ch. Mannix of Fran-Jo, ROM.

1974 U.S. and Can. Grand Victrix Ch. Lor-Locke's Tatta of Fran-Jo, ROM, the dam of Ch. Hutch of Fran-Jo, Ch. Tatta Too of Lor-Locke Fran-Jo, Ch. Aphoebe of Fran-Jo, Ch. Giradet of Fran-Jo, Regas of Fran-Jo on the way to the title, and three other ROM contributors. Joan and Fran Ford, owners, Fran-Jo Kennels, Grove City, Ohio.

immediately of the aforementioned Mannix, plus such outstanding dogs as 1967-1970 Select Champion Lakeside's Gilligan's Island, ROM, multi-Best in Show dog; Champion Cobert's Reno of Lakeside, ROM, the sire of fifty-three American and thirty Canadian champions, now the top ranking *living* ROM Sire; 1972 American Grand Victor Champion Lakeside's Harrigan, ROM; 1969 Best in Maturity Champion My Molly B of Fran-Jo; 1969 Select Champion Eko-Lan's Morgan, ROM; 1969 Canadian Grand Victrix and 1970 Select Champion Christa von Langenau, ROM; 1974 Futurity Victor and Select Champion Alator's Baccarat; 1970 Futurity Victrix Champion Winaki's Jahtzee von der Lo-Roc; 1971 Canadian Grand Victor and American Select, 1971 Maturity Victor Champion Haag and Haag's Dapper Dan; 1973 Futurity Victrix and Select Champion Doppelt-Tay's Gilda.

Fran-Jo Kennels, as of November 1982, are the breeders or owners of the following: 1966 Maturity Victor and Select, 1967 United States and Canadian Grand Victor, American and Canadian Champion Lance of Fran-Jo, ROM; 1965 Futurity Victrix Champion Lonie of Fran-Jo, ROM; Champion My Molly B of Fran-Jo (by Lance); Champion Gailand's Magic of Fran-Jo (by Lance); 1970 Maturity Victor and Select, 1971 American Victor Champion Mannix of Fran-Jo, ROM (by Lance); Champion Misheim's Abbey, ROM (by Lance); 1971 Best in Maturity, Champion Robbie of Fran-Jo; Champion Kolheim's Mia of Fran-Jo; Champion Beau of Fran-Jo, ROM (by Lance); 1972 Best in Maturity, Champion Bobette of Fran-Jo (by Lance); 1973 Best in Futurity, Champion Zeto of Fran-Jo, ROM, (by Lance); Champion Elfie of Fran-Jo, ROM; Champion Eisenberg's Ericka of Fran-Jo; 1975 Canadian Grand Victor

119

Champion Shaft of Delshire, Select Best in Maturity; Champion Jerry of Delshire; 1974 Maturity Victrix, 1974 American and Canadian Grand Victrix Champion Lor-Locke's Tatta of Fran-Jo, ROM; 1975 Best in Maturity, Champion Bridget of Fran-Jo, ROM; Champion Hutch of Fran-Jo; Select Champion Tatta Too Lor-Locke Fran-Jo; 1977 Best in Maturity Champion Raisin of Fran-Jo; Champion Apple Candy of Fran-Jo; 1977 Best Opposite in Maturity, Champion Dottie of Fran-Jo; 1979 Best in Futurity, 1980 Best in Maturity, 1981 Select Champion Papillon of Fran-Jo; 1980 American Grand Victor Champion Aspen of Fran-Jo, ROM, 1978 Best in Futurity; 1979 Best in Maturity, Champion Annie of Fran-Jo; Champion Aphoebe of Fran-Jo; Champion Giradet of Fran-Jo; and Zeus of Fran-Jo, ROM, by Lance and Hilgrove's Arle, ROM. This list shows that Fran-Jo has breeder-owned eleven Registry of Merit Sires, twenty-seven champions, three American Grand Victors, one American and Canadian Grand Victrix, two Canadian Grand Victors, one Futurity Victrix, two Maturity Victors, and one Maturity Victrix.

The breeding program at Fran-Jo has been based entirely on Lance. The Fords found it both safe and successful to line-breed and in-breed on him with no serious repercussions. Of course, one must always use caution, discretion, and knowledge in following this course; but under those circumstances the results can be, and in this case have been, quite outstanding.

Of Lance, Joan Ford says, "He was a great dog to live with. Super temperament, a lot of character and tons of devotion. No dog ever was more loved by his owners, and how proud we are to have been blessed with him and his progeny."

In the Fran-Jo breeding program, the Fords have kept only the best—the ones they felt would finish—from each litter. Only a couple of litters are bred there each year, enabling the Fords to keep their puppies longer to see them develop; puppies do go through many changes during that first year and require a lot of attention. Joan takes care of the dogs herself, with Fran's help on weekends when he is free, and a close friend looks out for the kennel when the Fords are at dog shows. In caring for her dogs, Joan is especially particular about cleanliness and top quality food for them.

Lance receives a standing ovation at his last dog show, in the Parade of Greats, at Atlanta, Georgia. A Shepherd who will live forever through the quality of his descendants!

Appropriate to dogs so beloved and so outstanding in their influence on the breed, this is the final resting place of Grand Victor Ch. Lance of Fran-Jo, ROM, and his son Grand Victor Ch. Mannix of Fran-Jo, ROM. Truly the beginning of an era, Lance was born on February 27th 1964 and died on February 2nd 1973. Joan E. and Francis L. Ford, Sr., owners.

This head-study is of Mimi Saltz's Ch. Ozark of Gan Edan, by Ch. Gabriel of Gan Edan (Ch. Beau of Fran-Jo, ROM, ex Bee-Jay's Holiday of Gan Edan) from Andoro's Aria (Ch. Zar-Zal's Ilko ex Ellyn Hill's Diamond Flush, ROM).

Gan Edan

Gan Edan Kennels are owned by Art and Mimi Saltz and are located at Lake Zurich, Illinois. The Saltzes' interest in German Shepherd Dogs began with a Utility Dog who was put through her titles by Art; this led to the eventual purchase of Bee Jay's Holiday of Gan Edan, ROM, a daughter of Champion Britmere's Timothy of Lahngold ex Trulander's Crimson of Marsa. This bitch was shown a little in the conformation classes, winning blue ribbons consistently, while a puppy. At five and a half years of age she was bred for the first time, and in three litters during her lifetime produced Champion Ember of Gan Edan, Champion Gabriel of Gan Edan, and others who were major-point winners. Holiday was the love and "watch person" of the Saltzes until her death when she was thirteen years old. Mrs. Saltz credits her with the sound minds, marvelous dispositions, and beautiful elastic gaits of the succeeding generations at Gan Edan.

Art and Mimi Saltz have certainly been highly successful breeders. Their greatest pride, of course, is the current star, Grand Victor Cham-

Ch. Ozark of Gan Edan is the sire of Am. and Can. Grand Victor Ch. Sabra of Gan Edan. Bred and owned by Art and Mimi Saltz, Lake Zurich, Illinois.

Grand Victor Ch. Sabra of Gan Edan, by Ch. Ozark of Gan Edan, ROM (Ch. Gabriel of Gan Edan ex Andora's Aria) ex Fran-Jo's Dawn of Gan Edan, ROM (Ch. Zeto of Fran-Jo, ROM, ex Lonnie of Jo Mar). Sabra has enjoyed a spectacular show career which has included being the 1981 U.S. Grand Victor, a Canadian Grand Victor, a Maturity Victor, and a U.S.A. Select. He finished his American title in five shows, going Best of Breed in all but his first. He represents the third generation of champion males bred at Gan Edan, a source of pride to breeders and owners Art and Mimi Saltz, Lake Zurich, Illinois.

pion Sabra of Gan Edan, who represents three homebred generations of champion males from this kennel. Sabra is by Champion Ozark of Gan Edan, a son of Champion Gabriel of Gan Edan who is, in turn, Holiday's son sired by Champion Beau of Fran-Jo, ROM (Grand Victor Champion Lance of Fran-Jo, ROM, ex Fran-Jo's Kelly of Waldesruh).

Sabra has enjoyed a truly spectacular show career, finishing in five majors, going Best of Breed from the classes. Before his third birthday, he had completed his American championship and had become a Grand Victor Champion in Canada, an American Select, and an American Maturity Victor—all this in only ten shows. Then came the 1981 National! Sabra was shown four or five times that year, always taking Best of Breed, and he emerged from the National in this same style, thus earning for himself the title of 1981 Grand Victor in the United States. This dog, in addition to his excellence of type and conformation, is a "sensible, level-headed, loving companion," to quote Mrs. Saltz, bringing happiness to his owners at home as well as in the show ring. His stud career will soon be showing exciting results, too, we predict, as he is in great demand among Shepherd breeders who are using him on their finest bitches.

Mrs. Saltz comments on Gan Edan's good fortune in having James A. Moses as their handler, adviser, and friend. His help toward their success has been inestimable.

Hessian

Hessian German Shepherds, owned by Helen and Art Hess at Goshen, Ohio, has been a proud name in the German Shepherd world since the 1950's and remains so today through the descendants of the great Shepherds which made it famous and through the continuing enthusiasm of owners Art (now a popular A.K.C. specialist judge of the breed) and Helen whose love for the breed will never diminish. In doing research for this book, I have found reference to the remarkable similarity of the Hessian dogs and to the fact that it was often noted that dogs of this strain could be immediately recognized for this reason. I have noted, too, frequent mention of the ground-covering gait and smooth, correct ac-

tion of these dogs. It makes us especially happy to have several action photos of these dogs included among our illustrations for the study and benefit of our readers.

It all began some thirty years ago when the lady who became Helen Hess, a former photographer's model with the beauty title "Miss Cicero," was working in Chicago. Among the employees of the same firm was a blind man whose "eyes" were his trained German Shepherd guide dog, an animal who won Helen's heart with the beauty, loyalty, intelligence, and devotion she noted each day. She never forgot this dog. Following Helen's marriage to Art Hess (a school teacher and professional musician associated with such famous combos as Dorsey,

The very famous winner, Ch. Quell vom Fredeholz, ROM, was the sire of the first bitch owned by Hessian Kennels, Ch. Kern Delta's Exakta, and was highly important in the development of the Hessian strain. Quell belonged to Mr. and Mrs. Anton Korbel of California.

Dunham, and "Scat" Davis) and their move to the Cincinnati, Ohio area (where they have remained since leaving Chicago), Art entered the field of sales which necessitated frequent absence from home and it was decided that Helen needed a dog as companion and guard. Of course, a German Shepherd was her choice of breed.

Through a newspaper advertisement, Helen Hess found what she describes as "a beautiful seven-week-old red male with erect ears," who grew to fill the bill exactly as a guard dog since he "hated everyone but us." Good citizenship came about through a course in obedience training, at which he proved so eager, adept, and intelligent that he was awarded "Highest Scoring Dog in any Class Shown for the First Time" at Queen City in 1953. This experience may be called the event that triggered the first stirring of interest in the competitive side of dog ownership for Art and Helen.

Soon a second Shepherd joined the family, this one outstanding in true German Shepherd temperament. The Hesses did a bit of exhibiting with both dogs in the conformation ring as well as in obedience, going through the usual ups and downs of new exhibitors still getting the "feel" of it all and learning more each day about their breed.

As they learned, the Hesses noted with admiration two leading Shepherd winners whom they considered to be very representative of the finest combination of German and American bloodlines. A litter in which they were par-

This is "Lizzie," or Ch. Kern Delta's Exakta, ROM, the Christmas gift puppy from Art to Helen Hess on which the future breeding program of Hessian Shepherds was founded. Bred to her grandsire, Grand Victor Ch. Alert of Hi-Noah's, ROM, in her first litter she produced the lovely Hessians Quella, ROM.

1964 Canadian Grand Victor, Am. and Can. Ch. Hessians Caribe making a good win for owners Helen and Art Hess, Hessian Kennels, Goshen, Ohio.

ticularly interested was one at the Kern Delta Kennels which belong to Joe and Nadine Henley of Bakersfield, California. These puppies were from a bitch named Champion Gale of Steven's Rancho (Grand Victor Champion Alert of Mi-Noah's, ROM, ex Champion Storm of Stevens Rancho) and were sired by the exciting top show winner Champion Quell vom Fredeholz, ROM, a son of Pirol von der Buchenhohe ex Nixie von Fredeholz, imported from Germany by the Anton Korbels of California. As a Christmas gift for Helen, from this litter Art purchased "Lizzie," little bitch puppy who grew up to become Champion Kern Delta's Exakta, ROM, a fabulous producer acknowledged as one of the most successful of her time. Her first litter, sired by her grandsire, Grand Victor Champion Alert of Mi-Noah's, ROM, was born in 1956 and produced her first champion and the first one bred by the Hesses, Champion Hessians Saxon, who went back to the West Coast to Kern Delta.

For her second litter, Exakta was again bred back to her grandsire, Alert, producing another champion, this one the lovely Hessians Exakta's Image, who remained with the Hesses and who became Art's particular handling triumph. Image gained her title in eleven shows, including two Bests of Breed, a Working Group second, and a Best of Breed at the German Shepherd Dog Specialty of Greater Cincinnati.

Hessians Quella, ROM, from the first litter bred at Art and Helen Hess's Hessian Kennels.

Also from the Alert-Exakta combination the Hesses produced their noted bitch Hessians Quella, ROM, who was in the ribbons on all of the twenty-three occasions she was shown, including Reserve Winners, when only fourteen months old, at a five-point major Specialty. Sadly, Quella's show career was abruptly ended by a shoulder injury, a misfortune for which she more than compensated by her success in the whelping box. She became a Registry of Merit member at an early age, and it is interesting that, as far as the Hesses know, she is the dam of the only bitch ever bred in the United States to be sent to Germany to obtain, successfully, the Schutzhund I training degree. This one is Hessians Ballencia. Quella also holds the unique position of being the only dam, to the Hesses' knowledge, who has produced an American Grand Victrix and a Canadian Grand Victor, American and Canadian Champion: 1963 American Grand Victrix Champion Hessians Vogue, ROM, and 1964 Canadian Grand Victor and American and Canadian Champion Hessians Caribe. She is also the dam of the Select bitch, Champion Hessians Tinsel, Champion Hessians Elegance, Champion Hessians Glory, and Champion Hessians Belle.

A 1966 picture of Ch. Hessians Belle. One of the top moving Shepherds of her day, she was among the first to introduce the fleet-moving gait of modern times. Bred by Art and Helen Hess. Owned by John Berry. Handled to championship by Peggy Lee, who was a non-professional at the time.

U.S. Grand Victrix Ch. Hessians Vogue, ROM, attained this honor in 1963. This beautiful bitch is, indeed, as the standard reads "stamped with a look of quality and nobility." In addition, she is famous for the excellence of her spectacular movement. She is half-sister, on her dam's side, to Canada's Top Dog in 1964, Can. Grand Victor and Am. and Can. Ch. Hessians Caribe. Helen and Art Hess, owners, Hessian Kennels, Goshen, Ohio.

Ch. Hessians Tinsel, Select, with Art Hess. This bitch, by Ch. Hessians Baldur, ROM, Select, ex Hessians Quella, ROM, is of the same breeding combination that produced Can. Grand Victor, Am. and Can. Ch. Hessians Caribe, Ch. Hessians Glory, Ch. Hessians Belle, Ch. Hessians Elegance, and the SchH I bitch Hessians Ballencia. Hessian Kennels, owners, Art and Helen Hess.

Ch. Hessians Baldur, ROM, Select, by Ch. Atlas v. Elfenhain ex Ch. Kern Delta's Exakta, ROM, typifies the magnificent German Shepherds owned by Art and Helen Hess, Hessian Kennels.

For the third litter from the foundation bitch, Champion Kern Delta's Exakta, ROM, a different sire was selected; this time the dog used was a very handsome import, Champion Atlas von Elfenheim, by Champion Grimm von der Fahrmuhle ex Lexa von Osnabruckerland. From this came Champion Hessians Titan, another who went to the West Coast where he made a respected name for himself.

The Atlas-Exakta combination also produced one of the very best of the Hessians, Select Champion Hessians Baldur, ROM, who is the sire of Canadian Grand Victor, American and Canadian Champion Hessians Caribe, Select bitch Champion Hessians Chantilly, Select bitch Champion Hessians Tinsel, Champion Hessians Curtzan, Champion Hessians Exaktor, Champion Hessians Brigette, Champion Hessians Lona, Select Champion Hessians Elegance, Champion Hessians Glory, Champion Hessians Belle, and Champion Lurene's Hope.

Baldur's son, Hessians Lothario, has several offspring out of two different dams purchased by the United States Army for breeding purposes. Lothario's dam is Grand Victrix Champion Hessians Vogue, ROM.

Champion Kern Delta's Exakta, ROM, proved her value in the show ring as well as in the whelping box. Starting out at puppy matches,

127

Ch. Hessians Exaktor handled here by Art Hess for a good win under the noted Shepherd breeder and authority Reginald Cleveland.

own career and through the careers of her spectacular offspring and their progeny!

The 1970 Grand Victrix in the United States, Champion Bel Vista's Solid Sender, is another to the Hesses' credit, being from Hessians Helene von Bel Vista, a bitch whom they sold.

Hessians Quella, ROM, produced the 1963 Grand Victrix of the United States, Champion Hessians Vogue, ROM, as the result of a breeding to Champion Kurt von Bid-Scono, who was by the superb Grand Victor Champion Troll vom Richterbach, ROM. The dog, Grand Victor Champion Alert of Mi-Noah's, ROM, so very influential in the Hessian breeding program as the grandsire of Exakta to whom she was twice bred back, was by Champion San Miguel's Baron of Afbor, ROM (Champion San Miguel's Ilo of Rocky Reach, ROM, ex Afra of Pangamore) ex Mi-Noah's Ophelia of Long Worth, by Alert of Long Worth (Champion Odin von Busecker-Schloss ex Orla of Liebestraum) from Champion Long Worth's Ophelia of Greenfair, ROM, (she by Grand Victor Champion Pfeffer von Bern, ROM, ex Champion Lucie von der Drei-Kronen).

Hessians Glitter, daughter of Ch. Hessians Exaktor ex Ch. Hessians Tinsel, winning the German Shepherd Dog Club of Miami Valley Specialty Show in 1969 with her breeder-owner-handler Helen Hess.

she delighted her owners by going Best of Breed at both the Cincinnati and Northern Kentucky events and then, at ten months of age, was Best of Breed at another match, beating fifty or more puppies including several with points toward their championships. At sixteen months, "Lizzie" (as Exakta was known) went on the Florida Circuit with a well-known professional handler at his request, where she won Best of Breed at the Miami Specialty over well-known champions. Helen and Art missed her, though, so she returned home to complete her title at the International with a record including four majors (two of them five-pointers). Adding frosting to the cake, she was recognized as one of the top Specialty Show winning bitches in 1956 and was one of the three finalists competing for the Grand Victrix title in 1957. What a very satisfactory Christmas gift "Lizzie" became both in her

Imp-Cen

Imp-Cen Kennels, at St. Mary's, Pennsylvania, is a fairly new project, the first Imp-Cen dog having been registered in 1974. It is also a small kennel; the Shepherds there are family pets and companions as well as show dogs. The interest in them is shared, as a family, by Connie Halliday, her husband Jeff, and their three children, all of whom participate in caring for the dogs.

Dog shows for the Hallidays are family outings, and the dogs are owner-handled. The Hallidays raise only one litter each year or so, putting a lot of time and energy into the planning and care of the puppies. The goal here is for tops in temperament and trainability as well as for type. Most of the puppies are sold through the recommendation of people with whom the Hallidays are personally acquainted.

Steinhuegel's Yasko, owned by Connie Halliday, Imp-Cen Kennels.

Imp-Cen's Shadow earning his third leg on the C.D. degree, pictured with owner and children. Shadow belongs to Connie Halliday, Imp-Cen Kennels, St. Mary's, Pennsylvania.

The name Imp-Cen was coined from the names of Mrs. Halliday's first two Shepherds, Imp and Centaur. Neither of these were show-quality dogs, but they were all Shepherd in heart and spirit. Like many others, Mrs. Halliday started out in obedience, in this case with Imp-Cen's Shadow, who gained his C.D. in three straight shows.

Having been bitten by the show-ring bug, the Hallidays decided that their next dogs should be selected with this in mind, and they purchased two from Mrs. Anne Given's Steinhuegel Kennels in Nashville, Tennessee. These were Steinhuegel's Yasko and Steinhuegel's Vista, both of whom were consistent competitors, winning or placing in their classes in their very limited show careers.

Through the support, guidance, and friendship of both Mrs. Given and Mrs. Mary Wingate (Hexengasse Kennels), Mrs. Halliday is starting now to establish her Imp-Cen line using what she considers to be the finest German and American bloodlines.

The favorite bitch at Imp-Cen, Kummervoll's Holly, is pointed and is a Best of Breed winner. Both of her only two puppies to be shown are

Imp-Cen's Elsa taking Best of Opposite Sex at Olean Kennel Club, May 1980. Handled by ten-year-old Christina Halliday. Owned by Imp-Cen's Kennels, Connie Halliday.

130

Gerra von der Hexengasse, dam of Imp-Cen's Lonie v. Hexengasse and Gisa v. Hexengasse and grandam of Imp-Cen's Golden Horizon. Owned by Connie Halliday, Imp-Cen Kennels, St. Mary's, Pennsylvania.

Lacey vom Steinhuegel and Christina Halliday winning Best Junior Novice Handler at the German Shepherd Dog Club of America National Specialty, November 1980, judged by Virginia McCoy. Lacey belongs to Christina's mother, Mrs. Connie Halliday, Imp-Cen Kennels.

winners. Imp-Cen's Elsa, sired by Steinhuegel's Yasko, has two points to date and was handled to them by the Hallidays' ten-year-old daughter Christina. Holly's son, Imp-Cen's Golden Horizon, had numerous first place and Best of Breed puppy match wins in 1981. Horizon is sired by Imp-Cen's Lonie vom Hexengasse, who has two reserve wins out of four times shown and will be campaigned during 1982 it is hoped, to his championship.

Behind the Imp-Cen Shepherds are some very distinguished bloodlines. Steinhuegel's Yasko, by Pohlo vom Steinhuegel ex Vera vom Fleischerheim, descends from German Siegers Ajax vom Haus Dexel, Hanko vom Hetschmule and Youth Siegers Klodo aus der Eremitenklause and Sam von der Schrinklergrenze. Lacey vom Steinhuegel, by Select Champion Steinhuegel's Siggo ex Irela von der Mindelaue, goes back to Ajax vom Haus Dexel, Klodo aus der Eremitenklause, and Champion Bernd von Kallengarten and Jalk von Fohlenbrunnen. Imp-Cen's Lonie vom Hexengasse and Gisa vom Hexengasse are by Champion Fashion vom Sonnenbachtal ex Gerra von der Hexengasse. Kummervoll's Holly is by Champion Torque of Frohlich ex Kummervoll's De De of Chenango, C.D. The other Shepherds at Imp-Cen represent equally excellent backgrounds with which Mrs. Halliday is working.

Jonlyn

Jonlyn German Shepherds, at Atlantic City, New Jersey, are owned by Mr. and Mrs. John Berry. As a Christmas gift for his wife, John Berry purchased from Mr. and Mrs. Arthur Hess of the famed Hessian Kennels a lovely bitch who became Champion Hessian's Belle, the start of Jonlyn. Little did they realize Belle's potential at the time or the fact that she would become both famous and successful and a source of enormous pleasure to them. Eventually she was bred to James and Eleanor Cole's German import, Champion Fels von der Rottumbruke of Dornwald, producing in the litter another beautiful bitch, Jonlyn's Georgy Girl, among others.

Georgy Girl went to professional handler Peggy Lee for her Bellemere Kennels, and breeding her to Champion Dot Wall's Vance, ROM, the two kennels joined forces, producing Champion Jonlyn's Samantha, a bitch who gained her title with ease. From the same litter there was also a very handsome dog, Jonlyn's Dustin of Bellemere, who was halfway to his title, including a Specialty four-point major, when the owners who had purchased him lost interest in showing; and thus he never had the opportunity to finish.

Samantha herself produced an excellent son in Jonlyn's Kojak, a Group winner, who also never got to finish—a pity, for, like Dustin, this dog deserved its title.

Ch. Jonlyn's Samantha, by Ch. Dot Wall's Vance, ROM, ex Jonlyn's Georgy Girl, pictured at the Jersey Shore German Shepherd Dog Club Specialty, October 1972. Judge, Mr. Doyle Williams. Owned by the Jonlyn Kennels of Mr. and Mrs. John Berry and bred by Peggy Lee who is handling.

Kubistraum

Kubistraum is a fairly recent kennel operation, located at St. Joseph, Wisconsin, and owned by Verna M. Kubik. The breeding program here is founded on Falkora's Catalina, C.D., ROM, an outstanding bitch who was purchased from Linda Dries Kofstad in 1970. Mrs. Kubik has at home whelped seven litters and has co-bred four others. These litters so far have yielded fifteen dogs with American Kennel Club championship points or major reserves. Five have earned their A.K.C. championship, one is a Canadian champion, and two Kubistraum dogs, Falkora's Catalina and Champion Kubistraums Kane, have completed their Register of Merit requirements. Another, Falina von Meredith, co-owned with Michael Wakeling, needs only a fourth qualifier to complete her Register of Merit title.

Champion Kubistraums Kane, whelped March 11th 1975, came from the first litter bred at Kubistraum. To have produced and to own such a dog is, as Mrs. Kubik puts it, "like living a dream." This litter, the "K" litter, was sired by Champion Cobert's Reno of Lakeside, ROM, (Grand Victor Champion Lance of Fran-Jo, ROM, ex Cobert's Melissa, ROM) out of Falkora's Catalina, ROM (Grand Victor Cham-

Ch. Rollingreen's Showoff, by Ch. Kubistraum's Kane, ROM, ex Rollingreen's Miss Wille, Best in Maturity, SW, 1980. One of a litter of three, all of which completed their championship titles. Verna M. Kubik.

pion Hollamar's Judd, ROM, ex Canadian Champion Jubilee von Celler Schloss), and this litter earned for its dam the designation of Number Eight Brood Bitch in the 1976 Futurity tabulations.

Kane completed his A.K.C. championship title at fourteen months of age with four major wins, was Best in Futurity for the Southwest region in 1976, and was Best in Maturity for the Mid-Pacific region in 1977. He has been a Top Ten Producer for the Futurity-Maturity tabulation each of the five years 1977 through 1981 and is currently the third highest living Register of Merit Sire for German Shepherd Dogs. To date, he is the sire of twenty-one A.K.C. champions, several Canadian champions, and over forty-five Register of Merit qualifiers. Four Kane litters so far have produced multiple champions, and at least eleven litters have produced more than one Register of Merit qualifier.

The successful bloodline combination of the old Long-Worth-Edgetowne behind Robin of Nikral, ROM (Catalina's grandam) and Grand Victor Champion Hollamar's Judd, ROM, with Bernd through Judd and Cobert's Melissa, has resulted in a highly successful foundation background for the Kubistraum breeding program.

Ch. Kubistraums Colt of Rimfire, by Ch. Cobert's Reno of Lakeside, ROM, ex Falina von Meredith, a Ch. Kubistraums Kane, ROM, daughter. Verna M. Kubik, St. Joseph, Wisconsin.

Ch. Lakeside's Gilligan's Island, owned by Daniel Dwier, winning one of his eighty-seven Working Group firsts under Mrs. Winifred Heckmann at the Old Dominion Kennel Club. Bred by Mr. Dwier, this fabulous dog won his first major when only six months of age and was Futurity Victor at eighteen months. His sudden and premature death in 1972 brought to an abrupt halt a show career which additionally included thirty-six Bests in Show, five of them during the six weeks prior to his death, at which time he was the Top Winning Dog of all breeds in the United States. Gilligan's Island was sold to Mrs. Helene Klotzman in 1971, by whom he was then campaigned. Kim Knoblauch was his handler.

German Shepherds and kids go well together! Here is the famous Cobert's Melissa (left) with Hy-Hopes Cenator of Lakeside and five young friends. Photo courtesy of Sharon Dwier.

Top producing German Shepherd bitch of the breed, Cobert's Melissa, ROM. An informal photo courtesy of Sharon Dwier.

Lakeside

Lakeside German Shepherd Dogs, located at Kresson, New Jersey, are owned by Daniel Dwier who has produced some truly noteworthy dogs.

Anyone who loves German Shepherd Dogs must be familiar with the fabulous Champion Lakeside's Gilligan's Island, who stormed all-breed dog show competition as the 1960's moved into the 1970's. Gilligan, who won his first major when only six months old and was a Futurity Victor at a year and a half, went on to compile a record consisting of thirty-six all-breed Bests in Show (five of them during the six weeks preceding his death), eighty-seven Working Group firsts, eighteen Specialty Show Bests of Breed, and a grand total of 151 Bests of Breed. His sudden and early death in 1972 came as a jolt to the entire Dog Fancy, for this dog was dearly loved and admired. He had been sold in 1971 to Helene Klotzman, for whom he was widely campaigned by Kim Knoblauch. This truly was a dog in a million!

Daniel Dwier is also co-breeder, with Connie Beckhardt, of the great Champion Cobert's Reno of Lakeside, ROM, while Champion Cobert's Golly Gee of Lakeside is a litter-sister to Gilligan. Numerous other German Shepherd celebrities carry the "Lakeside" prefix, too.

Some of the famous progeny of Cobert's Melissa, ROM, at the Southern New Jersey German Shepherd Dog Club 1971 Annual Specialty Show. Left to right: Ch. Lakeside's Gilligan's Island, ROM; his litter-sister Ch. Cobert's Golly Gee of Lakeside, ROM; and Ch. Cobert's Reno of Lakeside, ROM. Photo courtesy of Sharon Dwier.

Lakeside's Chico, pointed from the Puppy Classes, a most beautiful young German Shepherd Dog owned by Daniel and Sharon Dwier, Lakeside Kennels, Kresson, New Jersey.

Liebestraum

Liebestraum German Shepherd Dogs were, for their owner Grant E. Mann, exactly what their name translates to be—a "dream of love." Ever since the early 1920's, Grant Mann was happily involved with Shepherds, reaching his greatest success as a breeder some twenty years after his first acquisitions. His very first one, which he had eagerly anticipated, did not long remain with him, according to an account we have read: the dog was brought home and placed within a supposedly perfectly safe fenced enclosure, from which it jumped out and disappeared, never again to be seen by any member of the Mann family—quite a let-down, we are sure, for a puppy that had been awaited with keen anticipation! The unfortunate event, however, did not in the least discourage Mr. Mann from his desire to become a German Shepherd Dog owner, we are happy to report.

Although Liebestraum is no longer an active kennel, it was a particularly interesting one owing to Mr. Mann's various accomplishments for the breed, which placed him in a quite unique position. He was the only American breeder to open a branch of his kennel in Germany, and he devoted enormous time and energy to raising German Shepherd Dogs, almost exclusively at one period, for Leader Dogs League of Rochester, Michigan. Also very worthy of mention is the work he did in the American Breed Survey for German Shepherd Dogs, Inc., as its Chairman.

To start at the beginning, Grant Mann was a native of Michigan and remained in the Detroit area until his retirement in 1966, when he moved to Iowa. Harbor Beach, Michigan, was his birthplace, and in 1933, as Liebestraum became an active kennel with its own breeding program, he moved to Southfield, Michigan, where the kennel had more spacious surroundings. The first of his more than sixty champions was one co-owned with Marie J. Leary from Connecticut, Champion Luana von Liebestraum; and as we have noted elsewhere in this book, Miss Leary's Cosalta dogs were greatly involved in Liebestraum's early breeding program. Almost before owning his first Shepherd, Grant Mann had been a member of the German Shepherd Dog Club of Detroit, which fostered an early interest in both training and showing of

This is probably the last photograph ever taken of the late Grant Mann, taken by Tom Monahan in Livonia, Michigan, about two years before Mr. Mann's death. With him is his lovely German Shepherd, Indra von Liebestraum. Mr. Mann was born February 4th 1902 and passed away on August 31st 1980. Photo courtesy of Mary Schuetzler.

one's dogs. Nearly all of the Liebestraum champions had earned working degrees as well, and the majority of them were trained and handled by their owner.

When, after twenty years of careful breeding, Grant Mann reached the height of success, he did so in a very big way. First there was the Grand Victrix Champion Leda von Liebestraum, who brought great joy to her owner as she became the 1946 American Grand Victrix and then gained the Canadian Grand Victrix title, too.

Leda was followed, in 1947, by American and Canadian Grand Victrix Champion Jola of Liebestraum, repeating the Canadian victory in 1949. In 1951, a third homebred bitch also attained success, Grand Victrix Champion Tawnee of Liebestraum.

137

1956 Grand Victor Ch. Bill v. Kleistweg, ROM. Photo courtesy of Mary Schuetzler.

Int. Ch. Lux v. Liebestraum, Best of Breed Motor City Specialty, November 1958. Top winning Group and Best in Show dog of the mid-1950's. F. A. "Chum" Porter, handling. Owner, Robert Williamson, Waldsee Kennels.

It was in 1955 that Grant Mann made a truly exciting move for an American breeder; he opened a branch of his kennel in Germany. The name of this German branch was "Mannstraum" (Mann's dream), and Mr. Mann's purpose in opening it was to be situated so that he could avail himself of the opportunity of using some of the outstanding German stud dogs, who would never be permitted to leave the country no matter what the price offered, on his bitches. At the 1955 German Sieger Show, Mr. Mann saw and purchased a dog who brought still further laurels to his kennel by becoming the 1956 American Grand Victor Bill von Kleistweg, ROM. Bill sired many worthy champions in the United States, including the sensational American and Canadian Grand Victrix Champion Robin of Kingscroft and her litter-sister, 1958 Grand Victrix of Canada Champion Lark of Kingscroft. Many words of praise have been spoken regarding the quality of these two!

Two years after coming to the United States, Champion Bill von Kleistweg was sold to a breeder in Cuba, where he continued to be an important influence on the breed.

Grant Mann had tremendous admiration for the German Koer reports, which prompted him, assisted by several other devoted Shepherd fanciers, to found the American Breed Survey Society for German Shepherd Dogs, Inc., in 1958. He dedicated eight years to this project, during which time four volumes of information were brought out by the group. The work, however, became really tremendous, and eventually the project was discontinued owing to lack of assistance.

Under the auspices of the Roy Freuhauf Foundation, Mr. Mann at one period raised German Shepherds almost entirely for the Leader Dog League of Rochester, Michigan, the dogs being trained as guide dogs for the blind. It was during this same period that he established his Mannstraum Kennels in Germany.

Following a serious illness in 1967, Grant Mann moved to Iowa. His interest in Shepherds went along with him in the form of two lovely bitches. After a year of complete rest and relaxation, the old urge to raise a litter or two more overtook him, and Champion Brin of Liebestraum and Champion Braack of Liebestraum were the result.

Can. Ch. Jalk von Liebestraum, Am. and Can. C.D., by Ch. Ravenhaus Noah, ROM, ex Dyna von Liebestraum (she a Grand Victor Lance of Fran-Jo, ROM, daughter), was the last Liebestraum champion and titled dog. Grant E. Mann, owner. Judged here by Robert Wills. Handled by Karen Mayo.

Fredda von Olsonkamp, with her owner-handler Ken Rayner, Hopewell, New Jersey, winning at Washington, D.C., in 1963.

Markenhaus

The story of Markenhaus Shepherds is really a family story as far as both the people and the dogs involved are concerned. It is the story of Ken Rayner, Sr., his wife Marion, their son and daughter, Sue and Ken, Jr., and of a line of Shepherds developed from a carefully thought-out breeding program in which dogs and bitches truly complementing one another were selected for use, with special emphasis not only on conformation but also on such important matters as fertility, vigor, and longevity. Ken Rayner has always believed in his breed, to which he has dedicated a lifetime, and could never accept "fad" breeding as do some others. Type and soundness always have been requisites in the dogs he breeds as well as in the dogs he handles. To please him, a Shepherd must have "heart," a quality often difficult to find, along with the other traits important to the full potential and beauty of these magnificent dogs.

Ch. Sommerset's Banner Boy winning at the German Shepherd Dog Club of Maryland 16th Annual Specialty, April 1967. Ken Rayner handling.

Ch. Paprika of Clover Acres, bred and owned by P. and D. Murphy. Handled by Ken Rayner in 1972.

Ch. Barwyck's Starsky, owned by Fred Willson, sired by Ch. Ravenhaus Noah ex Von Witzen's Cameo. Here with Ken Rayner handling.

Here is Ch. Barwyck's Starsky gaining points towards the title, this time handled by Chips Rayner.

And here is Ch. Barwyck's Starsky winning again, this time under the handling of Sue Rayner for Winners at Elmira, June 1980.

Ken Rayner's story is an interesting and unique one in that midway in life, when he turned his avocation into his vocation, he left a very comfortable business. As an amateur Shepherd owner and breeder, he enjoyed handling his own dogs in the ring, doing it so well that soon other owners, impressed by his ability, began to request his services to show their dogs too. It reached the point where one day his wife jokingly observed that by the time he got to their own Shepherds, he had used up all his energy on other people's dogs—so why not apply for a license and start showing dogs professionally. He replied just as jestingly. Then in 1965, with two young children and a wife already dog-oriented, a small breeding kennel (the Rayners are located at Hopewell, New Jersey), and A.K.C. approval of Ken as a handler, the Rayner family literally "went to the dogs."

Ken Rayner had spent the early years of his life in an orphanage, where he developed a keen

Ch. Blisse v. Markenhaus, C.D., at eight years old going Best of Breed. Handled by a young Chips Rayner.

competitive spirit through sports and earned scholarships for himself through high school and college. This competitive spirit is essential if one is to show dogs successfully. It stood Ken Rayner in good stead, helping him to become one of the foremost all-breed handlers specializing in Shepherds; and it carried through to his children, too, as his son "Chips" (Ken, Jr.,) is also an all-breed handler while his daughter Sue is a professional handler specializing in Shepherds.

Ken's early knowledge of German Shepherds came from such pillars of the breed as Marie J. Leary, Reginald Cleveland, and Lloyd Brackett. His breeding program, although short, was successful; and he willingly shared his knowledge with others—he was the person responsible for some highly successful breeding programs carried on by clients who followed his advice and suggestions. Ken is a completely professional man who as a handler feels it only fair to his clients that he no longer participate actively with his own dogs, preferring rather to concentrate on doing his best by theirs, both in the ring and by his help to them as breeders. Honesty and in-

Ch. Blisse v. Markenhaus, C.D., by Ch. Condor v. Stoerstrudel ex Fredda v. Olsonkamp, making a puppy win in the beginning. Ken Rayner handling.

Markenhaus Donner was bred, owned, and handled by Ken Rayner, Markenhaus Kennels, Hopewell, New Jersey. This fine male died at an early age. He was the result of "B" litter bred to Hart-Wald's Flint. Photos of Donner and his grandsire, Grand Victor Ch. Condor v. Stoerstrudel, show consistency of type and also show that "A" and "B" lines and German lines blended properly produced correct type.

Donner's sire, Hartwald's Flint, owned by I. Wachter, sired by Ch. Tan-Zar's Blitz ex Ch. Xantes of Rocky Reach. Flint carried all American bloodlines of top successful breeding kennels such as Long Worth, Rocky Reach, and Mi-Noah. Photo courtesy of Ken Rayner.

Donner's grandsire, Grand Victor Ch. Condor v. Stoerstrudel, ROM, by Bello v. Hollewinkil ex Birke v. Saturner-See, an import of entirely German lines. Owned by Tom and Jane Bennett. Photo courtesy of Ken Rayner.

143

Ch. Doc of Dowsiri, one of the many Shepherds Ken Rayner has finished to well-deserved championships.

Sue Rayner winning Best of Breed at Carroll Kennel Club 1980 with one of the many German Shepherds she and her family handle so successfully.

Ayrwood's Hector, bred and owned by Betty Ayres, an Igor son, shown going Best Puppy with Sue Rayner, who took over and completed Hector's championship when her Dad, Ken Rayner, suffered an injury.

tegrity are characteristics for which Ken Rayner is well known, as is his fierce protective interest over his clients' dogs. While he is the first to offer congratulations on a win by a better dog, he has sometimes found it difficult to accept a questionable win on a lesser dog. Winning has always been the name of the game to him, as it is with any dedicated exhibitor; but at the same time he has always watched over novice fanciers, willingly helping them to learn what is correct, both in and out of the ring.

When Ken Rayner has visited kennels in Germany, he has impressed those astute breeders with what they describe as his "eye of an eagle" in his evaluation of German Shepherds; and we believe that his deep love of animals is very evident when one visits Markenhaus, for there one finds the house and kennels geared to the comfort of his canine charges. Any of the dogs are apt to appear in the most unexpected places to the surprise of guests. In fact, his love for and care of dogs preceded his expertise at handling and was rewarded by some pillars of the breed sending him Shepherds who previously had never been allowed to live in a handling kennel.

Meadowmill

Meadowmill German Shepherds, owned by Helen Miller Fisher and located at Lake Elmo, Minnesota, had its beginning on Valentine's Day, February 14th 1950, starting with the purchase of a six-week-old puppy as a Valentine gift. Helen was deciding between a Collie and a German Shepherd, and the Shepherd puppy won out. This first pet puppy developed into a long-haired monorchid, but that did not in the least discourage Helen, who proceeded to put C.D. and C.D.X. titles on him before he reached ten months of age!

Almost immediately thereafter a three-month-old "show-prospect" puppy was purchased. This puppy also did not live up to expectations, barely getting through to C.D. and not in the least the anticipated show type. The next move was to turn to Germany.

With the help of Jack Sinykin and Ernie Loeb, two fine imports were purchased. The first of these was the splendid Bundesleistung-Sieger (Top Working Dog) Falko von der Diederichsenstiftung, followed six months later by the

A most beautiful informal pose of the famous Ch. Falko von der Diederichsenstiftung SchH III, FH, C.D., C.D.X., U.D.T., who was the Top Working Dog in all of Europe for 1951, imported the following year by Helen Miller Fisher for her Meadowmill Kennels at Lake Elmo, Minnesota.

Three greats from the 1950's owned by Helen Miller Fisher. Left to right are Meadowmills Charmaine (Ch. Cuno von der Teufelslache ex Techie of La Salle); Ch. Bella vom Luisenschloss, whelped in Germany in 1949, by Kunz aus der Spitzenstadt ex Gunda vom Ostmarksfelsen; and Ch. Falko von der Diederichsenstiftung, the Top Working Dog in Europe when imported into the U.S. in 1952.

great Champion Cuno von der Teufelslache, SchH III, FH, ROM. Cuno, a superb dog who gained his American championship in three five-point shows, became a dominant sire, a tremendous asset not only to Meadowmill Kennels but also to the breed in general in the United States. A pair of bitches, Champion Kola von Beckhold (a Pfeffer von Bern daughter) and Champion Bella vom Luisenschloss were also purchased; and Meadowmill thus had assembled its foundation stock.

Virginia McCoy, of Long Worth Kennels, drove up to Minnesota with a bitch to breed to Cuno and stayed a week at Helen's house. It was really Virginia's idea, Helen tells us, that since Helen's name was Miller at the time and since she lived in the country surrounded by fields and meadows, these facts should be combined and

Ch. Bella vom Luisenschloss, by Kunz aus der Spitzenstadt ex Gunda vom Ostmarksfelsen, was imported from Germany in the early 1950's. Owned by Helen Miller Fisher, Meadowmill Kennels.

the kennel should be called "Meadowmill." This name was registered with the American Kennel Club by Helen in 1954.

Helen Fisher has always operated her kennel as a very small one, in sharp contrast to the huge wealthy kennels of the 1950's. She never has more than twenty of her own Shepherds on the place at one time, including the "old people" and puppies. She now raises about one litter each year and finishes, on the average, about one champion annually. She has cut back some of these activities since becoming a judge in 1965. However, she still manages to raise, show, and finish a champion each year. As she says, "I love the puppies so much that I cannot give it up, and of course one does hate to see the kennel bloodlines just die out."

Of all her dogs, Helen Miller Fisher feels that five of them are especially memorable. These are Champion Falko von der Diederichsenstiftung, SchH III, FH, C.D., C.D.X., U.D.; Champion Cuno von der Teufelslache, SchH III, FH,

ROM; Champion Meadowmill's Appolo; Champion Von Nassau's Buck Private; and Champion Meadowmill's Legend.

Champion Falko von der Diederichsenstiftung, SchH III, FH, C.D., C.D.X., U.D., is especially memorable for his intelligence, working ability, and fantastic companionship. This dog was exceptional, in that he was purchased as the Top Working Dog of all Europe in 1951. King Farouk of Egypt was on the throne at that time, and he presented the trophy for Falko's impressive award. Falko was acquired when he was three years of age. How disappointing it must have been that even though he was rated *Angekort* (inspected and certified suitable for breeding) and had sired eight litters in Germany, he became sterile shortly after his arrival at Meadowmill and never produced in the United States. Helen Fisher spoke in German to Falko for nearly a full year after his arrival and then gradually converted him to English. She says of him, "He was a brilliant dog. Not only did he do his Schutzhund work, but he went through to

Helen Miller Fisher with her famed "Cuno dog," Ch. Cuno von der Teufelslache, SchH III, FH, ROM, snapped informally at a dog show.

German Shepherd Dog Club of Wisconsin Special-ty, 1957. Ch. Ciro of Fieldstone, a Cuno son, taking Best of Breed. Handled by Helen Miller Fisher.

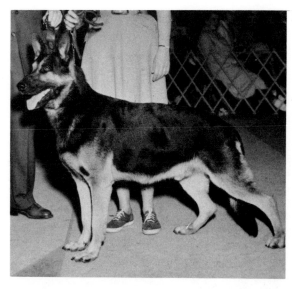

Ch. Meadowmill's Appolo, by Ch. Chimney Sweep of Long Worth ex Ch. Meadowmill's Jem, com-pleted his title on March 20th 1961 under judge E. Vary. Helen Miller Fisher, breeder-owner-handler.

get his C.D., C.D.X., and Tracking Dog degrees before I knew anything about tracking, and . . . at that time, I was not yet aware that one used a halter; he wore a choke chain and lead. The dog passed in spite of me."

Twice Falko has been credited with having saved his owner's life when burglars broke into the house while she was alone there. Helen also recalls, "Falko raised my son, A tough dog, solid, but gentle at the same time. My son, as a baby, taught himself to walk hanging onto Falko." This lovely Shepherd reached the age of twelve years. In tribute to him, Helen Fisher com-ments, "Truly a great mind and temperament."

Champion Cuno von der Teufelslache, SchH III, FH, ROM, was a son of Bingo von der Stellerburg, SchH III, ex Ulme vom Maschtor, SchH I. Cuno was three years old when he came to the United States. His arrival was not without excitement, as he was lost for three days in Customs in New York!

Cuno was imported by the Fishers in 1952 and was undoubtedly one of the really *great* Shep-herds of all time who, from everything we have heard about him, would be considered as great today as he was then. He completed his Ameri-can championship in three five-point shows, two of them in the East and one in the Midwest. Helen Fisher comments,

You must remember that, in the early 1950's, the Twin Cities was not an Interna-tional Airport and we did not have many airlines coming in here. So for all practical purposes, Cuno might as well have been in Alaska so far as remoteness was concerned. Because we showed in the East (Morris and Essex, Baltimore, etc.) we had some East-ern bitches bred to him, but no bitches from the West. Lloyd Brackett was the first big breeder to use Cuno. He took film of him out East at the shows which I now have, thankfully, as very few people took pictures, much less film, in those days.

Despite the difficulty of getting their bitches to him, Shepherd breeders were quick to recognize Cuno's potential as a sire, and by the time he was five years old (two years after his arrival in the United States) he was a Registry of Merit Sire. According to American Kennel Club records, Cuno was used at stud only twenty-eight times, from which litters he produced eigh-teen champions. This was quite remarkable con-sidering the fact that most people had to bring their bitches to him by car and he was shown very sparingly since the Fishers' closest shows, other than those at Minneapolis and St. Paul, were four hundred miles away in the Chicago area. This made the effort to show him consider-

Ch. Meadowmill's Score of Waldhorn, by Ch. Cuno von der Teufelslache, SchH III, ROM, ex Ch. Waldhorn's Prima of Long Worth, a handsome Shepherd of the 1950's. Photo courtesy of Helen Miller Fisher.

This is "the Cuno dog," at three years of age, after having been lost three days in Customs after arriving by plane in New York. Note excellent shoulder and short hock, though he was not groomed and was standing naturally. Helen Miller Fisher, owner.

able, particularly since the Fishers were new in the game at the time and thus did not realize the importance of campaigning and advertising.

You will find some beautiful photos of Cuno progeny in this book.

Champion Meadowmill's Appolo, a son of Champion Chimney Sweep of Long Worth, C.D., and a grandson of Champion Cuno von der Teufelslache, SchH III, FH, ROM, was whelped in August 1956. This splendid dog, who completed his title in March 1961, was a Group winner and a Best in Show winner.

Champion Von Nassau's Buck Private, one of Grand Victor Lakeside Harrigan's best sons (and Harrigan had many about which to boast) was a Group winner at a time when Shepherdists were particularly anti-Group minded.

The newest star, Champion Meadowmill's Legend, is considered by his owner to be "a legend in his own time." This fantastic young dog finished at sixteen and a half months of age, won Best Puppy at his early Specialties, and as we write this is starting out well in Group placements. He is a son of Champion Kubistraum's Kane ex Meadowmill's Molly Brown.

The late Noah Boomer, owner of Mi-Noah Kennels and of the 1953 Grand Victor Ch. Alert of Mi-Noah, C.D., ROM, here is awarding honors to Meadowmill's Reno (Ch. Zeto of Fran-Jo son, double Lance breeding), owned and handled by Helen Miller Fisher.

Ch. Von Nassau's Buck Private, one of Harrigan's top winning sons, was purchased at six months of age by Helen Miller Fisher from Von Nassau Kennels. Heré she is handling him to Best of Breed at Lake Minnetonka in 1976 under judge Bill Bungraaff, who is now an A.K.C. Field Representative.

BEST OF BREED
LAKE MINNETONKA
JUNE 5. 1976
OLSON PHOTO

Nanhall

Nanhall German Shepherd Dogs are located at Greensboro, North Carolina, where the owners, Fran and T. Hall Keyes, operate an outstanding boarding and training kennel in addition to being actively involved in breeding.

Hall Keyes grew up with Airedales and German Shepherds, and as a boy he enjoyed the companionship of the great Utz von Haus Schutting; but it took another great Shepherd, 1962 Grand Victrix Champion Bonnie Bergere of Ken Rose, U.D.T., ROM, for him to realize his dream of his own outstanding Shepherd line. It was while he was in the retail business that Hall and Dr. Wade Sanders created a German Shepherd type indicative of Nanhall quality. Many famous dogs have descended from Bonnie, a number of whom, although used for breeding on a very limited basis, in their turn produced fine champions.

Ch. Fenja v.d. Maienklause, SchH II, owned and finished by Fran Keyes, Nanhall Kennels, Greensboro, North Carolina. This bitch, sired by Kiddo a.d. Eremitenklause ex Inga aus der Lehmann-swiege, was Reserve Youth Siegerin in Germany.

1962 Grand Victrix Ch. Bonnie Bergere of Ken Rose, U.D.T., ROM, sired by Ch. Lake Trail Terrywoods Cito ex Ch. Ginger Girl of Long Worth. Dam of 1961 Grand Victrix Ch. Nanhall's Donna, C.D., the youngest German Shepherd champion and the youngest Grand Victrix. Owned by Nanhall Kennels and Dr. Wade Sanders; handled by T. Hall Keyes III and Gin Vaughn.

150

Ch. Ginger Girl of Long Worth, ROM, one of the greats of the breed, handled here by owner T. Hall Keyes to win the Veterans Class at the German Shepherd Dog Club of America National Specialty in November 1966.

Ch. Nanhalls Tangle, Number One German Shepherd Bitch 1979, 1980, and 1981; Number Two German Shepherd, Phillips System, 1980; a Group and Specialty Show winner; and a direct descendant of 1962 Grand Victrix Ch. Bonnie Bergere of Ken Rose, U.D.T., ROM. Owner-handled by Fran Keyes, Nanhall Kennels, to Best of Breed at the German Shepherd Dog of Greater Tulsa Specialty Show in May 1977 under judge Ann Mesdag.

Ch. Nanhalls Malachi, by Ch. Bernd v. Kallengarten, ROM, ex Ch. Nanhall's Elf. Owned, bred, and shown by T. Hall Keyes of Nanhall Kennels and Dr. Wade Sanders, Greensboro, North Carolina.

Ch. Nanhalls Elf, by Ch. Field Marshall of Arbywood, ROM, ex Grand Victrix Ch. Bonnie Bergere of Ken Rose, ROM. Bred and owned by Dr. Wade Sanders and Nanhall Kennels.

Ch. Gail of Waldesruh, ROM, by Ch. Fant Wikinger-blut (son of Ch. Ulk Wikingerblut) ex Dina of Waldesruh (daughter of Ch. Biff of Ken Rose, brother to Grand Victrix Ch. Bonnie Bergere of Ken Rose, U.D.T., ROM). Shown and owned by Nanhall Kennels and Dr. Wade Sanders.

Ch. Nanhalls Quell, by Ch. Fortune of Arbywood, ROM, ex Grand Victrix Ch. Bonnie Bergere of Ken Rose, U.D.T., ROM. Bred and owned by Dr. Wade Sanders and Nanhall Kennels.

Above: Ch. Nanhalls Dirk, C.D., a son of Ch. Field Marshall of Arbywood, ROM, ex Bonnie. Owned by Nanhall Kennels and Dr. Wade Sanders. **Below:** Ch. Nanhalls Heloise, by Ch. Nordraak of Matterhorn, ROM, ex Bonnie. Owned and shown by T. Hall Keyes (Nanhall Kennels) and Dr. Wade Sanders.

Bonnie finished her championship in two months of showing and, Fran Keyes tells us, is a top award-winning German Shepherd, having attained her U.D.T and ROM in addition to her conformation ring successes. Her daughter, 1961 Grand Victrix Champion Nanhalls Donna, gained her title when only eleven months old, making her the youngest German Shepherd to achieve her championship and the youngest Grand Victrix on record.

The latest German Shepherd whom the Keyes have finished is Champion Nanhalls Tangle. Although she was shown sparingly, Tangle became a Group and Specialty winner, was the top German Shepherd bitch for three successive years, and was the Number Two German Shepherd, Phillips System, in 1981.

Almost every dog owned by Hall Keyes has gained at least one obedience title. The Keyes feel that in Shepherds, obedience and conformation should be unified. Good obedience increases brain capacity, desire, and animation. "Then," says Fran Keyes, "you can have your good show-dog." As far as obedience is concerned, the byword at Nanhall is "kindness," and the success with which they have met in their training classes has been very rewarding.

Through the years, although the Keyeses have had very few litters, one thing has remained consistent: the most important thing of all is the Nanhall type!

Proven Hill

Proven Hill German Shepherds, owned by Judy and Ray Teidel, Jr., are located at Woodstock, Illinois. Their first litter was whelped December 26th 1966, but it took a total of ten litters plus two and a half years of experience before the arrival of the first litter Judy Teidel considered to be of true quality. Unfortunately, the Teidels found in the beginning that many breeders are not very informative or helpful to the novice. Thus, newcomers often must rely entirely on reading, research, and the "trial and error" method in order to gather the knowledge necessary for success.

It is Judy Teidel's feeling that a successful breeder must have the gift of a "good eye" for a quality dog. All the information in the world cannot really help a breeder who cannot evaluate a litter in an open-minded manner. It also takes years of experiments to see for oneself what lines can become compatible with those you have in order to obtain the desired outcome. Every determined and successful breeder must first have in mind a picture of the style and type that appeals to him, as well as the basic structure and movement necessary to attain this quality.

After fifteen years of breeding, the Teidels feel that they have finally reached their goal in this respect. The foundation of their stock has been

Judy Teidel's first show dog, Colene of Ellyn Hill. German Shepherds are wonderful companions and protectors of children. Proven Hill Shepherds, Judy and Ray Teidel, Jr., Woodstock, Illinois.

Ch. Proven Hill's Jason, by Grand Victor Ch. Lance of Fran-Jo, ROM, ex Here I Am of Stahl Farm. First of the champions bred at Proven Hill Kennels, Judy and Ray Teidel, Jr.

based on Grand Victor Champion Lance of Fran-Jo, ROM, a dog believed to produce quality with almost any line on which he was used. Numerous breeders have founded their kennels on this line; thus there are available many Shepherds going back to Lance, making various choices possible for line-breeding to him.

The litter whelped at Proven Hill on April 16th 1969, the one Judy Teidel refers to as her first of "real quality," was sired by Lance, and from this litter a male puppy was kept. This was the future Champion Proven Hill's Jason, and the dam was Here I Am of Stahl Farm. Jason completed his championship in a whirlwind campaign and at the age of two and a half years almost finished in one weekend when he obtained fourteen points in thirty-seven hours in three shows. He finished at his next show undefeated in the Open Class. This was the first of the Teidels' champions, and that final point was gained in November 1971.

Lance's very first litter produced Proven Hill's Randy, who as a young puppy had been

154

sold to an older couple but, when eight months old, was returned to Mrs. Teidel due to the death of the husband. Randy subsequently was bred to a full brother (owned by Mrs. Teidel) of the double Grand Victor Champion Yoncalla's Mike, ROM, and then to Grand Victor Champion Hollamor's Judd, ROM. But it was from her third litter, sired by Select Champion Dot-Walls Vance, ROM, that she "hit the jackpot," producing the 1974 Best in Futurity winner, Proven Hill's Kandy Man, and his sister who went fourth in her class. Then Randy was bred to a promising young son of the great Grand Victor Champion Mannix of Fran-Jo, ROM; this young son was destined to become Grand Victor Champion Scorpio of Shiloh Gardens, ROM. This litter contained only three puppies, two males and one female. The female puppy was a true "super star" and still remains the pride of Proven Hill Kennels. Co-ownership on her was sold when she was seven months old, and by the time she reached fifteen months of age, she had completed her title to become Scorpio's first champion offspring. This bitch, Select Champion Proven Hill's Sunshine, was Best in

Proven Hill's A Sun Hawk, by Ch. Doppelt-Tay's Hawkeye, ROM, ex Select Ch. Proven Hill's Sunshine. Proven Hill Shepherds, Judy and Ray Teidel, Jr., Woodstock, Illinois.

Futurity in 1975 and went Best of Opposite Sex in Maturity in 1976 to Grand Victor Champion Langenau's Watson, ROM, a Scorpio son.

In December of 1977, Sunshine had a litter of four males by Champion Doppelt-Tay's Hawkeye, ROM. Mrs. Teidel kept one male, Sun Hawk, who was to be the beginning of a whole new winning animal at Proven Hill, possessing the extreme suspension of side gait which Mrs. Teidel so deeply admires. Mrs. Teidel says,

> I first spotted Hawkeye in the Junior Dog Class at a Futurity and knew that this was the movement I had been seeking, the puppy seeming to "float" across the floor. Not quick, short, choppy steps. An extreme hindquarter is necessary to transmit to the front, and the front reach should far extend ahead of the dog. The topline should slope and the back must be firm.

Sun Hawk's first litter was out of a Lance daughter. This produced first-prize winning Intermediate Bitch at the Southwest Futurity in 1980, Proven Hill's Discovery. Then later, a daughter of Champion Eko-Lan's Morgan, ROM, was bred to him, producing First Intermediate Dog at the Northeast Futurity, Proven Hill's Jock Hoheneichen. Jock started out by winning Best of Opposite Sex Puppy in Match.

May 18th 1974, Best in Mid-Western Futurity and First Intermediate Dog, Proven Hill's Kandy Man, by Ch. Dot Wall's Vance, C.D., ROM, ex Proven Hill's Randy. Handler, Gary Staser. Owned by Proven Hill Kennels, Judy Teidel.

Judy Teidel has loaned us this photo of the great producing stud dog, Select Ch. Doppelt-Tay's Hawkeye, ROM, used extensively in her breeding program.

Midwestern Futurity Intermediate Bitch, King Haven Doli of Proven Hill, by Ch. Lakeside's Gilligan's Island ex Ch. Jola v. Celler Schloss. Owned by Judy Teidel, Proven Hill German Shepherds. Handled by Robert A. Denton.

Judy Teidel, owner of Proven Hill Kennels, with a ten-week-old Shepherd puppy.

At his first A.K.C. point show he was Winners Dog from the 9 to 12 Month Puppy Class, a four-point major. On the next day he was Best in Sweepstakes and first in the 9 to 12 Month Puppy Class. He won another class, then won his class in Futurity, then Reserve Winners, and then another four-point major. Undoubtedly these laurels will have been considerably augmented by the time you read this book.

Sun Hawk was bred back to Sunshine, a mother-son breeding, which produced Proven Hill's Jillian, Best of Opposite Sex at the Midwest Futurity in 1981. The day following the Futurity, Jillian went Best in Sweepstakes and Reserve Winners Bitch in a five-point entry. Sad to say, Sun Hawk died the following week of a bacterial infection.

Now Sunshine has been bred to Jock, and they have an outstanding son with which Mrs. Teidel hopes to continue the Sun Hawk producing ways with some grandson-to-grandmother breedings. This will be inbreeding, regarding which Mrs. Teidel remarks, "If you are fortunate to have a dominant producing animal who does not carry many faults when bred to several different animals, then I would inbreed. Sunshine does not produce so many undesirable traits that I decided to inbreed on her to build my future stock."

Judy Teidel pays special tribute to her first show dog, Colene, who gave her the inspiration to try "this dog show game"; to her first champion and great love of her life, Jason; and to her star producer, Sunshine, who gave her Sun Hawk, who in turn gave her Jock and Jillian. Now Jock and Sunshine have given her Sunshine Kid who should carry on in the family tradition.

In 1975, Toma of Lor-Locke and Fran-Jo was purchased by Mrs. Teidel. A son of Grand Victor Champion Scorpio of Shiloh Gardens, ROM, and the 1974 Grand Victrix Champion Lor-Locke's Tatta of Fran-Jo, ROM, Toma was bred to Sun Hawk and Lance daughters and has produced several champions.

To date, the homebred champions at Proven Hill have included Champion Proven Hill's Jason, Champion Proven Hill's I Remember (a Jason daughter), Champion Proven Hill's Sunshine, Champion Proven Hill's E.S.P: (a Jason son out of a Mannix daughter), and Champion Proven Hill's Uncola (Toma out of a Lance daughter).

At nine months old, Proven Hill Jock Hoheneichen, winner of eight points including both majors and First Intermediate Dog, N.E. Region, 1981. This grandson of Select Ch. Proven Hill's Sunshine is pictured here winning his class at the Topline German Shepherd Dog Club in 1981. Judy and Ray Teidel, Jr., Proven Hill Shepherds, Woodstock, Illinois.

157

Scherzar

Scherzar German Shepherds began in 1968 and are now located on sixty acres in Castro Valley, a northern California rural community. Janice L. Staley's interest in the breed had its beginning through the merits of a show-quality pup who was originally purchased to be a pet and a watch dog. The pup was line-bred and sired by Champion Gallant of Arbywood, ROM, and became a multiple Best Puppy winner at matches, also acquiring three points toward her championship before her retirement from the show ring due to an injury. This brief encounter with the German Shepherd Dog world led to the Staleys' desire to breed a dog that would conform as closely as possible to the standard for the breed.

Most of the Staleys' early litters were line-bred on the famous Arbywood "F" litter, through Champion Gallant of Arbywood, ROM, whose sire was Champion Fels of Arbywood, ROM, with outcrosses made into German lines through Klodo aus der Eremitenklause, ROM. In 1975, the Staleys changed their breeding program with the acquisition of their top foundation bitch, Scherzar's Mischief Maker, whose pedigree included lines to Grand Victor Champion Yoncalla's Mike, ROM, and the Waldesruh "K" litter (through Kristie of Waldesruh). At the same time they continued their line-breeding on the Arbywood "F" litter through Grand Victor Champion Lance of Fran-Jo, ROM, whose sire was Champion Fortune of Arbywood, ROM, and more recently through the use of Lance's son, Champion Cobert's Reno of Lakeside, ROM. The success of this pedigree combination became immediately apparent when their first litter from these lines contained their first champion, Scherzar's Rhianon.

Champion Rhianon was a consistent winner starting from her first puppy show when she was eleven weeks old. She won her class and earned Best Puppy awards nearly every time shown and then won the Best in Futurity Regional honors at eleven months of age. At this tender age, Rhianon won a five-point major and went Best of Breed. Due to her youth, she was then shown

Scherzar's Nefertiti, by Ch. Kubistraum's Kane, ROM, ex Scherzar's Mischief Maker, taking Winners Bitch and Best of Opposite Sex under judge Ron Whitehead at the German Shepherd Dog Club of Sacramento Valley 20th Annual Specialty Show on April 11th 1981. Owned by Janice L. Staley, Scherzar Shepherds, Castro Valley, California.

The superlative German Shepherd, Grand Victor Ch. Lance of Fran-Jo, Top Sire in the breed, by Ch. Fortune of Arbywood, ROM, ex Frohlich's Elsa von Grunestahl, ROM, has been a dog of very special beneficial influence on the breed. Owned by Joan and Fran Ford, Grove City, Ohio.

in the American-bred Class, and she still managed to complete her title in just twelve shows, when she was twenty-two months of age. She also won the award of Best in Regional Maturity Bitch just after completion of her title. Rhianon was sired by Champion Philberlyn's Iphis, ROM, a Champion Gallant of Arbywood, ROM, son, and is therefore line-bred to the Arbywood "F" litter through both Champion Fels and Champion Fortune, with the lines to Grand Victor Champion Yoncalla's Mike and Waldesruh "K" through her mother, Mischief Maker.

Recognizing the quality of the litter through Mischief Maker, the Staleys did a similar breeding which resulted in their top winning male, Scherzar's Wildfire, who had attained eleven points, including three majors, before his untimely death in 1981.

Mischief Maker's next litter was by the great producing Grand Victor Champion Lance son, Zeus of Fran-Jo, ROM, who has produced Scherzar's Barbary Coast, a Best of Breed win-

ner working toward his championship which by now he undoubtedly has completed.

The next litter from Mischief Maker was by the top producing Champion Kubistraum's Kane, ROM, a son of Champion Cobert's Reno of Lakeside, ROM. From this litter the Staleys have four top-winning Best Puppy contenders, one of whom is Scherzar's Nefertiti, who by now must have gained her championship as she was doing well at the shows at last report. She was Best in Futurity Bitch as had been her half-sister, Champion Rhianon. Nefertiti is a striking example of the type currently being achieved at Scherzar from these bloodlines.

Mischief Maker is very close to her Register of Merit listing and has earned recognition as a top brood bitch in the National Futurity tabulations. The Staleys feel that through her and the combination of the bloodlines they have with which to work they are producing a total German Shepherd—one of sound, correct, balanced structure with the true German Shepherd temperament.

Schutzenhaus

Schutzenhaus German Shepherd Dogs are owned by Mary E. Schuetzler, who with her late husband, Art, founded them some years back at Farmington, Michigan.

Mary Schuetzler's present stock comes down principally from the Nocturne Acres Kennels owned by Helen and Ed Gleason. Her dogs include Canadian Champion Nocturne's Ruffian, American and Canadian C.D., who is a younger full-sister to the 1974 Maturity Victor Champion Nocturne's Hale of Krisselhof, they being by Grand Victor Champion Hollamar's Judd.

Canadian Champion Schutzenhaus Rebel, from Ruffian by Champion Rebel Canyon's Artful Dodger, is a current winner bred by Mary Schuetzler and doing well for new owner Kenneth K. Milchrist. There also are several young dogs nearing show age for whom her hopes are high.

Can. Ch. Schutzenhaus Rebel, by Ch. Rebel Canyon's Artful Dodger ex Can. Ch. Nocturne's Ruffian, Am. and Can. C.D., pictured in April 1982 taking Best of Winners at Kent Kennel Club Dog Show. Bred by Art and Mary Schuetzler, Schutzenhaus Shepherds. Owned by Kenneth K. Milchrist, Trenton, Michigan.

Nocturne's Harmony, whelped January 28th 1973, by Grand Victor Ch. Hollamor's Judd, ROM, ex Nocturne's Ember, a Grand Victor Ch. Lance of Fran-Jo, ROM, daughter. Owned and bred by Helen Gleason, Georgetown, Indiana.

Tee Em

Tee Em Kennels, owned by Mr. Frederic W. (Ted) Meisner at Methuen, Massachusetts, has been raising German Shepherd Dogs for the past twenty years and during that time has had many splendid Shepherds. For the past few years Mr. Meisner, although active in breeding Shepherds, was inactive with Shepherds in the show ring. Now, however, his dogs are back in competition. Among them are two very handsome young males, both of whom have majors and other points (won in Specialty Show competition) toward their titles. These are Tee Em's Tax-A-Tion, a son of Champion Clover Acres X-Citation bred by Charles Noyes, and Tee Em's Huckster.

Mr. Meisner, in addition to being a Shepherd breeder, is a very dedicated member of the fancy. As a well-known canine authority who leads a full and busy life, he is a teacher of animal

Debonair's Showgirl, by Debonair's Showgum ex Debonair's Patience, owned by Frederic W. (Ted) Meisner, Tee Em Kennels, Methuen, Massachusetts.

Tee-Em's Tax-A-Tion, by Ch. Clover Acres X-Citation from Dalmar's Esprit of Spring Rock, here is taking Winners Dog from the Novice Class for a four-point major at German Shepherd Dog Club of Rhode Island Specialty. Owned by Frederic W. (Ted) Meisner, Tee Em Kennels.

Tee Em's Nadia, by Cobert's Whisper Jet ex Ch. Sharob's Dixie of Lonestar, U.D., the dam of the noted Ch. Tee Em's Aikara of Cobert, here is taking Best of Winners at North Shore Kennel Club 1980. Owned by Frederic W. (Ted) Meisner, Tee Em Kennels.

psychology in the neighborhood school system, is the Chairman of the Advisory Board at Essex Agricultural School (high school and college level), teaches obedience classes one night a week at his huge Tee Em Kennels, gives private obedience lessons, runs two weekly obedience classes for two different YMCA's in two cities, conducts a "Dear Abby"-type column on pets under the nom-de-plume of "Doggy Daddy" (about which he says, "That's a heck of a name for an ex-Marine, but an editor thought it up"), and does frequent three-minute prime-time features on hints about dogs and their care (under contract to Colony Cable Television).

A professional handler of all breeds of dog, Ted Meisner also is "into" talking birds (parrots and mynah birds)—not commercially but just for his own pleasure. In July 1981, he made a national television appearance which concerned his kennel and birds.

Tee Em Kennels employs about eighteen people on a steady basis and has three families living in separate houses on the property. It is a modern, beautiful, and extremely popular boarding and training establishment where at least several hundred dogs are usually in residence and it is not at all unusual for twenty-five or more dogs to come in for grooming in a single day.

A view from the air of Tee Em Kennels owned by Frederic W. (Ted) Meisner at Methuen, Massachusetts. This mammoth operation has been called the "largest kennel on the East Coast" and is where Mr. Meisner's Shepherds are raised. Ted Meisner operates a tremendous boarding and trimming business, plus an obedience and conformation training school with which he has been highly successful. The kennel employs eighteen people, and three families live in separate houses on the grounds.

A youthful Von Mibach Timmee's Ember, U.D., in 1979 winning Best of Breed at Bucks County, owner-handled by Valerie D. Mee, Smithtown, New York.

Timmee

Valerie D. Mee and her daughter, Terri, both derive a good deal of satisfaction and pleasure from the Timmee German Shepherds which Mrs. Mee owns and raises at Smithtown, New York.

Two splendid bitches are the background here. These bitches, Von Mibach Timmee's Ember, U.D., and Abby vom Linderhof, C.D., are successful in the obedience ring, as their titles indicate; have points toward conformation championship; and have worked with Terri in Junior Showmanship, at which she has been extremely successful.

Ember, who was born August 14th 1977, is a daughter of Champion Dante Manor Gaucho von Ausland from a Select Champion Rex Edlu Mibach granddaughter. She was owner-handled to her Utility Dog degree by Mrs. Mee and worked enthusiastically with Terri Mee to help her earn the German Shepherd Dog Club of America's Top Junior Handler Award for 1979.

The younger bitch, Abby vom Linderhof, C.D., is a year old at the time of this writing, yet she has already attained her first obedience degree! She is a combination of German bloodlines ("H" litter Lauerhof and "Q" litter Wienerau) and America's Lance and Shaft bloodlines. The Mees look forward to her further achievements as she matures, for she is a bitch of much promise.

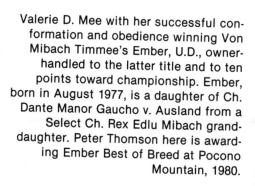

Valerie D. Mee with her successful conformation and obedience winning Von Mibach Timmee's Ember, U.D., owner-handled to the latter title and to ten points toward championship. Ember, born in August 1977, is a daughter of Ch. Dante Manor Gaucho v. Ausland from a Select Ch. Rex Edlu Mibach granddaughter. Peter Thomson here is awarding Ember Best of Breed at Pocono Mountain, 1980.

Van Cleve

The Van Cleve German Shepherds at Lithonia, Georgia, came about in the early 1960's when Dr. and Mrs. Carmen L. Battaglia, their owners, began serious testing, tracing, and data collection on stud dogs and brood bitches. As a result of that effort, Dr. Battaglia wrote a book entitled *Dog Genetics—How To Breed Better Dogs* (also published by T.F.H.) which, along with a series of articles that followed, served to describe the collected facts and data and known theories and techniques that worked for Dr. Battaglia and for others.

Basically, the strategy used at Van Cleve was to begin with quality brood bitches who had pedigree depth against the dreaded diseases so prevalent in Shepherds, namely hip dysplasia, torsion, bloat, and heart disease. These brood bitches were then taken for breeding to dogs who could improve on the basic structure of the dam, with the specific goal being to produce con-

Van Cleve's I'm A Country Boy, by Grand Victor Ch. Scorpio of Shiloh Gardens, ROM, ex a Reno-Watson cross, here is winning Teenage Dog at the Atlanta National Futurity in 1980 for Dr. and Mrs. C. L. Battaglia, Van Cleve Kennels, Lithonia, Georgia.

Van Cleve's Heaven Scent combines the bloodlines of Scorpio, Reno, and Watson. Owned by Dr. and Mrs. Carmen L. Battaglia.

sistent quality throughout each litter. Dr. Battaglia's evaluation of more than twenty-seven litters has been very rewarding. The major focus was on side gait and foot timing, coupled with clean movement coming and going, strong back, length of neck, and sound temperament. The bloodlines Dr. Battaglia used concentrated on Champion Cobert's Reno of Lakeside, ROM, due to his dominance toward sound structure, temperament, and longevity; dams with Reno bloodlines were bred with Grand Victor Champion Langenau's Watson due to his sire's line to Grand Victor Champion Lance of Fran-Jo, ROM, and his dam's line to Grand Victor Champion Hollamor's Judd, ROM. Several brood bitches have been retained from these breedings, and Dr. Battaglia is happy to say that progeny produced to date are virtually free from the diseases mentioned, are sound structurally, have good temperament, and show pleasing-to-excellent conformation characteristics.

One of the splendid brood bitches at Van Cleve Kennels, Dr. and Mrs. Carmen L. Battaglia of Lithonia, Georgia.

Ch. Cobert's Reno of Lakeside, ROM, with a group of his progeny winning the Stud Dog Class at the Northern New Jersey German Shepherd Dog Club Specialty. Connie Beckhardt, owner, Cobert Kennels, Tenafly, New Jersey.

Von-Wag-Non's Gotta Lot of Love, by Grand Victor Lance of Fran-Jo, ROM, ex Von Nassau's Giralda. Charles Wagnon, owner, Lithonia, Georgia. Photo by Os Hillman.

Von-Wag-Non's In His Presence at four months of age. This daughter of Von-Wag-Non's Sundown ex Von-Wag-Non's Ali of Laurel Farm is co-owned by breeder Charles Wagnon with Os and Diane Hillman of Atlanta, Georgia. Photo by Os Hillman.

Charles Wagnon of Von-Wag-Non Kennels with Von-Wag-Non's Sundown, sired by Ch. Cobert's Reno of Lakeside, ROM, ex Von Nassau's Giralda. Photo by Os Hillman.

Von-Wag-Non

Charles Wagnon, of Lithonia, Georgia, founded his Von-Wag-Non Kennels in the mid-1960's. Since childhood he had wanted a Shepherd, so at the first opportunity as an adult, that is what he got. His first ones were nice Shepherds but not quite the quality he wanted, so after about six years he purchased a bitch, Von Nassau Giralda, from Von Nassau Kennels on the West Coast. When "Gira" was two years old, Mr. Wagnon bred her to the noted Grand Victor Champion Lance of Fran-Jo, ROM, and this combination forms the background of his present kennel.

Later, Giralda was bred into the Waldesruh lines, which blended well with Mr. Wagnon's Lance progeny, and from this litter came Von-Wag-Non's Jingle Bells, who produced a lovely champion bitch. Another line popular with this breeder is that of Champion Bernd von Kallengarten. Studs used by Mr. Wagnon to date, whose bloodlines are to be found in his kennel, include Grand Victor Champion Lance of Fran-Jo, ROM; Grand Victor Champion Lakeside's Harrigan, ROM; Champion Cobert's Reno of Lakeside, ROM; Champion Dot-Wall's Vance, C.D., ROM; Champion Ravenhaus Noah, C.D., ROM; Champion Wonderland's Are von Eva-Heim; Champion Van Cloves Edge; and Grand Victor Champion Aspen of Fran-Jo.

Von-Wag-Non's Sundown, with owner Charles Wagnon of Lithonia, Georgia. Photo by Os Hillman.

Charles Wagnon owns this dog, Von-Wag-Non's Lincoln, by Von-Wag-Non's Gotta Lot of Love ex Von-Wag-Non's Jingle Bells. Photo by Os Hillman.

Walkoway

Walkoway is a young kennel at Sherrard, Illinois, featuring German Shepherd Dogs and Bearded Collies. With limited breeding so far, owners Ed and Chris Walkowicz feel that they have a bright future in German Shepherds with a sound background, since all of their breedings are based on complete soundness of the individuals involved and of their progenitors.

Owned at Walkoway are Champion Brandy von Rosshaus, C.D., by Select Champion Cobert's Reno of Lakeside, ROM, ex Grand Victrix Champion Cathwar's Lisa von Rob, ROM, who is one of a litter of three from these two famed Shepherds, all three of which finished. This litter was bred by Marge and Pete Ross.

Mr. and Mrs. Walkowicz take enormous pride and pleasure in owning Brandy, who has been dominant in producing the good temperament, attitude, ear set, and prettiness so noticeable in the Cobert lines. Mr. and Mrs. Walkowicz are intently watching the development of future "hopefuls," which include several from Brandy's last litter by Champion Doppelt-Tay's Hawkeye. They are Walkoway's Hot Fudge Sundae, Walkoway-Willow Run's Houston, Walkoway's Hepburn, and Heiden's Olympics of Walkoway.

Also at Walkoway is Walkoway's Eager Beaver, a sister to Gateshaus Enforcer von Purdue, with major points; and Christian's Quest o'Walkoway, C.D., a Brian of Stone Ridge son,

bred by Mr. and Mrs. Walkowicz. Jennarick's Favor von Howlhaus, carrying Jamaica-Judd-Harrigan blood, also has points and belongs to the Walkoway Kennels, while Nocturne's Calli of Cave Mill, by Grand Victor Champion Lance of Fran-Jo, ROM, ex Wonderland's Anna, is another owned here.

Walkoway Shepherds have distinguished themselves in both obedience competition and conformation competition.

Ch. Brandy von Rosshaus, C.D., bred by Marge and Pete Ross. Owned by Walkoway Kennels, Ed and Chris Walkowicz, Sherrard, Illinois.

Merry Christmas from Ch. Brandy von Rosshaus, C.D., with her puppies. Walkoway Kennels, owners, Ed and Chris Walkowicz.

Ch. Amber's Flair, ROM, by Zeus of Fran-Jo, ROM (Grand Victor Ch. Lance of Fran-Jo, ROM, ex Ch. Mirheim's Abbey, ROM) from Amber's Dina (also by Lance ex a daughter of Ch. Fels of Arbywood). A great producing bitch owned by Franklyn and Rosalind Schaefer, Wellspring Kennels, Sands Point, New York.

Wellspring

The Wellspring German Shepherd Dogs were established in the mid-1960's by Franklyn and Rosalind Schaefer at Sands Point, New York. It was as the culmination of a thirteen-year search for a truly great foundation bitch, during which time they had finished several champions and bred into various lines with some success (all the while developing a mental picture of the bitch that they would love to own), that the Schaefers saw a three-month-old puppy which they instantly recognized as exactly what they had been wanting.

With the helpful intervention of friends, Barbara Amidon, Flair's breeder, was persuaded that the Schaefers should have her, much to the delight and gratitude of her new owners.

Flair immediately showed enormous potential in the show ring as well as in the whelping box. Before her second birthday she had completed

her championship, which ended her show career because the Schaefers preferred to breed her rather than campaign her as a Special.

Flair is a daughter of Zeus of Fran-Jo, ROM (Grand Victor Champion Lance of Fran-Jo, ROM, ex Champion Mirheim's Abbey, ROM) from Amber's Dina (Lance ex a Champion Fels of Arbywood daughter). She has, to date, produced three litters, the Wellspring "H" litter, the "I" litter, and the "K" litters, all sired by Multiple Select Champion Doppelt-Tay's Hawkeye, ROM (by Champion Eko-Lan's Paladen ex a Lance daughter).

The "H" litter contained Champion Wellspring's Howard Johnson and his sisters Champion Wellspring's Holiday Inn and, close to the title, Wellspring's Happy Hour. The "I" litter contained Champion Wellspring's Iroquois; Champion Wellspring's Ironsides, Select 1979; American and Canadian Champion Wellspring's

Ch. Wellspring's Howard Johnson, handled by Fred Olsen for Franklyn and Rosalind Schaefer, making an important win at the German Shepherd Dog Club of America National Specialty, November 1st 1980. Judge, K. Olbis Steen.

Ch. Wellspring's Holiday Inn, by Ch. Doppelt-Tay's Hawkeye, ROM (Ch. Eko-Lan's Paladen, ROM, ex a Grand Victor Ch. Lance of Fran-Jo, ROM, daughter) from Ch. Amber's Flair, ROM. Bred and owned by Franklyn and Rosalind Schaefer, Sands Point, New York.

Am. and Can. Ch. Wellspring's Idaho, another by Hawkeye ex Flair, bred by Wellspring Kennels, Mr. and Mrs. Franklyn Schaefer.

Idaho; and the females, Champion Wellspring's Indiana, Select 1979; and Maturity Victrix and Champion Wellspring's Independence. The puppies from the "K" litter should debut this spring. It is interesting that Flair was also bred to her son, Howard Johnson, in an effort to preserve dominant qualities.

At six years of age, Flair rules her domain in a cheerful, noisy fashion. Her weakness, we understand, is an occasional trip to Carvel, where she relishes a soft-freeze. She was awarded Number One German Shepherd Dam for 1980 by the *Kennel Review* System.

The Schaefers are of the firm belief that Flair may well eventually become the Highest Producing German Shepherd Bitch in history. Considering the fact that she already has seven American champions and a new young Canadian champion to her credit and the fact that the young progeny just starting out are of very exciting quality, it would by no means seem an impossible dream that she would eventually beat the existing record, which is held now by Robin of Nikrai with eleven champions.

Woodlee

The Woodlee German Shepherds are owned by Shirley Braunstein of North Woodmere, New York, and are based strongly on the Covy-Tucker Hill bloodlines.

Among the winners in this kennel are American and Canadian Champion Covy-Tucker Hill's Manhattan, Champion Covy-Tucker Hill's Barbarino, Champion Schokrest-Covy-Tucker Hill J.R., and American and Canadian Champion Wil-Lynn's Debbie. Manhattan, as we go to press, is gaining a noteworthy record in the show ring, handled by Jimmy Moses.

Right: Am. and Can. Ch. Covy-Tucker's Manhattan, owned by Shirley Braunstein, North Woodmere, New York.

Below: Ch. Coby-Tucker Hill's Barbarino owned by Shirley Braunstein.

Ch. Windward's Maverick, a son of Ch. Maverick of Jo Mar ex Ch. Scotmar's Special Magic, full brother to Ch. Windward's Molly, both owned by Windward Kennels in Hawaii.

CHAPTER FOUR

German Shepherd Dogs in Hawaii

Windward's Gantry, by Ch. Caraland's Attilla ex Eko Lan's Pennie, is close to titular honors and will probably be a champion by the time you read this. Owned by Windward Kennels, Kailua, Hawaii.

The official beginning in Hawaii for the German Shepherd breed started in 1933 when Mr. Harold Castle, noted Shepherd and Great Dane breeder, and Mr. Arthur Zane, nationally known judge, founded the German Shepherd Dog Club of Hawaii.

There are certain difficult problems to live with and overcome for German Shepherd breeders (actually, those active in any breed) in Hawaii. These are, first of all, the isolation caused by being in the middle of the Pacific Ocean; second, the four-month quarantine period which certainly limits importation for many people; and third, the high cost of real estate and the scarcity of zoning for dog kennels.

Patrick H. Ayers, of Kailua, as a new fancier at the time, visited large kennels where he was distressed to note poor temperament among the Shepherds due principally, in his opinion, to lack of human contact.

It was due to the aforementioned problems and conditions that Mr. Ayers hit upon the idea of founding Windward Kennels. This presently consists of sixteen partners with each partner having between one and four (the limit permitted) dogs in their care. In this manner, each animal becomes part of the family.

There are now three Specialties for German Shepherds and five all-breed dog shows annually held in Hawaii. The German Shepherd dogs campaigned by Windward Kennel partners must be appealing to both the specialist judge and the all-rounder, because since finishing their first champion in 1969, Windward Kennels have shown and finished many German Shepherds. These include Champion Crusader's Autumn Von Saar, by Champion Gallant of Arbywood, ROM, ex Crusader's Shangrilla, a Champion Ulk Wikingerblut daughter; Champion Scotmar's Special Magic, by American Grand Victor and American and Canadian Champion Hollomar's Judd ex Scotmar's Aurora, a Champion Santana's Man O War daughter; Champion Maverick of Jo Mar, by Champion Ekolan Shilo, Maturity and Futurity Grand Victor, ex Lisha of Jo Mar, a Champion Eko-Lan Morgan daughter; Champion Caralands Attilla, by Champion Eko-lan's Paladen ex Smoketree's Americana; Champion Windwards Maverick and his sister Champion Windwards Molly, by Champion Maverick of Jo Mar ex Champion Scotmar's Special Magic; and Champion Windwards Ruby of Nocturne, by American and Canadian Grand Victor and American Champion Hollomar's

German Shepherds owned by Kaneohe Kennels, Mr. H. K. L. Castle of Hawaii, during the 1930's. All famous dogs, they are Ch. Tokay of Picardy, center, flanked by his sons, Questor and Quixote of Kaneohe. All three carried C.D. titles.

Ch. Windward's Maverick is one of the excellent Shepherds owned by Windward Kennels, Kailua, Hawaii.

Judd, ROM, from Scotmar Magic Moment, a bitch who has certainly produced well for them.

Currently being campaigned are a son of Champion Caraland Attilla from Champion Scotmar's Special Magic, Windwards Falcon, as well as Windwards Gantry, by Attilla from Eko-Lan's Pennie and Nocturne Night Fever, Grand Victor, by American Grand Victor Champion Boababs Chaz ex Nocturnes Harmony.

Right: Windward's Falcon, a young dog on the way to the title, by Ch. Caraland Attilla ex Ch. Scotmar's Special Magic. Owned by Windward Kennels.

Below: Ch. Windward's Ruby of Nocturne is by U.S. and Can. Grand Victor Ch. Hollomars Judd, ROM, ex Scotmar Magic Moment, a Santana's Man of War daughter. Owned by Windward Kennels.

Ch. Windward's Molly, a lovely bitch by Ch. Maverick of Jo Mar from Ch. Scotmar's Special Magic. Owned by Windward Kennels of Kailua, hawaii.

German Shepherd Dog Club of Hawaii, Inc., October 5th 1975. Judge, Mr. Frederick Migliore awarding Winners Dog, Best of Winners, and Best of Breed to Ch. Maverick of Jo Mar (by Ch. Ekolan Shilo, Maturity and Futurity Grand Victor ex Lisha of Jo Mar, a Ch. Eko-Lan Morgan daughter). Owned by Patrick and Sandra Ayers, Kailua, Hawaii.

Ch. Wellspring's Beatrix, one of the handsome Shepherds belonging to Mr. and Mrs. Franklyn Schaefer, Sands Point, New York.

GERMAN SHEPHERD
G CLUB OF MIAMI VALLEY
SPECIALTY SHOW
SEPT. 23 - 1979
WINNERS DOG
JUDGE
HERR GUNTHER BAUER
HOTO BY THACKER

Lakesides Chico taking Winners Dog at the German Shepherd Dog Club of Miami Valley Specialty Show, September 1979. Judge, Herr Gunther Bauer. Photo courtesy of Sharon Dwier.

Right: Markenhaus Elf, bred and owned by Ken Rayner, sired by Ch. Condor v. Stoerstrudel ex Fredda v. Olsonkamp. Shown winning a Futurity Class at a very young age, handled by Chips Rayner also at a very young age. **Below:** Terri Mee, named the Top Junior Handler of German Shepherds in 1979 by the German Shepherd Dog Club of America, with the lovely year-old bitch Abby vom Linderhof, C.D., a representative of top German bloodlines (H Lauerhof litter, Q Wienerau litter) and America's top bloodlines (Lance, Shaft, and so on). Abby is owned by Terri's mother, Valerie D. Mee, Smithtown, New York.

Ch. Meadowmill's Legend at nineteen months winning one of many Group placements for breeder-owner-handler Helen Miller Fisher. By Ch. Kubestraum's Kane ex Meadowmill's Molly Brown.

Opposite, above: Hermsdorf's High Flyer at fifteen months of age. Owned by Hermsdorf's German Shepherds, Peter and Bruni Zylberstein, Pickering, Ontario, Canada. **Below:** Ch. Quasar of Clover Acres, by Ch. Tannenwald's Igor ex Frolich of Clover Downs, pictured going Best Puppy at the German Shepherd Dog Club of America Specialty in October 1971. Handler, Chips Rayner. Judge, R.C. Smith.

Proven Hill's Jillian, Best of Opposite Sex in Futurity, 1981, by Proven Hill's A Sun Hawk ex Select Ch. Proven Hill's Sunshine, a mother-son breeding. Judy Teidel, owner, Proven Hill Kennels, Woodstock, Illinois.

Debonaire's Huckster, owned by Mr. Frederic W. (Ted) Meisner, taking Best of Winners at the German Shepherd Dog Club of Rhode Island in the spring of 1982.

Sue Rayner with her special, Ch. Du Chiens Desert Song, by Ch. Doppelt-Tay's Hawkeye ex Covy Tucker Hills Lucy Locket, owned by P. Phillips.

Ch. Beech Hills Benji von Masco, by Ch. Masko v. Konigstein ex Beech Hills No Trouble At All, winning the Working Group at Hartford 1982 on the way to Best in Show there. Ken Rayner Sr., handling for owner Mary Ellen Thomas.

Ch. Asler de Urquioli at the Federacion Canina de Venezuela 30th Anniversary Show in May 1982 winning Best Puppy in Show from judge Ed Dixon for owners Maria I. de Urquijo and Pierangelo Fiandrino and breeder Juan Olivier. Presenting the trophy to Mrs. Urquijo and Mr. Fiandrino is Hernan Perez, President of the F.C.V.

MEJOR
CACHORRO
VENEZOLANO DE
LA EXPOSICION

Canadian Select Ch.
Hermsdorf's Hellen, owned by
Gilles Pigeon, Laval City,
Quebec, Canada.

The fabulous Latin-American Ch.
Roda von Haussman, C.D.X.,
seven times Best in Show and
thirty times Best in Specialty
Show. She was Best in Show at
the Latin American Championship Show in 1981, winning Best
in Show there under judge Mr.
Herbert Oster from Germany. Mr.
Ramon Podesta, breeder-owner,
Santiago, Chile.

Von Jobeck's Brady winning a Junior Teenage Dog first at the German Shepherd Dog Club National Futurity, May 1972. Handled by Gerlinde Hockla for owner Joan Beck.

Ch. Scherzar's Rhianon, at two years of age, winning the Best Maturity Bitch, Mid-Pacific Region. Janice L. Staley, owner, Scherzar Shepherds, Castro Valley, California.

Famous owner of Cosalta Kennels, Miss Marie J. Leary, awarding honors to Blanka von Finsternwald with Gerlinde Hockla at the German Shepherd Dog Club of Massachusetts, April 1967.

Head-study of Gerlinde Hockla's beautiful bitch Antje of Lone Birch, dam of Blanka and Biene von Finsternwald.

Ch. Kamera Den's Crusader, bred and owned by W. and G. Herr.

Can. Ch. Nocturne's Ruffian, Am. and Can. C.D., by Ch. Nocturne's Gallant Gent, C.D., ex Nocturne's Harmony, younger full-sister to 1974 Maturity Victor Ch. Nocturne's Hale of Krisselhof (by Grand Victor Ch. Hollamor's Judd). Bred by Ed and Helen Gleason of Nocturne Acres Kennels. Owned by Mary E. Schuetzler, Schutzenhaus Shepherds, Farmington, Michigan.

GERMAN SHEPHERD DOG
CLUB OF TOLEDO
JULY 4, 1982
JUDGE — J. POEPPING
VETERAN BITCH
PHOTO — TOM MONAHAN

Ch. Ayrwood's Joshua, by Ch. Tannenwald's Igor, ROM (Jardo's Kurt of Cosalta ex Bruni of Tannenwald) from Glenhart's Della of Ayrwood, C.D. (Von Glaver's Barn Stormer ex Glenhart's Pride of Ayrwood, C.D.X.), owned by Dan and Betty Jean Lemler, Vonshore Kennels, Lexington, Missouri.

Gerlinde Hockla winning the Bred-by-Exhibitor Class with her Gero von Finsternwald at the German Shepherd Dog Club of Western Massachusetts Specialty Show in April 1974. Judge, Harry Polonitza.

Ch. Van Cleve's Edge, Southeast Futurity Victor, a son of Grand Victor Ch. Langenau's Watson. Here winning Best of Breed at Atlanta Kennel Club in 1979 for Dr. and Mrs. Carmen L. Battaglia, Lithonia, Georgia.

CHAPTER FIVE

1982 Can. Grand Victrix, Can. Ch. Covy's Altana of Tucker Hill, by Ch. Covy's Mazarati of Tucker Hill ex Covy Tucker Hill's Vigor n Zip. Owned by M. Charlton, Cappy Pottle, and Gloria Birch, the latter two co-breeders with J. and M. Scanlon.

German Shepherd Dogs in Canada

The German Shepherd Dog enjoys sound popularity in Canada, where we have noted many outstanding members of this breed as we have attended various dog shows. Canadian breeders have imported, and presently work with, the finest American bloodlines and those from the German kennels which they have incorporated into their own breeding programs; and they are producing very noteworthy Shepherds who are making good records in keen competition.

Canadian Kennels

On the following pages we bring you stories of several successful Canadian kennels: Holmsdorf, which has particularly distinguished itself in conformation competition; Leeven Rob, which has distinguished itself in both the show and obedience rings; and Vellmar, which owns a record-setting Best in Show dog. Other successful Canadian breeders of Shepherds include Brian and Grace Davidson of Caledon East, Ontario, who own Wencinschell Kennels, home of Canadian Grand Victor, Canadian Maturity Victor, American and Canadian Champion Wencin-

schell's Challenger, by Grand Victor Champion Padechma's Persuasion (Zeus of Fran-Jo ex Champion Padechma's Galaxie) from Atrice Von Bennerhaus (American and Canadian Champion Von Nassau's Dayan ex the Harrigan daughter, Von Nassau's High and Mighty). This kennel also houses Wencinschell's Grand Slam, carrying Harrigan five times in his pedigree, who was Winners Dog and Select Number Two at the 1979 Canadian National.

There also are Tessalto Kennels, owned by Nicole MacDuff and Michel McClere, who have an elegant bitch, Kolbrook's Rolls Royce; Brunorman's Kennels, owned by Nora and Bruce Bayles of Terra Cotta, Ontario, who have some fine dogs; and Herrlickheit Kennels, breeders of the Kinsellas' nine-month-old Champion Herrlickheit's Krista, who created quite a sensation during the summer of 1981.

Throughout Canada there are many, many other successful Shepherd breeders making important wins in both conformation and obedience. Interest here has been of long duration when one considers that the 1982 Specialty Championship Dog Show of the German Shep-

193

herd Dog Club of Canada was this organization's sixtieth such event and the Specialty Obedience Trial its eighth.

Canada publishes its own German Shepherd magazine, *The Canadian Shepherd Journal*, an attractive and useful periodical which is published six times a year.

Hermsdorf

Hermsdorf Kennels, owned by Peter and Bruni Zylberstein of Pickering, Ontario, have been breeding Shepherds since about 1975 and have, indeed, met with notable success during this comparatively short span of time.

Their most exciting product to date is the handsome "Condor," or, more formally, 1981 Canadian Grand Victor, American and Canadian Champion Hermsdorf's Eldorado. This

outstanding dog is a son of Champion Covy's Shamrock of Tucker Hill, C.D.X. (Grand Victor Champion Lakeside's Harrigan, ROM, ex Covy's Eve of Tucker Hill) from the Zylbersteins' great producing bitch Dornonville's Kora (Wynthea's Tut-E-Nuf ex Dornonville's Suzie, she by Champion Glucklich von der Funzig-Eichen). Eldorado gained his American championship with four four-point majors, twice going Best of Breed over Specials and twice Best of Winners. In Canada, three five-point majors gave him championship honors, and he was the 1980 Canadian National Best Puppy and the 1981 Canadian Grand Victor. All of these achievements were accomplished when Eldorado was less than two years old. He was handled in the United States by James Moses and in Canada by Michel Chaloux. This dog, a

1981 Can. Grand Victor, Am. and Can. Ch. Hermsdorf's Eldorado, "Condor" to his friends, by Ch. Covy's Shamrock of Tucker Hill, C.D.X., from Dornonville's Kora. Bred and owned by Hermsdorf's German Shepherds, Peter and Bruni Zylberstein, Pickering, Ontario, Canada.

Hermsdorf's Hercules, at six months of age, is by Cobert's Sirocco of Windigail, ROM, ex Dornonville's Kora and is one of the splendid German Shepherds bred and owned by Hermsdorf Kennels, Peter and Bruni Zylberstein.

Hermsdorf's Holly (above) and Hermsdorf's Harley (below), both by Cobert's Sirocco of Windigail, ROM, ex Dornonville's Kora. Both owned by Gord Novikoff of Canada.

Lonya Zylberstein, daughter of Peter and Bruni Zylberstein, is a young partner in the Hermsdorf German Shepherds at Pickering, Ontario. With her is her friend Hermsdorf's Jade, by Can. Grand Victor Ch., Am. Ch. Hermsdorf's Eldorado ex Can. Select Ch., Futurity Victor and Young Dog Siegerln, Carissima's La Davina.

tremendous source of pleasure to his owners at home as well as being a fabulous show dog, is also a super protector and a good pet whom they truly enjoy.

Hermsdorf owns several bitches on which their breeding program is based. Primarily they line-breed or type breed, but they have also successfully outcrossed to leading German and American bloodlines. They raise two or three litters each year.

The star producing bitch at this kennel is Dornonville's Kora. Not only is she the dam of Eldorado, but also her "H" litter, sired by Cobert's Sirocco of Windigail, ROM, is considered by Peter Zylberstein to be the best yet raised at this kennel. This litter is bringing Kora close to her Registry of Merit rating. Out of eight puppies, five are currently being shown. One is already a Canadian Select Champion and the others almost certainly will have finished by the time you are reading this book. At least one of them, Hermsdorf's High Flyer, will also be campaigned in the United States. The other four are Hermsdorf's Hercules, Canadian Select Champion Hermsdorf's Hellen (owned by Gilles Pigeon), Hermsdorf's Harley (owned by Gord Novikoff), and Hermsdorf's Holly (also owned by Mr. Novikoff).

Leeven Rob

It was in May of 1978, with the purchase of a most exciting puppy bitch, that Lu McLea and her husband Rob, of Echo Bay, Canada, decided to establish their Leeven Rob Shepherds. Lu had owned the breed for close to twenty years and Rob had done so for about a dozen years, but it was not until four years ago that the moment seemed right for them officially to become Shepherd breeders.

The new puppy bitch that triggered present activities really started them on their way in a most auspicious manner. Lu began working with her in obedience when the baby Shepherd was a mere fourteen weeks old and found her to be so amazing an animal that by the time she had reached nineteen and a half months old she had officially become Canadian Obedience Trial Champion Lana vom Kreuzberg. Shortly after that she was tested for Tracking Dog degrees in the United States and Canada, gaining them in both places with flying colors.

All of this had been accomplished in less than six months and Lana received the *Dog World* Award of Distinction in honor of her superior talents—a very nice start for these new breeders.

Ch. Poplar Valley's D'Artagnon has eleven A.K.C. points as well as his Canadian title. Owned by Joe and Cherie Sobieralski of Miami, Florida, "D'Art" has figured prominently in the breeding program of Lu McLea's Leeven Rob Kennels at Echo Bay, Ontario.

Can. Obedience Trial Champion Lana v. Kreuzberg, U.D.T., Am. C.D., T.D., at age three and a half years. Owned by Lu McLea, Leeven Rob Kennels.

Since it is important to the McLeas to have a dog that can be trained easily and that is as well a handsome representative of the breed according to the standard, their search for the next addition to their canine family was extensive, and they found it so difficult to locate the kind of dog they wanted that they decided their best bet would be to breed it. Their aim has been to produce "beauty plus brains," and their entire breeding program is directed toward this goal.

Their search for a handsome stud led them to a dog named Poplar Valley's D'Artagnon, a Canadian champion with eleven points toward his title in the United States. Lu McLea describes him as a "real stallion dog with floating gait and built as close to the standard as is possible." His dam is a true working dog, being one of eight bitches in charge on a hog farm in Berne, Indiana. The owners of D'Artagnon are Joe and Cherie Sobieralski, formerly of Castalia, Ohio, but now living in Miami, Florida. They approved of the McLeas' plan to breed Obedience Trial Champion Lana to their Bench Show Champion D'Artagnon, and the mating took place. This first litter produced some exciting pups, including a bitch who qualified for her Canadian Tracking Dog degree at seven and a half months of age with only twenty-nine days of training. All nine puppies from that litter are stable in temperament and are very trainable; and five of them are additionally very showable. One bitch belongs to the McLeas' son and, at nineteen months of age, was Best of Breed at Sudbury in 1982. The breeding has been repeated and hopes are high for similar success.

The fulcrum of the McLeas' breeding program is a German import, Oskar von Busecker-Schloss, described as a "beautiful dog with stable temperament and highly intelligent." These qualities have been passed on to his progeny and the McLeas find them most desirable.

One of the goals at Leeven Rob is to breed a Best in Show dog. We wish the McLeas success in fulfilling this ambition, and we feel quite certain they will make it!

Leeven Rob's Amber, twenty months of age and started toward her Canadian championship, by Can. Ch. Poplar Hill's D'Artagnon ex Obedience Trial Ch. Lana v. Kreuzberg. Owned by Leeven Rob Kennels, Lu and Rob McLea, Echo Bay, Ontario, Canada.

Poplar Valley's Sassafras has been leased by Leeven Rob Kennels from her owners, the Sobieralskis, for breeding to her half-brother Poplar Valley's Sinbad, both sired by Can. Ch. Poplar Valley's D'Artagnon.

Poplar Valley's Sinbad, a son of Can. Ch. Poplar Valley's D'Artagnon, is the principal stud dog at Leeven Rob Kennels. Lu and Rob McLea, owners.

Shaina's Cinderella at six months of age. One of the lovely puppies sired by Poplar Valley's Sinbad in his first litter, the dam a Ch. Erko v. Dinkelland granddaughter. Lu and Rob McLea owners, Leeven Rob Kennels.

Vellmar

Ingrid and Robert Keim, owners of Vellmar German Shepherds at Penhold, Alberta, Canada, have a record of which to be proud in that gained by their homebred-owner-handled Canadian Champion Lido von Vellmar, representing their fifth generation of homebreds, based mostly on leading German bloodlines. This magnificent dog has twenty all-breed Bests in Show on his record, which his owners believe gives him an all-time high in this respect for any German Shepherd in Canadian history.

Lido's accomplishments and successes in the show ring have made him the Number Five Top Dog, All Breeds, in Canada for 1980; Number Two Working Dog in Canada 1981; and Number One German Shepherd Dog in Canada in 1981.

This magnificent dog, Can. Ch. Lido von Vellmar, bred, owned, and handled by Ingrid Keim of Vellmar Kennels, Penhold, Alberta, Canada, is the Number One German Shepherd Dog in Canada for 1981, the Number One German Shepherd Dog male in Canada for 1980, the Number Two Working Dog in Canada for 1981, and the Number Five Top Dog All-Breeds in Canada for 1981.

1976 Grand Victor and 1977 Can. Grand Victor Ch. Padechma's Persuasion, by Zeus of Fran-Jo, ROM, ex Ch. Padechma's Galaxie. Photo courtesy of Mary Schuetzler.

Can. Ch. Herrlickheit's Krista, a champion at nine months old, by Ch. Mirheim's Serpico (Am. Ch. Doppelt-Tay's Hawkeye, ROM, ex Mirheim's Elli of Fran-Jo) ex Ch. Debra Lee of Sentar (Ch. Hardt v. Steuerufer, SchH III, Can. and Am. C.D., ex Ch. Herr-lickheit's Emma Peel). Here Krista is winning Best Puppy in Sweep-stakes at Barrie Kennel Club (134 entered) in August 1981. Krista was bred by Monica Hudson, is owned by Morgan and Jean Kinsella of Orangeburg, Ontario, and is handled by Paul Hudson.

Barking at the suspect. A Shepherd in schutzhund training under the auspices of the German Shepherd Schutzhund Club of Canada.

The German Shepherd Schutzhund Club of Canada

We have noted with interest the activities of the German Shepherd Schutzhund Club of Canada; and since they are proceeding along the lines approved by the S.V., we are using this Canadian club to exemplify Schutzhund work for the uninitiated and to advise our readers of the good job along these lines being performed by this enthusiastic group. We feel sure that you will find it both informative and interesting.

The German Shepherd Schutzhund Club of Canada was started in 1979 by a group of German Shepherd enthusiasts with the following objectives:

1. To do all in its power to protect and improve the German Shepherd Dog breed.

2. To urge its members to accept the standards of the German Shepherd Dog as approved by the WUSV.

3. To promote and encourage conformation shows and breed surveys according to the WUSV standard for German Shepherd Dogs in order to provide guidelines in breeding for its members and all other owners and breeders of German Shepherd Dogs.

4. To educate the general public with regard to the importance of strong, steady temperament and to the fact that it must be a prerequisite in any breeding program.

5. To promote Schutzhund training for working dogs and to encourage sportsmanlike behavior in training and competitions.

6. To promote Schutzhund training among the youth.

7. To give advice, assistance and encouragement to groups seriously interested in forming a Schutzhund training club.

8. To conduct Schutzhund trials according to regulations laid down by the Schaefer Verein, such trials to be judged by a person licensed as a judge by the Schaefer Verein.

9. To conduct one annual Canadian Schutzhund III Championship event each year.

10. To hold seminars, given by qualified Schutzhund trainers or Schaefer Verein teaching judges, in order to upgrade the knowledge and expertise of members and other interested participants.

The German Shepherd Schutzhund Club of Canada is more than just a schutzhund club. It is

Stopping the suspect.

also a breed club that is very concerned with correct structure in their dogs. At the present time, this group holds not only an Annual Schutzhund III Championship but also an annual breed show and survey. All trials and shows held by them are judged by licensed Schaefer Verein judges. Numerous seminars conducted by Germany's top teaching judges are held each year. Through these activities, the club's participants gain a better and more complete understanding of the German Shepherd Dog and particularly the schutzhund sport.

Approximately twelve trials are held each year for Schutzhund I through Schutzhund III, with tests and training degrees known as FH. Five conformation shows are held annually as well. Nearly every trial is accompanied by a seminar. There are presently twelve German Shepherd Dog Clubs in Canada that belong to the National Federation, three each in British Columbia and Alberta, two in Quebec, and one each in Saskatchewan, Manitoba, Ontario, and New Brunswick. There are also individual members who belong to the national club from all parts of Canada.

The number of participants in the schutzhund sport in Canada is still quite small, but it is beginning to grow at an ever increasing rate of speed. People are slowly realizing the value of a well-trained dog who can be depended on in any situation. Temperament is one of this group's prime areas of concern; and only those dogs who are steady, easy-going, and willing to work with their handlers in a very demanding sport are wanted.

The concept of schutzhund evolved about eighty-five years ago in Europe, and although the exercises have over the years changed slightly, the sport still consists of three phases: tracking, obedience, and protection. The dog must perform all tasks asked of him quickly and with a great deal of spirit. He must bite hard when required, showing no hesitation. Depending on the schutzhund degree being sought, the exercises consist of the following:

Tracking—The dog must follow a person's path, 400-1500 yards long with two to four turns in it, after twenty to sixty minutes have elapsed following laying of the track. He must find and indicate to his handler two or three lost articles, and this must be done regardless of weather conditions.

Obedience—The dog must follow his handler's orders to heel, jump, retrieve, retrieve over a six-foot wall, and go away from his master when

Bringing back the five-pound dumbbell.

Helen Miller Fisher put on interesting and extremely popular Working Dog demonstrations (schutzhund) for clubs, shows, Rotary Clubs, and others, with her great imported Working Dog, Falko, during the 1950's.

There are a number of outstanding dogs owned and handled by Canadians. One of the most well-known schutzhund dogs in Canada is a German Shepherd crossbreed by the name of Sheba, of whom we make special mention because in 1980 she and her handler, Doug Deacon of British Columbia, won the U.S. National Schutzhund III Championships, came in second in the Canadian National Schutzhund III Championships, and won the North American Schutzhund III Championship. Sheba is now retired, and her handler, Douglas Deacon, is now working a handsome, registered German Shepherd who has an excellent background in this field.

One of the other outstanding dogs and handlers who belong to the German Shepherd Schutzhund Club of Canada is Brix von Helgemeg, SchH III, sired by Negus von Kirschental, SchH, FH, ex Kessi von Anger, SchH I. Brix is a multiple Schutzhund III dog owned by Paul Erickson of Vancouver, British Columbia. He

Ulk stops the suspect! This is Ulk vom Bungalow, SchH III, FH, owned by Fred Sharpf of Langley, British Columbia, an outstanding Schutzhund dog.

ordered to do so. He must do this both on and off lead. The dog must not be intimidated by any distractions, including the sound of a gunshot or the presence of a group of strangers milling about.

Protection—The dog must, without handler assistance, respond properly in critical situations. He must alert his handler to an intruder by barking at a strange person who is standing perfectly still. He may not bite the unmoving person. He must by biting hard stop the intruder from escaping and attacking the dog's handler. He must let go when the intruder stops struggling or when commanded to do so by his handler. He must bite hard immediately, even when being threatened by the intruder with a stick. The dog must distinguish between a harmless bystander and a potentially dangerous person. He must display courage and fighting spirit throughout these exercises.

Schutzhund training is a sport that is open to all breeds of dogs as long as they can perform the required tasks; German Shepherd Dogs, however, are probably the most popular breed.

Quido vom Gerspenz, SchH II, by Hasko vom Hattsteiuburg ex Dori von Aeteieck, placed SG-8 Youth Class at the 1978 Sieger Show in Munich, while at the B.C. Sieger Show in 1979 he was V-3; in 1980, V-2; and in 1981, V-1. Owned by Frank Mensing of Langley, British Columbia.

has competed in two Canadian National Schutzhund III Championships.

Bodo vom Grundautal, SchH III, is by Klodo von der Wienerau, SchH II, ex Hadi Blue-Irish, SchH II. Owned by Eric Morphy of Birkland Kennels in Langley, British Columbia, Bodo is a multiple Schutzhund III dog as well as having attained the following honors: 1978, second in the U.S. National Schutzhund III Championship; 1979, second in the Canadian National Schutzhund III Championship; 1979, third in the U.S. National Schutzhund III Championship; 1979, twenty-third in the Europa Meistershaft.

Ulk von Bungalow is a multiple Schutzhund III dog owned by Fred Sharpf of Langley, British Columbia. A summary of his successes appears with the caption of his picture. A magnificent and intelligent dog, he is widely admired by Canadian breeders.

Friga vom Allerswald, SchH III, is presently owned by Audrey Morphy of Birkland Kennels in Langley, British Columbia. She is an outstanding solid black bitch, a daughter of Quicke vom Itztal, and is highly valued as a brood bitch. She placed V-22 at the 1977 Bundesiegerpruefung.

Quido vom Gerspenz, SchH II, owned by Frank Mensing of Langley, British Columbia, is by Hasko vom Hattsteiuburg ex Dori von Aeteieck. In 1978, he placed SG-8 Youth Class at the Sieger Show in Munich and was V-3, V-2, and V-1 respectively in 1979, 1980, and 1981 at the British Columbia Sieger Show.

Tanja von der Jungen Hansen, SchH III, is owned by Barry and Cathy Gay of Saskatoon, Saskatchewan. An outstanding producing bitch with a strong working pedigree (Condor von Distelkamp, SchH III, ex Kitty von der Jungen Hansen), she is one of the comparatively few bitches to have achieved Schutzhund III in Canada and she is also V-rated in conformation.

These are just a few of the most outstanding Canadian dogs who are working today. All are from excellent German working lines and are producing young dogs who are now developing the outgoing, confident, and friendly manner and high energy of animals which make the finest material for the schutzhund sport.

We are indebted to Cathy Gay for the information in this discussion of the schutzhund sport in Canada. Her time and interest in having gathered it together for us are sincerely appreciated.

Can. Grand Victor, Am. and Can. Select Ch. Ravenhaus Noah, ROM. Photo courtesy of Mary E. Schuetzler.

CHAPTER SIX

German Shepherd Dogs in England and Australia

Ch. Fenton of Kentwood, winner of Best in Show at Crufts.

The German Shepherd Dog made his way to England following the close of World War I when, as had been the case in the United States, many servicemen met the breed in Germany, admired its intelligence, loyalty, and other fine traits and wanted to bring a puppy home. The one problem was the stigma attached, at that period, to the breed because of its name—German Shepherd Dog! Lest this have a negative effect on the breed's reception there, the British decided to change the name to Alsatian Wolf Dog, which led to a whole other set of problems, owing to the inclusion of the word "wolf."

The Alsatian's rise to popularity during the early twenties was phenomenal, and by midway in that decade the breed rose to the top position on the list of popular breeds. As is bound to happen when a breed is overly popular, this rise was accompanied by many Alsatians winding up in the hands of careless owners and people not aware of the responsibility that accompanies ownership of so large, powerful, and active a breed, dogs who are instinctively geared for guard work and whose activities need to be correctly channeled. Suddenly, the press was filled with tales of unfortunate incidents involving the breed—and then it was that "wolf dog" became the cry. Actually, however, there is very little probability that any cross with wolves ever existed within the breed, plus the fact that even had it been true, the outcross would have been in the very remote past, much too long ago to have had any effect on the temperaments of the dogs of the 1920's period!

Aghast at the manner in which their well-intended act had backfired, the British switched back to the title "German Shepherd Dog" for the breed; unfortunately, however, this did not succeed in erasing the "wolf dog" pictures from the minds of the public. And just as the Alsatian's rise in popularity had brought the breed from less than one hundred to more than five thousand registrations annually between the end of World War I and the middle of the 1920's, so the pendulum swung in the opposite direction, with registrations falling back rapidly. Fortunately, this state of affairs lasted only a

205

Ch. Churlswood Tosca of Brinton, a fine English champion bitch.

short time, and an upward trend started again as people realized more and more the virtues of these magnificent dogs and the foolishness of the hysteria which had caused them to slip from favor. Slowly but surely the climb in registrations continued until as the 1970's approached, Alsatians or German Shepherds (whichever name one called them) were again on the top of the popularity polls in Britain's dog circles.

German Shepherd Dogs, the name by which the breed is now called in England, have continued to flourish since that time, and there are some lovely examples of the breed in the hands of dedicated fanciers today. Ambrook German Shepherds are owned by Mr. and Mrs. Tuckwell. Their Shepherds include the lovely Lynlee Peppercorn from Ambrook, by Champion Spartacist of Hendrawen ex a daughter of Champion Ramacon Philanderer. In addition to being a

show winner, Peppercorn has scored well in obedience and is a fully trained guard dog.

Then there is the handsome big winner, Champion Langfauld's Amos, who hails from the kennels of Hugh and Zoe de Zutter in Clydebank, Scotland.

Royvon's German Shepherds, belonging to Roy and Yvonne James in Wales, include some very beautiful and highly successful dogs of whom we have heard good things.

Mr. and Mrs. Wilkinson are breeders in Hampson near Lancaster. Kelowna German Shepherds belong to Miss M. O'Grady and are at Halesowen in West Midlands.

Mrs. Beck, who owns Letton German Shepherds at Privett, in Hampshire, also operates a branch of the kennel in South Africa.

Borderfame is another breeding establishment, raising dogs which are used for work on the police force, in the Royal Air Force, and for civilian duty. These belong to Mr. and Mrs. S. A. Emmerson in Derbyshire.

We understand that in Great Britain there currently (late 1982) is a somewhat sharp difference of opinion between the multiple breed and the specialist judges as to what exactly constitutes correct type in the breed ring. The focus in this matter is the topline. The breed, or specialist, judges prefer to place tremendous emphasis upon a decidedly pronounced (almost to the point of exaggeration) curve in the topline, leading detractors of this preference to refer to Shepherds so constructed as "banana dogs." We hope that these differences of opinion are but a passing phase and that a reconciliation between the two schools of thought will have taken place by the time you are reading this, for in *any* breed of dog, there actually can be but one correct basic type; and when sharp differences in its interpretation arise, only problems can be the result.

In Australia, the popularity of German Shepherd Dogs has suffered little fluctuation over the years, although there was a time, starting in the mid-1920's, when the importation of German Shepherd Dogs into Australia was prohibited. Fortunately, those already owning the breed there guarded it well, and thus it continued to progress despite the ban on importation. Now these lovely dogs are regarded with such high esteem by Australian owners that the breed consistently holds a position as one of the most popular breeds in Australia.

Reading a summary description of the activities of the Australian dog world during 1982, we note that German Shepherd Dogs have ranked high in show entries at the country's most prestigious events. The Melbourne Royal drew 199 of them; and entries for the breed on many other occasions averaged between one and two hundred. We also note German Shepherds accounting for important wins. One such win was made by a young bitch, Paladeen Xamber, who was awarded Best of Opposite Sex to Best in Show at Brisbane's National Show where the total entry was close to 4,000.

An English champion male, Ch. Archer of Brinton.

Ch. Klodo del Juncal pictured at twelve years of age. This is the foundation dog from Ramon Podesta's von Haussman Kennels, Santiago, Chile. A sire of tremendous importance to the breed, when Klodo died at age fifteen he left behind countless winning descendants.

CHAPTER SEVEN

German Shepherd Dogs in South America

Am., Ven., Puerto Rican Ch. Wellspring Iroquois, owned by Mrs. Maria de Peter, Caracas, Venezuela, won the Best of Breed and Working Group at Federacion Canofila de Puerto Rico, May 1982. A multiple Best in Show winner, this dog has five times won the breed in Venezuela and four times led the Group.

Nowhere in the world is there to be found more intense and dedicated interest in breeding dogs than in South America. Our friends there have a really deep desire not only to import and own typical animals of superior quality but also to breed them and produce noteworthy dogs from their imported bloodlines in their own country. With steadily increasing frequency, breeders from South America are visiting the United States, giving us the opportunity to know them personally and thus to learn to appreciate their ambitions and their high ideals. These people never are satisfied with second best. Their aim is for superior dogs, and they invest not only considerable amounts of money but also a great deal of time, energy, and study into expanding their knowledge in order to obtain the finest stock from which to work. We have deep admiration for the South American breeders and for the progress they are making with the advancement of their favorite breeds.

German Shepherds are among the major canine interests in South American countries, with numerous breeders who can truly point

with pride to their accomplishments. One of these is Mr. Ramon Podesta, owner of the Von Haussman Kennels at Santiago, Chile.

Although Mr. Podesta now successfully owns a number of breeds, it was exclusively with German Shepherds that the Von Haussman Kennels was established back in 1964. Now Mr. Podesta is generally considered to be the top Shepherd breeder in Chile. From 1975 through the time of this writing (the end of 1982), Mr. Podesta's dogs have been major all-breed Best in Show winners and leaders at German Shepherd Specialties not only in Chile but also in Colombia and Uruguay.

Von Haussman breeding is highly regarded throughout the South American canine world and representatives from this kennel are top winners in Brazil, Paraguay, Venezuela, Colombia, and Argentina. Mr. Podesta's kennels are the home of about thirty Shepherds in addition to around two hundred dogs of other breeds. This gentleman operates a huge but quality-filled operation with spacious grounds and magnificent facilities for all of his dogs.

All of the Shepherds at Von Haussman are free of hip dysplasia problems and all are temperament-tested and -approved.

One of Mr. Podesta's best known German Shepherds is Latin American Champion Roda von Haussman, winner of that honor in 1981, when she competed in the Latin American Championship Show against the Best Male and Best Female from every South American country, winning Best in Show under Mr. Herbert Oster, widely respected judge from Germany. Born in April 1978, Roda is a homebred daughter of two German imports, Cen von Holtkamper See and Burga von Valdsee. She has a C.D.X. degree, and at the time of this writing, she has already won seven all-breed Bests in Show plus Best in Show at thirty Specialty events—certainly with more to come!

Cen von Holtkamper See (the sire of Roda) is also owned by Mr. Podesta, who imported him from Germany in 1975. A true representative of the Canto-Winerau bloodlines, while still in Germany he was a class winner in keen competition; and when shown in Chile he did considerable Best of Breed winning including Specialties, being undefeated among Shepherds there. This dog, we are told, is the Number One German Shepherd sire in Chile.

Hussein von Haussman, bred by Mr. Ramon Podesta, was trained and shown by the Chilean Air Force to whom Mr. Podesta presented him. A dog who has gained many friends for the breed, he was the winner of the National Specialty in Chile in 1978, and in 1980 he was sent as Chilean representative to the Latin-American Championship Show.

Above: Cen von Holtkampersee, the sire of Roda and Rashid von Haussman. Imported and owned by Mr. Ramon Podesta, Santiago, Chile. **Below:** Rashid von Haussman, litter-brother to Roda von Haussman. Bred and owned by Mr. Ramon Podesta.

Rashid von Haussman, litter-brother to Roda, is the Number One German Shepherd Male in Chile and the Number One C.D.X. winner. Undefeated in Best of Breed competition, he will be the Chilean male representative at 1982's Latin American Championship Show, where Roda also will return in an effort to defend her 1981 title. Rashid, despite his youth, is already proving himself as a sire, his sons starting out well as class winners at Specialty shows.

Hussein von Haussman, bred by Mr. Podesta, by Black Khole und Staldt ex Kieb da Casa Dos Arcos (Quanto-Winerau bloodlines), was the Chilean representative male German Shepherd at the 1980 Latin American Championship Show and was C.D.X. in 1980 and 1981. He

Evi von Silverstar with her owner, Ramon Podesta. Evi, an imported bitch who produced several litters and whose puppies are always reserved far in advance of their birth, is a Group and Specialty Show winner.

won the National Specialty for his area in 1978; and, as is the case with most of the Von Haussman dogs, his progeny are winning throughout the country. It is interesting that Hussein is owned by the Air Force of Chile, by whom he was trained and shown, generating considerable dog show enthusiasm for this group! It is Hussein who leads all of the parade marches during national festivities.

The lovely bitch Evi von Silverstar was imported to Chile from Germany by Mr. Podesta and became the leading imported female there in 1979, 1980, and 1981. A multiple Group-winner, she has more than twenty Specialty

Bests of Breed as well, with time off in between to raise several outstanding litters. She is a daughter of Frei von Holtkampersee.

The great Champion Klodo del Juncal, who lived to be fifteen years old, was the foundation dog of the Von Haussman Shepherds. It was he who taught Mr. Podesta to love this breed, and he left behind him an important legacy in the form of many outstanding descendants.

Bijou von Haussman, a homebred born in 1979, is one of the kennels young hopefuls. She was Best Puppy in 1979 and Best Young Female in 1980; and as this is written, she remains undefeated in Best of Breed competition.

It is easy to see how well Mr. Podesta has used the stock in his kennel to produce in each succeeding generation more outstanding representatives of the German Shepherd breed; and he is constantly on the lookout for worthy kennel additions whose bloodlines may complement and blend well with those already there. Mr. Podesta is a noted all-breed judge who travels extensively and thus is in touch with what takes place in German Shepherd circles throughout the world.

In Brazil there is a famous German Shepherd kennel which was established in the late 1950's by Mrs. Vera Lucia de Castro Barbosa. This is Dois Pinheiros, the home of a great many celebrated, handsome, outstanding representatives of the German Shepherd breed. Included among the noted winners here is four times champion, Kassie de Dois Pinheiros, by the German im-

Bijou von Haussman, by Cen von Holtkampersee ex Anka von Haussman, was bred and owned by Mr. Ramon Podesta of Chile.

Four times Ch. Kassie de Dois Pinheiros, by Olaf v. Schinklergrenze (German import) ex three times Ch. Gina de Dois Pinheiros, a multiple Best in Show winner bred by Mrs. Vera Lucia de Castro Barbosa of Brazil.

The lovely Cilly von Overledingerland, one of the many handsome German Shepherds owned by Mrs. Vera Lucia de Castro Barbosa in Brazil.

port, Olaf von Schinklergrenze ex three times champion, Gina de Dois Pinheiros. This bitch was the Brazilian vice-representative to the South American Championship Show of 1971 and was the winner of Best in Show at the Dog Festival of the Kennel Club Paulista at Sao Paulo. Kassie was bred by her owner.

In 1973, Champion Veus von Unterhain, who had come from Germany following his placing sixth in the *Jugendklasse* of the Siegerschau in Germany in competition against 120 dogs in the class, was successfully carrying the banner for Mrs. Barbosa. Sired by Quanto von Wienerau, VA, ex Celly von Wienerau, VA, Veus quickly made his presence felt in Brazil and for five consecutive years won the award for Best Imported Sire. Included among his progeny were the three females chosen to compete in the South American Championship Show in 1980, 1981, and 1982, two of which gained the championship title in 1980 and 1982. Veus also sired the 1982 winner of the title Best Sire in the Nation. His contributions to the quality of the breed in Brazil have been tremendous.

The lovely bitch Cilly von Overledingerland, by Arko von Pelambachtal, VA, ex Kathia von Noort, V, is another importation which has proven a true asset to the Dois Pinheiros Kennel. She is the dam of the Southeast Junior Champion of 1980, the Vice-Champion Junior of 1981, and Reserve Best in Show in the Latin American Show of 1982.

Danka de Dois Pinheiros, a homebred bitch by Champion Veus von Unterhain ex Zola von der Rader-Nachtweide, is the winner of several Specialties and is Brazilian and South American Champion 1982.

One of the most popular stud dogs is Bax von Spiegels-Berge, recently imported from Germany. He is by Dax von Kopenkamp, VA, ex Airin von Spiegels-Berge, V.

Then there is the very notable Lupe de Dois Pinheiros, by Champion Veus von Unterhain ex triple Champion Kassie de Dois Pinheiros, who represents the fourth generation of Mrs. Barbosa's breeding program. She is the dam of numerous well-known dogs, including three Best in Show winners.

We are indebted to Arq. Antonio Quiroga N, Secretario Administrativo of the Federacion Canina de Venezuela at Caracas who, through

Above: Ch. Veus von Unterhain, German import, owned by Vera Lucia de Castro Barbosa, Brazil. **Below:** Danka de Dois Pinheiros, Brazilian and South American Champion, 1982, winner of multiple Specialties. Mrs. Vera Lucia de Castro Barbosa, owner.

the interest of our mutual friend, the famous all-breed judge Richard Guevara, very kindly sent me information and photographs of some of the Shepherds who recently have been outstanding in his country.

Among the especially successful Shepherd fanciers in Venezuela is Mrs. Maria de Urquijo, the breeder of many Best of Breed and Group-placing dogs, including a Best in Show winner, I believe the only one of the latter so far bred in Venezuela. This is Venezuelan Champion Olga de Ondarreta, whose pedigree should especially interest readers in the United States as she is by Champion Winaki's Hombre of Lakeside (Grand Victor Champion Lance of Fran-Jo, ROM, ex Cobert's Melissa, ROM) from Lur de Ondarreta (Oleg von der Doeheimerhohe ex Cora vom Alten Kloster). In addition to the Best in Show win, this gorgeous bitch has gained a second in Best in Show, three times Best Venezuelan-bred in Show, and numerous Best of Breed and Group placements.

Mrs. Maria de Peter has owned two superb dogs who have accounted for prestigious winning, too. They are American and Venezuelan Champion Von Nassau's Sherpa and American and Venezuelan Champion Arap von Wallensteinpark, both Best in Show winners in the United States and Venezuela.

Ven. Ch. Olga de Ondarreta, by Ch. Winaki's Hombre of Lakeside, is the only Venezuelan-bred Best in Show winning German Shepherd Dog at present in the breed. Maria de Urquijo, owner, Caracas, Venezuela.

Ch. Wellspring's Iroquois taking Best of Breed at the Lehigh Valley German Shepherd Dog Club Specialty Show in the U.S., March 1980. Judged by Mrs. Lawrence, bred by Betty Radzevich and M. Lombardo of the United States, and owned by Mrs. Maria de Peter, Caracas, Venezuela.

Three other Best in Show dogs with splendid records in Venezuela include Champion Winaki's Hombre of Lakeside, the sire of the Venezuelan-bred Best in Show winner; Champion Waltzer von Feimerech, SchH I; and Venezulan and American Champion Von Nassau's Ronan. All are owned by Mr. F. Castro.

Federico and Beatris Tovar Segovia (he is a doctor who gave up his career in medicine to dedicate more time to his horses) own some of the finest racehorses in Venezuela and also some top German Shepherds, including such Best in Show dogs as Champion Winaki's Hombre of Lakeside and a number of splendid German importations.

Other particularly successful German Shepherd breeders in Venezuela include Mrs. Bethy Hernandez, Mrs. Francisca de Estever, and Mr. Francisco Drobsky.

Hussein von Haussman was bred by Mr. Ramon Podesta and is owned by the Air Force of Chile.

Ch. Sir Lance Talbot, owned by Eduardo A. Hurtado of Valencia, Venezuela, was bred in the United States by Roy L. Blaylock and Robert Gibson. This dog has a number of Best of Breed and Group placements to his credit, plus having been Best Sire in Show.

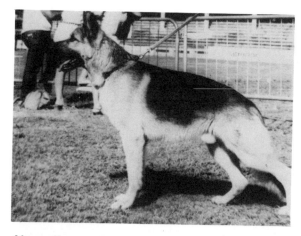

Above: Bax von Spiegels-Berge, by Dax von Kopenkamp, VA, ex Airin von Spiegels-Berge, V, belongs to Mrs. Vera Lucia de Castro Barbosa, noted Brazilian Shepherd breeder. **Below:** Lupe de Dois Pinheiros, by Ch. Veus v. Unterhain ex triple Ch. Kassie de Dois Pinheiros, represents the fourth generation of Mrs. Vera Lucia de Castro Barbosa's breeding program.

Mrs. Vera Lucia de Castro Barbosa with her daughter and some of the famous German Shepherd Dogs at her Dois Pinheiros Kennels in Brazil.

Am., Can., Ven., Mex., and Col. Ch. Warlock's Avenger of Sregor was imported to Caracas, Venezuela, from the U.S. by Mr. F. Castro Perez and was later sold to Mr. Adrian Aguirre Canedo of Mexico City, for whom he became Number One in Mexico. This dog's sudden death from a heart attack at an early age resulted in a tremendous loss to the breed.

Ganges Do Bacara was the Latin-American Champion for 1980 and 1981. Owned by Mr. Matheus Paladino, Sao Paulo, Brazil.

1961 Grand Victrix Ch. Nanhall's Donna, C.D., by Ch. Field Marshall of Arbywood, C.D., ROM, ex 1962 Grand Victrix Ch. Bonnie Bergere of Ken Rose, U.D.T., ROM, the youngest German Shepherd Dog champion to finish to date (at eleven months) and the youngest Grand Victrix to date (at fifteen months). Owned, bred, and handled by T. Hall Keyes of Nanhall Kennels, Greensboro, North Carolina, and Dr. Wade Sanders.

CHAPTER EIGHT

The German Shepherd Dog Club of America

1977 Maturity Victor Select Ch. Covy-Tucker Hill's Durango, ROM, by Covy's Oregano of Tucker Hill, ROM, ex Covy-Tucker Hill's Turtle Dove, ROM. Owners, R. and B. Schafer, Cappy Pottle, and Gloria Birch; bred by Cappy Pottle and Joy Houston. This dog comes from a solid ROM line-bred pedigree.

The principles on which the German Shepherd Dog Club of America was founded back in 1913 are the principles which still serve as its guide:

To promote the breeding of the German Shepherd Dog; to define precisely and publish definition of the true type, and to urge the adoption of such types on breeders, judges, dog show committees, etc., as the only recognized and unvarying standard by which the German Shepherd Dog is to be judged, and which may in the future be uniformly accepted as the sole standard of excellence in breeding and awarding prizes of merit; to do all in its power to protect and advance the interests of the breed by offering prizes, supporting certain shows, encouraging the development of working qualities and taking any other steps that may seem advisable to promote the most conspicuous characteristics as a Police Dog, War Dog, Red Cross Dog and Herding Dog; to encourage therefore all trials and demonstrations in which these qualities may be shown so as to interest the public generally, but especially the police and other municipal organizations in our ideals.

The German Shepherd Dog Club of America, as parent club for the breed, has more than one hundred regional clubs under its wing. The regional clubs are located in every part of the country, and the relationship between them and the parent club is strong. These regional clubs sponsor training classes in breed and obedience and have educational programs which newer fanciers should enjoy. New owners of Shepherds should discuss joining one of these clubs with the breeder of their dog, who no doubt can supply the information necessary for membership application.

The German Shepherd Dog Club of America itself sponsors a National Specialty Show each year, a National Obedience Specialty, a National Tracking Test, and Regional Futurity-Maturity Shows; and, of course, it keeps the Register of Merit (about which a detailed discussion follows). The National Specialties, both conformation and obedience, are held, on a rotation basis, in various sections of the country each year. In several areas of the country, Regional Futurity Shows are held for dogs six to eighteen months of age and Maturity Shows are held for selected mature dogs eighteen to thirty months of age.

One of the parent club's most useful and interesting services to the Shepherd Fancy is the publication of *German Shepherd Dog Review*, its official organ. This magazine has, very justly, won any number of awards since its inception in 1924. Everyone interested in the breed should be among its readers.

A great many people have been involved with the advancement of the German Shepherd Dog in this country, and the German Shepherd Dog Club published a Roll of Honor in their 1979 Membership List, which Connie Beckhardt kindly loaned to me when I began work on this book. I feel that these people should be mentioned here, as each has played a vital role in the breed's development and each contributed considerable devotion, time, and effort in one or more phases to its progress.

Roll of Honor

Mrs. Charles W.G. Baiter
Frank Barnikow
Miss Blanche Beisswenger
Mrs. Thomas L. Bennett

Lloyd C. Brackett
Reginald M. Cleveland
Miss Adele Colgate
William E. Cotton
Mrs. M. Hartley Dodge, Jr.
Lee Duncan
Will Ebeling
Mrs. Anne T. Eristoff
Dr. Werner Funk
John Gans
Dr. Karl A. Glaser
James E. Grossin
Mrs. Margaret Horn
Herr Hans Kremhelmer
Miss Marie J. Leary
Ernest Loeb
Manuel R. Lombardo
Grant E. Mann
Miss Fanny B. McIlvain
Miss Joan R. Michler
Miss Margaret Pooley
Dr. William E. Redlich
A.C. (Bob) Reuter
Burr L. Robbins
Dr. Christopher Rummel
John B. Simson
Melvin H. Steinbrenner
Miss Mary Ellis Turner
Mrs. Irma Werner
Robert E. Williamson

Waymarsh's Bretta of Ayrwood, by Ch. Treffer of Clover Acres ex Ayrwood's Fame and Fortune, winning under judge Ernest Loeb. Handled by Chips Rayner for breeder-owner Marie Sagendorf.

Ch. Ajax of La Salle, by Ch. Cuno von der Teufelslache, SchH III, ROM, ex Ch. Linnette of Long Worth, at the German Shepherd Dog Club of America National Specialty in 1958. The judge is the late Dr. William Redlich, noted Shepherd authority. The handler, Mrs. Helen Miller Fisher. Owner, Jack L. Sinykin of the famed La Salle Kennels.

Ch. Den-Lea's By Jiminey, bred, owned, and handled by Denise Kodner, became a famous Group winner, a most outstanding achievement for a black Shepherd bitch. Here, Jiminey is going Best of Breed at Steel City Kennel Club, entry of seventy-five, under Lloyd Brackett, famous Shepherd breeder.

Ch. Wellspring's Indiana, 1979 Select, Maturity Victrix, by multiple Select Ch. Doppelt-Tay's Hawkeye, ROM, ex Ch. Amber's Flair, ROM, taking Maturity Best of Opposite Sex at the German Shepherd Dog Club of America 1979 National Specialty judged by Mrs. Virginia McCoy. Owned by Franklyn and Rosalind Schaefer, Sands Point, New York.

Register of Merit

When you see the identification "ROM" following the name of a German Shepherd Dog (male or female), you should know that this indicates that the dog or bitch has been admitted to the German Shepherd Dog Club of America Register of Merit, which was established by the parent club back in 1950 in order to assist breeders with a readily available reference guide to information regarding the most successful producing German Shepherd sires and dams.

For listing as a Register of Merit Sire, a dog must have sired a total of ten or more progeny who among them have earned one hundred or more points under a schedule worked out by the German Shepherd Dog Club of America and who include among their number five who have achieved either American Kennel Club championship or their own ROM designation.

To become a Register of Merit Dam, a bitch must have produced four or more offspring who have earned a total of forty points and who include two or more who have gained either American Kennel Club championship or their own ROM listing.

The schedule of points by which this is computed has been worked out by the German Shepherd Dog Club of America, which has occasionally revised the schedule over the years, and the latest figures as this book is written are as follows:

Best of Breed or Opposite Sex from Specials class—6 points at a three-point show; 8 points at a four-point show; 10 points at a five-point show.

Best of Breed or Opposite Sex from regular classes—3 points at a three-point show; 4 points at a four-point show; 5 points at a five-point show.

Winners Dog or Winners Bitch—3 points at a three-point show; 4 points at a four-point show; 5 points at a five-point show.

Reserve Winners Dog or Reserve Winners Bitch —1 point at a three-point show; 2 points at a four-point show; 3 points at a five-point show.

Champion—10 points.

Select Ratings at the National Specialty— 10 points.

Registry of Merit progeny—15 points.

An informal head-study of U.S. and Can. Select Ch. Bel Vista's Joey Baby, ROM, owned by the Poeppings, Bel Vista Shepherds, Lebanon, Illinois.

Grand Victor or Grand Victrix—15 points.
Best in the National Futurity or Maturity— 5 points.
Best of Opposite Sex in the National Maturity— 5 points.
Best in Futurity or Best of Opposite Sex at a Regional Futurity—3 points.
Best in Maturity or Best of Opposite Sex at a Regional Maturity—4 points.

Obedience titles are recognized with Register of Merit points, provided that the obedience-titled progeny has also won at least Reserve Winners at conformation classes at a show with major A.K.C. championship points. The current schedule of points is as follows:

Companion Dog (C.D.)—5 points.
Companion Dog Excellent (C.D.X.)—10 points.
Utility Dog (U.D.)—15 points.
Tracking Dog (T.D.)—5 points.
Obedience Trial Champion (O.T.Ch.)—5 points.
Victor or Victrix at the National Specialty— 15 points.

The listings of Register of Merit Sires and Dams are divided into two groups: active and inactive. When points on a dog or bitch are unchanged over a three-year period, then that dog or bitch is automatically placed on the inactive list. A dog or bitch who is deceased remains on the active list so long as the progeny's continued wins make this appropriate.

Canadian shows with a proven entry of at least one hundred German Shepherd Dogs in competition, Alaska, Hawaii, and Puerto Rico are also included in the ROM point system.

The latest tabulations available to me as this book goes to press are for 1980 and are courtesy of Ms. Cappy Pottle who so kindly loaned me copies of the German Shepherd Dog Club of America 1980 Register of Merit and Futurity and Maturity tabulations to assist me in compiling accurate information for this book. The Active Register of Merit Sires for 1980 reads as follows:

Grand Victor Ch. Lance of Fran-Jo—3256 points
Grand Victor Ch. Lakeside's Harrigan— 2031 points
Ch. Eko-Lan's Paladen—1681 points
Ch. Cobert's Reno of Lakeside—1601 points
Grand Victor Ch. Yoncalla's Mike—1055 points
Zeus of Fran-Jo—936 points
Grand Victor Ch. Hollamor's Judd—912 points

Ch. Doppelt-Tay's Jesse James, ROM, owned by Jesse and Lorraine Clifford, taking Best of Opposite Sex at the German Shepherd Dog Club of Detroit Specialty, June 1966. Photo courtesy of Mary Schuetzler.

Grand Victor Ch. Scorpio of Shiloh Gardens— 866 points

Ch. Tannenwald's Igor—828 points

Ch. Doppelt-Tay's Hawkeye—720 points

Ch. Zeto of Fran-Jo—647 points

Ch. Caralon's Hein von der Lockenheim, C.D. —646 points

Ch. Lakeside's Gilligan's Island—644 points

Grand Victor Ch. Mannix of Fran-Jo—595 points

Grand Victor Ch. Langenau's Watson— 563 points

Ch. Kubistraum's Kane—527 points

Ch. Doppelt-Tay's Hammer—492 points

Covy's Oregano of Tucker Hill—435 points

Ch. Ravenhaus Noah—417 points

Ch. Dot-Wall's Vance—414 points

Ch. Fritz De Cloudt, C.D.—363 points

Grand Victor Ch. Caesar v. Carahaus— 334 points

Covy-Tucker Hill's Zinfandel—287 points

Ch. Peddacre's Uno, U.D.—246 points

Ch. Arbor's Benno—227 points

Ch. Haydelhaus' Augie v. Zahnarzt—225 points

Ch. Marty von Bid-Scono—196 points

Ch. Von Nassau Dayan—196 points

Ch. Beau of Fran-Jo—195 points

Ch. Junger Haus Ceasar—190 points

Grand Victor Ch. Telleheide's Gallo—188 points

Ch. Kovaya's Judd—176 points

Ch. Val-Don's Quaker—163 points

Two outstanding greats of the breed photographed the day before the 1970 National in Denver, Colorado. 1966 and 1968 Grand Victor Ch. Yoncalla's Mike, ROM, handled by Bert Penny, and 1970 Grand Victor Ch. Hollamor's Judd, ROM, handled by Jim Norris. Photo courtesy of Mary E. Schuetzler.

Covy-Tucker Hill's Zinfandel, ROM, by Grand Victor Ch. Lakeside's Harrigan ex Ch. Tucker Hill's Angelique, C.D., ROM. Owned by Cappy Pottle and Gloria F. Birch, Cotati, California.

At this time, there are eighty dogs listed on the Inactive Register of Merit Sires. The first ten dogs on this list are as follows:

Ch. Ulk Wikingerblut—2222 points
Grand Victor Ch. Troll v. Richterbach—2035 points

Ch. Bernd vom Kallengarten—1375 points
Ch. Vol of Long-Worth—1126 points
Ch. Nordraak of Matterhorn—905 points
Ch. Wotan v. Richterbach, C.D.X.—901 points
Ch. Field Marshall of Arbywood—819 points
Ch. Falko von Cellar Schloss—780 points
Ch. Fortune of Arbywood—734 points
Grand Victor Ch. Ingo Wunschelrut—733 points

Ch. Tannenwald's Igor, ROM, early in his career. A truly great day at the German Shepherd Dog Club of Staten Island. Ken Rayner handling.

Ch. Lakeside's Gilligan's Island, ROM, winning first in the Working Group at Westchester Kennel Club under Langdon Skarda. Kim Knoblauch handling for breeder-owner Daniel Dwier, Lakeside Kennels, Kresson, New Jersey.

Ch. Rebel Canyon's Artful Dodger, by Bravado of Verdugo Hills ex Bodina, C.D., has ROM points and is the first German Shepherd champion in southern Nevada. Born in May 1972 and owned by Audrey Clark of Las Vegas. Photo by Joan Ludwig.

Ch. Tucker Hill's Angelique, C.D., ROM, on the occasion of her seventh Select award. A U.S. Maturity Victrix, "Angel" is by Gauss vom Stauderpark, SchH III, ex Jodi of Tucker Hill. Owners, Cappy Pottle, Jean Stevens, and Gloria F. Birch.

The Active Register of Merit Dams for 1980 is as follows:

Cobert's Melissa—745 points
Select Ch. Tucker Hill's Angelique, C.D.— 408 points
Arnhild's Black Frost—396 points
Ch. Amber's Flair—279 points
Just A Joy of Billo—270 points
Langenau's Quessa—260 points
Ch. Kovaya's Contessa, C.D.—256 points
Ch. Ponca Hill's Sudana—173 points
Ellyn Hill's Diamond Flush—166 points
Tessandra of Maplewild Hill, C.D.—163 points
Yoncalla's Patti of Sunny Bee—161 points
Ch. Amber's Valiant Robin—151 points
Del-Deena of Waldesruh—151 points
Gracelyn's Gay Blade—146 points
Grand Victor Ch. Aloha of Bid-Scono—135 points
Ch. Cobert's Windsong—132 points
Von Auckland's Melody Rocket—128 points
Ch. Elfie of Fran-Jo—127 points
Jill of Seebree—121 points
Ch. Lakeside's Just Jamaica—121 points
Ch. Covy's Tartar of Tucker Hill—109 points
Ch. Von Nassau's Galaxy, C.D.—108 points
Samian's Image—106 points
Grand Victrix Ch. Covy's Rosemary of Tucker Hill—105 points

Fran-Jo's Dawn of Gan-Edan—102 points
Kristie of Waldesruh—100 points
Doppelt-Tay's Legal Tender—99 points
Grand Victrix Ch. Cathwar's Lisa v. Rob— 97 points
Ch. Mirheim's Abbey—96 points
Ch. Cobert's Golly Gee of Lakeside—95 points
Barithaus' Ramblin' Rose—88 points
Johnsondale's True Luv—87 points
Wonderland's Anna of Cave Hill—86 points
Eko-Lan's Rhyme—80 points
Ch. Covy's Felita of Tucker Hill—79 points
Kenwood's Clove of Bay Meadow—73 points
Smoketrees Americana—71 points
Kismet's Deliah—69 points
Cobert's Rhythm of Lakeside—68 points
Grand Victrix Ch. Lor-Locke's Tatta of Fran-Jo —66 points
Ch. Kovaya's Jill, C.D.—63 points
Echowood's Raquel of Louron—60 points
Glenhart's Della of Ayrwood—58 points
Edelheim's Bianka Tulpenheim—57 points
Kovaya's Amanda of Shadowbrook—56 points

To review the most successful ROM sires, who have had so tremendous and beneficial an

Eko-Lan's Rhyme winning the Novice Bitch Class at Kenilworth Kennel Club, 1972, for Mrs. M. Dolan and Carol Lordo. Judged by John P. Murphy; handled by Gerlinde Hockla.

Ch. Kovaya's Jill, C.D., ROM, by Grand Victor Ch. Yoncalla's Mike, ROM, ex Ch. Kovaya's Contessa, C.D., ROM. Bred by Gloria Birch and Sally Holcombe; owned by G. and J. Head and Gloria Birch.

influence on the German Shepherd breed, "pride of place" as the greatest all-time producer goes to the late Grand Victor Champion Lance of Fran-Jo, who at the time the accompanying list was compiled had 3256 points.

In second place comes the late Champion Ulk Wikingerblut with 2222 points. Close behind Ulk, and with only a few points separating them, are Grand Victor Champion Troll von Richterbach with 2035 points and Grand Victor Champion Lakeside's Harrigan with 2031 points.

The Highest Living Register of Merit Sire, Champion Eko-Lan's Paladen, ROM, bred and owned by Fred Migliore, was listed here as having 1681 points, a number which is still growing. As of 1980, Paladen had nine times been included in the Top Ten Sires. Running almost neck and neck with Paladen in 1980 was Champion Cobert's Reno of Lakeside, each of them

having produced thirty-seven champions as of that year. Reno's 1980 points totalled 1601. This splendid dog was bred by Daniel P. Dwier and Connie Beckhardt and is co-owned by Mrs. Beckhardt with Vito Moreno. He is a son of Grand Victor Champion Lance of Fran-Jo, ROM. Champion Eko-Lan's Paladen is a Lance grandson; thus both Paladen and Reno are carrying on in the best family tradition. (As this book goes to press, Reno has moved into the Highest Living ROM Sire position.)

Among the bitches, Cobert's Melissa, in first place with 745 points, had produced eight champions, plus two additional winning progeny, by the time this list was assembled. The Highest Living Register of Merit Producing Bitch as of 1980 was Champion Amber's Flair, bred by Barbara Amidon and owned by Franklyn and Rosalind Schaefer.

227

The very dedicated lady Mary Schuetzler of Farmington, Michigan, has assembled this magnificent collection of photos of the German Shepherd Dog Club of America Grand Victors and Grand Victrixes which goes on display at all German Shepherd Dog Club National Specialties. Quite a job to haul around, as Mrs. Schuetzler remarks, but what a treasure this is for all fanciers of the breed to study and enjoy.

Grand Victors and Grand Victrixes

When you read the designation "Grand Victor" or "Grand Victrix" preceding the name of a German Shepherd Dog in the United States, you will know that that dog or bitch has gained the honor of winning either Best of Breed or Best of Opposite Sex to Best of Breed at the annual National Specialty Show of the German Shepherd Dog Club of America. The winners of these top awards at the National receive this designation, with the dog taking either Best of Breed or Best of Opposite Sex becoming that year's Grand Victor, while the bitch that takes either Best of Breed or Best of Opposite Sex likewise becomes that year's Grand Victrix in the United States.

These titles have been bestowed upon the principal winners at the National Specialty since 1918 (the title for the top dog and top bitch initially was "Grand Champion"; the present title name was adopted in 1925), with the following exceptions: in 1932, the German judge refused to bestow the awards on the basis that none of the Shepherds in competition were worthy of the honor; in 1936, the judge, again from Germany, withheld the Grand Victor award on these same grounds although the judge did select a Grand Victrix; and in, 1964, a disagreement over the date led to no National Specialty being held.

The following list contains the names of the Grand Victor and Grand Victrix for each year from 1918 to the present. (In all cases the name of the Grand Victor is listed first.)

1918—Komet v. Hoheluft
Lotte v. Edelweis

1919—Apollo v. Hunenstein
Vanhall's Herta

1920—Rex v. Buckel
Boda v.d. Fuerstenburg

1921—Ch. Grimm v.d. Mainkur, PH
Dora v. Rheinwald

1922—Ch. Erich v. Grafenwerth, PH
Debora v. Weimar

1923—Ch. Dolf v. Dusternbrook, PH
Boda v.d. Fuerstenburg

1924—Ch. Cito Bergerslust, SchH
Irma v. Doernerhof, SchH

1925—Same as above
Same as above

1926—Ch. Donar v. Overstolzen, SchH
Ch. Asta v.d. Kaltenweide, SchH

1927—Ch. Arko v. Sadowaberg, SchH
Ch. Inky of Willowgate

1928—Ch. Arko v. Sadowaberg, SchH
Ch. Erich's Merceda of Shereston

1929—Ch. Arko v. Sadowaberg, SchH
Ch. Katja v. Blaisenberg, ZPr

1930—Ch. Bimbo v. Stolzenfels
Christel v. Stimmberg, PH

1931—Ch. Arko v. Sadowaberg, SchH
Ch. Gisa v. Koenigsbruch

1932—Not awarded
　　Not awarded

1933—Golf v. Hooptal
　　Ch. Dora of Shereston

1934—Ch. Erekind of Shereston
　　Ch. Dora of Shereston

1935—Ch. Nox of Glenmar
　　Ch. Nanka v. Schwyn

1936—Not awarded
　　Ch. Frigga v. Kannenbaeckerland

1937—Ch. Pfeffer v. Bern, ZPr,MH, ROM
　　Ch. Perchta v. Bern

1938—Ch. Pfeffer v. Bern, ZPr,MH, ROM
　　Ch. Giralda's Geisha

1939—Ch. Hugo of Cosalta, C.D.
　　Ch. Thora v. Bern of Giralda

1940—Ch. Cotswald of Cosalta, C.D.
　　Ch. Lady of Ruthland, ROM

1941—Ch. Nox of Ruthland, ROM
　　Ch. Hexe of Rotundina

1942—Ch. Noble of Ruthland
　　Ch. Bella of Haus Hagen

1943—Major of Northmere
　　Ch. Bella v. Haus Hagen

1944—Ch. Nox of Ruthland, ROM
　　Ch. Frigga v. Hoheluft, ROM

1945—Ch. Adam of Veralda
　　Ch. Olga of Ruthland

1946—Dex of Talladega, C.D.
　　Ch. Leda v. Liebestraum, ROM

1947—Ch. Dorian v. Beckgold
　　Ch. Jola v. Liebestraum, ROM

1948—Ch. Valiant of Draham C.D., ROM
　　Ch. Duchess of Browvale

1949—Ch. Kirk of San Miguel
　　Doris v. Vogtlandshof

1950—Ch. Kirk of San Miguel
　　Ch. Yola of Long-Worth

1951—Ch. Jory of Edgetowne, C.D., ROM
　　Ch. Tawnee v. Liebestraum

1952—Ch. Ingo Wunschelrute, ROM
　　Ch. Afra v. Heilholtkamp, ROM

1953—Ch. Alert of Mi-Noah's, ROM
　　Ch. Ulla of San Miguel

1954—Ch. Brando of Aichtal
　　Ch. Jem of Penllyn

1955—Ch. Rasant v. Holzheimer Eichwald, SchH II
　　Ch. Sola Nina of Rushagen, ROM

1956—Ch. Bill v. Kleistweg, ROM
　　Ch. Kobeil's Barda

1957—Ch. Troll v. Richterbach, SchH III, ROM
　　Ch. Jeff-Lynnes Bella

1958—Ch. Yasko v. Zenntal, SchH III
　　Ch. Tan-Zar Desiree

1959—Ch. Red Rocks Gino, C.D., ROM
　　Ch. Alice v.d. Guten Fee, SchH I, ROM

1960—Ch. Axel v. Poldihaus, ROM
　　Ch. Robin of Kingscroft

1961—Ch. Lido v. Mellerland
　　Ch. Nanhall's Donna

1962—Ch. Yorkdom's Pak
　　Ch. Bonnie Bergere of Ken-Rose, U.D.T., ROM

1963—Ch. Condor v. Stoerstrudel, SchH I, ROM
　　Ch. Hessian's Vogue, ROM

1964—No Competition
　　No Competition

1965—Ch. Brix v.d. Grafenkrone, SchH III, ROM
　　Ch. Marsa's Velvet of Malabar

1922 Grand Victor Ch. Erich Grafenwerth, imported early in 1921 to the Hamilton Farm Kennels of J.C. Brady. Whelped July 7, 1918, Erich was truly the *great* dog of his era: Sieger of Germany for 1920, highly successful in the U.S.A. show ring, and a prepotent sire of highest quality. Photo courtesy of Mary Schuetzler.

1976 Grand Victor Ch. Padechma's Persuasion.
Photo courtesy of Mary E. Schuetzler.

1966—Ch. Yoncalla's Mike, ROM
　　　Ch. Hanarob's Touche

1967—Ch. Lance of Fran-Jo, ROM
　　　Ch. Hanarob's Touche

1968—Ch. Yoncalla's Mike, ROM
　　　Ch. Valtara's Image

1969—Ch. Arno v.d. Kurpfalzhalle, SchH III
　　　Ch. DeCloudt's Heidi, C.D.

1970—Ch. Hollamor's Judd, ROM
　　　Ch. Bel Vista's Solid Sender

1971—Ch. Mannix of Fran-Jo, ROM
　　　Ch. Aloha v. Bid-Scono

1972—Ch. Lakeside's Harrigan, ROM
　　　Ch. Cathwar's Lisa v. Rob

1973—Ch. Scorpio of Shiloh Gardens, ROM
　　　Ch. Ro San's First Love

1974—Ch. Tellaheide's Gallo
　　　Ch. Lor-Locke's Tatta of Fran-Jo

1975—Ch. Caesar v Carahaus, ROM
　　　Ch. Langenau's Tango of Fran-Jo

1976—Ch. Padechma's Persuasion
　　　Ch. Covy's Rosemary of Tucker Hill,
　　　ROM

1977—Ch. Langenau's Watson
　　　Ch. Charo of Shiloh Gardens

1978—Ch. Baobab's Chaz
　　　Ch. Jo-San's Charisma

1979—Ch. Schokrest On Parade
　　　Ch. Anton's Jesse

1980—Ch. Aspen of Fran-Jo
　　　Ch. Lacy Britches of Billo

1981—Ch. Sabra of Gan Edan
　　　Ch. Anton's Jenne

While it is a tremendous honor to have one Grand Victor or Grand Victrix designation on your dog's record, just think how thrilling it must be to have the victory with the same dog on more than one occasion! A few have done just that, and in this writer's opinion, these German Shepherds deserve very special acclaim.

The leader among the multiple Grand Victors was Champion Arko von Sadowaberg who distinguished himself by gaining that title in 1927, 1928, 1929, and 1931. Arko, owned by Mr. Mahoney of the Jessaford Kennels, is the only German Shepherd to have been crowned Grand Victor or Grand Victrix more than twice.

To date, the dogs who gained the Grand Victor identification on two occasions have been Champion Cito Bergerslust, SchH, in 1924 and 1925; Champion Pfeffer von Bern, ZPrMH, ROM, in 1937 and 1938; Champion Nox of Ruthland, ROM, in 1941 and 1944; Champion Kirk of San Miguel, in 1949 and 1950; and Champion Yoncalla's Mike, ROM, in 1966 and 1968.

The bitches who were designated Grand Victrix on more than one occasion have been Boda von der Fuerstenburg twice, in 1920 and 1923; Irma von Doernerhof, SchH, in 1924 and 1925; Champion Dora of Shereston, in 1933 and 1934; Champion Bella von Haus Hagen, in 1942 and 1943; and Champion Hanarob's Touche, in 1966 and 1967.

1982 Grand Victor Ch. Kismet's Impulse v. Bismarck, by Ch. Marty von Bid-Scono ex Ch. Von Bismarck's Dark Angel, Best of Breed under judge Ernest Loeb at the National Specialty in October 1982. Owned by Robert and Mary Ellen Kish. Handler, James Moses.

1982 Grand Victrix Ch. Merkel's Vendetta, Best of Opposite Sex at the National Specialty on October 16th 1982, judged by Ernest Loeb. George Collins, President of the German Shepherd Dog Club of America, presenting the trophy to handler Terry Hower. Owners, Anthony LaPorte, Jr., and Joan Fox.

1928 Grand Victrix Erich's Merceda of Shereston, who did not become a champion. Photo courtesy of Mary E. Schuetzler.

1926 Grand Victor Ch. Donar v. Overstolzen, SchH, by Dutch Sieger Orpal v. Gruneneck ex Blanka v.d. Urftalsperre, was also the 1924 German Sieger. Photo courtesy of Mary Schuetzler.

1926 Grand Victrix Ch. Asta v.d. Kaltenweide, SchH (German Siegerin 1922, 1923, and 1924), by Ch. Erich v. Grafenwerth, PH (1922 Grand Victor, 1920 German Sieger) ex Flora v. Oeringen.

1935 Grand Victor Ch. Nox of Glenmar. Photo courtesy of Mary E. Schuetzler.

1935 Grand Victrix Ch. Nanka v. Schwyn. Photo courtesy of Mary E. Schuetzler.

1929 Grand Victrix Ch. Katja v. Blasienberg, ZPr, C.D. (1928 and 1929 German Siegerin), by Samson v. Blasienberg ex Anni v. Blasienberg.

1939 Grand Victor Ch. Hugo of Cosalta, C.D. Photo courtesy of Mary E. Schuetzler.

1938 Grand Victrix Ch. Giralda's Geisha, C.D., owned by Giralda Farm, Madison, New Jersey. Photo courtesy of Mary E. Schuetzler.

1940 Grand Victor Ch. Cotswald of Cosalta, C.D. Photo courtesy of Mary E. Schuetzler.

1941 Grand Victrix Ch. Hexe of Rotundina. Photo courtesy of Mary Schuetzler.

1940 Grand Victrix Ch. Lady of Ruthland, ROM, by Grand Victor Ch. Pfeffer v. Bern, ROM, ex Grand Victrix Ch. Frigga v. Kannenbackerland. Photo courtesy of Mary E. Schuetzler.

1942 Grand Victor Ch. Noble of Ruthland, by Grand Victor Ch. Pfeffer v. Bern, ROM, ex Carol of Ruthland, ROM.

1942 and 1943 Grand Victrix Ch. Bella von Haus Hagen. Photo courtesy of Mary Schuetzler.

This magnificent and very famous German Shepherd, Ch. Frigga von Hoheluft, ROM, was the U.S. Grand Victrix in 1944. Bred by John Gans of Staten Island and owned by Bernard W. Daku, Frigga was born May 21st 1941, sired by Ch. Nox of Ruthland, U.S. Grand Victor 1941, ex Champion Lady of Ruthland, U.S. Grand Victrix 1940. Frigga made many prestigious show wins, including Best of Breed and second in the Working Group at Westminster, Best of Breed at the German Shepherd Dog Specialty in 1944, Best of Breed at the New England Shepherd Specialty, and first in the Working Group at Orange Kennel Club.

1945 Grand Victor Ch. Adam of Veralda. Photo courtesy of Mary E. Schuetzler.

The 1946 National Specialty, judge Arthur Zane. Grand Victor Ch. Dex of Talladega, C.D., and Grand Victrix Am. and Can. Ch. Leda v. Liebestraum, ROM. Photo courtesy of Mary E. Schuetzler.

1947 Grand Victrix Ch. Jola v. Liebestraum, ROM, owned by Mr. and Mrs.
Grant E. Mann.

1952 Grand Victrix Ch. Afra vom
Heilholtkamp, ROM. Photo courtesy of Mary E. Schuetzler.

1947 Grand Victor Ch. Dorian v. Beckgold. Photo courtesy of Mary E. Schuetzler.

1950 Grand Victrix Ch. Yola of Long Worth. Photo courtesy of Mary Schuetzler.

1952 Grand Victor Ch. Ingo Wunschelrute, ROM. Photo courtesy of Mary Schuetzler.

1951 Grand Victrix Ch. Tawnee v. Liebestraum. Photo courtesy of Mary E. Schuetzler.

1953 Grand Victrix Ch. Ulla of San Miguel, ROM, by Judo v. Liebestraum ex Ch. Christel of San Miguel, owned by Rancho San Miguel Kennels. Photo courtesy of Mary Schuetzler.

1953 Grand Victor Ch. Alert of Mi-Noah's, ROM. Photo courtesy of Mary Schuetzler.

1954 Grand Victrix Ch. Jem of Penllyn. Photo courtesy of Mary Schuetzler.

1955 Grand Victor Ch. Rasant v. Holzheimer Eichwald, SchH II. Photo courtesy of Mary Schuetzler.

1957 Grand Victrix Ch. Jeff-Lynne's Bella. Photo courtesy of Mary E. Schuetzler.

1957 Grand Victor Ch. Troll vom Richterbach, SchH III, ROM, by Axel v.d. Deininghauserheide, SchH III, DPH, FH, ex Lende v. Richterbach, SchH III. Owner, Irving Appelbaum. Troll's influence as a sire has been tremendous—a dog of great importance to the Shepherd as we know it in America today. Photo courtesy of Mary E. Schuetzler.

1958 Grand Victrix Ch. Tan-Zar Desiree. Photo courtesy of Mary E. Schuetzler.

1959 Grand Victor Ch. Red Rocks Gino, C.D., ROM, by Ch. Edenvale's Nikki, C.D., ex Kay of Ayron. Photo courtesy of Mary Schuetzler.

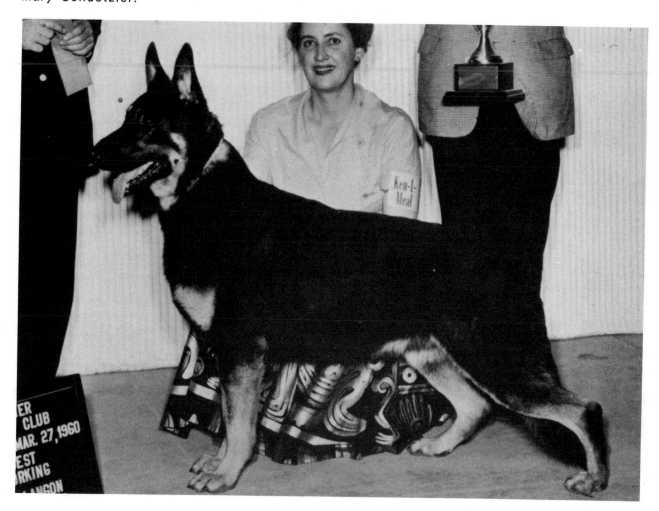

1961 Grand Victor Ch. Lido vom Mellerland. Photo courtesy of Mary Schuetzler.

1963 Grand Victor Ch. Condor von Stoerstrudel, SchH I, ROM, by Bello v. Hollewinkel ex Birke v. Saturner-See. Photo courtesy of Mary Schuetzler.

1960 Grand Victor Ch. Axel vom Poldihaus, ROM, owned by Otto Meier and Erna McCoy (handling) of Waldeslust Kennels, Reg. Here being judged by Lloyd Brackett, famous German Shepherd authority and owner of Long Worth Kennels. Photo courtesy of Mary Schuetzler.

1963 Grand Victrix Ch. Hessian's Vogue, ROM, shows us an example of the outstanding movement for which she was famous. Helen and Art Hess, owners, Goshen, Ohio.

1965 Grand Victor Ch. Brix v. d. Grafenkrone, SchH III, ROM. Photo courtesy of Mary Schuetzler.

1969 Grand Victor Ch. Arno v.d. Kurpfalzhalle, SchH III, by Fant v. Eichengarten ex Peggi v. Aichral. Photo courtesy of Mary Schuetzler.

1969 Grand Victrix Ch. DeCloudt's Heide, C.D. Photo courtesy of Mary E. Schuetzler.

1962 Grand Victor Ch. Yorkdom's Pak, with a friend. Photo courtesy of Mary Schuetzler.

This lovely bitch winning Best of Breed at the German Shepherd Dog Club of America's 54th Annual Specialty in 1968, on that same day became Grand Victrix Champion Valtara's Image. Gustave Schindler had judged the bitch classes that day and had selected her for Winners Bitch. Ernest Loeb, in this photo loaned to us by Mr. Schindler, is awarding her the Best of Breed—an exciting finish to a quality-filled event.

1966 and 1968 Grand Victor Ch. Yoncalla's Mike, ROM. Photo courtesy of Mary E. Schuetzler.

1972 Grand Victrix Ch. Cathwar's Lisa v. Rob, ROM, by Ch. Lakeside's Gilligan's Island, ROM, ex Ch. Dorjo's Donka. Photo courtesy of Mary E. Schuetzler.

1970 Grand Victor Hollamor's Judd, ROM. Photo courtesy of Mary E. Schuetzler.

1973 Grand Victrix Ch. Ro San's First Love. Photo courtesy of Mary E. Schuetzler.

1971 Grand Victrix Ch. Aloha von Bid-Scono, ROM. Photo courtesy of Mary E. Schuetzler.

1974 Grand Victor Ch. Tellaheide's Gallo, ROM, by Ch. Tellaheide's Enoch ex Baroness Bella von Friden. Photo courtesy of Mary Schuetzler.

1972 U.S. Grand Victor, 1973 Can. Grand Victor, Am. and Can. Ch. Lakeside's Harrigan, ROM (by Grand Victor Ch. Lance of Fran-Jo, ROM, ex Cobert's Melissa, ROM) was one of the mighty Lance's greatest sons, not only as a Grand Victor but also as one of the highest producing sires. He died at six years of age, a tremendous loss to the breed. Owned by Ann Mesdag, Von Nassau Kennels.

Above: 1976 U.S. Grand Victrix Ch. Covy's Rosemary of Tucker Hill, ROM. Owned by Cappy Pottle and J. Stevens.
Below: 1977 Grand Victor Ch. Langenau's Watson, ROM, by 1973 Grand Victor Ch. Scorpio of Shiloh Gardens, ROM, ex Langenau's Quessa, ROM. Photo courtesy of Mary Schuetzler.

1979 Grand Victor Ch. Schokrest On Parade, by Covy's Oregano of Tucker Hill, ROM, ex Ch. Philberlyn's Rhoda von Marin. Photo courtesy of Mary E. Schuetzler.

1980 Grand Victrix Ch. Lacy Britches of Billo. Photo courtesy of Jo Hanna Smith.

1979 Grand Victrix Ch. Anton's Jesse, by Zeus of Fran-Jo, ROM, ex Arn- hild's Black Frost, ROM, litter-sister to the 1981 Grand Victrix Ch. Anton's Jenne. Photo courtesy of Mary E. Schuetzler, who tells us that these are the only two litter-sisters to gain the Grand Victrix titles. A brother and sister combination, Grand Vic- tor Ch. Pfeffer von Bern and his litter-sister Grand Victrix Ch. Perch- ta von Bern, gained their awards in 1937.

1981 Grand Victrix Ch. Anton's Jenne, litter- sister to 1979 Grand Vic- trix Ch. Anton's Jesse. Photo courtesy of Mary E. Schuetzler.

1976 Obedience Victrix Natasha von Hammhausen, U.D. Photo courtesy of Mary E. Schuetzler.

Another worthy win for 1964 Can. Grand Victor, Am. and Can. Ch. Hessian's Caribe, who gained his Grand Victor title from a judge from Germany at the Canadian National Specialty Show and ranked third among Working Group winners, Phillips Rating System, with Best in Show and Working Group firsts and multiple Working Group placements during his show career. Helen and Art Hess, owners, Hessian Kennels, Goshen, Ohio.

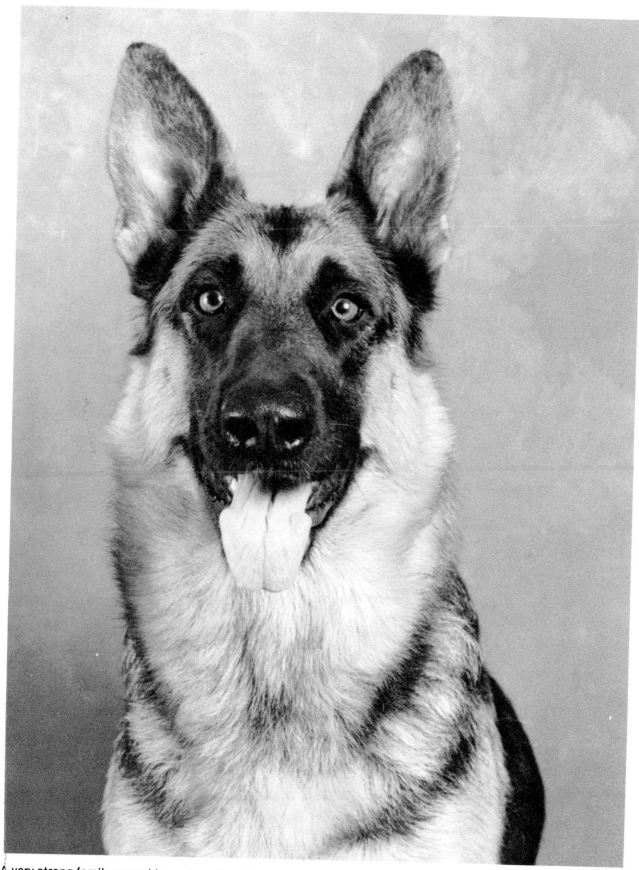

A very strong family resemblance is noticeable in Helen Gleason's breeding down through her line. This beautiful head-study is of Can. Ch. Nocturne's Ruffian, Am. and Can. C.D., who is owned by Mary E. Schuetzler of Schutzenhaus Shepherds but was bred by Mrs. Gleason. Ruffian is a daughter of Nocturne's Harmony and is the dam of Can. Ch. Schutzenhaus' Rebel.

Select Ch. Linnloch Sundown von Freya, sired by Covy-Tucker Hill's Zinfandel, ROM, ex Linnloch Klassie v. Vel-Bren, the Number One Shepherd winner in the United States in 1980. Breeders, Mrs. Dorothy Linn and Diane Garcia. Owners, Mary C. Roberts and James Halferty, Covina, California. Pictured winning under Ted Gunderson with Mary Roberts handling.

Opposite: Am. and Can. Grand Victor Ch. Sabra Dennis of Gan Edan owned by Mimi Saltz, Lake Zurich, Illinois.

Grand Victor Ch. Lance of Fran-Jo, ROM, the sire of sixty champions, with his handler Jimmy Moses. This dog holds the record as the Top Producing Sire in German Shepherd history. Owned by Fran-Jo Kennels, Joan and Fran Ford, Grove City, Ohio.

U.S. and Can. Grand Victor Ch. Lakeside's Harrigan, ROM, here completing his championship, handled by his owner Ann Mesdag, just five months prior to winning Grand Victor in 1972 at the National Specialty. This son of Lance ex Cobert's Melissa was Top Producer in Shepherds for several years.

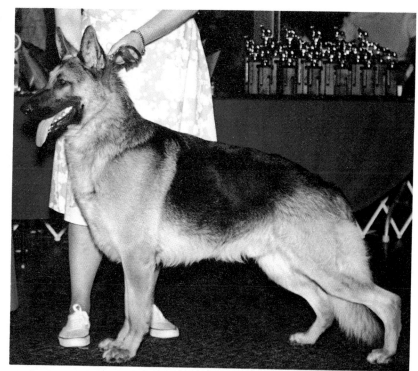

1974 Futurity Victrix, two times Select Ch. Covy's Tartar of Tucker Hill, ROM, by Grand Victor Ch. Lakeside's Harrigan, ROM, ex the seven times Select Ch. Tucker Hill's Angelique, C.D., ROM. Owners, Cappy Pottle and Gloria Birch, Cotati, California.

Grand Victor Ch. Schokrest On Parade, at six and a half years age, was winner of a Working Group under German Shepherd authority Ernest Loeb at Macon Kennel Club in April 1982. This splendid dog was Best Puppy at the National in 1976, completed his championship in 1978, and in 1979 gained his greatest triumph becoming that year's Grand Victor of the United States by taking Best of Breed at the National. Breeder-owner Lorraine Schowalter, co-owner Roy Ivens. Sired by Covy's Oregano of Tucker Hill, ROM, ex Philberlyn's Rhoda of Marin, a granddaughter of Grand Victor Ch. Mannix of Fran-Jo, ROM, and Am. and Can. Grand Victor Ch. Lance of Fran-Jo, ROM.

Opposite, above: Grand Victor Ch. Lor Locke's Tatta of Fran-Jo, ROM, American and Canadian Grand Victor for 1974, another famed homebred from Fran-Jo Kennels, Joan and Fran Ford. **Below:** 1980 Grand Victor Ch. Aspen of Fran-Jo, ROM, the third Grand Victor from Fran-Jo Kennels owned by Joan and Fran Ford. A homebred who is line-bred on Grand Victors Ch. Mannix and Lance, and Lonie of Fran-Jo.

GERMAN SHEPHERD DOG
CLUB OF AMERICA
NATIONAL SPECIALTY
NOV. 1, 1980
JUDGE — K. OLBIS STEEN
GRAND VICTOR

PHOTO — TOM MONAHAN

1971 Grand Victor Ch. Mannix of Fran-Jo, ROM, producer of two American Grand Victors and one American Grand Victrix, they being Grand Victor Ch. Scorpio of Shiloh Gardens, ROM; Grand Victor Ch. Caesar of Cara Haus; and Grand Victrix Ch. Langenau's Tango. Fran-Jo German Shepherds, Joan and Fran Ford.

Ch. Nocturne's Hale of Krisselhof, Maturity Victor and Select Number Two at the National Specialty in 1974, here taking Best of Opposite Sex at the Motor City Specialty Club in November 1977. Handler, T. Hower. Breeders, Ed and Helen Gleason. Owners, Tom and Cecelia Jones. Mrs. B. Amidon, judge. Photo courtesy of Mary Schuetzler.

German Shepherd Dog Club of America National Specialty, November 1st 1980. Judge, K. Olbis Steen. Select Bitch Number Six, Champion Bel Vista's Hera of Sylmar. Bel Vista Kennels, owners, Joe and Charlotte Poepping, Lebanon, Illinois.

Select Number Three 1981, Am. and Can. Ch. Covy-Tucker Hill's Don Quixote completed his American championship before two years of age and his Canadian championship with three five-point majors. For Best of Breed competition he has been shown only at leading shows under the breed's top Specialty judges and is, at the time of this writing, undefeated in these classes. He combines the cream of top producing Shepherds in his pedigree, being by Cobert's Sirocco of Windigail, ROM (Select Am. and Can. Ch. Cobert's Reno of Lakeside, ROM, ex Ch. Cobert's Windsong, ROM) ex Covy-Tucker Hill's Carmelita, ROM (Coby-Tucker Hill's Zinfandel, ROM, ex Ch. Covy's Felita of Tucker Hill, ROM). Bred by M. and G. Krumm, Cappy Pottle and Gloria Birch; co-owned by the latter two ladies with Richard and Helen Franklin of Brentwood Bay, British Columbia.

Opposite, above: Am. and Can. Ch. Covy-Tucker Hill's Finnegan, ROM, Number One Shepherd Dog in the U.S., 1976 through 1979, winner of twenty-six Bests in Show, and sire of fourteen champions, here adds to his laurels with another Best in Show, this at Mount Ogden Kennel Club under judge Isidore Schoenberg. Handled by Mary Roberts who co-owns him with her husband Ralph. **Below:** Select Ch. Covy's Mercedes of Tucker Hill, owned by Gloria Estabrook, Cappy Pottle, and Gloria F. Birch (bred by the latter two), one of three champions from the "car" litter who gained her title in January 1981, going on to four Bests of Breed and numerous Bests of Opposite Sex. She was awarded the Select title at the 1981 National Specialty in Tulsa, Oklahoma.

269

Select Ch. Tara Bella's Jeb of Stoneway, son of Grand Victor Ch. Langenau's Watson, ROM. Judge, Ralph Roberts. Handler, James Moses.

Select Ch. Bel Vista's Joey Baby winning the 1981 Veterans Class at the National Specialty in 1981. Joe and Charlotte Poepping, owners, Lebanon, Illinois.

Ch. Hessians Tinsel, Select bitch, handled here by breeder-owner-handler Art Hess as she makes a notable win. Hessian Shepherds belong to Art and Helen Hess and are located at Goshen, Ohio.

CHAPTER NINE

Standards for German Shepherd Dogs

Am. and Can. Ch., 1981 Select, Ch. Covy-Tucker Hill's Monte Alban, a Best in Show winner, Am. and Can. C.D.X., the youngest U.D. Champion Select in History—all when under twenty-three months of age. By Cobert's Sirocco of Windigail, ROM, ex Ch. Covy's Rosita of Tucker Hill. Owned by Freeman and Theresa Spencer and breeders Gloria Birch and Cappy Pottle.

The standard for a breed of dog is a detailed description of the ideal specimen of that particular breed—a word picture intended to describe in detail exactly how this dog should look, act, and gait, as well as what features are the ones important to breed character. This standard describes every feature of the dog, from nose to tail-tip, from topline to paws, placing each in its proper perspective when one surveys the dog as a whole.

The standard of each breed is the product of many years' observation. Our modern standards are based on those which preceded them, the earliest descriptions of the dogs under discussion, usually from the country of their origin. The earliest standards were principally concerned with a dog's working ability as well as his proper conformation to fulfill the tasks for which he had been created. With the passage of time and the increasing appreciation of dogs as companions and as competitors in dog shows, the need came to refine the standards, with the hope of retaining the original desirable traits while at the same time adding modifications and refinements to lead to a more pleasing appearance.

American Standard

The task of drawing up, revising, or rewriting a breed standard in the United States is in the hands of that breed's parent specialty club, whose responsibility it is to preserve correct type within a breed. Final approval of the club's efforts then must come from the American Kennel Club. The standard for the German Shepherd Dog was approved by the A.K.C. on February 11th 1978.

GENERAL APPEARANCE: The first impression of a good German Shepherd Dog is that of a strong, agile, well-muscled animal, alert and full of life. It is well balanced, with harmonious development of the forequarter and hindquarter. The dog is longer than tall, deep-bodied, and presents an outline of smooth curves rather than angles. It looks substantial and not spindly, giving the impression, both at rest and in motion, of muscular fitness and nimbleness without any look of clumsiness or soft living. The ideal dog is stamped with a look of quality and nobility—difficult to define, but unmistakable when present. Secondary sex characteristics are strongly marked,

Ch. Treffer of Clover Acres, the epitome of correct type, temperament, and quality in the breed, by Ch. Tannenwald's Igor ex Clover Downs Dixie. Owned by Ray Picard and handled by Ken Rayner.

and every animal gives a definite impression of masculinity or femininity, according to its sex.

CHARACTER: The breed has a distinct personality marked by direct and fearless, but not hostile, expression, self-confidence, and a certain aloofness that does not lend itself to immediate and indiscriminate friendships. The dog must be approachable, quietly standing its ground and showing confidence and willingness to meet overtures without itself making them. It is poised, but when the occasion demands, eager and alert; both fit and willing to serve in its capacity as companion, watchdog, blind leader, herding dog, or guardian, whichever the circumstances may demand. The dog must not be timid, shrinking behind its master or handler; it should not be nervous, looking about or upward with anxious expression or showing nervous reactions, such as tucking of tail, to strange sounds or sights. Lack of confidence under any surroundings is not typical of good character. Any of the above deficiencies in character which indicate shyness must be penalized as very serious faults and any dog exhibiting pronounced

indications of these must be excused from the ring. It must be possible for the judge to observe the teeth and to determine that both testicles are descended. Any dog that attempts to bite the judge must be disqualified. The ideal dog is a working animal with an incorruptible character combined with body and gait suitable for the arduous work that constitutes its primary purpose.

HEAD: The head is noble, cleanly chiseled, strong without coarseness, but above all not fine, and in proportion to the body. The head of the male is distinctly masculine, and that of the bitch distinctly feminine. The muzzle is long and strong with the lips firmly fitted, and its topline is parallel to the topline of the skull. Seen from the front, the forehead is only moderately arched, and the skull slopes into the long, wedge-shaped muzzle without abrupt stop. Jaws are strongly developed.

EARS: Ears are moderately pointed, in proportion to the skull, open toward the front, and carried erect when at attention, the ideal carriage being one in which the center lines of the ears, viewed from the front, are parallel to each other and perpendicular to the ground. A dog with cropped or hanging ears must be disqualified.

EYES: Of medium size, almond shaped, set a little obliquely and not protruding. The color is as dark as possible. The expression keen, intelligent and composed.

TEETH: 42 in number—20 upper and 22 lower—are strongly developed and meet in a scissors bite in which part of the inner surface of the upper incisors meets and engages part of the outer surface of the lower incisors. An overshot jaw or a level bite is undesirable. An undershot jaw is a disqualifying fault. Complete dentition is to be preferred. Any missing teeth other than first premolars is a serious fault.

NECK: The neck is strong and muscular, clean-cut and relatively long, proportionate in size to the head and without loose folds of skin. When the dog is at attention or excited, the head is raised and the neck carried high; otherwise typical carriage of the head is forward rather than up and but little higher than the top of the shoulders, particularly in motion.

FOREQUARTERS: The shoulder blades are long and obliquely angled, laid on flat and not placed forward. The upper arm joins the shoulder blade at about a right angle. Both the upper arm and the shoulder blade are well muscled. The forelegs, viewed from all sides, are straight and the bone oval rather than round. The pasterns are strong and springy and angulated at approximately a 25-degree angle from the vertical.

FEET: The feet are short, compact, with toes well arched, pads thick and firm, nails short and dark. The dewclaws, if any, should be removed from the hind legs. Dewclaws on the forelegs may be removed, but are normally left on.

PROPORTION: The German Shepherd Dog is longer than tall, with the most desirable proportion as 10 to 8½. The desired height for males at the top of the highest point of the shoulder blade is 24 to 26 inches; and for bitches, 22 to 24 inches. The length is measured from the point of the prosternum or breastbone to the rear edge of the pelvis, the ischial tuberosity.

German Shepherd breeder and popular Working Group judge Bob Slay at his first Specialty judging assignment awarding Best of Breed to Ch. Lakeside's Gilligan's Island, bred by Daniel Dwier and Connie Beckhardt.

BODY: The whole structure of the body gives an impression of depth and solidity without bulkiness.

CHEST: Commencing at the prosternum, it is well filled and carried well down between the legs. It is deep and capacious, never shallow, with ample room for lungs and heart, carried well forward, with the prosternum showing ahead of the shoulder in profile.

RIBS: Well sprung and long, neither barrel-shaped nor too flat, and carried down to a sternum which reaches to the elbows. Correct ribbing allows the elbows to move back freely when the dog is at a trot. Too round causes interference and throws the elbows out; too flat or short causes pinched elbows. Ribbing is carried well back so that the loin is relatively short.

ABDOMEN: Firmly held and not paunchy. The bottom line is only moderately tucked up in the loin.

TOPLINE: *Withers:* The withers are higher than and sloping into the level back. *Back:* The back is straight, very strongly developed without sag or roach, and relatively short. The desirable long proportion is not derived from a long back, but from over-all length with relation to height,

Ch. Andiron Ricochet of Dolmar taking Best of Breed at the Macon Kennel Club in October 1981. Judge, Sharon Griffin Dwier; handler, Scott Yergin. Co-bred by Mrs. Marge Dolan and Andrea Washburn. This lovely Shepherd was Winners Bitch two years in a row at Westminster in the beginning of the 1980's.

Ch. Hessians Baldur, ROM, Select, illustrates correct movement for the breed. Baldur is the sire of eleven American champions, including a Canadian Grand Victor; four or five Canadian champions, and the sire of the only American-bred bitch to achieve the German training title, Hessian's Ballencia, SchH II, who also won a five-point major plus other points when brought to the U.S. at six years of age. Hessian Kennels, owners, Art and Helen Hess.

which is achieved by length of forequarter and length of withers and hindquarter, viewed from the side. *Loin:* Viewed from the top, broad and strong. Undue length between the last rib and the thigh, when viewed from the side, is undesirable. *Croup:* Long and gradually sloping.

TAIL: Bushy, with the last vertebra extended at least to the hock joint. It is set smoothly into the croup and low rather than high. At rest, the tail hangs in a slight curve like a saber. A slight hook—sometimes carried to one side—is faulty only to the extent that it mars general appearance. When the dog is excited or in motion, the curve is accentuated and the tail raised, but it should never be curled forward beyond a vertical line. Tails too short, or with clumpy ends due to

ankylosis, are serious faults. A dog with a docked tail must be disqualified.

HINDQUARTERS: The whole assembly of the thigh, viewed from the side, is broad, with both upper and lower thigh well muscled, forming as nearly as possible a right angle. The upper thigh bone parallels the shoulder blade while the lower thigh bone parallels the upper arm. The metatarsus (the unit between the hock joint and the foot) is short, strong and tightly articulated.

GAIT: A German Shepherd Dog is a trotting dog, and its structure has been developed to meet the requirements of its work. *General Impression:* The gait is outreaching, elastic, seemingly without effort, smooth and rhythmic, covering the maximum amount of ground with the minimum number of steps. At a walk it covers a great deal of ground, with long stride of both hind legs and forelegs. At a trot the dog covers still more ground with even longer stride, and moves powerfully but easily, with co-ordination and balance so that the gait appears to be the steady motion of a well-lubricated machine. The feet travel close to the ground on both forward reach and backward push. In order to achieve ideal movement of this kind, there must be good muscular development and ligamentation. The hindquarters deliver, through the back, a powerful forward thrust which slightly lifts the whole animal and drives the body forward. Reaching far under, and passing the imprint left by the front foot, the hind foot takes hold of the ground; then hock, stifle and upper thigh come into play and sweep back, the stroke of the hind leg finishing with the foot still close to the ground in a smooth follow-through. The overreach of the hindquarter usually necessitates one hindfoot passing outside and the other hindfoot passing inside the track of the forefeet, and such action is not faulty unless the locomotion is crabwise with the dog's body sideways out of the normal straight line.

TRANSMISSION: The typical smooth, flowing gait is maintained with great strength and firmness of back. The whole effort of the hindquarter is transmitted to the forequarter through the loin, back and withers. At full trot, the back must remain firm and level without sway, roll, whip or roach. Unlevel topline with withers lower than the hip is a fault. To compensate for the forward motion imparted by

Lovely flowing movement by Ch. Hessians Exaktor. Helen and Art Hess, Hessian Kennels.

the hindquarters, the shoulder should open to its full extent. The forelegs should reach out close to the ground in a long stride in harmony with that of the hindquarters. The dog does not track on widely separated parallel lines, but brings the feet inward toward the middle line of the body when trotting in order to maintain balance. The feet track closely but do not strike or cross over. Viewed from the front, the front legs function from the shoulder joint to the pad in a straight line. Viewed from the rear, the hind legs function from the hip joint to the pad in a straight line. Faults of gait, whether from front, rear or side, are to be considered very serious faults.

COLOR: The German Shepherd Dog varies in color, and most colors are permissible. Strong rich colors are preferred. Nose black. Pale, washed-out colors and blues or livers are serious faults. A white dog or a dog with a nose that is not predominantly black must be disqualified.

COAT: The ideal dog has a double coat of medium length. The outer coat should be as dense as possible, hair straight, harsh and lying close to the body. A slightly wavy outer coat, often of wiry texture, is permissible. The head, including the inner ear and foreface, and the legs and paws are covered with short hair, and the neck with longer and thicker hair. The rear of the forelegs and hindlegs has somewhat longer hair extending to the pastern and hock, respectively. Faults in coat include soft, silky, too long outer coat, woolly, curly, and open coat.

DISQUALIFICATIONS: Cropped or hanging ears. Undershot jaw. Docked tail. White dogs. Dogs with noses not predominantly black. Any dog that attempts to bite the judge.

Am. and Can. Ch. Covy-Tucker Hill's Finnegan, ROM, by Covy's Oregano of Tucker Hill, ROM, ex Covy's Fate of Tucker Hill, was the Number One Shepherd in the United States 1976-79. Owned by Ralph S. and Mary C. Roberts; bred and co-owned by Cappy Pottle and Gloria F. Birch.

1977 Select Number Three, Ch. Covy-Tucker Hill's Fall Storm, litter-brother to Finnegan.

This is Abadee Kennels' Ch. Cito, described by owner Gustave Schindler as one of the best moving and intelligent dogs he has ever seen or known.

Meisterplatz's Britta vom Kornfeldshof illustrates Shepherd intelligence and beauty. Handled by Denise Kodner.

British Standard

CHARACTERISTICS: The characteristic expression of the Alsatian gives the impression of perpetual vigilance, fidelity, liveliness and watchfulness, alert to every sight and sound, with nothing escaping attention; fearless, but with decided suspiciousness of strangers—as opposed to the immediate friendliness of some breeds. The Alsatian possesses highly developed senses, mentally and temperamentally. He should be strongly individualistic and possess a high standard of intelligence. Three of the most outstanding traits are incorruptibility, discernment and ability to reason.

GENERAL APPEARANCE: The general appearance of the Alsatian is a well-proportioned dog showing great suppleness of limb, neither massive nor heavy, but at the same time free from any suggestion of weediness. It must not approach the greyhound type. The body is rather long, strongly boned, with plenty of muscle, obviously capable of endurance and speed and of quick and sudden movement. The gait should be supple, smooth and long-reaching, carrying the body along with the minimum of up-and-down movement, entirely free from stiltiness.

HEAD AND SKULL: The head is proportionate to the size of the body, long, lean and clean cut, broad at the back of the skull, but without coarseness, tapering to the nose with only a slight stop between the eyes. The skull is slightly domed and the top of the nose should be parallel to the forehead. The cheeks must not be full or in any way prominent and the whole head, when viewed from the top should be much in the form of a V, well filled in under the eyes. There should be plenty of substance in foreface, with a good depth from top to bottom. The muzzle is strong and long and, while tapering to the nose, it must not be carried to such an extreme as to give the appearance of being overshot. It must not show any weakness, or be snipy or lippy. The lips must be tight fitting and clean. The nose must be black.

EYES: The eyes are almond-shaped as nearly as possible matching the surrounding coat but darker rather than lighter in shade and placed to look straight forward. They must not be in any way bulging or prominent, and must show a lively, alert and highly intelligent expression.

Select Ch. Cobert's Golly Gee of Lakeside, ROM, takes Best of Opposite Sex under the noted authority from Germany, Dr. C. Rummel. One of the magnificent German Shepherds from Cobert Kennels, Connie and Theodore Beckhardt.

The gorgeous, typey bitch, Ch. Hessians Tinsel, noted for her extraordinary gait, was Select at the 1967 National Specialty where her sire, Ch. Hessians Baldur, ROM, Select, appeared in the Parade of Great Dogs. Tinsel is the only American-bred bitch pictured in the British publication, *The Complete Alsatian*, by English judge Nem Elliott, portraying her great reach and movement as shown here. A homebred, owner-handled member of the Hessian Shepherds Kennel, Art and Helen Hess.

EARS: The ears should be of moderate size, but rather large than small, broad at the base and pointed at the tips, placed rather high on the skull and carried erect—all adding to the alert expression of the dog as a whole. (It should be noted, in case novice breeders may be misled, that in Alsatian puppies the ears often hang until the age of six months and sometimes longer, becoming erect with the replacement of the milk teeth.)

MOUTH: The teeth should be sound and strong, gripping with a scissor-like action, the lower incisors just behind, but touching the upper.

NECK: The neck should be strong, fairly long with plenty of muscle, fitting gracefully into the body, joining the head without sharp angles and free from throatiness.

FOREQUARTERS: The shoulders should slope well back. The ideal being that a line drawn through the centre of the shoulderblade should form a right-angle with the humerus when the leg is perpendicular to the ground in stance. Upright shoulders are a major fault.

They should show plenty of muscle, which is distinct from, and must not be confused with coarse or loaded bone, which is a fault. The shoulderbone should be clean. The forelegs should be perfectly straight viewed from the front, but the pasterns should show a slight angle with the forearm when regarded from the side, too great an angle denotes weakness and while carrying plenty of bone, it should be of good quality. Anything approaching the massive bone of the Newfoundland, for example, being a decided fault.

BODY: The body is muscular, the back is broadish and straight, strongly boned and well developed. The belly shows a waist without being tucked-up. There should be a good depth of brisket or chest, the latter should not be too broad. The sides are flat compared to some breeds, and while the dog must not be barrel ribbed, it must not be so flat as to be actually slab-sided. The Alsatian should be quick in movement and speedy but not like a Greyhound in body.

HINDQUARTERS: The hindquarters should show breadth and strength, the loins being broad and strong, the rump rather long and sloping and the legs, when viewed from behind, must be quite straight, without any tendency to cow-hocks, or bow-hocks, which are both extremely serious faults. The stifles are well turned and the hocks strong and well let down. The ability to turn quickly is a necessary asset to the Alsatian, and this can only be if there is a good length of thigh-bone and leg, and by the bending of the hock.

FEET: The feet should be round, the toes strong, slightly arched and held close together. The pads should be firm, the nails short and strong. Dewclaws are neither a fault nor a virtue, but should be removed from the hind legs at 4 to 5 days old, as they are liable to spoil the gait.

TAIL: When at rest the tail should hang in a slight curve, and reach at least as far as the hock. During movement and excitement it will be raised, but in no circumstances should the tail be carried past a vertical line drawn through the root.

COAT: The coat is smooth, but it is at the same time a double coat. The under-coat is woolly in texture, thick and close and to it the animal owes its characteristic resistance to cold. The outer-coat is also close, each hair straight, hard, and lying flat, so that it is rain-resisting. Under the body, to behind the legs, the coat is longer and forms near the thigh a mild form of breeching. On the head (including the inside of the ears), to the front of the legs and feet, the hair is short. Along the neck it is longer and thicker, and in winter approaches a form of ruff. A coat either too long or too short is a fault. As an average, the hairs on the back should be from 1 to 2 inches in length.

COLOUR: The colour of the Alsatian is in itself not important and has no effect on the character of the dog or on its fitness for work and should be a secondary consideration for that reason. All white or near white unless possessing black points are not desirable. The final colour of a young dog can only be ascertained when the outer coat has developed.

WEIGHT AND SIZE: The ideal height (measured to the highest point of the shoulder) is 22 to 24 inches for bitches and 24 to 26 inches for dogs. The proportion, of length to height, may vary between 10:9 and 10:8.5.

FAULTS: A long, narrow, Collie or Borzoi head. A pink or liver-coloured nose. Undershot or overshot mouth. Tail with curl or pronounced hook. The lack of heavy undercoat.

NOTE: Male animals should have two apparently normal testicles fully descended into the scrotum.

A handsome study of German Shepherd Dog beauty and intelligence. This photo of 1962 Grand Victor Ch. Yorkdom's Pak comes to us courtesy of Doris Heidt through the thoughtfulness of Mary Schuetzler.

Ch. Meadowmill's Legend on the day he completed his title with his breeder, owner, handler, and friend, Helen Miller Fisher.

CHAPTER TEN

Judging the German Shepherd Dog

by Helen Miller Fisher

Ch. Ciro of Fieldstone, by Ch. Cuno von der Teufelslache, SchH III, ROM, ex Freia von der Wilkan (a Rolf von Osnabrucherland daughter), was Best of Breed and won the Working Group at Duluth Kennel Club in 1957. Helen Miller Fisher handling under the very famous judge, the late Mrs. Marie Meyer Nolan.

Judging the German Shepherd Dog requires an appreciation of the fact that the approach and emphasis are quite different from most other breeds. Recognizing that the dog was originally bred for herding sheep in Germany, nearly all emphasis is placed on the gait of the animal.

To appreciate why such importance is placed on the gait, let us touch briefly on the history. In the early and middle nineteenth century in Germany, the name "Shepherd Dog" was given to any dog that had the ability to work and herd the livestock. It didn't matter that they were drop-or prick-eared, long- or short-coated or had any special appearance. The only uniform qualities emerging from this conglomeration of animals were that the better dogs were of medium size and had ground-covering gait. Looks were of no importance. Late in the nineteenth century the Verein fur Deutsche Schaferhunde, S.V., was established. Under the leadership of Capt. Max von Stephanitz, this vast conglomeration of herding dogs was, by dictatorial selection and in-breeding, fused into what we now know as the German Shepherd Dog. Von Stephanitz was an organizer and a strict disciplinarian. The German Shepherd fanciers of today like to think of

him as the "Father" of our breed. Because of him, the gait *was* and still *is* of the greatest importance. He was very rigid in his belief in the working ability of the breed, and he aimed all the controlled breeding in that direction. The result was a working, efficient machine. Unsoundness of gait in any form was not tolerated, as this would interfere with the fitness of the German Shepherd Dog's working ability. The standard was written to describe the ideal dog fit for hard service. The standard has not been altered essentially in any way since that time. Consequently, the emphasis on gait is still of prime importance and consideration. The beauty and nobility as we know it today came later, originating from Flora Berkemeyer, the foundation bitch of the Riedekenburg strain. Flora was a beautiful accident of her time, and thank goodness she was dominant in passing on the grace and beauty she possessed.

Since we have such a complete descriptive standard for our breed, it is assumed that judging German Shepherd Dogs would be relatively easy. Nothing is farther from the truth. Taking for granted the usual variation in interpretation of the standard, there is a much larger problem.

German Shepherd Dog Club of Maryland 1953. Judge, Herr Klien from Germany. Dog, Ch. Cuno von der Teufels-lache, SchH III, FH, ROM, owned by Helen Miller Fisher and handled by Bill Fisher. An historic picture, especially interesting as the dogs were not stacked by the handlers in those days as is now the custom.

You must remember that in Germany, where the Verein fur Deutsche Schaferhunde reigns supreme, the German Shepherd Dog is king. Dog shows, whether they be just for the German Shepherd Dog or for all breeds, are designed primarily for the number one breed—German Shepherd Dogs. Small indoor rings are almost unheard of. Dogs are shown in large (seventy to one hundred feet) outside rings. Because of this, the novice, amateur or professional can see the dog at its proper gait at a proper distance and learn how the German Shepherd Dog functions in motion.

From the beginning in this country, the German Shepherd Dog has been forced to try and function in rings designed for Terrier and Toy breeds. Since our primary governing body in this country is the American Kennel Club, the emphasis is on the all-breed show, with the German Shepherd Dog having to accept the same size ring as the rest of the dogs. Many clubs try to accommodate Shepherds by allowing a slightly larger ring if there is room, but that is the exception. This inadequate ring size has had two disastrous effects. First, the German Shepherd Dog exhibitors have rebelled; and in the last fifteen years, they have refused to show the good dogs at the all-breed shows. Specialty shows have sprung up like toadstools all over the country. We now have 120 regional clubs, each having two Specialty shows per year. The serious Shepherd exhibitor chooses these shows rather than the all-breed events, because at these Specialties, like in Germany, there is room for the dog to be correctly judged: on its gait.

The second, and worst, effect of the small rings, however, has been that since judges can't see and learn the proper gait, they are forced to accept what they see in the ring as correct gait, and so it is passed on from one generation of judges to the next. As a result, German Shepherd Dogs are often judged on their looks, expression and coats and a few trotting steps taken in the ring; and judges feel they understand the breed. Unfortunately, they do not. No matter how descriptive our standard is, the naked truth is that you must see the powerful suspension and the effortless ground-covering, hard-driving gait in a large ring and from a reasonable distance to understand and appreciate the true German Shepherd Dog gait.

With this emphasis on gait, and accepting reasonable variations in interpretations of the standard by different judges, how do we judge the German Shepherd Dog?

First of all, the judging procedure differs slightly from other breeds. If a spectator, exhibitor or another judge watches, he can easily tell why the dog is placed where he is, simply by the procedure we use.

When the dogs enter the ring, they may or may not be stacked or set up in show pose. If they are stacked, it is for two reasons: to let the judge get a quick overall general impression of the animals and also for audience education. This is of very short duration, however, and the dogs are then gaited around the ring. During this preliminary gaiting, dogs are placed in position according to their side gait. If a large class needs to be divided in order to evaluate properly the side gaiting, the dogs are broken into groups of six to eight dogs. This preliminary compara-

Ch. Meadowmill's Jem, whelped October 17th 1954, by Ch. Cuno von der Teufelslache, SchH III, ROM, ex Erika of La Salle (Ch. Stark of Grafmar daughter), completed her championship in 1957. Bred, owned, and handled by Mrs. Helen Miller Fisher.

tive gaiting tells the judge more than just the side gait. The German Shepherd Dog is a natural dog with a short coat that lies close to the body. Because of this, during this selective gaiting, the judge can also pass judgment on size, secondary sex characteristics, back and croup faults, and pastern and hock problems. He can also probably predict which dogs will be unsound both in the coming and going gait, as well as in temperament. The skitterish animal flying at the end of its lead is apt to be unapproachable on the temperament test.

The temperament test is a simple one and takes only an extra thirty to forty-five seconds per dog to do. We feel this is very necessary in our breed. Our parent club, the German Shepherd Dog Club of America, has sent out letters requesting all judges to temperament-test the German Shepherd Dog.

The judge stands in the center of the show ring and the individual dog is brought halfway to him on a loose lead. No command of "Stay" or "Hold" is given by the handler. The dog stands free and away from the handler and is not posed. The judge then approaches the dog in a firm but non-aggressive manner, usually talking to the dog at the same time. If the dog cannot be approached or slinks behind his owner, the dog is dismissed from the ring. The dog should either stand firm and have eye contact with the judge or wander around at the end of the lead totally disregarding the judge. The judge should be able to pat the German Shepherd Dog and the dog's reactions should range from total disinterest to inquisitiveness or outright friendliness. The dog is then stacked and ready for the individual examination by the judge.

Very little importance is placed on the German Shepherd Dog's head. Our preference is to have definite secondary sex characteristics, upright and well-placed ears, dark brown eyes and full dentition with proper bite. However, there are people whom we describe as "Gait Purists." Like other breeds, we have judges that fall into each end of the scale, with the majority of us falling somewhere in the center. The "Gait Purists" judge strictly on side movement, often forgiving soft ears, light eyes, ugly heads and, yes, even some unsoundness in the coming and going gait. As long as the animal has that famous

Ch. Meadowmill's Score of Waldhorn (Ch. Cuno von der Teufelslache, SchH III, ROM, ex Ch. Waldhorn's Prima of Long Worth), owned and handled by Helen Miller Fisher, winning under judge John Seiler at the German Shepherd Dog Club of Minneapolis and St. Paul Specialty Show in October 1956. Mr. Seiler is now an A.K.C. Field Representative.

Meadowmill's Charmaine, whelped March 20th 1953, by Ch. Cuno von der Teufelslache, SchH III, ROM, ex Techie of La Salle. This beautiful bitch, with thirteen points, unfortunately never finished. She was owned by Helen Miller Fisher.

Ch. Meadowmill's Appolo, by Can. Grand Victor, Am. and Can. Ch. Chimney Sweep of Long Worth, C.D., ROM, ex the Cuno daughter, Ch. Meadowmill's Jem, taking Best of Winners at the German Shepherd Dog Club of Minneapolis and St. Paul Specialty in 1959 under judge Virginia McCoy. Helen Miller Fisher, breeder, owner, and handler.

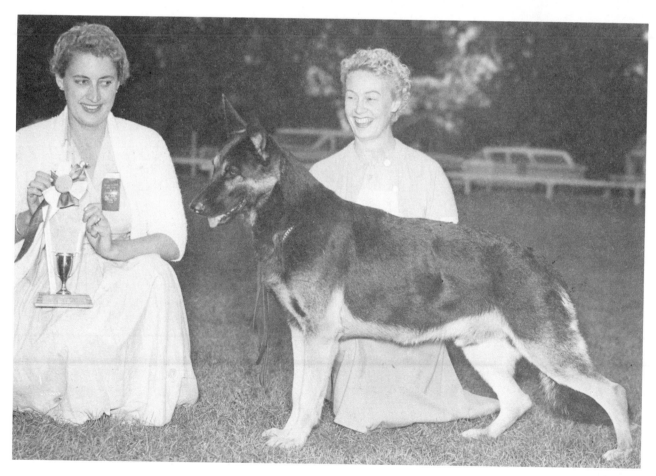

Meadowmill's Venus, whelped August 18th 1958, by Ch. Atlas vom Plastendamm (German import) ex Meadowmill's Charmaine, owned by Helen Miller Fisher, Meadowmill Kennels.

Ch. Llano Estacado's Cicely, by Ch. 'Nother Sweep of Long Worth ex Ch. Llano Estacados Arrogante, representing some of the most famous Shepherd breeding of the 1950's, as Long Worth Kennels were owned by Lloyd Brackett and Llano Estacado by Langdon Skarda. Owned by Helen Miller Fisher.

This is Ch. Caralon's Phantom v. Le Barland at fourteen months of age, owned by Caralon Kennels and Timothy H. Hills. Photo courtesy of Helen Miller Fisher, who says of him: "This dog was a Hein son and a great all-black dog. He finished very quickly, and the handlers voted him 'closest to the standard of any dog living'—that and being all black make him unusual."

"flying trot," all else is forgotten. Unfortunately, we now have some heads that are too refined and some ears that "wave at you" as the dog moves. We have always contended that the "Shepherd doesn't work on its head"; nevertheless, we should not ignore these head faults simply because we emphasize gait. On the other hand, there are judges who are tooth and eye freaks who heavily penalize a dog with a missing tooth or a light eye and ignore a proper body with correct movement. The impression of the head should be one of regal elegance, of nobility with just a touch of arrogance. We all love a gorgeous, typy head; but, in truth, we sometimes sacrifice it to an outstanding moving dog.

As we continue examination of the dog, we note length of neck. Obviously the neck will be too short if the shoulder is upright, so the whole forequarter is appraised in one piece, not as neck, brisket, shoulder, forearm, and so on. The standard describes these correctly, but in actual judging, you never "piecemeal" a dog. The dog is examined as a whole, not in sections.

Other than examining teeth and testicles, very little "hands on" examination of the German Shepherd Dog is needed by an informed judge. Many times judges will feel the withers area to see if the shoulder blade is laid on as well as laid back properly. Normally, this is simply to confirm what you have seen in motion. To clarify terms, "laid on" refers to the closeness of the two shoulder blades at the point of the withers. The width of two fingers or less is desirable. "Laid back," on the other hand, refers to the angle (preferably a 90°, or right, angle) the shoulder and upper arm make where they join. The importance of both of these is evident in the extension of the foreleg in motion. Since the German Shepherd Dog is longer than he is tall by 10 to 8½, it is important to note that the length is not in the back itself. The back should be short. Think of the dog as a train with a

German Sieger and Am. Ch. Lierberg's Bodo at the German Shepherd Dog Club of Los Angeles Specialty in 1967. Owned by Eric Renner, this was a famous West Coast winner. Helen Miller Fisher comments on him: "Bodo had just been brought to this country from winning the German Sieger title. Had been over here only three weeks when I judged him in his third show and awarded him the points to complete his American championship. A fantastic dog with a temperament that wouldn't quit. One of the last imports to do any American winning with the exception of one or two that Ernie Loeb brought over."

coupling between two of the cars. This compares to the front and rear parts of the dog connected by the spinal cord. The area between the last rib and the rear assembly is called the loin. We use the term "coupled" here to describe this area and how well the front and rear are coordinated. Normally, the desired width is four fingers slightly spread apart. This short coupling and short back contribute to the overall firm, solid topline with no roach or whipping or sagging. So while we want a dog that is longer than tall, we *don't* want a *long back*. We appraise

not only the length of the topline but also the slope. Even standing in a natural stance, not a show pose, the slope should be such that a drop of water placed on the head should easily run down the length of the topline dropping off at the croup, which is also long and sloping—all one fluid line.

At the same time we are considering the topline, we appraise the bottomline. Here the depth of brisket and the length of the chest cavity is noted. Desirable depth, or brisket, is at least to the elbows. A minimum tuck-up is allowed.

Nothing looks worse than a tuck-up similar to a Greyhound. Feet are noted and they should be thick and compact. Here is where some German Shepherd Dog owners get a little lazy. Toenails are often left too long, with exhibitors counting on the grass of the outside rings to cover what they forgot to do. Pasterns should be springy but not let down. Anything over a 25° angle from the vertical will result in a paddling action when the dog is in motion.

When viewed in a show stance, the hindquarters should be broad and well muscled with the upper and lower thigh meeting in a right angle. The German Shepherd Dog in repose will naturally stand with one hind leg in back of the other. Because of his extreme rear angulation,

Ch. Kubistraums Idyll, by Ch. Kubistraums Kane, ROM, ex Kane's dam, Falkora's Catalina, C.D., ROM, was the single puppy whelped by Catalina when she was eight and a half years old. Here, Idyll is winning American-Bred Bitch at the German Shepherd Dog Club of Greater Kansas City Show, 1980. Judged by Helen Miller Fisher. Owned by Verna M. Kubik of St. Joseph, Wisconsin.

this stance is the most comfortable for him when at rest. The show pose tends to overemphasize this, sometimes to the extreme, with the leg closest to the handler brought toward the front of the dog and resting nearly flat on its hock and the leg closest to the judge stretched back with the hock set perpendicular to the ground. A check for testicles and a brief fingering to the tail to check for ankylosis and the individual examination is done. To an experienced judge, less than thirty seconds has been spent on a "hands on" examination. Now the gaiting judgment begins.

Gait is examined as the dog is moved away from and brought back to the judge on a straight line and is somewhat harder to observe in German Shepherd Dogs than other breeds. Most of the show dogs are trained to gait out in a flying trot in front of the handler at the end of a six-foot lead. When the handler attempts to slow the dog down for the individual coming and going, the dog often pulls to the side, or the handler has to forcibly lift him up to slow him down and the dog then does all sorts of peculiar things with his front. Also in the going-away gait, the dog accustomed to digging in to thrust forward will appear to be wide apart behind, rather than appear to be single tracking. Dogs that are too extreme in the rear also are very unstable in gait and will

"knit and purl" as they attempt to single track. As in any other breed, this is where you pick up the paddling, toeing in, the elbows out and so on, but again it is simply to confirm or reject what you have seen on that initial selective side gaiting. The dog is then sent around one time by himself to show off his side gait. This is his "time to shine." This is why large rings are so important. It sometimes takes this beautifully well-oiled machine six or seven steps to get in motion. In many all-breed rings, the space allowed the German Shepherd Dog is so small that the dog barely gets started and into his gait when he has to break his stride for a turn or a stop. As a result, the gait, which is the most desirable and necessary attribute of the German Shepherd Dog, is not only not seen but is also not given its proper importance in judging the dog. Suspension cannot be judged and the flying trot cannot be seen under these circumstances.

It is during this individual side gaiting that you can really see that powerful rear drive—the moving thrusting force that propels and transmits the power through to the front and forehand. The well-muscled thigh and leg reach under the dog in a powerful stride and overreach or overstep the front leg. The length of the rear overstep should be equalized by the extension

Ch. Hoobin's Gray Boy wins the breed first time out at an all-breed show. This startling blue youngster, only two years old, finished his title with four majors, shown in the classes only fourteen times. Owners, Mary and Lee Hoobin and Llano Estacado Kennels. The noted all-breed judge Langdon Skarda judged and admired this unusually colored but excellent dog to the extent that he not only put him to a good win but also later purchased him and that under Mr. Skarda's ownership he promptly became a Best in Show winner, confirming well Mr. Skarda's high opinion of his quality.

An especially outstanding puppy, Schutzenhaus Destiny, bred and owned by Mary Schuetzler, here is winning the 6-9 Month Class at six and a half months of age under Helen Miller Fisher at Detroit Kennel Club in March 1983. Handled by Tom McCoy, Destiny is by Ch. Wellsprings Howard Johnson ex Can. Ch. Nocturne's Ruffian.

and reach of the forehand. With feet close to the ground, the front paw often extends beyond the nose of the dog. The standard describes it as "outreaching," effortless and ground-covering, but the most exciting aspect of the German Shepherd Dog gait is the suspension. This is what enables the dog to cover ground with so little effort. It is exciting and thrilling to watch, and it must be seen in a large space to be properly understood.

After each individual gait, comparative selective gaiting is done again. Dogs are moved up or dropped back in position based on the final appraisal of the whole dog. Good qualities are measured against the faults that were discovered in the individual examination. Performance and attitude of the dog are highly critical at this point. The dog that "turns on" and "asks for" that final nod by the judge often overcomes apparent minor faults just by his will to win. When

the moment of truth is at hand, the final judgment is made on side gait.

I have deliberately avoided the word "type" in my discussion, because in my opinion the word "type" is over-used and over-abused. It simply means that the appearance or looks of the dog verifies its use. In the case of the German Shepherd, the dog was bred to herd. It is a utility working dog and soundness and correctness of gait were, and are, of prime importance. The German Shepherd Dog's stance and gait are particular only to this breed. No other breed has the elastic suspension of gait, either at a walk or a flying trot. The gait is exciting and beautiful, but its primary importance is in the purpose for which the German Shepherd Dog exists. He has the ability to cover ground, to walk or trot with the fewest steps and the least amount of effort, equally able to guide a blind person for hours, walk a police beat or herd livestock all day.

Fredda von Olsonkamp, by Ch. Buddha's Fissmertemple ex Waldenmark's Iris. She is the foundation bitch at Markenhaus, owned by Ken Rayner, and this lovely picture of her was made when she was eleven years old. Fredda was born in April 1961 and lived to be sixteen years old.

CHAPTER ELEVEN

Selection of a German Shepherd Dog

The future Grand Victor Ch. Lance of Fran-Jo, ROM, as a four-month-old puppy with his breeder-owner Joan Ford winning Best in Match over 105 entries. Even at this early age, his quality and excellence were very apparent and outstanding.

Once you have made the decision that the German Shepherd Dog is the breed of dog you wish to own, the next important step for you is to determine the right Shepherd to best satisfy your needs. Do you prefer to start out with a puppy, with an adult dog, or with one partially mature? Do you prefer a male or a female? What type of dog do you wish—one for show or for competition in obedience? Are you looking for a Shepherd for breeding, possibly as the foundation for a kennel? Do you simply want one for companionship, to be a family pet?

A decision should be reached about these matters prior to your contacting breeders; then you can accurately describe your requirements and the breeder can offer you the most suitable dog for your purposes. Remember that with any breed of dog, as with any other major purchase, the more care and forethought you invest when planning, the greater the pleasure and satisfaction likely to result.

Referring to a dog as a "major investment" may possibly seem strange to you; however, it is an accurate description. Generally speaking, a sizable sum of money is involved, and you are assuming responsibility for a living creature, taking on all the moral obligations this involves. Assuming that everything goes well, your Shepherd will be a member of your family for a dozen or more years, sharing your home, your daily routine, and your interests. The happiness and success of these years depend largely on the knowledge and intelligence with which you start the relationship.

Certain ground rules apply to the purchase of a dog, regardless of your intentions for its future. Foremost among these is the fact that no matter what you will be doing with the dog, the best and most acceptable place at which to purchase a German Shepherd Dog is a kennel specializing in that breed. Even though pet shops occasionally have Shepherd puppies for sale, they are primarily concerned with *pet* stock, puppies without pedigrees. When you buy from a breeder you are getting a dog that has been the result of parents very carefully selected as individuals and as to pedigree and ancestry. For such a breeding, a dog and a bitch are chosen from whom the breeder hopes to achieve show type dogs that upgrade both his own kennel's quality

Ch. Celebrity's Theme Song, by Ch. Vox Wikingerblut, ROM, ex Trulanders Celebrity, ROM, 1966-1977. One from a litter of four champions. Ralph S. and Mary C. Roberts, owners.

and that of the breed generally. Much thought has been given to the conformation and temperament likely to result from the combination of parents and bloodlines involved, for the breeder wants to produce sound, outstanding dogs that will further the respect with which he is regarded in the German Shepherd Dog world. A specialist of this sort is interested in raising *better* dogs. Since it is seldom possible to keep all the puppies from every litter, fine young stock becomes available for sale. These puppies have flaws so slight in appearance as to be unrecognizable as such by other than the trained eye of a judge or a specialist on Shepherds. These flaws in no way affect the strength or future good health of these Shepherds; they simply preclude success in the show ring. The conscientious breeder will point them out to you when explaining why the puppy is being offered for sale at "pet price." When you buy a Shepherd like this, from a knowledgeable, reliable breeder, you get all the advantages of good bloodlines with proper temperament, careful rearing, and the happy, well-adjusted environment needed by puppies who are to become satisfactory, enjoyable adults. Although you are not buying a show dog or show prospect, puppies raised in the same manner have all the odds in their favor to become dogs of excellence in the home and in obedience.

If you are looking for a show dog, obviously everything I have said about buying only from a specialized Shepherd breeder applies with even greater emphasis. Show-type dogs are bred from show-type dogs of proven producing lines and are the result of serious study, thought, and planning. They do *not* just happen.

Throughout the pages of this book are the names and locations of dozens of reliable Shepherd breeders. Should it so happen that no one has puppies or young stock available to go at the moment you inquire, it would be far wiser to place your name on the waiting list and see what happens when the next litter is born than to rush off and buy a puppy from some less desirable source. After all, you do not want to repent at leisure.

Another source of information regarding recognized Shepherd breeders is the American Kennel Club, 51 Madison Avenue, New York, NY 10010. A note or phone call will bring you a list of breeders in your area.

Information can also be obtained from professional handlers. They have many contacts and might be able to put you in touch with a breeder and/or help you choose a dog.

The moment you even start to think about purchasing a German Shepherd Dog, it makes sense to look at, observe, and study as many

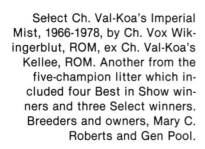

Select Ch. Val-Koa's Sentry, by Ch. Vox Wikinger-blut, ROM, ex Ch. Val-Koa's Kellee, ROM, 1966-1977. One from the five-champion litter of Ch. Vox and Ch. Kellee which included four Best in Show winners and three Select winners. Breeders-owners, Mary C. Roberts and Joseph Totora.

members of the breed as possible prior to taking the step. Acquaint yourself with correct type, soundness, and beauty before making any commitments. Since you are reading this book, you have already started on that route. Now add to your learning by visiting some dog shows if you can. Even if you are not looking for a show dog, it never hurts to become aware of how such a dog appears and behaves. Perhaps at the shows you will meet some breeders from your area with whom you can discuss the breed and whom you can visit.

If you wish your Shepherd to be a family dog, the most satisfactory choice often is a bitch (female). Females make gentle, delightful companions and usually are quieter and more inclined not to roam than males. Often, too, they make neater house dogs, being easier to train. And they are of at least equal intelligence to the males. In the eyes of many pet owners, the principal objection to having a bitch is the periodic "coming in season." Sprays and chlorophyll tablets that can help to cut down on the nuisance of visiting canine swains stampeding your front door are available; and, of course, I advocate spaying bitches who will not be used for show or breeding, with even the bitches who are shown or bred being spayed when their careers in competition or in the whelping box have come to a close. Bitches who have been spayed, preferably

Select Ch. Val-Koa's Imperial Mist, 1966-1978, by Ch. Vox Wikingerblut, ROM, ex Ch. Val-Koa's Kellee, ROM. Another from the five-champion litter which included four Best in Show winners and three Select winners. Breeders and owners, Mary C. Roberts and Gen Pool.

before four years old, remain in better health later on in life, because spaying almost entirely eliminates the dangers of breast cancer. Spaying also eliminates the messiness of spotting on rugs and furniture, which can be considerable during her periods with a member of a medium-sized or large breed and which is annoying in a household companion.

To many, however, a dog (male) is preferable. The males do seem to be more strongly endowed with true breed character. But do consider the advantages and disadvantages of both males and females prior to deciding which to purchase.

If you are buying your Shepherd as a pet, a puppy is usually preferable, as you can teach it right from the beginning the ways of your household and your own schedule. Two months is an ideal age at which to introduce the puppy into your home. Older puppies may already have established habits of which you will not approve and which you may find difficult to change. Besides, puppies are such fun that it is great to share and enjoy every possible moment of their process of growing up.

When you are ready to buy, make appointments with as many Shepherd breeders as you have been able to locate in your area for the purpose of seeing what they have available and discussing the breed with them. This is a marvelous learning experience, and you will find the ma-

Ch. Tannenwald's Igor, by Santa's Kurt of Cosalta ex Bruni of Tannenwald, at an early age. Pictured with Ken Rayner.

jority of breeders are willing and happy to spend time with you, provided that you have arranged the visit in advance. Kennel owners are busy folks with full schedules, so do be considerate about this courtesy and call on the telephone before you appear.

If you have a choice of more than one kennel where you can go to see the dogs, take advantage of that opportunity instead of just settling for and buying the first puppy you see. You may return to your first choice in the long run, but you will do so with greater satisfaction and authority if you have seen the others before making the selection. When you look at puppies, be aware that the one you buy should look sturdy and big-boned, bright-eyed and alert, with an inquisitive, friendly attitude. The puppy's coat should look clean and glossy. Do not buy a puppy that seems listless or dull, is strangely hyperactive, or looks half sick. The condition of the premises where the puppies are raised is also important as you want your puppy to be free of parasites; don't buy a puppy whose surroundings are dirty and ill kept.

One of the advantages of buying at a kennel you can visit is that you are thereby afforded the opportunity of seeing the dam of the puppies and possibly also the sire, if he, too, belongs to the breeder. Sometimes you can even see one or more of the grandparents. Be sure to note the temperament of these Shepherds as well as their conformation.

A three-month-old puppy from Dois Pinheiros Kennels in Brazil. Mrs. Vera Lucia de Castros Barbosa, owner.

Ch. Flash of Clover Acres and his litter-sister, Frolich of Clover Acres. Owned and bred by D. and P. Murphy; handled by father and son Ken and Chips Rayner. Bred to Ch. Tannenwald's Igor, Frolich produced several noted champions for the Murphys. Some of the progeny from this excellent bitch and fine stud dog are shown below.

Above: The younger generation! All of the puppies shown on this page were bred by D. and P. Murphy. Photos courtesy of Ken Rayner. **Below:** Q.T. of Clover Acres.

Above: Quell of Clover Acres. **Below:** Still another lovely puppy from the Ch. Tannenwald's Igor ex Frolich of Clover Acres litter, Quasar of Clover Acres. This litter bred and owned by D. and P. Murphy.

If there are no Shepherd breeders within your travelling range, or if you have not liked what you have seen at those you've visited, do not hesitate to contact other breeders who are recommended to you even if their kennels are at a distance and to purchase from one of them if you are favorably impressed with what is offered. Shipping dogs is done with regularity nowadays and is reasonably safe, so this should not present a problem. If you are contacting a well-known, recognized breeder, the puppy should be fairly described and represented to you. Breeders of this caliber want you to be satisfied, both for the puppy's sake and for yours. They take pride in their kennel's reputation, and they make every effort to see that their customers are pleased. In this way you are deprived of the opportunity of seeing your dog's parents, but even so you can buy with confidence when dealing with a specialized breeder.

Every word about careful selection of your pet puppy and where it should be purchased applies twofold when you set out to select a show dog or the foundation stock for a breeding kennel of your own. You look for all the things already mentioned but on a far more sophisticated level, with many more factors to be taken into consideration. The standard of the German Shepherd Dog must now become your guide, and it is essential that you know and understand not only the words of this standard but also their application to actual dogs before you are in a position to make a wise selection. Even then, if this is your first venture with a show-type Shepherd, listen well and heed the advice of the breeder. If you have clearly and honestly stated your ambitions and plans for the dog, you will find that the breeders will cooperate by offering you something with which you will be successful.

There are several different degrees of show dog quality. There are dogs that should become top-flight winners which can be campaigned for Specials (Best of Breed competition) and with which you can hope to attain Working Group

Promising and appealing Hamilton Farm German Shepherd puppies owned by Mr. and Mrs. James R. Brady.

A young future star, Santo Von Burgerland, typical of the fine Shepherd puppies raised at Burgerland Kennels, Dr. and Mrs. Zoltan Puskas.

placements and possibly even hit the heights with a Best in Show win. There are dogs of championship quality which should gain their titles for you but are lacking in that "extra something" to make them potential Specials. There are dogs that perhaps may never finish their championships but which should do a bit of winning for you in the classes: a blue ribbon here and there, perhaps Winners or Reserve occasionally, but probably nothing truly spectacular. Obviously the hardest to obtain, and the most expensive, are dogs in the first category, the truly top-grade dogs. These are never plentiful as they are what most breeders are working to produce for their own kennels and personal enjoyment and with which they are loathe to part.

A dog of championship quality is easier to find and less expensive, although it still will bring a good price. The least difficult to obtain is a fair show dog that may pick up some points here and there but will mostly remain in class placements. Incidentally, one of the reasons that breeders are sometimes reluctant to part with a truly excellent show prospect is that in the past people have bought this type of dog with the promise it will be shown, but then the buyer has changed his mind after owning the dog awhile, and thus the dog becomes lost to the breed. It is really not fair to a breeder to buy a dog with the understanding that it will be shown and then renege on the agreement. Please, if you select a dog that is available only to a show home, think it over carefully prior to making a decision; then buy the dog only if you will be willing to give it the opportunity to prove itself in the show ring as the breeder expects.

If you want a show dog, obviously you are a person in the habit of attending dog shows. Now this becomes a form of schooling rather than just a pleasant pastime. Much can be learned at the

A future star on the way to his title. Treffer of Clover Acres, by Ch. Tannenwald's Igor ex Clover Acres Dixie, as a young dog taking the points from judge H. Hardin. Owned by Ray Picard.

Shepherd ringside if one truly concentrates on what one sees. Become acquainted with the various winning exhibitors. Thoughtfully watch the judging. Try to understand what it is that causes some dogs to win and others to lose. Note well the attributes of the dogs, deciding for yourself which ones you like, giving full attention to attitude and temperament as well as conformation. Close your ears to the ringside "know-it-alls" who have only derogatory remarks to make about each animal in the ring and all that takes place there. You need to develop independent thinking at this stage and should not be influenced by the often entirely uneducated comment of the ringside spoilsports. Especially make careful note of which exhibitors are campaigning winning homebreds—not just an occasional "star" but a series of consistent quality dogs. All this takes time and patience. This is the period to "make haste slowly"; mistakes can be expensive, and the more you have studied the breed, the better equipped you will be to avoid them.

As you make inquiries among various breeders regarding the purchase of a show dog or a show prospect, keep these things in mind. Show-

Ayrwood's Holly of Waymarsa, by Ch. Tannenwald's Igor ex Glenhart's Della of Ayrwood. An excellent producing bitch who has eight points towards her own title. Ken Rayner, handler. Owned by Marie Sagendorf.

Basko von Bergluft, C.D., a son of Klodo aus der Eremitenklause, ROM, ex Long Haven's Friendship, C.D.X., pictured at four months of age. Note the tremendous bone of this handsome youngster. Bred and owned by Dorit S. Rogers.

A puppy picture of the outstanding Ch. Hessians Baldur, ROM, Select, shows the promise of future greatness at an early age. Helen and Art Hess, owners, Hessian Kennels.

Weberhaus War Witch of Ember, by Select Ch. Falk of Ravinswood ex Waldeslust's Helma. Breeders, Weberhaus Kennels and Jacqueline Di Bernardo; owner, Diana Riddle.

prospect puppies are less expensive than fully mature show dogs. The reason for this is that with a puppy there is the element of chance, for one never can be absolutely certain exactly how the puppy will develop, while the mature dog stands before you as the finished product— "what you see is what you get"—all set to step out and win.

There is always the risk factor involved with the purchase of a show-type puppy. Sometimes all goes well and that is great. But many a swan has turned into an ugly duckling as time passes, and it is far less likely that the opposite will occur. So weigh this well and balance all the odds before you decide whether a puppy or a mature dog would be your better buy. There are times, of course, when one actually has no choice in the matter; no mature show dogs may be available for sale. Then one must either wait awhile or gamble on a puppy, but please *be aware that gambling is what you are doing.*

If you do take a show-prospect puppy, be guided by the breeder's advice when choosing from among what is offered. The person used to working with a bloodline has the best chance of predicting how the puppies will develop. Do not trust your own guess on this; rely on the experience of the breeder. For your own protection, it is best to buy puppies whose parents' eyes have been certified clear and who have been O.F.A.-certified free of hip dysplasia.

Although initially more expensive, a grown show dog in the long run often proves to be the far better bargain. His appearance is unlikely to change beyond weight and condition, which depend on the care you give him. Also to your advantage, if you are a novice about to become an exhibitor, is that a grown dog of show quality almost certainly will have been trained for the ring; thus, an inexperienced handler will find such a dog easier to present properly and in winning form in the ring.

Five Oaks Bar-Jonah, by Ch. Val-don's Quaker ex Fritzlund's Dixie, typical of the progeny from Fritzlund bitches. Ken Rayner handling to Best of Winners at Schooley's Mountain in 1980. Bred by Rev. Moore and owned by Ron Dob.

Future champion Farmils Chantz at eight weeks of age. Owned by Charles and Doris Farrell, Farmil Shepherds.

Spenrock Maxmilan, by Grayarlin Pierrot ex Halstor's Lola of Rock Maple, C.D., at one year of age. Bred by Janet Churchill. Betty Dumaine, owner.

If you plan to have your dog campaigned by a professional handler, have the handler help you locate and select a future winner. Through their numerous clients, handlers usually have access to a variety of interesting show dogs; and the usual arrangement is that the handler buys the dog, resells it to you for the price he paid, and at the same time makes a contract with you that the dog shall be campaigned by this handler throughout the dog's career.

If the foundation of a future kennel is what you have in mind as you contemplate the purchase of a Shepherd, concentrate on one or two really excellent bitches, not necessarily top show bitches but those representing the finest producing Shepherd lines. A proven matron who has already produced show-type puppies is, of course, the ideal answer here; but, as with a mature show dog, a proven matron is more difficult to obtain and more expensive since no one

Ch. Kern Delta's Exakta, ROM, great producing early bitch in the development of the Hessian German Shepherds, Helen and Art Hess.

Jan Churchill with her Spenrock Buccaneer just starting out at the puppy matches.

really wants to part with so valuable an asset. You just might strike it lucky, though, in which case you will be off to a flying start. If you do not find such a matron available, do the next best thing and select a young bitch of outstanding background representing a noted producing strain, one that is herself of excellent type and free of glaring faults.

Great attention should be paid to the background of the bitch from whom you intend to breed. If the information is not already known to you, find out all you can about the temperament, character, field ability, and conformation of the sire and dam, plus eye and hip rating. A person just starting in dogs is wise to concentrate on a fine collection of bitches and to raise a few litters sired by leading *producing* studs. The practice of buying a stud dog and then breeding everything you have to that dog does not always work out. It is better to take advantage of the availability of splendid stud dogs for your first few litters.

In summation, if you want a family dog, buy it young and raise it to the habits of your household. If you are buying a show dog, the more mature it is the more certain you can be of the future. If you are buying foundation stock for a breeding program, bitches are better than dogs,

At ten years of age, Margo von Bid-Scono, is the dam of two champions. William Endries, owner, Ender-Haus Kennels.

Ch. Hessians Exaktor, by Ch. Hessians Baldur, ROM, Select, ex Grand Victrix Ch. Hessians Vogue, ROM, as a puppy. Hessian German Shepherds, owned by Helen and Art Hess.

Gerlinde Hockla with her beautiful eight-week-old puppy, Antje of Lone Birch.

but they must be from the finest *producing* bloodlines.

Regarding price, you should expect to pay up to a few hundred dollars for a healthy pet German Shepherd puppy and more than that for a show-type puppy with the price rising accordingly as the dog gets older. A grown show dog can run well into four figures if of finest quality, and a proven brood matron will be priced according to the owner's valuation and can also run into four figures.

When you buy a purebred Shepherd dog or puppy that you are told is eligible for registration with the American Kennel Club, you are entitled to receive, from the seller, an application form that will enable you to register your dog. If the seller cannot give you the application, you should demand and receive an identification of your dog consisting of the breed, the registered names and numbers of the sire and dam, the name of the breeder, and the dog's date of birth. If the litter of which your Shepherd is part has been recorded with the American Kennel Club, then the litter number is sufficient identification.

Do not accept a verbal promise that registration papers will be mailed to you. Demand a registration application form or proper identification. If neither is supplied, do not buy the dog. These words are to be especially heeded if you are buying show dogs or breeding stock.

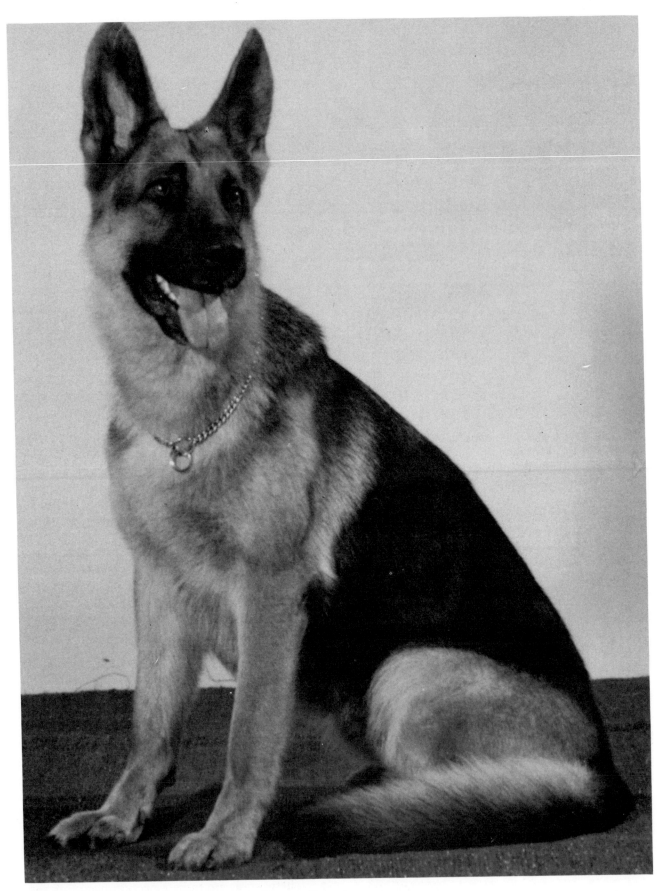

A fine bitch belonging to Valerie Mee, Timmee Kennels.

CHAPTER TWELVE

Caring for a German Shepherd Puppy

The great Ch. Lakeside's Gilligan's Island at five months old. Owned by D. Dwier. Photo courtesy of Sharon Dwier.

Ownership of a dog entails a great deal of responsibility. You must be willing and prepared to provide your pet with shelter, food, training, and affection. With proper attention and care, your pet will become a loving member of the family and a sociable companion to be enjoyed for many years to come.

Advance Preparation

The moment you decide to become the owner of a German Shepherd puppy is not one second too soon to start planning for the new family member in order to make the transition period more pleasant for yourself, your household, and the puppy.

The first step in preparation is a bed for that puppy and a place where you can pen him up for rest periods. I am a firm believer that every dog should have a crate of its own right from the very beginning. This will fill both of the previously mentioned requirements, and the puppy will come to know and love this crate as his special haven. Crates are ideal, for when you want the puppy to be free, the crate door stays open. At other times, you securely latch it and know that the puppy is safe from harm, comfortable, and out of mischief. If you plan to travel with your dog, his crate comes along in the car; and, of course, to travel by plane, the dog must be put in a crate. If you show your dog, or take him to obedience trials, what better place to keep him when you are not working with him than in his crate? No matter how you look at it, a crate is a very sensible, sound investment in your puppy's comfort, well being, and safety—not to mention your own peace of mind.

The crates we prefer are the sturdy wooden ones with removable side panels. These wooden crates are excellent for cold weather, with the panels in place, and they work equally well for hot weather when the solid panels are removed, leaving just the wire sides for better ventilation. Crates made entirely of wire are all right in the summer, but they provide no protection from drafts or winter chills. I intensely dislike solid aluminum crates due to the manner in which aluminum reflects surrounding temperatures. If it is cold, so is the metal of the crate. If it is hot, that too is reflected, sometimes to the point that one's fingers can be burnt when handling it. For this reason I consider them unsuitable.

When you choose the puppy's crate, be certain that it is roomy enough not to be outgrown as your Shepherd matures. He should have sufficient height in which to stand up comfortably and sufficient area to stretch out full length when relaxed. When the puppy is young, give him shredded newspapers as his first bed. In time, the newspapers can be replaced with a mat or turkish towels. Carpet remnants are great for the bottom of the crate as they are inexpensive and in case of accidents can be easily replaced. Once the dog has matured past the chewing stage, a pillow or a blanket for something soft and comfortable is an appreciated luxury in the crate.

Sharing importance with the crate is a safe area where the puppy can exercise and play. If you are an apartment-dweller, a baby's playpen works well for a young puppy and a portable exercise pen (which will come in handy if you show your dog) is good for a mature dog. If you have a yard of your own, then the fenced area in which he can stay outdoors safely should be ready and waiting upon his arrival. It does not need to be a vast area, but it should have shade and be secure. Do have the fenced area planned and installed *before* bringing the puppy home if you possibly can do so; this is far more sensible than putting it off until a tragedy occurs. If you have close neighbors, stockade fencing works out well, as then the neighbors are less aware of the dog and the dog cannot see and bark at every-

This seven-month-old puppy has a proud heritage. Hermsdorf's Joy is by Can. Grand Victor Ch. and Am. Ch. Hermsdorf's Eldorado ex Can. Select and Futurity Victor and Young Dog Siegerin Carissima's La Davina. Hermsdorf Kennels, owners, Peter and Bruni Zylberstein, Ontario.

This handsome youngster is Bow Creek's Camelot, by Ch. Tannenwald's Igor, at ten months of age. Photo courtesy of Ken Rayner.

thing that passes near the area. If you live in the country, then regular chain-link fencing is fine. To eliminate the possibility of the German Shepherd jumping the fence when he matures, the fence should be six feet high. As an absolute guarantee that a dog cannot dig his way out under the fence, an edging of cinder blocks tight against the inside bottom of it is very practical protection. If there is an outside gate, a key and padlock are a *must* and should be *used at all times.* You do not want to have the puppy or dog set free in your absence either purposely or through carelessness. I have seen people go through a fence and then just leave the gate ajar. So for safety's sake, keep the gate locked so that only someone responsible has access to its opening.

The ultimate convenience, of course, is if there is a door in your house situated so that the fence can be installed around it, thereby doing away with the necessity for an outside gate. This arrangement is ideal, because then you need never be worried about the gate being left unlatched. This arrangement will be particularly appreciated during bad weather when, instead of escorting the dog to wherever his fenced yard is, you simply open the house door and he exits directly into his safe yard.

If you have only one dog, however, do not feel that he will get sufficient exercise in the fenced area; most dogs just sit there when they're alone. Two or more dogs will play and move them-

"Just thinking." Three-month-old Abby vom Linderhof, owned by Valerie D. Mee, in a pensive mood.

the latter found as soup bones at most butcher shops or supermarkets) are safe and provide many hours of happy entertainment, at the same time being great exercise during the teething period. Rawhide chews can be safe, too, if made under the proper conditions. There was a problem, however, several years back owing to the chemicals with which some of the rawhide chew products had been treated, so in order to take no chances, avoid them. Also avoid plastic and rubber toys, *particularly* toys with squeakers. If you want to play ball with your Shepherd, select a ball that has been made of very tough construction; Shepherds have strong jaws. Even then do not leave the ball with the puppy alone; take it with you when you finish the game. There are also some nice "tug of war" toys which are fun when you play with the dog. But again, do not go off and leave them to be chewed in privacy.

Imp-Cen's Golden Horizon at three months of age. Imp-Cen Kennels, owned by the Hallidays.

selves around; but from my own experience, one dog by himself does little more than make a leisurely tour once around the area and then lie down. You must include a daily walk or two in your plans if your puppy is to be rugged and well.

When you go to pick up your Shepherd, you should take a collar and lead with you. Both of these should be appropriate for the breed and age of the dog, and the collar should be one that fits him now, not one he has to grow into. Your new Shepherd also needs a water dish (or two, one for the house and one for outside) and a food dish. These should preferably be made from an unbreakable material. You will have fun shopping at your local pet shop for these things, and I am sure you will be tempted to add some luxury items of which you will find a fascinating array. For chew things, either Nylabone or real beef bones (leg or knuckle cut to an appropriate size,

Janet Churchill holds a lovely seven-week-old German Shepherd puppy, Halstor's Lola of Rock Maple, C.D.

Joining the Family

Remember that as exciting and happy as the occasion may be for you, the puppy's move from his place of birth to your home can be a traumatic experience for him. His mother and littermates will be missed. He will perhaps be slightly frightened or awed by the change of surroundings. The person he trusted and depended on will be gone. Everything, thus, should be planned to make the move easy for him, to give him confidence, to make him realize that yours is a pretty nice place to be after all.

Never bring a puppy home on a holiday. There just is too much going on, with people and gifts and excitement. If he is honoring "an occasion" (a birthday, for example), work it out so that his arrival will be a few days before or, better still, a few days after the big occasion. Then he will be greeted by a normal routine and will have your undivided attention. Try not to bring the puppy home during the evening. Early morning is the ideal time, as then he has the opportunity of getting acquainted, and the first strangeness wears off before bedtime. You will find it a more peaceful night that way, I am sure. Allow the puppy to investigate his surroundings under your watchful eye. If you already have a pet in the household, carefully watch that things

Too many changes all at once can be difficult for a puppy. Therefore, no matter how you eventually wind up doing it, for the first few days keep him as nearly as you can on the routine to which he is accustomed. Find out what brand of food the breeder used, how frequently and when the puppies were fed, and start out by doing it that way yourself, gradually over a period of a week or two making whatever changes suit you better.

Of utmost precedence in planning for your puppy is the selection of a good veterinarian whom you feel you can trust. Make an appointment to bring the puppy in to be checked over on your way home from the breeder's. Be sure to obtain the puppy's health certificate from the breeder, along with information regarding worming, shots, and so on.

With all of these things in order, you should be nicely prepared for a smooth, happy start when your puppy actually joins the family.

Judy Teidel owns this attractive puppy saying "Merry Christmas" with a very pretty little girl.

are going smoothly between them, so that the relationship gets off to a friendly start; otherwise, you may quickly have a lasting problem. Be careful not to let your older pet become jealous by paying more attention to the newcomer than to him. You want a friendly start. Much of the future attitude of each toward the other depends on what takes place that first day.

If you have children, again, it is important that the relationship start out well. Should the puppy be their first pet, it is assumed that you have prepared them for it with a firm explanation that puppies are living creatures to be treated with gentle consideration, not playthings to be abused and hurt. One of my friends raised her children with the household rule that should a dog or puppy belonging to one of the children bite one of the children, the child would be punished, not the dog, as Mother would know that the child had in some way hurt the dog. I must say that this strategy worked out very well, as no child was ever bitten in that household and both daughters grew up to remain great animal

Bergluft's "A" litter at seven weeks old. German Shepherd puppies bred and owned by Dorit S. Rogers.

Basko v. Bergluft, C.D., with a young friend. Mrs. Dorit S. Rogers, owner.

lovers. Anyway, on whatever terms you do it, please bring your children up not only to *love* but also to *respect* their pet, with the realization that dogs have rights, too. These same ground rules should also apply to visiting children. I have seen youngsters who are fine with their own pets unmercifully tease and harass pets belonging to other people. Children do not always realize how rough is too rough, and without intending to, they may inflict considerable pain or injury if permitted to ride herd on a puppy.

If you start out by spoiling your new puppy, your puppy will expect and even demand that you continue to spoil it in the future. So think it out carefully before you invite the puppy to come spend its first night at your home in bed with you, unless you wish to continue the practice. What you had considered to be a one-night stand may be accepted as just great and expected for the future. It is better not to start what you may consider to be bad habits which you may find difficult to overcome later. Be firm with the puppy, strike a routine, and stick to it. The puppy will learn more quickly this way, and everyone will be happier as a result.

Socialization and Training

Socialization and training of your new baby Shepherd actually starts the second you walk in the door with him, for every move you make should be geared toward teaching the puppy what is expected of him and, at the same time, building up his confidence and feeling of being at home.

The first step is to teach the puppy his name and to come when called by it. No matter how flowery or long or impressive the actual registered name may be, the puppy should also have a short, easily understood "call name" which can be learned quickly and to which he will respond. Start using this call name immediately, and use it in exactly the same way each time that you address the puppy, refraining from the temptation to alternate various forms of endearment, pet names, or substitutes which will only be confusing to him.

Using his name clearly, call the puppy over to you when you see him awake and looking about for something to do. Just a few times of this, with a lot of praise over what a "good dog" he is when he responds, and you will have taught him to come to you when he hears his name; he

Ch. Cobert's Just Jollie of Lakeside and Wulfie at home with Dr. Eugen Grabscheid. Photo courtesy of Connie Beckhardt.

knows that he will be warmly greeted, petted, and possibly even be given a small snack.

As soon as the puppy has spent a few hours getting acquainted with his new surroundings, you can put a light collar on the puppy's neck, so that he will become accustomed to having it on. He may hardly notice it, or he may make a great fuss at first, rolling over, struggling, and trying to rub it off. Have a tasty tidbit or two on hand with which to divert his attention at this period, or try to divert his attention by playing with him. Soon he no longer will be concerned about that strange new thing around his neck.

The next step in training is to have the puppy become accustomed to the lead. Use a lightweight lead, attached to the collar. Carry him outdoors where there will be things of interest to investigate; then set him down and see what happens. Again, he may appear hardly to notice the lead dangling behind him, or he may make a fuss about it. If the latter occurs, repeat the diversion attempts with food or a toy. As soon as the puppy has accepted the presence of the lead, pick up the end of it and follow after him. He may react by trying to free himself, struggling to slip his head through the collar, or trying to bite at the lead. Coax him, if you can, with kind words and petting. In a few moments, curiosity regarding his surroundings and an interesting smell or two should start diverting him. When this takes place, do not try at first to pull on him or guide

German Shepherd puppies, by Ch. Carlo von der Hardtperle ex Halstor's Lola of Rock Maple, C.D., playing on the lawn. Bred by their owner, Jan Churchill.

his direction. Just be glad that he is walking with the lead on and let him decide where to go. When he no longer seems to resent the lead, try gently to direct him with short little tugs in the direction you would like him to travel. Never jerk him roughly, as then he will become frightened and fight harder; and never pull steadily or attempt to drag him, as this immediately triggers a battle of wills with each of you pulling in an opposite direction. The best method is a short, quick, gentle jerk, which, repeated a few times, should get him started off with you. Of course, continue to talk encouragingly to him and offer him "goodies" until he gets started. Repetition of the command "Come" should accompany all of this.

Once this step has been mastered and walks are taken on the lead pleasantly and companionably, the next step is to teach him to remain on your left-hand side. Use the same process as you used to teach him to respond correctly while on the lead, this time repeating the word "Heel." Of course, all of this is not accomplished in one day; it should be done gradually, with short work periods each time, letting the puppy know when he pleases you. The exact length of time required for each puppy varies and depends on the aptitude of each individual puppy.

Housebreaking a puppy is more easily accomplished by the prevention method than by the cure. Try to avoid "accidents" whenever you can rather than punishing the puppy once

Ch. Lakeside's Chico moving out on the lead. A son of Ch. Lakeside's Gilligan's Island owned by Daniel Dwier. Photo courtesy of Sharon Dwier.

Proven Hills Young Toma, at nine weeks of age, with the somewhat guilty look of having been caught while up to mischief. Judy Teidel, owner.

they have occurred. Common sense helps a great deal. A puppy will need to be taken out at regularly spaced intervals: first thing in the morning directly from his bed, immediately after meals, after he has napped, or whenever you notice that he is "looking for a spot." Choose roughly the same place outdoors each time that you take the puppy out for this purpose, so that a pattern will be established. If he does not go immediately, do not just return him to the house as chances are that he will go the moment he is back inside. Try to be patient and remain out with him until you get results; then praise him enthusiastically and both of you can return indoors. If you catch the puppy having an "accident," pick him up firmly, sharply say, "No!" and rush him outside. If you do not see the accident occur, there is little point of doing anything beyond cleaning it up, as once it has happened and been forgotten, the puppy will likely not even realize why you are angry with him.

Your Shepherd puppy should form the habit of spending a certain amount of time each day in his crate, even when you are home. Sometimes the puppy will do this voluntarily, but if not, he should be taught to do so. Lead the puppy by the collar over to the crate, and then gently push him inside firmly saying "Down" or "Stay" as you fasten the door. Whatever command you use, always make it the same word for each act every time. Repetition is the big thing in training, and the dog must learn to associate a specific word or phrase with each different thing he is expected to do. When you mean "Sit," always say exactly that. "Stay" should mean that the dog should remain where he was when you gave the command. "Down" means something else again. Do not confuse the dog by shuffling the commands, as you will create confusion for him and a problem for yourself by having done so.

As soon as he has received his immunization shots, take your Shepherd puppy with you wherever and whenever possible. Nothing else can equal this close association for building up self-confidence and stability in a young dog. It is extremely important that you spend the time necessary for socialization, particularly if you are planning on the puppy becoming a show dog.

Take your Shepherd in the car, so that he will learn to enjoy riding without becoming carsick, as can happen to a dog unused to the car's motion. Take him everywhere you go, provided you are certain he will not be unwelcome or create any difficulties by his presence: visiting friends

Spenrock Buccaneer, by Ch. Carlo von Hardtperle ex Halstor's Lola of Rock Maple, C.D., relaxes at home. Bred and owned by Jan Churchill, Spenrock Kennels, Chesapeake City, Maryland.

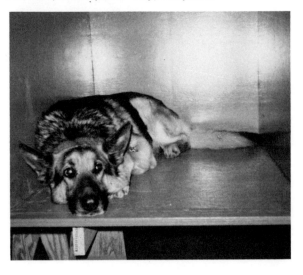

and relatives (if they like dogs and do not have house pets of their own who will consider your puppy an intruder), to busy shopping centers (always keeping him on his lead), or just walking around the streets of your town. If someone admires him, as always seems to happen under these circumstances, encourage that person to pet or talk with him; becoming accustomed to people in this manner always seems especially beneficial in instilling self-confidence. You want your puppy to develop a relaxed, happy canine personality and like the world and its inhabitants. The most debilitating thing for a puppy's self-confidence is excessive sheltering and pampering. Keeping a growing puppy always away from strange people and strange dogs may well turn him into a nervous, neurotic dog—surely the last thing anyone can enjoy as a pet.

Make obedience training a game with your puppy while he is extremely young. Try to teach him the meaning of and expected responses to the basic terms such as "Come," "Stay," "Sit," "Down," and "Heel," along with the meaning of "No" even while he is still too young for formal training, and you will be pleased and proud of the good manners that he will exhibit.

German Shepherds bask in being petted and appreciated by their owners. This is Angus of Rock Maple, by Grayarlin's Pierrot from Grayarlin's X-Etta, bred by Jan Churchill and owned by Julian B. Heron, Jr., in February 1962.

Hessians Quella as a puppy. Note the beautiful balance of this great bitch even at so early an age. Art and Helen Hess, owners, Hessian Kennels.

Feeding

There was a time when providing good, nourishing food for our dogs involved a far more complicated routine and time-consuming process than people now feel is necessary. The old belief was that the daily rations should consist of fresh beef, vegetables, cereal, egg yolks, and cottage cheese as basics, with such additions as brewer's yeast and other vitamin supplements.

During recent years, however, many attitudes have been changed regarding the necessity, or even the desirability, of this procedure. We still give eggs, cottage cheese, and supplements to the diet, but the basic methods of feeding dogs have changed; and the changes are definitely for the better in the opinion of many an authority. The school of thought now is that you are doing your dogs a definite service when you feed them some of the fine commercially prepared dog foods in preference to your own home-cooked concoctions.

The reasoning behind this new outlook is easy to understand. The production of dog food has grown to be a major industry, participated in by some of the best known, most highly respected names in the dog fancy. These trusted firms do turn out excellent products. People are feeding their dogs these preparations with confidence, and the dogs are thriving, prospering, and keeping in top condition. What more could we want or ask?

There are at least a half dozen absolutely splendid dry foods which can be mixed with water or broth and served to your dog, either "as is" or with the addition of fresh or canned meat. There is a variety of canned meat preparations for your dog, either 100% meat to be mixed with kibble or complete prepared dinners, a combination of both meat and cereal. There are several kinds of "convenience foods," these in packets which you open and dump out into the dog's dish. It is just that simple. The "convenience foods" are neat and easy for you when travelling, but generally speaking we prefer to feed a dry food mixed with hot water, to which we usually add canned meat (although leftover meat scraps or ground beef are sometimes added instead of the canned meat.) Actually we feel that the canned meat, with its added fortifiers, is more beneficial to

the dogs than the fresh meat. However, the two can be used alternately or, if you prefer and your dogs do well on it, by all means use ground beef.

Dogs enjoy variety in the meat part of their diet, which is easy to provide with the canned meat. The canned meats available include all sorts of beef (chunk, ground, stewed, and so on), lamb, chicken, liver, and numerous concoctions of several of these blended together.

There also is prepared food geared to every age bracket of your dog's life, from puppyhood on through old age, with special additions or modifications to make it especially nourishing and beneficial. The dogs of yesteryear never had it so good during the canine dinner hour because these foods are tasty and geared to meet the dog's gastronomical approval.

Additionally, contents and nutritional values are clearly listed on the labels, and careful instructions for feeding exactly the right amount for the size and weight of each dog are also given.

With the great choice of dog foods available today, we do not feel that the addition of vitamins is necessary; but if you do, there are several highly satisfactory vitamin products available at pet shops. These products serve as tasty treats along with being beneficial.

Ravenhaus Noah in 1975, who lives happily in a suburban neighborhood and brings great joy to his family.

These good friends are Halstor's Lola of Rock Maple, C.D., and an English Foxhound puppy, both owned by Janet Churchill.

320

Grand Victor Ch. Lance of Fran-Jo, ROM, relaxes after a busy day hosting a holiday party at the home of his owners, Joan and Fran Ford.

An informal photo of the great producing bitch Cobert's Melissa, ROM. Courtesy of Sharon Dwier.

Of course there is no reason not to cook up something for your German Shepherd's dinner if you would feel happier doing so, but it seems to us superfluous when such truly satisfying rations are available at so much less expense and trouble.

How often you feed is a matter of how a schedule works out best for you and for your dog or dogs. Many owners prefer to feed their dogs once a day. Others feel that twice daily is better for the digestion and more satisfying to the dog, particularly if he is a family member who stands around and watches the preparation of family meals. The important thing is that you *do not overfeed*, as overfeeding can bring on many canine problems.

From the time your puppy is fully weaned until he reaches about twelve weeks of age, he should be fed four times daily. His breakfast and his dinner should consist of about two to two and a half cups of moistened puppy kibble to which about one cup (slightly more if necessary to soften) of hot water or broth has been added, mixed with either a quarter-pound of fresh ground beef or a quarter-can of canned beef (these amounts are approximate as there is no

harm in slightly more of the beef and a bit less kibble if you prefer). At noontime and at bedtime the puppy should be given one can of evaporated milk mixed with one can of slightly warmed water.

As the puppy grows older, from three to six months of age, cut back to three meals daily, substituting the milk meals with a meal of meat and kibble. If the puppy cleans his dish with gusto and is not putting on too much weight, you will know the amount of food is right for him. If he is starting to look chubby, cut back a bit on the amount; you do not want your puppy to be fat. Too much weight can be overburdening on growing limbs and muscles and can also result in a sagging topline. So do guard against it. If the puppy is eating up everything but looking thin, slightly increase the amount of food, as he may not be getting all he needs. At six months of age, the pup should be fed twice daily, and at twelve months, if you wish, you may cut back to one daily feeding with a biscuit or two morning and evening. If you do feed just once daily, the meal should be given by early afternoon. Don't forget to have the puppy checked regularly for worms and to keep a watchful eye. Each puppy is an individual and needs to be treated as such.

Remember that fresh, cool water should always be available for your Shepherd. This is of utmost importance to his good health throughout his lifetime.

321

Ch. Gech Nerder Sachenstolz poses for a most beautiful head-study of a German Shepherd. Photo courtesy of Mrs. Denise Kodner.

CHAPTER THIRTEEN

Grooming Your German Shepherd Dog

Can. Grand Victor, Am. and Can. Ch. Hessians Caribe gained his Grand Victor title under a judge from Germany and is a fine representative of the breeding program at this famous kennel. He is a son of Select Ch. Hessians Baldur, ROM, ex Hessians Quella, ROM, she also the dam of U.S. Grand Victrix Ch. Hessians Vogue, ROM.

Keeping a German Shepherd's coat in good, healthy, lustrous, and obviously well cared for condition is really not too difficult a task. It can best be accomplished by a regimen of daily grooming, to which only a few minutes need be given each time, rather than by "crash grooming" at the last moment just before you plan to show the dog. If the coat is always well cared for, there should be little or no problem when show days roll around. And even if you do not show your dog, is it not a pleasure to have him looking his best rather than unkempt and raggedy?

As a double-coated breed, the German Shepherd's body is covered with a soft, dense, water-repellent undercoat which will vary in density according to the season of the year, weather conditions, and the climate in which you live. This undercoat serves as the dog's protection from heat or cold (insulating him against extremes in temperature either way); keeps rain, snow, and sleet from reaching his skin; and even serves to protect against many types of insects. Through this undercoat grows a second coat, the outercoat, which is of an entirely different texture, being harsh to the touch (sometimes even slightly wiry), preferably perfectly straight and lying flat to the body (although a slightly wavy outercoat, sometimes of wiry texture, is not to be penalized), and ranging in length between an inch and a half and two inches and a half, the latter preferred but length in excess of that undesirable.

Thicker, longer hair covers the neck and is more profuse on the hips and tail of a German Shepherd. There is also a longer, almost fringe-like growth of hair extending down the back of the legs, to the pastern on the forelegs and to the hock on the rear.

The head (including insides of ears), front and sides of legs, and paws are covered with short hair.

Since faults in evaluating a German Shepherd's coat include complete lack of undercoat; too soft, silky, or long (more than 2½ inches) an outercoat; and a coat that is "curly" as opposed to "slightly wavy" or too open a coat, certain precautions should be taken in the method of caring for your dog's coat.

First of all, moderation should be exercised in taking out the undercoat too strenuously, lest you find yourself with a temporarily flat-coated

This beautiful Shepherd is Ch. Ingo of La Salle, owned by La Salle Kennels. Photo courtesy of Denise Kodner.

removal of it will cause the outer coat to lie too flat against the dog, perhaps giving the impression that he does not normally carry a coat that is correct.

Instructions for bathing your dog are given in another chapter, and these instructions should be followed when you feel a bath is necessary. If you must bathe the dog prior to showing him, a day or two in advance is better than at the last moment as it gives the coat's natural luster and oils a chance to replace themselves. Should you wish to do so, there are various hair pomades which may be successfully used—but just very lightly to give a sheen, not so much as to create a sticky or greasy appearance or to come off on the judge's hands.

I am one of the people who believes that dogs should be bathed only when absolutely necessary, as frequent baths definitely will soften the texture of the outercoat. Usually a good rubdown with a Turkish towel whenever the dog comes in wet, a daily brushing with a quality hair brush, and a light combing daily should

Ch. Van Cleve's Colombo, son of Ch. Cobert's Reno of Lakeside, ROM, is one of the handsome German Shepherds owned by Van Cleve Kennels, Dr. and Mrs. Carmen L. Battaglia.

dog. The only time a Shepherd's coat should be seriously raked out with a fine tooth comb or other implement intended for this purpose should be at the "blowing of the coat" period. This comes usually once during the year in double-coated breeds (although sometimes more frequently depending on the dog living in areas of sharp temperature changes) and is easily recognizable by the fact that the dog will literally throw off clumps of the undercoat, to the extent that they can be removed with the fingers. Then it is wisest to get it over with as quickly as possible by stripping out the undercoat until this copious shedding has ended (usually a matter of a few days). This stripping encourages faster replacement. Also if the loose hair is permitted to just sit there, it causes the skin to itch and you may find your dog scratching these spots, or biting at himself, creating a sore and uncomfortable condition.

At periods other than during the shedding season, do be cautious about stripping out undercoat, for while it will grow in again, over-

A lovely photo by Jim Robinson of Ch. Jonlyn's Samantha. Samantha is owned by Jonlyn Kennels, John J. Berry.

keep your Shepherd clean, tidy, and at his handsome best.

Remember that if your dog comes in muddy, one of the easiest ways to clean the dog up is to let the mud dry and then brush it out of the coat.

Grooming tools should include an ordinary metal comb for just routine combing to clean the coat, a good quality bristle brush (one with a stiff bristle will do the best job) for daily use, a "grooming mitt" for a final rubdown when the job is finished, and an appropriate stripping comb or rake-like instrument for aiding in the periodic changing of the undercoat. Also, if yours is a show dog, a pair of curved scissors should be part of your equipment for trimming whiskers and eyebrows (which are removed for the show ring) or any other necessity which may demand the use of scissors.

Leuchtag's Happy of Ingomar, by Am. and Can. Ch. Lance of Fran-Jo, ROM, ex Ch. Yasmin of Stahl Farm. Breeders, Diana Riddle and Sarah L. Leughtag; owner, Diana Riddle, Ingomar Kennels, Zelienople, Pennsylvania.

Keeping the toenails neat and of a respectable length is another important part of grooming, and this should be attended to at least on a monthly basis or whenever the dog's nails appear too long. While some dogs, if they exercise consistently on cement, seem to keep toenail growth under control, the majority do not and for the well-being of such dogs the job must be done for them. Neglect here can cause lameness, sore feet, and a breaking down or splay foot condition; and at the very least, long hooks on a dog's toes are unattractive and turn the judge off quite promptly.

There are two ways of caring for your dog's nails: either with a nail clipper especially manu-

Ch. Harry Luftigen Hoe He making another fine win with Gerlinde Hockla. Edward Legee and Alfred Espinosa own this famous winning Shepherd.

Moiaussis Flirt of Fritzlund, by Ch. Treffer of Clover Acres ex Brunhilda of Fritzlund, winning at National Capital in 1979. Bred by Charles Fritz, owned by Jean Reagan, and handled by Ken Rayner.

Echo Knoll's Satan (above), owned by Zell Dee Kennels, and Echo Knoll's Stardust (below), owned by Harry Broderson, both by Ch. Treffer of Clover Acres. Photos courtesy of the Rayners.

Ch. Winooska of Ingomar, by Grand Victor Ch. Caesar von Carahaus, ROM, ex Select Ch. Nootka of Ingomar. Bred and owned by Diana Riddle and Jerome W. Rozanski.

factured for this purpose and on sale at your pet suppliers or with an electric nail grinder which files the nails quickly to a smooth finish. If you use the clipper, it is usually necessary to smooth the nails off with a metal nail file. But some dogs object to the noise made by the electric grinder, and some owners feel that they have better control over clippers. Whichever your choice, the important thing is that the nails are not neglected. Be careful not to cut or grind down into the quick (close examination will usually show you where it ends); but should an accident occur, have on hand some styptic powder with which to touch the tip of the nail should bleeding occur, as it will stop bleeding and pain almost instantly.

Teeth, too, should be watched and cleaned whenever necessary. Hard dog biscuits, Nylabones, or beef bones can help with this cleaning process; but the teeth should be checked on a weekly basis. When tartar is seen it should be removed either by yourself or by your veterinarian with a scraper made for this purpose. Do not permit tartar to build up.

Valrech Naida, one of the splendid German Shepherds owned by Val Wells.

This is Ch. Sabra Dennis of Gan Edan, whose titles include American and Canadian Grand Victor, Canadian Sieger, and American Maturity Victor and who was bred and owned by Mimi Saltz.

CHAPTER FOURTEEN

Showing Your German Shepherd Dog

Proven Hill's Kandy Man, Best in Mid-Western Futurity, 1974. Judy Teidel, owner.

The groundwork for showing your German Shepherd Dog has been accomplished with your careful selection and purchase of your future show prospect. If it is a puppy, we assume that you have gone through all the proper preliminaries of good care, which actually should be the same whether the puppy is a pet or a future show dog, with a few extra precautions in the case of the latter.

General Considerations

Remember that a winning dog must be kept in trim, top condition. You want him neither too fat nor too thin, so do not spoil his figure and his appearance, or his appetite for proper nourishing food, by allowing family members or guests to be constantly feeding him "goodies." The best "treat" of all is a small wad of ground raw beef or one of the packaged dog "goodies." To be avoided are ice cream, potato chips, cookies, cake, candy, and other fattening items which will cause the dog to gain weight. A dog in show condition must never be fat, nor must he be painfully thin to the point of his ribs fairly sticking through the skin.

The importance of temperament and showmanship cannot possibly be overemphasized. These two qualities have put many a mediocre dog across, while lack of them can ruin the career of an otherwise outstanding specimen. So, from the day your dog or puppy arrives home, socialize him. Keep him accustomed to being with people and to being handled by people. Encourage your friends and relatives to "go over" him as the judges will in the ring, so that at the shows this will not be a strange, upsetting experience. Practice showing his "bite" (the manner in which his teeth meet) deftly and quickly. It is quite simple to spread the lips apart with your fingers, and the puppy should be accustomed and willing to accept this from you or from the judge, without struggle. The puppy should also be accustomed to having his jaws opened wide in order for his teeth to be counted, since missing teeth, if other than premolars, is a serious fault. Some judges ask the exhibitors to handle the mouths, showing them bite and jaws, rather than doing it themselves. These are the considerate judges who prefer not to risk spreading any possible virus infections by taking their hands from one dog's mouth to another's; but the old-fashioned judges still persist in doing the latter, so the dog should be prepared for either.

Take your future show dog with you in the car, so that he will love riding and not become carsick when he travels. He should associate going in the car with pleasure and attention. Take him where it is crowded: downtown, shopping malls, or, in fact, anywhere you go where dogs are permitted. Make the expeditions fun for him by frequent petting and words of praise; do not just ignore him as you go about your errands or other business.

Do not overly shelter your future show dog. Instinctively you may want to keep him at home, especially while a young puppy, where he is safe from germs or danger; but this can be foolish on two counts. To begin with, a dog kept away from other dogs or other environments builds up no natural immunity against all the things with which he will come in contact at the dog shows. Actually it is wiser to keep him well up-to-date on all protective "shots" and then allow him to become accustomed to being among other dogs and dog owners. Also, a dog who never goes among people, to strange places, or among strange dogs, may grow up with a timidity of spirit that will cause you deep problems when his show career gets under way.

Ch. Job of Gan Edan, a son of Ch. Gabriel of Gan Edan (Ch. Beau of Fran-Jo, ROM, ex Bee Jay's Holiday of Gan Edan, ROM) ex Dawn, ROM, owned by Gan Edan Kennels, Art and Mimi Saltz.

Tannenwald's Ukon, by Ch. Tannenwald's Igor, pictured with Ken Rayner.

Keep your German Shepherd's coat in immaculate condition with daily grooming (which takes only a few minutes) and baths when they latter are necessary. For the latter, use a mild baby shampoo or whatever the person who bred your puppy may suggest. Several of the "brand name" products do an excellent job, and there are several which are beneficial toward keeping the dog free of fleas. Look for them at your pet supplier's. Be sure to rinse the dog thoroughly, leaving no traces of soap which may cause itching or skin irritation. It is a wise precaution to put a drop of castor oil in each eye to ensure no soap irritation. Use warm water (be sure it is not uncomfortably hot or chillingly cold) and a good spray. An electric hair dryer is a great convenience; use it after first blotting off the excess moisture with a Turkish towel. Do not let water find its way into the ear cavity. A wad of cotton in the ear guards against this possibility. Toenails also should be watched and trimmed every few weeks. It is important not to let nails grow too long as they can become painful and ruin the appearance of foot and pastern.

Assuming that you will be handling the dog personally, or even if he will be professionally handled, it is important that a few moments of each day be spent practicing dog show routine. Practice "stacking," or "setting him up," as you have seen the exhibitors do at the shows you've

Ch. Yasmin of Stahl Farm, by Ch. Bernd vom Kallengarten, ROM, ex Ch. Zara of Stahl Farm. Bred by Bernice D. Stahl and Sarah L. Kling; owned by Diana Riddle and Sarah L. Kling.

attended, and teach him to hold this position once you have him stacked to your satisfaction. Make the learning pleasant by being firm but lavish in your praise when he behaves correctly. Work in front of a mirror for setting up practice; this enables you to see the dog as the judge does and to learn what corrections need to be made by looking at the dog from that angle.

Teach your Shepherd to gait at your side, or moving out ahead of you as his learning progresses, on a loose lead. Since Shepherds are judged largely on movement, and this is so important a part of the total dog, showing a Shepherd is somewhat different from showing many other breeds. While, generally, exhibitors are advised to move their dogs at a moderate gait, Shepherd exhibitors are expected to move their dogs out freely, without restriction, on a long lead and in front of the handler. When you have mastered the basic essentials at home, then look for and join a training class for future work and polishing up your technique. Training classes are sponsored by show-giving clubs in many areas, and their popularity is steadily increasing. If you have no other way of locating one, perhaps your veterinarian may know of one through some of his clients; but if you are sufficiently aware of the dog show world to want a show dog, you will probably be personally acquainted with other fanciers who will share information of this sort with you.

Accustom your show dog to being in a crate (which you should be doing, even if the dog is to be only a pet). He should be kept in the crate "between times" for his own well-being and safety.

A show dog's teeth must be kept clean and free of tartar. Hard dog biscuits can help toward this. If tartar does accumulate, see that it is removed promptly by your veterinarian. Bones are not suitable for show dogs once they have their second teeth as they tend to damage and wear down the tooth enamel (bones are all right for puppies, as they help with the teething process).

Beyond these special considerations, your show-prospect Shepherd will thrive under the same treatment as accorded any well-cared-for family pet. In fact, most of the foregoing is applicable to a pet Shepherd as well as to a show Shepherd, for what it boils down to is simply keeping the dog at his best.

Echo Knoll's Disco Kid (above), owned by Harry Broderson, and Echo Knoll's Sundance Kid (below), owned by Joe Olivo, both by Ch. Treffer of Clover Acres. Photos courtesy of the Rayners.

Echo Knoll's Sonic, by Ch. Treffer of Clover Acres. Sagendorf, owner. Photo courtesy of the Rayners.

Ingo of La Salle, owned by La Salle Kennels. Photo courtesy of Denise Kodner.

Match Shows

Your German Shepherd's first experience in show ring procedure should be at match show competition. There are several reasons for this. First of all, this type of event is intended as a learning experience for both the puppies and for the exhibitors; thus you will feel no embarrassment if your puppy misbehaves or if your own handling technique is obviously inept. There will be many others in that same position. So take the puppy and go, and the two of you can learn together what it is like actually to compete against other dogs for the approval of the judge.

Another reason for beginning a show career at match shows is the matter of cost. Entries at the point shows nowadays cost over ten dollars. True, there are many clubs who reduce this fee by a few dollars for the Puppy Classes (but by no means do all of them), but even so it is silly to throw this amount away when you know full well your puppy will not yet have the ring presence to hold his own. For the match shows, on the other hand, the entry fee is usually less than five dollars, so using those shows as a learning ground for you and your puppy certainly makes better sense. Another advantage of match shows is that advance entries for them are seldom necessary, and even those clubs having them usually will accept additional entries the morning of the show. If you wake up feeling like

Spenrock Buccaneer, by Ch. Carlo von der Hardperle ex Halstor's Lola of Rock Maple, C.D., at eight months of age winning Best in Match at the Blue Ridge Kennel Club in 1966. Judge, Marie Moore. Breeder-owner-handler, Janet Churchill, Spenrock Kennels.

Astarte of Rellini, belonging to Kay Miller, at Greater Lowell Dog Show in 1968. Photo courtesy of Gerlinde Hockla.

taking the puppy for an outing, you can go right ahead. The entries at point shows, however, close about two and a half weeks in advance.

You will find the judges more willing to discuss your puppy with you at a match show than during the day of a full and hectic point show; one of their functions, when officiating at a match, is to help new exhibitors with comments and suggestions. We might wish that we could do so at the point shows; but, generally speaking, our schedules do not permit this time to be taken. Unless you stay until the judge's working day is ended, it is often difficult to get even a few words with him. The informality of match shows makes it far easier to get a judge's verbal opinion there; and since judges at these events are usually professional handlers or already licensed judges who are working toward applying for additional breeds, the opinions should be knowledgeable and helpful.

As with training classes, information regarding match shows can be obtained from breeders in your area, your local kennel club if there is one, your veterinarian, or, of course, the person in charge of your training class, if you belong to one. The A.K.C. can also furnish this information; and if your local newspaper carries a pet column, announcements of such coming events will almost certainly appear there.

Kingland's Duke, owned by Mrs. Edwin H. King, Midlothian, Virginia. Handled here in March 1964 by Robert S. Forsyth.

Point Shows

Entries for American Kennel Club licensed or member point shows must be made in advance. This must be done on an official entry blank of the show-giving club and then filed either in person or by mail with the show superintendent (or show secretary) in time to reach the latter's office prior to the published closing date and hour or the filling of the advertised quota. These entries should be written out clearly and carefully, signed by the owner of the dog or his agent (your professional handler), and must be accompanied by the entry fee; otherwise they will not be accepted. Remember, it is not when the entry blank leaves your hands or is postmarked that counts but the time that the entry arrives at its destination. If you are relying on the postal system, bear in mind that it is not always reliable, and waiting until the last moment may cause your entry to arrive too late for acceptance. Leave yourself a bit of leeway by mailing *early*.

A dog must be entered at a dog show in the name of the actual owner at the time of entry closing date for that specific show. If a registered dog has been acquired by a new owner, the dog must be entered in the name of that new owner at any show for which entries close following the date of purchase, regardless of whether or not the new owner has actually received the registration certificate indicating that the dog is registered in the new owner's name. State on the entry form whether or not the transfer application has been mailed to the American Kennel Club, and it goes without saying that the latter should be promptly attended to when you purchase a registered dog.

When you fill out your entry blank, be sure to type, print, or write legibly, paying particular attention to the spelling of names, correct registration numbers, and so on. Sign your name as owner *exactly*—not one time as Jane Doe, another as Jane C. Doe, and another as Mrs. John Doe.

Puppy Classes are for dogs or bitches that are six months of age and under twelve months, were whelped in the United States, and are not champions. The age of a puppy is calculated up to and inclusive of the first day of a show you are entering. For example, the first day a dog whelped on January 1st is eligible to compete in

Ch. Nanhalls Erla, by Ch. Field Marshall of Arbywood, ROM, ex Grand Victrix Ch. Bonnie Bergere of Ken Rose, U.D.T., ROM, winning the Best Puppy award in El Paso during September 1962. Bred by Nanhall Kennels and Dr. Wade Sanders.

Boston Blackie Express, TT-194-GSD, winning the 9-12 Month Puppy Class at the German Shepherd Dog Club of Central Ohio Specialty Show (right) and his Temperament Test Certificate (below). Owned by Mike Szabo, Jr., and Lanalee Jorgensen.

AMERICAN TEMPERAMENT TEST SOCIETY, INC.

CERTIFICATE

This Certifies that This

GERMAN SHEPHERD DOG

owned by MIKE SZABO, JR. & LANALEE JORGENSEN

having completed the requirements for the

TEMPERAMENT TEST

has been officially recorded as

BOSTON BLACKIE EXPRESS, TT-194-GSD

May 25, 1981

AMERICAN TEMPERAMENT TEST SOCIETY, INC.

Ch. Flash of Clover Acres, by Dittmeister's Ernst, C.D., ex Dittmeister's Cherokee. This handsome rich black and tan finished in nine shows, handled by Ken Rayner. Bred and owned by Donna and Paul Murphy.

a Puppy Class at a show is July 1st of the same year; and he may continue competing in Puppy Classes up to and including a show on December 31st of the same year, but he is *not* eligible to compete in a Puppy Class at a show held on or after January 1st of the following year.

The Puppy Class is the first one in which you should enter your puppy, for several reasons. To begin with, a certain allowance for behavior is made in recognition of the fact that they *are* puppies and lack show experience; a puppy who is immature or displays less than perfect ring manners will not be penalized so heavily as would be the case in an adult class such as Open. It is also quite likely that others in the Puppy Class will be suffering from the same puppy problems as your own; all of the puppies will be pretty much on equal footing where age and ring assurance are concerned. A puppy shown in the same class with fully matured Shepherds who are experienced in the show ring looks all the more young

Sarego's Una, by Ch. Tannenwald's Igor, with Ken Rayner.

and inexperienced and thus is far less likely to gain the judge's admiration than in a class where the puppy does not seem out of place. There are many good judges who will take a smashing good puppy right from the Puppy Class on through to Winners, but more often than not, this puppy started the day and was "discovered" by the judge right where it belonged, in the Puppy Class. Another bonus of using Puppy Class is the fact that numerous clubs offer a reduced entry fee to those competing in it; this certainly is beneficial because showing dogs is becoming increasingly expensive.

One word of caution on entering the Puppy Class: carefully check the classification, as in some cases it is divided into a 6-9 months old section and a 9-12 months old section; if this is the case you will have to ascertain that your puppy is entered in the correct section for the age he will be on the day of the show.

The Novice Class is for dogs six months of age and over, whelped in the United States or in Canada, who *prior to* the official closing date for entries have *not* won three first prizes in the Novice Class, any first prize at all in the Bred-by-Exhibitor, American-bred, or Open Classes, or one or more points toward championship. The provisions for this class are confusing to many people, which is probably the reason it is so infrequently used. A dog may win any number of first prizes in the Puppy Class and still retain his eligibility for Novice. He may place second, third, or fourth not only in Novice on an unlimited number of occasions but also in Bred-by-Exhibitor, American-bred, or Open and still remain eligible for Novice. But he may no longer be shown in Novice when he has won three blue ribbons in that class, when he has won even one blue ribbon in either Bred-by-Exhibitor, American-bred, or Open, or even a single championship point.

In determining whether or not a dog is eligible for the Novice Class, keep in mind the fact that previous wins are calculated according to the official published date for closing of entries, not by the date on which you may actually have made the entry. So if, in the interim, between the time you made the entry and the official closing date, your dog makes a win causing it to become ineligible for Novice, change your class *immediately* to another for which your Shepherd will be eligible. The Novice Class always seems to have the fewest entries of any class, and therefore it is a splendid "practice ground" for you and your young Shepherd while you both are getting the "feel" of being in the ring.

Ch. Beine v. Finsternwald taking four points on her way to her title in June 1971 at the Miami German Shepherd Dog Club Specialty. Handled by Herbert S. Kaiser, M.D., for owner Gerlinde Hockla.

Gerlinde Hockla with her handsome homebred dog, Gero v. Finsternwald, winning the Bred-by-Exhibitor Class at the German Shepherd Dog Club of Long Island Specialty, May 1973. The judge is Julius Due.

Ch. Wigar of Clover Acres winning American-bred Dog under judge F. Anderson at the German Shepherd Dog Club of Detroit Specialty, June 1974. Chips Rayner handling for owner Ray Picard of Florida.

Ch. Noon of Ingomar, by Grand Victor Ch. Scorpio of Shiloh Gardens, ROM, ex Leuchtag's Happy of Ingomar, winning American-bred Bitch. Bred by Diana Riddle, co-owner with Jerome W. Rozanski.

338

Bred-by-Exhibitor Class is for dogs whelped in the United States or, if individually registered in the American Kennel Club Stud Book, for dogs whelped in Canada that are six months of age and over, are not champions, and are owned wholly or in part by the person or the spouse of the person who was the breeder or one of the breeders of record. Dogs entered in this class must be handled *in this class* by an owner or by a member of the immediate family of the owner. Members of an immediate family for this purpose are husband, wife, father, mother, son, daughter, brother, or sister. This is the class which is really the "breeder's showcase," the one which breeders should enter with special pride, to show off their achievements. It is *not necessary* for the winner of Bred-by-Exhibitor to be handled by an owner or a member of the owner's family in the Winners Class, where the dog or bitch *may be handled by whomsoever the exhibitor may choose*, including a professional handler.

Ch. Matmar's Pro of Clover Acres, by 1968 Select Number Two Ch. Tannenwald's Igor ex Frolic of Clover Acres (litter-sister to multiple Group-winning Ch. Flash of Clover Acres), at fourteen months of age winning his second major by going Best of Winners from the American-bred Class at the German Shepherd Dog Club of Western New York Specialty in June 1974, judged by Helen A. Polonitza. Bred by D. and P. Murphy, owned by Matis Marcus, and handled by Chips Rayner.

This handsome young Shepherd is Brett of Ingomar, by Ch. Wellspring's Ironsides ex Ch. Nootka of Ingomar. Halfway to his championship as this is written, he should have gained the title by the time you read this. Here he is winning Open Dog at the 1981 Bay State German Shepherd Dog Club Show. Bred by Diana Riddle and Jerome W. Rozanski; owned by Diann C. and Deborah A. Coombs, Kallisto Kennels, Newburyport, Massachusetts.

The American-bred Class is for all dogs excepting champions, six months of age or older, who were whelped in the United States by reason of a mating which took place in the United States.

The Open Class is for any dog six months of age or older (this is the only restriction for this class). Dogs with championship points compete in it; dogs who are already champions can do so; dogs who are imported can be entered; and, of course, American-bred dogs compete in it. This class is, for some strange reason, the favorite of exhibitors who are "out to win." They rush to enter their pointed dogs in it, under the false impression that by so doing they assure themselves of greater attention from the judges. This really is not so; and it is my feeling that to enter in one of the less competitive classes, with a better chance of winning it and then getting a second crack at gaining the judge's approval by returning to the ring in the Winners Class, can often be a more effective strategy.

One does not enter for the Winners Class. One earns the right to compete in it by winning first prize in Puppy, Novice, Bred-by-Exhibitor, American-bred, or Open. No dog who has been defeated on the same day in one of these classes is eligible to compete in Winners, and every dog who has been a blue-ribbon winner in one of them and not defeated in any of the others *must* do so. Following the selection of the Winners Dog or the Winners Bitch, the dog or bitch receiving that award leaves the ring. Then the dog or bitch who placed second in the class, unless previously defeated by another dog or bitch at the same show, re-enters the ring to compete against the remaining first-prize winners for Reserve. The latter award means that the dog or bitch receiving it is standing by "in reserve" should the one that received Winners be disallowed through any technicality when the awards are checked at the American Kennel Club. In that case, the one that placed Reserve is moved up to Winners, at the same time receiving the appropriate championship points.

Winners Dog and Winners Bitch are the awards which carry points toward championship

Ch. Covy-Tucker Hill's Tecate, by Cobert's Sirocco of Windigail, ROM, ex Ch. Covy's Rosita of Tucker Hill, taking Reserve Winners Bitch at the Golden State German Shepherd Dog Club of San Jose Specialty, January 1982. Owned by J. and S. Davenport with breeders Cappy Pottle and Gloria Birch.

Ch. Covy-Tucker Hill's A'Tiffany, by Covy-Tucker Hill's Zinfandel, ROM, ex Covy's Gusty of Tucker Hill, was bred by Cappy Pottle and Gloria F. Birch and is co-owned by them with Hope Moncivais.

with them. The points are based on the number of dogs or bitches actually in competition; and the points are scaled one through five, the latter being the greatest number available to any dog or bitch at any one show. Three-, four-, or five-point wins are considered majors. In order to become a champion, a dog or bitch must win two majors under two different judges, plus at least one point from a third judge, and the additional points necessary to bring the total to fifteen. When your dog has gained fifteen points as described above, a certificate of championship will be issued to you, and your Shepherd's name will be published in the list of new champions which appears monthly in *Pure-Bred Dogs, American Kennel Gazette,* the official publication of the American Kennel Club.

The scale of championship points for each breed is worked out by the American Kennel Club and reviewed annually, at which time the number required in competition may be either changed (raised or lowered) or remain the same. The scale of points for all breeds is published an-

Ch. Lakeside's Gilligan's Island, ROM, by Grand Victor Ch. Lance of Fran-Jo, ROM, ex Cobert's Melissa, ROM, going Winners Dog at the 1969 National Specialty Show under Art Stromety. Photo courtesy of Connie Beckhardt.

nually in the May issue of the *Gazette*, and the current ratings for each breed within that area are published in every dog show catalog.

When a dog or a bitch is adjudged Best of Winners, its championship points are, for that show, compiled on the basis of which sex had the greater number of points. If there are two points in dogs and four in bitches and the dog goes Best of Winners, then *both* the dog and the bitch are awarded an equal number of points, in this case four. Should the Winners Dog or the Winners Bitch go on to win Best of Breed, additional points are accorded for the additional Shepherds defeated by so doing, provided, of course, that there were entries specifically for

Best of Breed competition, or Specials, as these specific entries are generally called. If your dog or bitch takes Best of Opposite Sex after going Winners, points are credited according to the number of the same sex defeated in both the regular classes and Specials competition. Many a one- or two-point class win has grown into a major in this manner.

Moving further along, should your Shepherd win the Working Group from the classes (in other words, if it has taken either Winners Dog or Winners Bitch, Best of Winners, and Best of Breed), you then receive points based on the greatest number of points awarded to any breed included within that Group during that show's

Ch. Covy's Toulouse of Tucker Hill, here taking Best of Winners at James River Kennel Club under judge Marie Moore. Toulouse, born June 11th 1975, is by Grand Victor Ch. Lakeside's Harrigan, ROM, ex Ch. Tucker Hill's Angelique, C.D., ROM. Owned by Dick and Trish Phillips of Morgantown, West Virginia, Cappy Pottle, and Gloria Birch.

competition. Should the dog's winning streak also include Best in Show, the same rule of thumb applies, and your Shepherd receives points equal to the highest number of points awarded to any other dog of any breed at that event.

Best of Breed competition consists of the Winners Dog and the Winners Bitch, who automatically compete on the strength of those awards, in addition to whatever dogs and bitches have been entered specifically for this class for which champions of record are eligible. Shepherds who, according to their owner's records, have completed the required number of points for a championship after closing of entries for the show but whose championships are unconfirmed, may be transferred from one of the regular classes to the Best of Breed competition, provided this transfer is made by the show superintendent or show secretary *prior to the start of judging at the show*.

This has proven an extremely popular new rule, as under it a dog can finish on Saturday and then be transferred and compete as a Special on Sunday. It must be emphasized that the change *must* be made a half hour *prior* to the start of the day's judging, which means to the start of *any* judging at the show, not your individual breed.

A father/son and father/daughter combination. Ken Rayner on the right with Ch. Tannenwald's Igor are the fathers, Chips Rayner on the left with Ch. Tannenwald's Kira, the son/daughter duo. Here Chips and Kira are taking the Best of Breed award as Ken and Igor wind up Best of Opposite Sex. Photo courtesy of the Rayners.

In the United States, Best of Breed winners are entitled to compete in the Variety Group which includes them. This competition is not mandatory; it is a privilege which German Shepherd exhibitors should value. The dogs winning *first* in each Variety Group *must* compete for Best in Show.

Non-regular classes are sometimes included at the all-breed shows, and they are almost invariably included at Specialty shows. These include Stud Dog Class and Brood Bitch Class, which are judged on the quality of the offspring (usually two) accompanying the sire or dam. The quality of the latter two is beside the point; it is the youngsters that count, and the qualities of *both* are averaged to decide which sire or dam is the best and most consistent producer. Then there is the Brace Class (which, at all-breed shows, moves along to Best Brace in each Variety Group and then Best Brace in Show), which is judged on the similarity and evenness of appearance of the two members of the brace. In other words, the Shepherds should look like identical twins in size, color, and conformation and should move together almost as a single dog, one

Ken Rayner with his magnificent current Special, Champion Beech Hills Benji von Masco, adding another first in the Working Group, this time under Bob Forsyth at the South Windsor Kennel Club, November 1981. Bred and owned by M. E. Thomas.

Select Ch. Linnloch Sundown von Freys winning Best in Show under Joseph E. Gregory at the 1980 Mid-Continent Kennel Club, Tulsa, Oklahoma. This Best in Show winner is co-owned by James L. Halferty of Pasadena, California, and Mary C. Roberts of Covina, California, who is handling.

person handling with precision and ease. The same applies to the Team competition except that four dogs are involved and, if necessary, two handlers.

The Veterans Class is for the older dog, the minimum age of whom is usually seven years. This class is judged on the quality of the dogs, as the winner competes for Best of Breed, and, on a number of occasions, has been known to win it. So the point is *not* to pick the oldest looking dog, as some seem to think, but the best specimen of the breed, exactly as throughout the regular classes.

Then there are Sweepstakes and Futurity Stakes, sponsored by many Specialty clubs, sometimes as part of their shows and sometimes as separate events. The difference between the two is that Sweepstakes entries usually include dogs and bitches from six to eighteen months of age, and entries are made at the usual time as others for the show, while for a Futurity the entries are bitches nominated when bred and the individual puppies entered at or shortly following their birth.

Ch. Van Cleve's Edge, Southeast Maturity Victor, owned by Dr. and Mrs. Carmen L. Battaglia, Lithonia, Georgia.

The mighty Ch. Cuno von der Teufelslache, SchH III, FH, ROM, at eight years of age, having just won the Veterans Class at a Specialty. Helen Miller Fisher, owner, Meadowmill Kennels.

Ch. Covy-Tucker Hill's Lufthansa, 1979 Futurity Victor, 1981 Champion, by Covy's Oregano of Tucker Hill, ROM, ex Ch. Covy's Felita of Tucker Hill, ROM. Owners R. and B. Glenz, San Jose, California. Breeders and co-owners, Cappy Pottle and Gloria F. Birch, Covy-Tucker Hill Kennels.

Ch. Wellspring's Independence, by multiple Select Ch. Doppelt-Tay's Hawkeye, ROM, winning the Northwest Regional Futurity, Iana Frost judging. Owned by Mr. and Mrs. Franklyn Schaefer, Sands Point, New York.

Junior Showmanship

If there is a youngster in your family between the ages of ten and seventeen, I can suggest no better or more rewarding a hobby than having a Shepherd to show in Junior Showmanship competition. This is a marvelous activity for young people. It teaches responsibility, good sportsmanship, the fun of competition where one's own skills are the deciding factor of success, proper care of a pet, and how to socialize with other young folks. Any youngster may experience the thrill of emerging from the ring a winner and the satisfaction of a good job done well.

Through the years, the German Shepherd Dog has always seemed especially popular with Junior Showmanship-minded youngsters. Being of such superb intelligence and being easily trainable, they are agreeable dogs for the youngsters to work with; and judging by the success of German Shepherds with their young handlers which we have noted, the breed seems well suited for this type of competition.

Entry in Junior Showmanship is open to any boy or girl who is at least ten years old and under seventeen years old on the day of the show. The Novice Junior Showmanship Class is open to youngsters who have not already won, at the time the entries close, three firsts in this class. Youngsters who have won three firsts in Novice

Amber von Finsternwald, owned by Gerlinde Hockla, handled here by her niece Janina Lauren. Judge, A. Peter Knoop.

Markenhaus Elf at eight years of age helping Sue Rayner win a Junior Showmanship Class. This was Sue's first time out in Juniors.

may compete in the Open Junior Showmanship Class. Any junior handler who wins his third first-place award in Novice may participate in the Open Class at the same show, provided that the Open Class has at least one other junior handler entered in it. The Novice and Open Classes may be divided into Junior and Senior Classes. Youngsters between the ages of ten and twelve, inclusively, are eligible for the Junior division; and youngsters between thirteen and seventeen, inclusively, are eligible for the Senior division. Any of the foregoing classes may be separated into individual classes for boys and for girls. If such a division is made, it must be indicated on the premium list. The premium list also indicates the prize for Best Junior Handler, if such a prize is being offered at the show. Any youngster who wins a first in any of the regular classes may enter the competition for this prize, provided the youngster has been undefeated in any class at that show.

The high point of each year's Junior Showmanship competition is when those talented juniors who qualify compete in these classes at the Westminster Kennel Club Dog Show in Madison Square Garden in New York City each February. The privilege of doing so is gained by the number of classes won during the preceding year, and the qualifications are explained in detail on the Westminster premium list and entry blank.

Junior Showmanship Classes, unlike regular conformation classes in which the dog's quality is judged, are judged entirely on the skill and ability of the junior handling the dog. Which dog is best is not the point—it is which youngster does the best job with the dog that is under consideration. Eligibility requirements for the dog being shown and other detailed information can be found in *Regulations for Junior Showmanship*, issued by the American Kennel Club.

A junior who has a dog that he or she can enter in both Junior Showmanship and conformation classes has twice the opportunity for success and twice the opportunity to get into the ring and work with the dog. Shepherds and juniors work well together, and this combination has often wound up in the winner's circle. There are no age restrictions on a child showing in breed competition, and a youngster may start at any age his parents think suitable. Of course, much depends upon the individual child, and I hardly need point out the irresponsibility of turning too young a child, or one not yet able to control it, loose at a dog show with one of *any* of the large, powerful breeds. Too many totally unexpected things could happen.

Best Junior Handler and Best Puppy. An exciting day for Janina Lauren and Amber von Finsternwald. Joe Bihari is the judge.

Ch. Sandheims Dru, by Ch. Nanhall's Taurus, owned by Dr. Wade Sanders.

Pre-Show Preparation

Preparation of the things you will need as a Shepherd exhibitor should not be left until the last moment. They should be planned and arranged for at least several days before the show in order for you to relax and be calm as the countdown starts.

The importance of the crate has already been discussed, and we assume it is already in use. Of equal importance is the grooming table, which we are sure you have already acquired for use at home. You should take it along with you, as your dog will need final touches before entering the ring. If you do not have one yet, a folding table with a rubber top is made specifically for this purpose and can be purchased from the concession booths found at most dog shows. Then you will need a sturdy tack box (also available at the show's concessions) in which to carry your brush, comb, scissors, nail clippers, whatever you use for last minute clean-up jobs, cotton swabs, first-aid equipment, and anything else you are in the habit of using on the dog, such as a leash or two of the type you prefer, some well-cooked and dried-out liver or any of the small packaged "dog treats" your dog likes for use as "bait" in the ring, and a Turkish towel.

Take a large thermos or cooler of ice, the biggest one you can accommodate in your vehicle, for use by "man and beast." Take a jug of water

(there are lightweight, inexpensive ones available at all sporting goods shops) and a water dish. If you plan to feed the dog at the show, or if you and the dog will be away from home more than one day, bring food from home so that he will have the type to which he is accustomed.

You may or may not have an exercise pen. Personally, I think that one is a *must*, even if you have only one dog. While the shows do provide areas for exercise of the dogs, these are among the best places to come into contact with any illnesses that may be going around, and I feel that having a pen of your own for your dog's use is excellent protection. Such a pen can be used in other ways, too, such as a place other than the crate in which to put the dog to relax and a place in which the dog can exercise at rest areas or motels during your travels. A word of caution: never tie a dog to an exercise pen or leave him unattended in it while you wander off, as the pens are not sufficiently secure to keep the dog there should he decide to leave, at least not in most cases. Exercise pens are also available at the

Ch. Tannenwald's Kira, by Ch. Tannenwald's Igor ex Ch. Weberhaus Gemina, taking Best of Opposite Sex at the German Shepherd Dog Club of Greater Washington, D.C., Specialty Show, August 1969. Bred by Weberhaus Kennels, owned by Gert Hoppe and Agnes Considine, and handled by Ken Rayner.

Ch. Ex von der Schlangenspitze taking Best of Breed at Staten Island in 1972. Gerlinde Hockla handling.

Ch. Covy's Rosita of Tucker Hill, a daughter of Covy-Tucker Hill's Zinfandel, ROM, ex Ch. Covy's Felita of Tucker Hill, ROM. Owned by Gloria F. Birch and Cappy Pottle.

dog show concession booths should you not already have yours when you reach the dog's first show. They come in a variety of heights and sizes.

Bring along folding chairs for the members of your party, unless all of you are fond of standing, as these are almost never provided by the show-giving clubs. Have your name stamped on the chairs so there will be no doubt as to whom the chairs belong. Bring whatever you and your family enjoy for drinks or snacks in a picnic basket or cooler, as show food, in general, is expensive and usually not great. You should always have a pair of boots, a raincoat, and a rain hat with you (they should remain permanently in your vehicle if you plan to attend shows regularly), as well as a sweater, a warm coat, and a change of shoes. A smock or big cover-up apron will assure that you remain tidy as you prepare the dog for the ring. Your overnight case should include a small sewing kit for emergency repairs, headache and indigestion remedies, and any personal products or medications you normally use.

In your car you should always carry maps of the area where you are headed and an assortment of motel directories. Generally speaking, we have found that Holiday Inns are the friendliest about taking dogs. Some Ramadas and some

Ch. Hilgrove's Iris as a class bitch winning at the German Shepherd Dog Club of Greater New Haven 1965 Specialty. Gloria Taylor, owner; Gerlinde Hockla, handler; Mr. Williamson, judge.

Howard Johnsons do so cheerfully (the Ramadas indicate on each listing in their directory whether or not pets are welcome). Best Western usually frowns on pets (not all of them but enough to make it necessary to find out which do). Some of the smaller chains welcome pets. The majority of privately owned motels do not.

Have everything prepared the night before the show to expedite your departure. Be sure that the dog's identification and your judging program and other show information are in your purse or briefcase. If you are taking sandwiches, have them ready. Anything that goes into the car the night before will be one thing less to be concerned with in the morning. Decide upon what you will wear and have it out and ready. If there is any question in your mind about what to wear, try on the possibilities before the day of the show; don't risk feeling you may want to change when you see yourself dressed a few moments

prior to departure time! In planning your outfit, wear something simple that will make an attractive background for your Shepherd, providing contrast to his color, calling attention to the *dog* rather than to yourself. Sports clothes always seem to look best at a dog show. What you wear on your feet is important, as many types of flooring are slippery, and wet grass, too, can present a hazard as you move the dog. Make it a rule to wear rubber soles and low or flat heels in the ring, so that you can move along smartly.

Your final step in pre-show preparation is to leave yourself plenty of time to reach the show that morning. Traffic can get extremely heavy as one nears the immediate vicinity of the show, finding a parking place can be difficult, and other delays may occur. You'll be in better humor if you can take it all in your stride without the pressure of watching every second because you figured the time too closely.

Day of the Show

From the moment of your arrival at the dog show until after your Shepherd has been judged, keep foremost in your mind the fact that he is your purpose for being there. You will need to arrive in advance of the judging in order to give him a chance to exercise after the trip to the show and take care of personal matters. A dog arriving in the ring and immediately using it for an exercise pen hardly makes a favorable impression on the judge. You will also need time to put the final touches on your dog, making certain that he goes into the ring looking his very best.

When you reach ringside, ask the steward for your arm-card with your Shepherd's entry number on it and anchor it firmly into place on your arm with the elastic provided. Make sure that you are where you should be when your class is called. The fact that you have picked up your arm-card does not guarantee, as some seem to think, that the judge will wait for you more

Again "the Bear Dog" in the limelight! Ch. Bar v. Weiherturchen with his handler Denise Kodner bringing home more laurels to owners Barbara and John Schermerhorn.

Ch. Cobert's Just Jollie of Lakeside, a daughter of Ch. Eko-Lan's Paladen, ROM, ex Cobert's Melissa, ROM. Bred by Connie Beckhardt.

than a minute or two. Judges are expected to keep on schedule, which precludes delaying for the arrival of exhibitors who are tardy.

Even though you may be nervous, assume an air of cool, collected calm. Remember that this is a hobby to be enjoyed, so approach it in that state of mind. The dog will do better, too, as he will be quick to reflect your attitude.

If you make a mistake while presenting the dog, don't worry about it—next time you'll do better. Do not be intimidated by the more expert or experienced exhibitors. After all, they, too, were once newcomers.

Always show your Shepherd with an air of pride. An apologetic attitude on the part of the exhibitor does little to help the dog win, so try to appear self-confident as you gait and set up the dog.

The judging routine usually starts when the judge asks that the dogs be gaited in a circle around the ring. During this period the judge is watching each dog as it moves along, noting style, topline, reach and drive, head and tail carriage, and general balance. This is the time to keep your mind and your eye on your dog, moving him at his most becoming gait and keeping your place in line without coming too close to the dog ahead of you. Always keep your dog on the inside of the circle, between yourself and the judge, so that the judge's view of the dog is unobstructed.

Calmly pose the dog when requested to set up for examination. If you are at the head of the line and many dogs are in the class, do not stop halfway down the end of the ring and begin stacking the dog. Go forward enough so that sufficient space is left for the other dogs. Simple courtesy demands that we be considerate and give others a chance to follow the judge's instructions, too.

Space your Shepherd so that on all sides of the dog the judge will have room in which to make his examination; this means that there must be sufficient room between each of the dogs for the judge to move around. Time is important when you are setting up your Shepherd, so practice in front of a full-length mirror at home, trying to accustom yourself to "getting it all together" correctly in the shortest possible time. When

you set up your Shepherd, you want his forelegs well under the dog, feet directly below the elbows, toes pointing straight ahead, and hindquarters extended *correctly*. Hold the dog's head up with your hand at the back inner corner of the lips, your left hand extending the tail to its proper position. You want the dog to look "all of a piece," head carried proudly on a strong neck, correct topline, hindquarters nicely angulated, the front straight and true, and the dog standing firmly on his feet.

Listen carefully as the judge instructs the manner in which the dog is to be gaited, whether it is straight down and straight back; down the ring, across, and back; or in a triangle. The latter has become the most popular pattern with the majority of judges. "In a triangle" means down the outer side of the ring to the first corner, across that end of the ring to the second corner, and then back to the judge from the second corner, using the center of the ring in a diagonal line. Please learn to do this pattern without breaking

Proud sire Select Am. and Can. Ch. Cobert's Reno of Lakeside, ROM, today's highest living Register of Merit Dog with fifty-three American and thirty Canadian champions to his credit, with some of his progeny in the Stud Dog Class at the National. Reno belongs to Connie Beckhardt, Cobert Kennels.

Another photo of Markenhaus Elf at eight years of age helping Sue Rayner get off on the right foot in her handling career.

at each corner to twirl the dog around you, a senseless maneuver we sometimes have noted. Judges like to see the dog move in an *uninterrupted* triangle, as they get a better idea of the dog's gait.

It is impossible to overemphasize that the gait at which you move your Shepherd is tremendously important, and considerable thought and study should be given to the matter. At home, have someone move the dog for you at different speeds so that you can tell which shows him off to best advantage.

Do not allow your Shepherd to sidetrack, flop, or weave as you gait him, and do not let him pull so that he appears to lean on the lead as you are gaiting him. He should move in a straight line, proudly, smoothly, and firmly. That is your goal as you work with him on a lead in preparation for his show career. Movement is the most important feature of a Shepherd; thus, it is essential that yours displays his movement to full advantage.

Baiting your dog should be done in a manner which does not upset the other Shepherds in the

Beautiful movement illustrated by a great German Shepherd. Ch. Beech Hills Benji von Masco demonstrates the excellent reach and drive which have helped make him so consistent a winner. Handled by Ken Rayner, Sr., this famed dog belongs to Mary Ellen Thomas.

ring or cause problems for their handlers. A tasty morsel of well-cooked and dried-out liver is fine for keeping your own dog interested, but discarded on the ground or floor, it can throw off the behavior of someone else's dog who may attempt to get it. So please, if you drop liver on the ground, pick it up and take it with you when you have finished.

One of the most controversial matters in connection with showing German Shepherds is whether or not the practice of "double handling" (*i.e.,* someone outside the ring "baiting" the dog) should be encouraged or permitted. In the eyes of the American Kennel Club, it should not. Within the German Shepherd world, however, opinion is divided:

some exhibitors feel it is both essential and appropriate while others agree that it should not be permitted. Double handling takes many forms, ranging from a low, familiar whistle from a friend or family member at ringside, which immediately alerts the dog to which the whistle was directed, to dashing frantically around the ring shaking a cow bell, which also attracts and alerts the dog. Objection to this is based on the fact that it disturbs other dogs in that ring, sometimes in other rings as well, and that it is, therefore, unfair to competing exhibitors. It also can be hazardous, as I know of many occasions when spectators, innocently wandering past the ring during German Shepherd judging, have just escaped being knocked to the ground by a

Ch. Chardo's Dock v. Auf Wiedersehn, by Select Am. and Can. Ch. Cobert's Reno of Lakeside, ROM, ex Hilltop's Chardo (a Ch. Stormhaven's Dolf, ROM, daughter), is owned by Ralph Ambrosio and Beverly Gannon and handled here by Fran Wasserman.

CHAMPION
DOCK

"One big, happy family." Ch. Von Nassau Sherpa celebrates a Best in Show with handler, Denny Kodner, and friends. Owned by Betty Radzevich.

frantic Shepherd person, intent only on keeping the bell ringing or the whistle going, dashing madly around the ring within which his or her dog is being gaited.

In defense of double handling, it is said to often be the only way to alert some dogs and bring their ears up and focus their attention. At the same time, I might remark, it gives dogs cause for some rather strange antics as they are constantly looking over their shoulders for their "baiter," trying to locate that person's position at ringside.

When the awards have been made, accept yours courteously, no matter how you may actually feel about it. To argue with a judge is un-thinkable, and it will certainly not change the decision. Be gracious, congratulate the winners if your dog has been defeated, and try not to show your disappointment. By the same token, please be a gracious winner; this, surprisingly, sometimes seems to be even more difficult.

If you already show your Shepherd, if you plan on being an exhibitor in the future, or if you simply enjoy attending dog shows, there is a book, written by me, which you will find to be an invaluable source of detailed information about all aspects of show dog competition. This book is *Successful Dog Show Exhibiting* (T.F.H. Publications, Inc.) and is available wherever the one you are now reading was purchased.

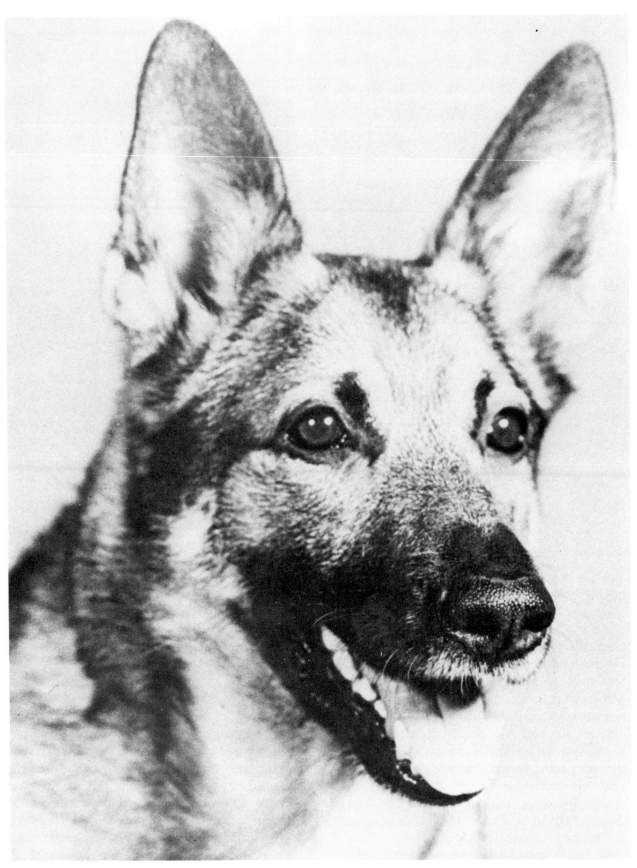

This is the first German Shepherd Dog Club of America Obedience Victrix, in 1968, Heide von Zook, U.D. Photo from Mary E. Schuetzler's collection.

CHAPTER FIFTEEN

Obedience and Working German Shepherd Dogs

Reno of Luan, C.D.X., T.D., was put through to obedience titles by his master in the wheelchair. I believe this is the first dog in the United States to have achieved this distinction. Photo courtesy of Denise Kodner.

German Shepherd Dogs have a well-deserved reputation for great intelligence, loyalty, and service. Properly trained and managed Shepherds have distinguished themselves not only in the show ring but also in other endeavors. Many, many Shepherds who are show champions also have earned one or more obedience titles; and many Shepherds have achieved success in various fields of specialized work, only one of which is described in detail here.

Obedience

For its own protection and safety, every dog should be taught, at the very least, to recognize and respond promptly and correctly to the basic commands "Come," "Heel," "Down," "Sit," and "Stay." Doing so might at sometime save the dog's life and, in less extreme circumstances, will certainly make him a better citizen, more well-behaved and far more pleasant as a companion.

If you are patient and enjoy working with your dog, study some of the excellent books available on the subject of obedience and start at an early age to teach your German Shepherd puppy these basic manners. If you need the stimulus of working with a group, find out where obedience training classes are available (usually your veterinarian, your dog's breeder, or a dog-owning friend can tell you) and you and your dog can join up. If you have difficulty locating such a class, the American Kennel Club will, upon request, provide you with this information.

As an alternative, you could, of course, let someone else do the training by sending your dog to class, but this is far less rewarding as you then lose the opportunity of working with the dog, developing the rapport and closeness which the two of you can enjoy by working together. Since there could hardly be found a more intelligent, easily trainable breed of dog than a German Shepherd, it certainly should prove worth your while to attempt the task yourself.

If the latter has been your decision, there are some basic rules which you should follow. You must remain calm and confident in attitude at all times. You must never lose your temper and frighten your dog or punish him unjustly. Never, ever, resort to cruelty. Be quick and lavish with your praise each time a command is correctly followed. Make it fun for the dog and he will be eager to please you by responding correctly. Repetition is the keynote, but it should not be continued without recess to the point of tedium. Limit the training sessions to ten- or fifteen-minute periods each time.

Formal obedience training can be followed, and very frequently is, by entering the dog in obedience competition to work toward an obedience degree, or several of them, depending on the dog's aptitude and your own enjoyment. Obedience trials are held in conjunction with the majority of conformation dog shows, both all-breed and Specialty, and as separate events as well. If you are working alone with your dog, you will need to obtain information on these from someone local, from a German Shepherd Dog Club to which you may belong, or from the American Kennel Club. If you have been working with a training class, you will find information readily available regarding dates and locations of trials.

The goals for which one works in the formal American Kennel Club member or licensed obedience trials are the following titles: C.D. (Companion Dog), C.D.X. (Companion Dog Excel-

Alf vom Kroppelberg receiving his *Dog World* Award as the Obedience Dog of 1954, during which year he completed all four working degrees in less than six months, was seven times highest scoring dog in trial, and twice won the highest combined score. His owner, Gustave Schindler, is on the right. Jack Baird, famous writer and obedience authority, is presenting Alf's certificate to Mrs. Winifred Strickland who trained and handled this magnificent dog. Alf was an import from Germany where he was classified V (excellent) during 1953.

lent), and U.D. (Utility Dog). These degrees are earned by receiving three qualifying scores, or "legs," at each level of competition. The degrees must be earned in order, with one completed prior to starting work on the next. For example, a dog must have earned C.D. prior to starting work on C.D.X. Then C.D.X. must be completed before U.D. work begins. The ultimate title possible to attain in obedience work is that of Obedience Trial Champion (O.T.Ch.). In order to qualify for this one, a dog must have received the required number of points by placing first or second in Open or Utility after having earned the Utility Dog rating. There is also a Tracking Dog title (T.D.) to be earned at tracking trials and a new, more difficult-to-attain degree, Tracking Dog Excellent (T.D.X.).

When you see the letters "C.D." following a dog's name, you will know that the dog has satisfactorily completed the following exercises: heel on leash, heel free, stand for examination, recall, long sit, and long stay. "C.D.X." means that tests have been passed in all of the exercises for Companion Dog plus heel free, drop on recall,

Imp-Cen's Fancy, owned by Bea Coble, in training for C.D.

At thirteen months of age, Von Mibach Timmee's Ember, U.D., owned by Valerie D. Mee. This lovely bitch, in addition to her U.D. degree has ten championship points and has assisted her owner's daughter, Terri, in becoming the German Shepherd Dog Club of America's selection for Top Junior Handler of 1979. A splendid example of the breed's beauty and versatility.

Arno von Bergluft, C.D.X., pictured going over the broad jump. Dorit S. Rogers, owner.

retrieve over high jump, broad jump, long sit, and long down. "U.D." indicates that the dog has additionally passed tests in scent discrimination (leather article), scent discrimination (metal article), signal exercises, directed retrieve, directed jumping, and group stand for examination.

The letters "T.D." indicate that the dog has been trained for and passed the test to follow the trail of a stranger along a path on which the trail was laid between thirty minutes and two hours previously. Along this track there must be more than two right-angle turns, at least two of which are well out in the open where no fences or other boundaries exist for guidance of the dog or handler. The dog wears a harness and is connected to the handler by a lead twenty to forty feet in length. Inconspicuously dropped at the end of the track is an article to be retrieved, usually a glove or wallet, which the dog is expected to locate and the handler to pick up. The letters "T.D.X." indicate that the dog has passed a more difficult version of the Tracking Dog test, with a longer track and more turns to be successfully worked through.

The owner of a dog holding the U.D. title and the T.D. title may then use the letters "U.D.T." following the dog's name. If the dog has gained his U.D. title and his T.D.X. title, then the letters "U.D.T.X." may follow his name, indicating that he is a Utility Dog and Tracker Excellent.

A most interesting photo of the six Burgerland Utility Dogs. Rex, U.D., Regina, U.D., Gigi, U.D., Ch. Princess, U.D., Sara, U.D., and Portas, C.D.X. Owners, Dr. and Mrs. Zoltan Puskas.

German Shepherd Dogs have distinguished themselves admirably in obedience work ever since it first became recognized in the United States. As you read this book, you will note the frequency with which show champions also carry one or more of the obedience titles. Beauty and brains are well combined in this breed, to be sure.

We have already mentioned the interest Miss Marie J. Leary had in obedience work and the fact that the majority of her famed Cosalta show champions carried obedience titles as well. Miss Leary was in the thick of activity when Mrs. Whitehouse Walker and Miss Blanche Saunders inaugurated the earliest obedience trials in the United States in Westchester County, New York, and her dogs were successful participants on a great many occasions.

The first A.K.C.-licensed obedience trial was held in conjunction with the North Westchester Kennel Club Dog Show in June of 1936. Of course, a German Shepherd was one of the first two dogs of any breed to win all of the obedience degrees. He topped off his U.D. by winning the first tracking test under A.K.C. rules. His name was Champion Schwarpels von Mardex, and he belonged to Walter P. Pheiffer. Miss Leary's Champion Anthony of Cosalta was the first German Shepherd Dog C.D.X.

Int. Ch. Anthony of Cosalta, C.D.X., was the first German Shepherd Dog show champion to win a C.D.X. Owned by Marie J. Leary, Cosalta Kennels. Photo courtesy of Mary Schuetzler.

360

It seems appropriate that the German Shepherd Dog Club of America, in 1968, should have inaugurated a special award for the German Shepherd dog or bitch who gained the highest combined obedience score at the National Specialty each year. The title which goes with the award is "Obedience Victor" or "Obedience Victrix," depending on the sex of the winner. To gain the award, a dog or bitch must have the highest combined score in Open B and Utility with a combined score of not less than 385, scores in each class of not less than 190, and proof of having won an award in a conformation class. Only German Shepherds bearing no disqualifying faults are eligible.

The list of German Shepherds who have been crowned Obedience Victor or Obedience Victrix is as follows:

1968—Heide von Zook, U.D.T.
1969—No winner
1970—Schillenkamp Duke of Orleans, U.D.T.
1971—Bihari's Uncle Sam, U.D.
1972—Ruglor's Reboza von Zook, U.D.
1973—Brunhild of Ravenna, U.D.T., SchH I.
1974—Kelnorth Lady Jessica, U.D.T.
1975—Penny auf der Heide, U.D.T.
1976—Natasha von Hammhausen, U.D.
1977—Herta von Hammhausen, U.D.
1978—Indra von Hoheneichen, U.D.
1979—O.T. Ch. Johnsondale's Kool Kaper, U.D.
1980—O.T. Ch. Von Jenin's Link, T.D.

1971 Obedience Victor Ch. Bihari's Uncle Sam, U.D. Photo courtesy of Mary E. Schuetzler.

1982 German Shepherd Dog Club of America Obedience Victrix Martin's Kassel vom Lohberg, U.D., bred, owned, trained, and handled by Robert J. Martin, Port Matilda, Pennsylvania, author of *Toward the R.H.D. for Dogs*.

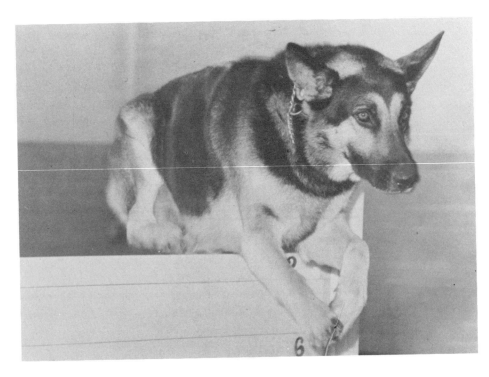

1976 Obedience Victrix Natasha von Hammhausen. Owner-breeder, Edward L. Hamm, Pennington, New Jersey. Photo courtesy of Mary E. Schuetzler.

Can. Obedience Trial Champion Lana vom Kreuzberg at sixteen months of age. Owned by Rob and Lu McLea, Leeven Rob Kennels, Echo Bay, Ontario, Canada.

1970 Obedience Victor Schillenkamp Duke of Orleans, U.D. Photo courtesy of Mary E. Schuetzler.

1979 Obedience Victrix Obedience Trial Ch. Johnsondale's Kool Kaper, U.D. Photo courtesy of Mary Schuetzler.

1974 Obedience Victrix Kenilworth's Lady Jessica, Am. and Can. U.D.T. Photo courtesy of Mary E. Schuetzler.

Police Dogs

The training of German Shepherds, and other selected breeds of dogs, for police work has been an accepted practice in Europe for many years. Dogs may have occasionally been used for this purpose in the United States, too, early in this country's history; but it took the foresight of the Police Department in Dearborn, Michigan, to really inaugurate the practice on a wide scale and to let the fact be known, making it the trailblazer for other cities to follow suit.

It all began for Dearborn during 1955 with the purchase of four partially trained purebred German Shepherds and the employment of a specialized trainer for these dogs, Charles Art, a former member of the Marine Corps, who worked with the Dearborn Police Department as a civilian. At one period, Mr. Art had no fewer than sixty dogs working with him, in preparation for use in Dearborn or police work in other cities.

When Mr. Art's dogs had completed their training course, they were proficient in the following:

1.) Patrolling or walking a beat with a police officer.
2.) Searching out and holding a prowler, burglar, or disorderly person.
3.) Entering buildings and holding suspicious persons.
4.) Disarming a bandit.
5.) Riding in a scout car.
6.) Jumping into a car upon command and holding its occupants.
7.) Going into a burning building.
8.) Going through a plate-glass window.
9.) Scaling fences and walls up to fourteen feet.
10.) Being vicious or gentle as commanded.
11.) Being obedient by lying down, sitting down, or walking quietly at the officer's side without a lead, upon command.

Each dog was trained with two officers, who were encouraged to have the dogs live with them at home. In the beginning, the dogs were used on night duty, going their rounds with four foot-patrolmen in busy districts of the city and especially where there were parks and public swimming pools. It was found that their presence helped tremendously in curbing vandalism and other forms of mischief.

This handsome German Shepherd is "Sgt. Orvie," one of the four breed members used by the Dearborn, Michigan, Police Department back in the 1950's. With him is the trainer, Charles Art, who was so highly successful in this field.

Following Dearborn in the establishment of a canine division were the police departments of Baltimore, Maryland, in 1956; St. Louis, Missouri, in 1958; Atlanta, Georgia, in 1959; and Chicago, Illinois, in 1961. Undoubtedly, this sudden increase in attention to the value and usefulness of dogs in police work was directly attributable to the very wide newspaper and television coverage accorded the success of the Dearborn team!

The most admired and imposing of the Dearborn Shepherds was the magnificent "Sergeant Orvie," the special charge of a young man, then Corporal, John Connolly who had joined the force in the late 1940's and who is still with the department, now as Chief of Police. John is, and all his life has been, a true "dog man." He is a very famous breeder of outstanding show Boxers and a widely respected judge of the Working breeds. "Sergeant Orvie" was Corporal Connolly's dog. The two of them worked well together and attracted a great deal of attention when they accompanied Public Safety Director Mrs. Marguerite C. Johnson (who had been largely instrumental in gaining approval of the acquisition of the dogs) to the Police Chiefs Convention in Philadelphia in 1955. At that time "Sergeant Orvie" was featured, with Corporal Connolly, in more than half a dozen television "spots." Additionally, the two appeared on all three of the Detroit television channels during 1955 and on the "International News John Daly Show" in October of that year; their last televised appearance was a fifteen-minute segment on "You Asked For It" on February 20th 1956. "Sergeant Orvie," wearing his vest adorned by six gold buttons and sporting his sergeant's stripes and his "No. 4" shield from the Dearborn Police Department, became one of the most widely known canine celebrities of his day.

After a full year of successful use in Dearborn, it was decided that the dogs were no longer needed in that city because the types of crimes warranting their continued employment were not taking place. Thus, the original four dogs were sold to the City of Portland, Oregon, where a total of fifteen police dogs were being purchased. Along with the dogs, Portland also hired Dearborn's trainer, Charles T. Art, to continue his work in their city.

At the International Association of Chiefs of Police Convention held at Philadelphia, Pennsylvania, in 1955, Cpl. (now Chief of Police) John Connolly (famous A.K.C. judge of Working Dogs) with the outstanding German Shepherd police dog "Sergeant Orvie" and Mrs. Marguerite Johnson, Commissioner of Police and Fire Departments in Dearborn, the only woman in the nation holding such a position (at that time) and the first to endorse the use of dogs for police detail in her city. Greeting them, on the right, Philadelphia City Councilman Wm. H. Broomhall. Note that "Sgt. Orvie" is wearing a vest adorned with six gold buttons, the No. 4 shield of the Dearborn Police Department, and the three stripes denoting his rank.

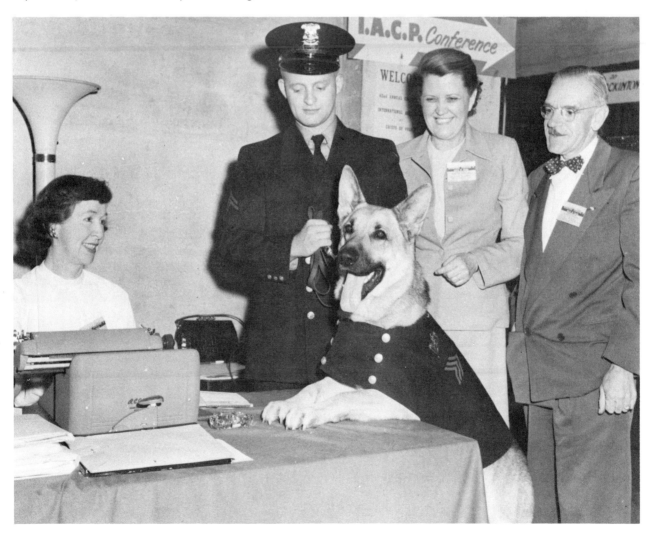

Cpl. John Connolly (now Chief of Police Connolly) and Cpl. Stan Hughes step out smartly in the mid-1950's with two of the famed German Shepherds who were members of the Dearborn, Michigan, Police Force in those days. On the left, "Sgt. Orvie"; on the right, "Basch." Both dogs were extremely useful in the work at Dearborn.

Nanhall German Shepherd Dogs at work. All owned by Fran and Hall Keyes, Nanhall Kennels.

Mrs. Harrison Eustice, New York City socialite of the 1920's-1930's, began training dogs for the Intelligence Division of the Swiss Army and ended training them to lead the blind. It was an article written by Mrs. Eustice for the *Saturday Evening Post* that called her work to the attention of Morris Frank, a blind youth from Tennessee, leading to his travelling to Switzerland to visit her and returning with his famous guide dog "Buddy." This was the event that led to the foundation by Mr. Frank of The Seeing Eye, a school which trains dogs for leading the blind. Mrs. Eustice is pictured with three of her canine pupils. Photo courtesy of Janet Churchill.

Wartime Britain. A young Shepherd learning the essentials of working under wartime conditions, one of the first of which is not bark while advancing. Photo courtesy of Janet Churchill.

A Red Cross German Shepherd during World War I. Photo courtesy of Janet Churchill.

These scenes feature the German Shepherd Dogs which were brought in by the U.S. Air Force to help with the rescue and clean-up work when Mt. St. Helens erupted in Washington. These specially trained Shepherds were of inestimable value in saving lives and have received recognition for a job well done. Photos courtesy of Mary E. Schuetzler.

Von Mibach Timmee's Ember, U.D., an obedience star with ten points toward her conformation title as this is written. Owned by Valerie D. Mee, Smithtown, New York.

Members of the German Schutzhund Club of Canada start their puppies tracking at an early age.

Opposite: A classic head-study of Can. Ch. Nocturne's Ruffian, Am. and Can. C.D., bred by Helen Gleason and owned by Mary E. Schuetzler. Schutzenhaus Shepherds, Farmington, Michigan.

Opposite and above: Gerlinde Hockla doing some schutzhund training.

Ulk vom Bungalow, SchH III, FH, by Caro vom Allerswald, SchH III, ex Pali vom Bungalow, SchH III, F H. A multiple Schutzhund III dog owned by Fred Scharpf of Langley, British Columbia. An outstanding dog in all phases of the sport, achieving a perfect score in both obedience and protection on different occasions. Among Ulk's achievements are a third at the Canadian Schutzhund III Championship, 1979; a second at the U.S. National Schutzhund III Championship, 1980; a twelfth at the Europe Meistershaft, 1980; a second at the Canadian National Schutzhund III Championship, 1980; a third at the U.S. National Schutzhund III Championship, 1980; and a second at the North American Schutzhund III Championships, 1980.

Opposite: Tanja v.d. Jungen Hansen, SchH III, by Condor v. Distelkamp, SchH III, ex Kitty v.d. Jungen Hansen, SchH II, an excellent producing bitch with a strong working pedigree, V-rated in conformation, and one of the few bitches in Canada to have achieved a SchH III. Owned by Barry and Cathy Gay of Saskatoon, Saskatchewan.

Barry and Cathy Gay, Saskatoon, Saskatchewan, own this handsome group of dogs pulling the sled in the winter. These versatile Shepherds also compete in races.

A magnificent German Shepherd, Ch. Treffer of Clover Acres, by Ch. Tannenwald's Igor ex Clover Acres Dixie, owned by Ray Picard. A prepotent sire, as was his father before him. Ken Rayner, handler.

Opposite: A stunning head-study of the great bitch Grand Victrix Ch. Covy's Rosemary of Tucker Hill, ROM, owned by Gloria Birch and Cappy Pottle, Cotati, California.

Scherzar's Mischief Maker, by Covy's Casino of Tucker Hill (Grand Victor Ch. Yoncalla's Mike, ROM, ex Ch. Kouays's Contessa, ROM) ex Tanbark's Dare Me of Love Creek (Grand Victor Ch. Lance of Fran-Jo, ROM, ex Kristie of Waldesruh, ROM). Mischief Maker is close to her own ROM title and has earned recognition as a top brood bitch in the National Futurity Tabulations. Owned by Scherzar German Shephards, Janice L. Staley, Castro Valley, California.

380

Head-study of the twelve-week-old puppy bitch, Von-Wag-Non In His Presence, co-owned by breeder Charles Wagnon and Os and Diane Hillman, Atlanta, Georgia. Photo by Os Hillman.

Dolmar's Uric, taking top honors in the 9-12 Month Puppy Class, went on to take Best Puppy in Specialty at the Bay State German Shepherd Dog Club on June 13th 1981. Handler, George Berstler. Dolmar's Uric is one of the fine youngsters at Dolmar Kennels in Woodbridge, Connecticut. Bred and owned by Mrs. M. Dolan.

Ch. Kubistraum's Kane, ROM, in 1981 for the fifth consecutive year featured as a Top Ten Stud Dog based on the Futurity-Maturity Tabulation System. A homebred proudly owned by Verna M. Kubic, St. Joseph, Wisconsin.

Opposite, above: Farmils Breena of Dolmar by Cobert's Whisper Jet ex Dolmars Ilese of Farmil, at eleven months of age. Bred by Doris Farrell and owned by John Mucci. **Below:** Select Ch. Proven Hill's Sunshine, famous producing daughter of Grand Victor Ch. Scorpio of Shiloh Gardens, ROM, ex Proven Hill's Randy. Judy and Ray Teidel, Jr., owners, Woodstock, Illinois.

NORTHEASTERN FUTURITY
G.S.D.C. OF WESTERN
NEW YORK
MAY 10, 1979
JUDGE — LAMAR KUHNS
TEENAGE BITCH
3
PHOTO — TOM MONAHAN

BEST OF OPP. SEX
TOPLINE GSDC, INC.
2ND ANNUAL SHOW
JULY 10, 1977

America's Highest Living ROM German Shepherd Dog, Ch. Cobert's Reno of Lakeside (Grand Victor Ch. Lance of Fran-Jo, ROM, ex Cobert's Melissa, ROM) co-owned by Vito Moreno and Connie Beckhardt.

CHAPTER SIXTEEN

Breeding German Shepherd Dogs

Top Ten Sire Covy-Tucker Hill's Zinfandel, ROM, by Grand Victor Ch. Lakeside's Harrigan, ROM, ex seven times Select Ch. Tucker Hill's Angelique, C.D., ROM. Owned by Cappy Pottle and Gloria Birch, co-breeders with Jean Stevens.

Breeding good dogs requires a lot of hard work. It is not easy to produce dogs who conform as closely as possible to the standard, and it takes years to develop a strain of good and successful dogs. A lot of time and effort must go into choosing the stud dog and brood bitch, and then more time must be spent with the litter once it arrives.

The Stud Dog

Choosing the best stud dog to complement your bitch is not an easy task. The principal factors to be considered are the stud's quality and conformation and his pedigree. The pedigree lists the various bloodlines involved with the ancestry of the dog. If you are a novice in the breed, I would suggest that you seek advice from some of the more experienced breeders who are old-timers in the fancy and thus would be able to discuss with you some of the various dogs behind the one to which you are planning to breed your bitch. Many times such people accurately recall in minute detail the dogs you need to know about, perhaps even having access to photos of them. And do be sure to carefully study the photos in this book, as they show

representatives of important German Shepherd bloodlines.

It is extremely important that the stud's pedigree be harmonious with that of your bitch. Do not just rush out and breed to a current winner, with no regard for whether or not he can reproduce his quality. Take time to check out the progeny being sired by the dog, or dogs, under your consideration. A dog that has sired nothing of quality for others probably will do no better for you, unless, of course, it is a young stud just starting out; such a stud may not have had the opportunity to produce much of anything, good or bad, thus far. Do you want to waste your bitch's time on an unknown quantity? Wouldn't you prefer to use a dog with a good producing record? You may get a little-known or unproven dog for a less expensive stud fee, but is that really sensible?

Breeding dogs is not a moneymaking proposition. By the time you pay a stud fee, take care of the bitch during gestation, whelp the litter, and raise and care for the puppies (including shots, and food, among other things) until they reach selling age, you will be fortunate if you break even on the cost of the litter. Therefore, it is

Two outstanding German Shepherds, the results of line-breeding on Grand Victor Ch. Lance of Fran-Jo, ROM: on the left, Ch. Dolmar's Cara of Spring Rock (Ch. Eko-Lan's Paladen, ROM, ex Eko-Lan's Rhyme) and on the right, Ch. Cobert's Reno of Lakeside, ROM (Lance ex Cobert's Melissa, ROM).

foolish to skimp on the stud fee. Let nothing influence your selection except that the dog be best suited to your bitch in background and conformation, with the best producing record, regardless of the cost. It is just as expensive to raise mediocre puppies as good ones, and you will certainly fare better financially if you have show-prospect puppies to sell than if you come up with nothing but pets, which you will probably wind up selling for far less than you had intended or you'll end up giving away to get them good homes. Remember, the only excuse for breeding and bringing puppies into the world is an honest effort to improve the breed. So in choosing the stud you use, remember that the best, most suitable one you can find with an impressive producing record will almost certainly be by far the greatest bargain in the long run.

You will have to decide on one of three courses to follow in planning the breeding of your bitch: inbreeding, line-breeding, or outcrossing. Inbreeding is normally considered to be father to daughter, mother to son, or sister to brother. Line-breeding is combining two dogs belonging originally to the same strain or family of Shepherds, descended from the same ancestors,

Quaker Oats Award Winner, Am. and Can. Ch. Covy-Tucker Hill's Finnegan, ROM, Number One U.S. Shepherd 1976, 1977, 1978, and 1979. Sired by Covy's Oregano of Tucker Hill, ROM, ex Covy's Fate of Tucker Hill (litter-sister to Ch. Covy's Felita of Tucker Hill, ROM). Owners, Ralph S. and Mary C. Roberts. Breeders, Gloria Birch and Cappy Pottle.

Bax von Spiegels-Berge is a recent German import and one of the currently popular stud dogs at Dois Pinheiros Kennels owned by Mrs. Vera Lucia de Castro Barbosa in Brazil.

such as half-brother to half-sister, niece to uncle, granddaughter to grandsire, and so on. Outcross breeding is using a dog and a bitch of completely different bloodlines with no mutual ancestors, or only a few, and these far back, if at all.

Each of these methods has advantages and disadvantages; each has supporters and detractors. I would say that line-breeding is probably the safest, the most generally approved, and the most frequently used with the desired results. Thus, I would say, it is perfect for the novice breeder because it is the easiest to figure out, especially until one has acquired considerable experience with the breed and the various bloodlines of which it consists.

Inbreeding should be left for the experienced, very sophisticated breeder who knows the line extremely well and thus is in a position to evaluate the probable results. Outcrossing is normally done when you are trying to bring in a specific feature or trait, such as better movement, better head type, superior bone or substance, or better personality or temperament.

Everyone sincerely interested in breeding dogs wants to develop a line of their own, but this is not accomplished overnight. It takes at least

Ch. Cobert's Cardinal is the result of full brother-sister breeding by Ch. Cobert's Reno of Lakeside, ROM, ex Ch. Cobert's Golly Gee of Lakeside, ROM. Winning under Mrs. Francis V. Crane for Connie Beckhardt.

several generations before you can claim to have done so, and during this time the close study of bloodlines and the observation of individual dogs are essential. Getting to know and truthfully evaluate the dogs with which you are working will go a long way in helping you preserve the best in what you have while at the same time remove weaknesses.

As a novice breeder, your wisest bet is to start by acquiring one or two bitches of the finest quality and background you can buy. In the beginning, it is really foolish to own your own stud dog; you will make out better and have a wider range of dogs with which to work if you pay a stud fee to one of the outstanding producing Shepherds available to service your bitch. In order to be attractive to breeders a stud dog must be well known, must have sired at least one champion (and usually one that has attracted considerable attention in Specials competition), and must have winning progeny in the ring; this

Ch. Rassela's Jim Grim, a grandson of Ch. Tannenwald's Igor by Ch. Quasar of Clover Acres ex Rassela's Alleluiah. Bred by Jan Trounson, owned by Gale McLaughlin, and handled by Ken Rayner.

represents a large expenditure of time and money before the dog begins to bring in returns on your investment. So start out by paying a stud fee a few times to use such a dog, or dogs, retaining the best bitch out of each of your first few litters and breeding those once or twice before you seriously think of owning your own stud dog. By that time, you will have gained the experience to recognize exactly what sort of dog you need for this purpose.

A future stud dog should be selected with the utmost care and consideration. He must be of very high standard as he may be responsible for siring many puppies each year, and he should not be used unless he clearly has something to contribute to the breed and carries no hereditary disease. Ideally, he should come from a line of excellent Shepherds on both sides of his pedigree, the latter containing not only *good* dogs but also ones which are *proven successful producers of quality*. The dog himself should be of sufficient quality to hold his own in competition in his breed. He should be robust and virile, a keen stud dog who has proved that he is able to transmit his best qualities to his progeny. Do not use an unsound dog or a dog with a major or outstanding fault. Not all champions seem able to pass along their individual splendid quality and, by the same token, occasionally one finds a dog who never finished but who does sire pup-

Ch. Oak Hill's Cosmic Cowboy, a very masculine, sound, easy moving dog owned by Peggy Lee, Absecon, New Jersey. Handled by Terry Hower. This exciting youngster by the great Select Ch. Cobert's Reno of Lakeside, ROM, finished under Shepherd expert Ernest Loeb with a four-point major. His dam is Oak Hill's Brielle who was sired by Grand Victor Ch. Padechma's Persuasion from a bitch that goes back to Ch. Dot-Wall's Vance and then into the famous Hessian line.

pies better than himself *provided that his pedigree is star-studded with top producing dogs and bitches.* Remember, too, that the stud dog cannot do it alone; the bitch must have what it takes too, although I must admit that some stud dogs, the truly dominant ones, can consistently produce type and quality regardless of the bitch or her background. Great studs like this, however, are few and far between.

If you are the proud owner of a promising young stud dog, one that you have either bred from one of your own bitches or that you have purchased after much serious thought and deliberation, do not permit him to be used for the first time until he is about a year old. The initial breeding should be to a proven matron, experienced in what is expected of her and thus not likely to give the stud a bad time. His first encounter should be pleasant and easy, as he could be put off breeding forever by a maiden bitch who fights and resents his advances. His first

breeding should help him develop confidence and assurance. It should be done in quiet surroundings, with only you and one other person (to hold the bitch) present. Do not make a circus of it, as the first time will determine your stud's attitude and feeling about future breeding.

Your young stud dog must allow you to help with the breeding, as later there will be bitches who will not be cooperative and he will need to develop the habit of accepting assistance. If, right from the beginning, you are there helping and praising him, he will expect and accept this as a matter of course whenever it may be necessary.

Before you introduce the dogs, be sure to have some K-Y Jelly at hand (this is the only lubricant that should be used) and either a stocking or a length of gauze with which to muzzle the bitch should it seem necessary, as you do not want either yourself or your stud dog bitten. Once they are "tied," you will be able to remove the

Can. Grand Victor, Am. and Can. Ch. Chimney Sweep of Long Worth, C.D., ROM, was a tremendously famous and successful winner of the early 1950's, as well as the sire of a long list of champions. Owned by Virginia McCoy. Photo courtesy of Denise Kodner.

muzzle, but, for the preliminaries, it is best to play it safe by muzzling her.

The stud fee is paid at the time of the breeding. Normally a return service is offered should the bitch fail to produce. Usually one live puppy is considered to be a litter. In order to avoid any misunderstanding regarding the terms of the breeding, it is wise to have a breeding certificate which both the owner of the stud and the owner of the bitch should sign. This should spell out quite specifically all the conditions of the breeding, along with listing the dates of the matings (usually the bitch is bred twice with one day in between, especially if she is a maiden bitch). The owner of the stud should also at this time provide the owner of the bitch with a copy of the stud dog's pedigree, if this has not previously been done.

Sometimes a pick-of-the-litter puppy is taken instead of a stud fee, and this should be noted on the breeding certificate along with such terms as at what age the owner of the stud dog is to select the puppy and whether it is to be a dog puppy, a bitch puppy, or just the "pick" puppy. All of this should be clearly stated to avoid any misunderstandings later on.

In almost every case, the bitch must come to the stud dog for breeding. Once the owner of the bitch decides to what stud dog she will preferably be bred, it is important that the owner of the stud be contacted immediately to discuss the stud fee, terms, approximate time the bitch is due in season, and whether she will be shipped in or brought to the stud owner. Then, as soon as the bitch shows signs of coming into season, another phone call to the stud owner must follow to finalize the arrangements. I have experienced times when the bitch's owner has waited until a day or two before the bitch should be bred to contact me, only to meet with disap-

Ch. Vox Wikingerblut, ROM, sired by Dick v. Backerkamp, SchH III, ex Quora Pressenblut, SchH I, was whelped September 5th 1962. Breeder, Erich Sander, Bad Essen, Germany. Owners, Ralph and Mary Roberts of California.

Ch. Wellspring's Howard Johnson, by Ch. Doppelt-Tay's Hawkeye, ROM, ex Ch. Amber's Flair, ROM, is making an important contribution to the breed as an excellent producer. Franklyn and Rosalind Schaefer.

pointment owing to the dog's absence from home.

It is essential that the stud owner have proper facilities for housing the bitch while she is there. Nothing can be more disheartening than to have a bitch misbred or, still worse, to have her get away and become lost. Unless you can provide safe and proper care for visiting bitches, do not offer your dog at public stud.

Owning a stud dog is no easy road to riches, as some who have not experienced it seem to think; making the dog sufficiently well known is expensive and time-consuming. Be selective in the bitches you permit this dog to service. It takes two to make the puppies; and while some stud dogs do seem almost to achieve miracles, it is a general rule that an inferior bitch from a

mediocre background will probably never produce well no matter how dominant and splendid may be the stud to whom she is bred. Remember that these puppies will be advertised and perhaps shown as sired by your dog. You do not want them to be an embarrassment to yourself or to him, so do not accept just any bitch who comes along in order to get the stud fee. It may prove far too expensive in the long run.

A stud fee is generally based on the going price of one show-type puppy and on the sire's record as a producer of winners. Obviously, a stud throwing champions in every litter is worth a greater price than a dog that sires mediocre puppies. Thus a young stud, just starting his career as a sire, is less expensive before proven than a dog with, say, forty or fifty champions already

A family portrait of Cuno with his son and daughter: far right, Ch. Cuno von der Teufelslache, SchH III, FH, ROM; center, Ch. Meadowmill's Charmaine, daughter; far left, Ch. Yukon of La Salle, son. Helen Miller Fisher, owner.

on the record. And a dog that has been used more than a few times but has no winning progeny should, it goes without saying, be avoided no matter how small the fee; he will almost certainly be a waste of your bitch's time.

I do not feel that we need to go into the actual breeding procedure here, as the experienced fancier already knows how it should be handled and the novice should not attempt it for the first time by reading instructions in a book. Plan to have a breeder or handler friend help you until you have become accustomed to handling such matters or, if this is not practical for you, it is very likely your veterinarian can arrange to do it for you or get someone from his staff to preside.

If a complete "tie" is made, that breeding should be all that is actually necessary. However, with a maiden bitch, a bitch who has "missed" (failed to conceive) in the past, or one who has come a long distance, most people like to give a second breeding, allowing one day to elapse in between the two. This second service

gives additional insurance that a litter will result; and if the bitch is one with a past record for misses, sometimes even a third mating takes place in an effort to take every precaution.

Once the "tie" has been completed, be sure that the penis goes back completely into its sheath. The dog should be offered a drink of water and a short walk, and then he should be put in his crate or kennel somewhere alone to settle down. Do not permit him to mingle with the other males for a while, as he will carry the odor of the bitch about him and this could result in a fight.

The bitch should not be allowed to urinate for at least an hour. In fact, many people feel that she should be "upended" (held with her rear end above her front) for several minutes following the "tie" in order to permit the sperm to travel deeper. She should then be offered water, crated, and kept quiet.

There are no set rules governing the conditions of a stud service. They are whatever the

Am. and Can. Ch. Covy-Tucker Hill's Hot Legs, daughter of Ch. Covy's Mazarati of Tucker Hill, belongs to Art Lopez, Cappy Pottle, and Gloria Birch. Bred by Cappy Pottle, Gloria Birch, and M. and J. Scanlon.

Ch. Covy's Mazarati of Tucker Hill, by Cobert's Sirocco of Windigail ex Grand Victrix Ch. Covy's Rosemary of Tucker Hill, ROM, a distinguished and highly successful sire of winners. Owners, Gary Cook, Cappy Pottle, Gloria Birch, and Gail Sprock. Breeders, Cappy Pottle and Gloria Birch.

owner of the stud dog chooses to make them. The stud fee is paid for the act, not for the litter; and if a bitch fails to conceive, this does not automatically call for a return service unless the owner of the stud sees it that way. A return service is a courtesy, not something that can be regarded as a right, particularly as in many cases the failure has been on the part of the bitch, not the stud dog. Owners of a stud in whom they take pride and whom they are anxious to have make records as the sire of numerous champions, however, are usually most generous in this respect; and I do not know of any instances where this courtesy has been refused when no puppies resulted from the breeding. Some stud owners insist on the return service being given to the same bitch only, while others will accept a different bitch in her place if the owner wishes, particularly if the original one has a previous record for missing.

When a bitch has been given one return breeding and misses again, the stud owner's responsibility has ended. If the stud dog is one who consistently sires puppies, then obviously the bitch is at fault; and she will quite likely never conceive, no matter how often or to how many different studs she is bred. It is unreasonable for the owner of a bitch to expect a stud's owner to give more than one return service.

Fritzlund's Farmboy, by Ch. Treffer of Clover Acres ex Brunhilda of Fritzlund, bred and owned by Charles Fritz. Ken Rayner handling.

Ch. Ayrwood's Joshua, by Ch. Tannenwald's Igor ex Glenhart's Della of Ayrwood, C.D., taking Best of Breed at Blennerhasset Kennel Club, 1978. Born April 1974, Joshua is owned by Dan and Betty Jean Lemler, Lexington, Missouri, and is handled by Ken Rayner.

Lawmark's A Delightful Demon, sired by Ch. Tannenwald's Igor, photographed with Ken Rayner.

Deb-Mar's Belle Star, a typical daughter of Ch. Tannenwald's Igor, closing out 1981 in style. Handled by Ken Rayner for breeder-owner D. Piagiantini.

Sarego's Udo, by Ch. Tannenwald's Igor. Photo courtesy of Ken Rayner.

Cinderella of Bow Creek, by Ch. Tannenwald's Igor, with Ken Rayner.

Rassela's Teaberry, by Ch. Quasar of Clover Acres ex Cinderella of Bow Creek, another generation of breeding on the Ch. Tannenwald's Igor line. Owned by M. Schlauter; handled by Chips Rayner.

Cobert's Melissa, ROM, the top producing dam in German Shepherd history, pictured at the 1976 National at Niagara Falls, New York. Melissa is a daughter of Ch. Falk of Bihari Wonder, C.D. (Ch. Bernd vom Kallengarten, ROM, ex Agnes Gold of Bihari Wonder) ex Select Ch. Cobert's Ernestine, C.D. (Ch. Bernd vom Kallengarten, ROM, ex Ch. Cobert's Amber). She is the dam of eight champions and six Register of Merit sons and daughters. Breeders, Connie and Theodore Beckhardt, Cobert Kennels. Owners, Daniel P. Dwier and Connie Beckhardt.

The Brood Bitch

One of the most important purchases you will make in dogs is the selection of your foundation brood bitch, or bitches, on whom you plan to base your breeding program. You want marvelous bloodlines representing top producing strains; you want sound bitches of basic quality, free of any hereditary problems. There is no such thing as a "bargain" brood bitch. If you are offered one, be wary and bear in mind that you need the *best* and that the price will be correctly in ratio to the quality.

Conscientious German Shepherd breeders feel quite strongly that the only possible reason for producing puppies is the desire to improve and uphold quality and temperament within the breed, certainly not because one hopes to make a quick cash profit on a mediocre litter, which never works out that way in the long run and can very well wind up adding to the nation's shocking number of unwanted canine waifs. The only reason for breeding a litter is the ambition to produce high-quality puppies of intelligence, show potential, and sound temperament. That is the thought to be kept in mind right from the moment you begin to yearn for puppies.

Your Shepherd bitch should not be bred until her second period in season; but if she starts her season at an extra early age, say, barely over six months of age and then for the second time just past one year of age, you would be wise to wait until her third heat. Many breeders prefer to

Ch. Covy's Felita of Tucker Hill, ROM, by Ch. Lakeside's Gilligan's Island, ROM, ex Ch. Kovaya's Contessa, ROM, is the dam of five champions and one ROM daughter. Bred and owned by Gloria F. Birch and Cappy Pottle, Covy-Tucker Hill Kennels. Winning here under judge Mrs. James A. (Eleanor) Cole.

wait and finish their bitch's championship and then breed her, as pregnancy can be disastrous to a show coat and getting it back in shape again takes time. The waiting period can be profitably spent carefully watching for the ideal stud to complement her own qualities and be compatible with her background. Keeping this in mind, attend dog shows and watch the males who are winning and, even more important, siring the winners. Subscribe to *German Shepherd Dog Review* and some of the all-breed magazines and study the pictures and stories accompanying them to familiarize yourself with dogs in other areas of which you may have not been aware. Be sure to keep in mind that the stud should be strong in the bitch's weak points; carefully note his progeny to see if he passes along the features you want and admire. Make special note of any offspring from bitches with backgrounds similar to your bitch's; then you can get an idea of how well the background fits with his. When you see a stud dog that interests you, discuss your bitch with the owner and request a copy of his dog's

pedigree for your study and perusal. You can also discuss the stud dog with other knowledgeable breeders, including the one from whom your bitch was purchased. You may not always get an unbiased opinion (particularly if the person giving it also has an available stud dog), but discussion is a fine teacher. Listen to what they say and consider the value of their comments. As a result, you will be better qualified to reach a knowledgeable and intelligent decision on your own.

When you have made a tentative choice, contact the stud's owner to make the preliminary arrangements regarding the stud fee (whether it will be in cash or a puppy), approximate time the

Above: Fritzlund's Dixie of Five Oaks, a top producing daughter of Ch. Treffer and Brunhilda of Fritzlund. Owned by Rev. James Moore. **Below:** Fritzlund's Dark Lady, another top producing bitch by Ch. Treffer of Clover Acres ex Brunhilda of Fritzlund. Owned by Jackie Zerrlaut.

bitch should be ready, and so on. Find out, too, the requirements (such as a copy of your bitch's pedigree, health certificates, and tests) the stud owner has regarding bitches accepted for breeding. If you will be shipping the bitch, find out which airport and airline should be used.

The airlines will probably have special requirements, too, regarding conditions under which they will or will not take dogs. These requirements, which change from time to time, include such things as crate size and type they will accept. Most airlines have their own crates available for sale which may be purchased at a nominal cost, if you do not already have one that they consider suitable. These are made of fiberglass and are the safest type in which to ship a dog. Most airlines also require that the dog be at the airport two hours before the flight is scheduled to depart and that the dog is accompanied by a health certificate from your veterinarian, including information about rabies inoculation. If the airline does not wish to accept the bitch because of extreme temperature changes in the weather but will do so if you sign a waiver stating that she is accustomed to them and should have no problem, think it over carefully before doing so, as you are thus relieving them

of any responsibility should the bitch not reach her destination alive or in good condition. And always insure the bitch when you can.

Normally the airline must be notified several days in advance for the bitch's reservation, as only a limited number of dogs can be accommodated on each flight. Plan on shipping the bitch on her eighth or ninth day, but if at all possible arrange it so that she avoids travelling on the weekend when schedules are not always the same and freight offices are likely to be closed.

It is important that whenever possible you ship your bitch on a flight that goes directly to the airport which is her destination. It is not at all unusual, when stopovers are made along the way, for a dog to be removed from the plane with other cargo and either incorrectly loaded for the next leg of the flight or left behind. Take every precaution that you can against human error!

It is simpler if you can plan to bring the bitch to the stud dog. Some people feel that the trauma of the plane trip may cause the bitch not to conceive; others just plain prefer not sending them that way. If you have a choice, you might do better to take the bitch in your own car where she will feel more relaxed and at ease. If you are doing it this way, be sure to allow sufficient time

Covy-Tucker Hill's Carmelita, ROM at a little over five years of age, by Covy-Tucker Hill's Zinfandel, ROM, ex Ch. Covy's Felita of Tucker Hill, ROM. This Number Five Futurity Maturity Dam and Number Seven Highest Living ROM Dam in 1981 was bred by Cappy Pottle and Gloria F. Birch who co-own her with Morgan and Gloria Krumm.

Dixie of Clover Acres, bred and owned by the Murphys from a repeat breeding of Ch. Tannenwald's Igor and Clover Acres Frolich. This bitch is the dam of Ch. Treffer of Clover Acres.

This bitch, Ch. Fleetwood's Fawn, C.D., bred to Ch. Tannenwald's Igor, produced Bow Creek Kennels' "C" and "E" litters. Nancy Monahan is owner of Fawn, here handled by Ken Rayner to a good win at Harrisburg Kennel Club in 1968.

for the drive to get her to her destination at the correct time for the breeding. This usually is any time from the eighth to the fourteenth day, depending on the individual bitch and her cycle. Remember that if you want the bitch bred twice, you must allow a day in between the two services. Do not expect the stud's owner to put you up during your stay. Find a good, nearby motel that accepts dogs, and make a reservation for yourself there.

Just prior to your bitch's season, you should make a visit to your veterinarian with her. Have her checked for worms, make sure that she is up-to-date on all her shots, and attend to any other tests the stud owner may have requested. The bitch may act and be perfectly normal up until her third or fourth week of pregnancy, but it is better for her to have a clean bill of health before the breeding than to bother her after it. If she is

Ch. Cobert's Windsong, at about thirteen months of age, winning under judge Francis Ford, of the Fran-Jo Kennels, at the National Futurity Show, South Pacific Region, May 1974. In her first litter, Windsong produced two champion bitches and a Register of Merit male; and in her second litter, she produced two champion bitches. Co-owned by Gail Sprock (who is handling) and Connie Beckhardt.

National Futurity Show
Southern Pacific Region
Hosted by: Grand Canyon G.S.D.C.
May 5 1974 Judge: Mr. Fran Ford

overweight, right now is when you should start getting the fat off her; she should be in good hard condition, neither fat nor thin, when bred.

The day you've been waiting for finally arrives, and you notice the swelling of her vulva, followed within a day or two by the appearance of a colored discharge. Immediately call the stud's owner to finalize arrangements, advising whether you will ship her or bring her, the exact day she will arrive, and so on. Then, if she is going by plane, as soon as you know the details, advise the stud owner of the flight number, the time of arrival, and any other pertinent information. If you are shipping the bitch, the check for the stud fee should be mailed now. If the owner of the stud dog charges for his trips to the airport, for picking the bitch up and then returning her, reimbursement for this should either be included with the stud fee or sent as soon as you know the amount of the charge.

If you are going to ship your bitch, do not feed her on the day of the flight; the stud's owner will do so when she arrives. Be sure that she has had access to a drink of water just before you leave her and that she has been exercised prior to being put in her crate. Place several layers of newspapers, topped with some shredded papers, on the bottom of the crate for a good bed. The papers can be discarded and replaced when she reaches her destination prior to the trip home.

Rugs and towels are not suitable for bedding material as they may become soiled, necessitating laundering when she reaches her destination. A small towel may be included to make her feel more at home if you wish. Remember to have her at the airport two hours ahead of flight time.

If you are driving, be sure to arrive at a reasonable time of day. If you are coming from a distance and get in late, have a good night's sleep before contacting the stud's owner first thing in the morning. If possible, leave the children and relatives at home; they will not only be in the way, but also most stud owners definitely object to too many people around during the actual breeding.

Once the breeding has been completed, if you wish to sit and visit for a while, that is fine; but do not leave the bitch at loose ends. Take her to her crate in the car where she can be quiet (you should first, of course, ascertain that the temperature is comfortable for her there and that she has proper ventilation). Remember that she should not urinate for at least an hour following the breeding.

If you have not already done so, pay the stud fee now, and be sure that you receive your breeding certificate and a copy of the dog's pedigree if you do not have one.

Now you are all set to await, with happy anticipation, the arrival of the puppies.

Pedigrees

To anyone interested in the breeding of dogs, pedigrees are the basic component with which this is best accomplished. It is not sufficient to just breed two nice-looking dogs to one another and then sit back and await outstanding results. Chances are they will be disappointing, as there is no equal to a scientific approach to the breeding of dogs if quality results are the ultimate goal.

We have selected for you pedigrees of German Shepherd dogs and bitches who either are great producers or have come from consistently outstanding producing lines. Some of these dogs are so dominant that they have seemed to "click" with almost every strain or bloodline. Others, for best results, need to be carefully line-bred. The study of pedigrees and breeding is both a challenge and an exciting occupation.

Even if you have no plans to involve yourself in breeding and just anticipate owning and loving a dog or two, it is fun to trace back the pedigree of your dog, or dogs, to earlier generations and thus learn the sort of ancestors behind your own. Throughout this book you will find a great many pictures of dogs and bitches whose names appear in these pedigrees, enabling you not only to trace the names in the background of your German Shepherd but also to see what the forebears look like.

BERGLUFT, reg.

P. O. BOX 148, SEWICKLEY, PA. 15143

PEDIGREE

NAME _____ARNO VON BERGLUFT C.D.X._____

A.K.C. REG. NO. _WA-622858___ SEX __M__ DATE WHELPED _July 18, 1965_

BREEDER _____Dorit S. Rogers, P. O. Box 148, Sewickley, PA 15143_____

SIRE Wotan von Reverie WA-33228	Arno vom Haus Schwingel SchH III	Watzer von Bad Melle SchH III	Axel v.d. Deininghauser-heide SchH III, DPH, FH
			Immo von Bad Melle SchH II
		Edda vom grauen Dorn SchH I	Kuno vom Jungfernsprung SchH III, FH
			Brigga vom Rautheck SchH II
	Drossel vom glasernen Bild SchH I	Casar v.d. Malmannsheide SchH III, FH	Hein vom Richterbach SchH III
			Donka vom Muschelteich SchH III
		Burga v.d. Schlangenspitze SchH II	Bruno v.d. Riedperle
			Wolga vom Corneliushof SchH III, FH
DAM Michelle of Tom Bett WA-140073	Totana's Fal	Ch. Iro von Urari SchH III, FH	Cello v.d. Barnberger
			Esther von Urari
		Ursel vom Richterbach SchH I	Axel v.d. Deininghauser-heide SchH III, DPH, FH
			Hexe vom Richterbach
	Mona V	Ch. Xantos of Rocky Reach II	1953 Grand Victor Ch. Alert of Mi-Noah
			Ch. Karah vom Kupferhof CD
		Sycamore Lane's Schatzi	Donner of Da-Rie-Mar-Hill
			Lundhine's Gretchen

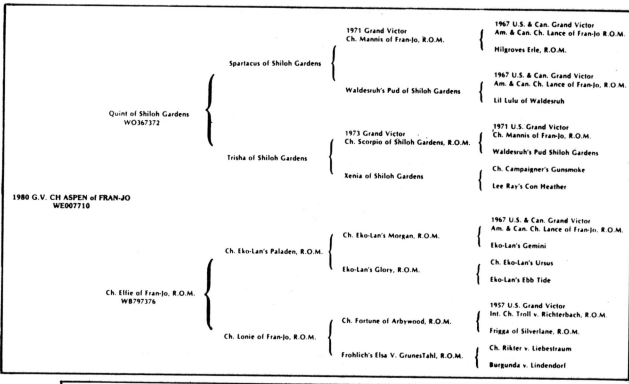

1980 G.V. CH ASPEN of FRAN-JO
WE007710

- Quint of Shiloh Gardens WO367372
  - Spartacus of Shiloh Gardens
    - 1971 Grand Victor Ch. Mannix of Fran-Jo, R.O.M.
      - 1967 U.S. & Can. Grand Victor Am. & Can. Ch. Lance of Fran-Jo R.O.M.
      - Hilgroves Erle, R.O.M.
    - Waldesruh's Pud of Shiloh Gardens
      - 1967 U.S. & Can. Grand Victor Am. & Can. Ch. Lance of Fran-Jo, R.O.M.
      - Lil Lulu of Waldesruh
  - Trisha of Shiloh Gardens
    - 1973 Grand Victor Ch. Scorpio of Shiloh Gardens, R.O.M.
      - 1971 U.S. Grand Victor Ch. Mannix of Fran-Jo, R.O.M.
      - Waldesruh's Pud Shiloh Gardens
    - Xenia of Shiloh Gardens
      - Ch. Campaigner's Gunsmoke
      - Lee Ray's Con Heather
- Ch. Elfie of Fran-Jo, R.O.M. WB797376
  - Ch. Eko-Lan's Paladen, R.O.M.
    - Ch. Eko-Lan's Morgan, R.O.M.
      - 1967 U.S. & Can. Grand Victor Am. & Can. Ch. Lance of Fran-Jo, R.O.M.
      - Eko-Lan's Gemini
    - Eko-Lan's Glory, R.O.M.
      - Ch. Eko-Lan's Ursus
      - Eko-Lan's Ebb Tide
  - Ch. Lonie of Fran-Jo, R.O.M.
    - Ch. Fortune of Arbywood, R.O.M.
      - 1957 U.S. Grand Victor Int. Ch. Troll v. Richterbach, R.O.M.
      - Frigga of Silverlane, R.O.M.
    - Frohlich's Elsa V. GrunesTahl, R.O.M.
      - Ch. Rikter v. Liebestraum
      - Burgunda v. Lindendorf

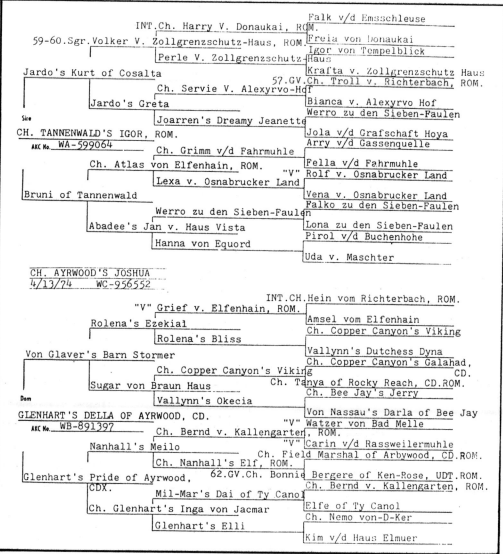

Sire

CH. TANNENWALD'S IGOR, ROM.
AKC No. WA-599064

- Jardo's Kurt of Cosalta
  - 59-60.Sgr.Volker V. Zollgrenzschutz-Haus, ROM.
    - INT.Ch. Harry V. Donaukai, ROM.
      - Falk v/d Emsschleuse
      - Freia von Donaukai
    - Perle V. Zollgrenzschutz-Haus
      - Igor von Tempelblick
      - Krafta v. Zollgrenzschutz Haus
  - Jardo's Greta
    - Ch. Servie V. Alexyrvo-Hof
      - 57.GV.Ch. Troll v. Richterbach, ROM.
      - Bianca v. Alexyrvo Hof
    - Joarren's Dreamy Jeanette
      - Werro zu den Sieben-Faulen
      - Jola v/d Grafschaft Hoya
- Bruni of Tannenwald
  - Ch. Grimm v/d Fahrmuhle
    - Ch. Atlas von Elfenhain, ROM.
      - Arry v/d Gassenquelle
      - Fella v/d Fahrmuhle
    - "V" Lexa v. Osnabrucker Land
      - Rolf v. Osnabrucker Land
      - Vena v. Osnabrucker Land
  - Abadee's Jan v. Haus Vista
    - Werro zu den Sieben-Faulen
      - Falko zu den Sieben-Faulen
      - Lona zu den Sieben-Faulen
    - Hanna von Equord
      - Pirol v/d Buchenhohe
      - Uda v. Maschter

CH. AYRWOOD'S JOSHUA
4/13/74   WC-956552

Dam

GLENHART'S DELLA OF AYRWOOD, CD.
AKC No. WB-891397

- Von Glaver's Barn Stormer
  - Rolena's Ezekial
    - "V" Grief v. Elfenhain, ROM.
      - INT.CH.Hein vom Richterbach, ROM.
      - Amsel vom Elfenhain
    - Rolena's Bliss
      - Ch. Copper Canyon's Viking
      - Vallynn's Dutchess Dyna
  - Sugar von Braun Haus
    - Ch. Copper Canyon's Viking
      - Ch. Copper Canyon's Galahad, CD.
      - Ch. Tanya of Rocky Reach, CD.ROM.
    - Vallynn's Okecia
      - Ch. Bee Jay's Jerry
      - Von Nassau's Darla of Bee Jay
- Glenhart's Pride of Ayrwood, CDX.
  - Nanhall's Meilo
    - Ch. Bernd v. Kallengarten, ROM.
      - "V" Watzer von Bad Melle
      - "V" Carin v/d Rassweilermuhle
    - Ch. Nanhall's Elf, ROM.
      - Ch. Field Marshal of Arbywood, CD.ROM.
      - 62.GV.Ch. Bonnie Bergere of Ken-Rose, UDT.ROM.
  - Ch. Glenhart's Inga von Jacmar
    - Mil-Mar's Dai of Ty Canol
      - Ch. Bernd v. Kallengarten, ROM.
      - Elfe of Ty Canol
    - Glenhart's Elli
      - Ch. Nemo von-D-Ker
      - Kim v/d Haus Elmuer

403

BERGLUFT, reg.

P. O. BOX 148, SEWICKLEY, PA. 15143

PEDIGREE

NAME _____ *BASKO VON BERGLUFT, C.D.* _____

A.K.C. REG. NO. _WA-816406_   SEX _M_   DATE WHELPED _October 24, 1966_

BREEDER _____ Dorit S. Rogers, P. O. Box 148, Sewickley, PA 15143 _____

SIRE V. Klodo a.d. Eremitenklause SchH III, Z Pr., A.D. WA-611847	Arras v. Adam- Riesezwinger SchH III, FH	Cito v. Coburger Land SchH II	Arno v.d. Bildhauergilde SchH II
			Ossy v. Schaefergruss SchH I
		Ella a.d. Eremitenklause SchH I	Ulf im Strudel SchH II
			Illa v. Haunstetten SchH III FH
	Halla a.d. Eremitenklause SchH III, FH	Iwo v. Johanneshauch SchH I	Benno v. Herbeder Schloss SchH III
			Ilse v. Sieghaus SchH II
		Freia a.d. Eremitenklause SchH I	Arno v.d. Pfaffenau SchH III
			Illa v. Haunstetten SchH III FH
DAM Long-Haven's Friendship C.D.X. WA-585468	Ch. Chief Master of Tatarus WA-141238	Eng. & Can. Ch. Vikkas Chieftan of Deanthorpe	Eng. Ch. Moonraker of Monteray
			Jolna of Jonquest
		Ballerina of Tatarus	Utz of Tatarus
			Damsel of Tatarus
	Valrich's Berna of Long-Haven WA-170833	Ch. Bernd v. Kallengarten SchH III ROM	Watzer v. Bad Melle SchH III
			Carin v.d. Rassweilermuhle
		Ch. Relita's Lucinda	Ch. Immo v. Niederschwarz- bach SchH II
			Elexis of Relita

CH-BLITZ VOM STEVERUFER

1. **Vater:**

Gr. Vic. Ch.
†Troll
vom
Richterbach

SchHIII FH
Angek. 1956-57

Rating V

HARLAN K. GIBBS, JR.

2. **Mutter:**

†Cita
vom der
Malmannsheide
862864

SchHI
angek. 1957-58

Rating V

†Axel von der
Deininghauserheide
SchHIII
DPH FH

Rating VA

†Lende vom
Richterbach
749438 SchHIII

Rating V

†Hein vom
Richterbach
700070 SchHIII

Rating V

†Donka vom
Muschelteich
763570 SchHIII

Rating V

†Immo vom
Hassenfang
568512 SchHIII

†Helma vom
Hildegardsheim
571076 SchHIII

†Fels vom
Vogtlandshof
694572 SchHIII

†Rosel vom
Osnabrucker Land
640725 SchHI

†Billo vom
Oberviehland
561004 SchHII FH

†Rosel vom
Osnabrucker Land
640725 SchHI

†Burkhard v. d.
Endmorane
668757 SchHII

†Asta
Siegeswillen
593094 SchHII

†Nestor v. Wiegerfelsen

†Dorte v. Hasenfang

†Gnom v. Kalsmont

†Tita v. d. Starrenburg

†Claudius vom Hain

†Barbel v. Haus Trippe

†Lex Preussenblut Land

†Maja v. Osnabrucker Land

†Odo z. d. Sieben Faulen

†Nute von Bern

†Lex Preussenblut

†Maja v. Osnabrucker Land

†Falter Preussenblut

†Favoritin Preussenblut

†Mix v. d. Hohenluft

†Dora v. Richterbach

CH CARLO VON DER HARDTPERLE

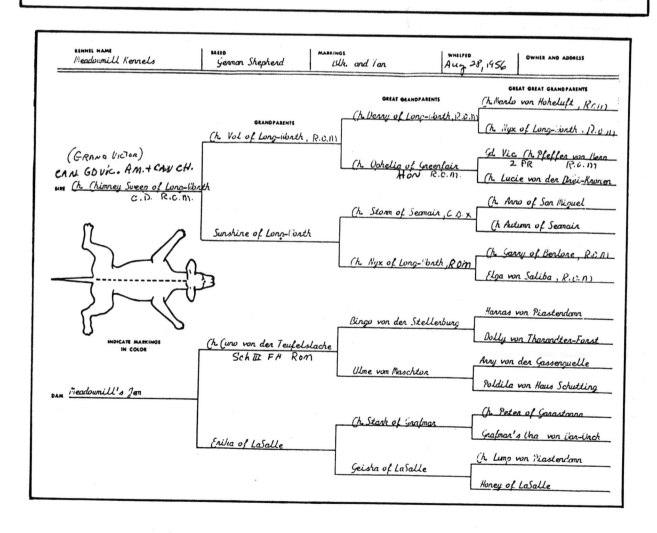

1. Vater:

†Klodo
aus der
Eremitenklause
970940 SchHIII
Angek. 1962-63
1960 Youth Seiger
Rating V

†Arras von
Adam-Riesezwinger
899377 SchHIII FH
‡1957-62
Rating V

†Halla aus der
Eremitenklause
932021 SchHIII FH
‡1959-64
Rating VA

†Cito vom
Coburger Land
751567 SchHII

†Ella aus der
Eremitenklause
833945 SchHI

†Iwo vom
Johanneshauch
820945 SchHI

†Freia aus der
Eremitenklause
858489 SchHI

†Arno von der Bildhauergilde

†Ossy vom Schafergruss

†Ulf im Strudel

†Illa von Haunstetten

†Benno vom Herbeder Schloss

†Ilse vom Sieghaus

†Arno von der Pfaffenau

†Illa von Haunstetten

2. Mutter:

†Carin
von der
Abtsburg
958575 SchHK
Angek. 1961-62
Rating V

†Axel von der
Asmusklinge
924088 SchHII
Rating V

†Britta von den
Drei Weiden
934933 SchHI
‡1959-60
Rating V

†Alf vom
Nordfelsen
739163 SchHIII

†Asta aus der
Sautanzgasse
820566 SchHI

†Falko vom
Haus Zurn
702131 SchHI

†Barbel aus der
Triebstrasse
858102 SchHI

†Axel v. d. Deininghauserheide

†Carin v. Bombergschen Park

†Casar vom Haus Dold

†Elly vom Alphorn

†Bero von der Kaiserfarm

†Burgel von Wernau

†Bero vom Geigerbrunnen

†Afra vom Rinschbachtal

KRAGSPOINT KENNELS
2905 HEMLOCK RD. YORK, PA.

KENNEL NAME	BREED	MARKINGS	WHELPED	OWNER AND ADDRESS
Meadowmill Kennels	German Shepherd	Blk. and Tan	Aug 28, 1956	

(GRAND VICTOR)
CAN. GD VIC. AM. + CAN CH.
SIRE Ch. Chimney Sweep of Long-Worth
C. D. R.O.M.

GRANDPARENTS
Ch. Vol of Long-Worth, R.O.M.

Sunshine of Long-Worth

GREAT GRANDPARENTS
Ch. Derry of Long-Worth, R.O.M.

Ch. Ophelia of Greenfair
Hon. R.O.M.

Ch. Storm of Seamair, C.D.x

Ch. Nyx of Long-Worth, R.O.M.

GREAT GREAT GRANDPARENTS
Ch. Marlo von Hoheluft, R.O.M.

Ch. Nyx of Long-Worth, R.O.M.

Gd. Vic. Ch. Pfeffer von Bern
2 PR R.O.M.

Ch. Lucie von der Drei-Kronen

Ch. Arno of San Miguel

Ch. Autumn of Seamair

Ch. Garry of Benlore, R.O.M.

Elga von Saliba, R.O.M.

INDICATE MARKINGS
IN COLOR

DAM Meadowmill's Jan

Ch. Cuno von der Teufelslache
Sch III FH Rom

Erika of LaSalle

Bingo von der Stellerburg

Ulme vom Maschtor

Ch. Stark of Grafmar

Geista of LaSalle

Harras von Piastendamm

Dolly von Tharandter-Forst

Any von der Gassenquelle

Poldila von Haus Schutting

Ch. Peter of Carastanna

Grafmar's Uba von Bar-Urch

Ch. Lump von Piastendamm

Honey of LaSalle

Cobert Kennels

MR. AND MRS. THEODORE BECKHARDT

6 ESSEX DRIVE
TENAFLY, NEW JERSEY 07670

Pedigree Certificate

CH. COBERT'S WINDSONG ROM

Name COBERT'S WHISPER JET OFA   A.K.C. # WC 464860   Sex: M   Breeder: Connie & Ted Beckhardt

Breed German Shepherd Dog   Color: Black with tan markings   Whelped: Apr. 29, 1973

SIRE	SIRE	SIRE	SIRE
	Grand Victor Ch. Mannix of Fran-Jo R.O.M.	Grand Victor Ch. Lance of Fran-Jo R.O.M. OFA	Ch. Fortune of Arbywood ROM
			DAM Frohlich's Elsa v Gruens
		DAM Hillgrove's Erle R.O.M.	**SIRE** Tahl ROM Ch.Bernd v Kallengarten ROM
Grand Victor Ch. Scorpio of Shiloh Gardens R.O.M.			**DAM** Ch Toni of Fieldstone
	DAM Waldesruh'a Pud of Shiloh Gardens	**SIRE** Grand Victor Ch. Lance of Fran-Jo R.O.M. OFA	**SIRE** Ch.Fortune of Arbywood ROM
			DAM Frohlich's Elsa v Gruens Tahl ROM
		DAM Lil Lulu of Waldesruh	**SIRE** Ch.Korporal of Waldesruh
			DAM Del-Dena of Waldesruh ROM
DAM	**SIRE** Grand Victor Ch. Lance of Fran-Jo R.O.M. O.F.A.	**SIRE** Ch. Fortune of Arbywood R.O.M.	**SIRE** G.V.Ch.Troll v Richterbach ROM
			DAM Frigga of Silver Lane ROM
		DAM Frohlich's Elsa v Gruens Tahl R.O.M.	**SIRE** Ch.Rikter v: Liebestraum
Select Ch.Cobert's Golly Gee of Lakeside OFA R.O.M.			**DAM** Burgunda v Lindendorf
	DAM Cobert's Melissa R.O.M.	**SIRE** Ch. Falk of Bihari Wonder C.D.	**SIRE** Ch.Bernd v KallengartenROM
			DAM Agnes Gold of Bihari Wonder
		DAM Select Ch.Cobert's Ernestine C.D.	**SIRE** Ch. Bernd v KallengartenROM
			DAM Ch.Cobert's Amber

THIS PEDIGREE IS CERTIFIED TO BE CORRECT TO THE BEST OF MY KNOWLEDGE AND BELIEF

Signed _____   Date _____

Cobert Kennels

MR. AND MRS. THEODORE BECKHARDT

6 ESSEX DRIVE
TENAFLY, NEW JERSEY 07670

Pedigree Certificate

Name: _CH_ COBERT'S TROLLSTIGEN _OFA_ A.K.C. # _WE330426_ Sex: _M_ Breeder: _Theodore Beckhardt_

Breed: _German Shepherd Dog_ Color: _Black with tan markings_ Whelped: _June 21, 1979_

SIRE	SIRE	SIRE	SIRE
Select Ch. Doppelt-Tay's Hawkeye R.O.M.	Ch. Eko-Lan's Paladen R.O.M. O.F.A.	Select Ch. Eko-Lan's Morgan R.O.M. O.F.A.	**SIRE** G.V. Ch. Lance of Fran-Jo R.O.M. O.F.A.
			DAM Eko-Lan's Gemini
		DAM Eko-Lan's Glory R.O.M.	**SIRE** Ch. Elwillo's Ursus O.F.A.
			DAM Eko-Lan's Ebb-Tide
	DAM Doppelt-Tay's Jessette	**SIRE** Am.&Can. Grand Victor Ch. Lance of Fran-Jo R.O.M. O.F.A.	**SIRE** Ch. Fortune of Arbywood R.O.M.
			DAM Frohlich's Elsa v Grunes-Tahl R.O.M.
		DAM Laurlloy's Admira	**SIRE** Ch. Doppelt-Tay's Jesse James R.O.M.
			DAM Classica v Ceages
DAM Ch. Cobert's Zephyr of Windigail _R.o.M_ O.F.A.	**SIRE** Select Am.& Can. Ch. Cobert's Reno of Lakeside R.O.M. O.F.A.	**SIRE** Am.&Can.Grand Victor Ch. Lance of Fran-Jo R.O.M.	**SIRE** Ch.Fortune of Arbywood R.O.M.
			DAM Frohlich's Elsa v Grunes-Tahl R.O.M.
		DAM Cobert's Melissa R.O.M.	**SIRE** Ch.Falk of Bihari Wonder CD
			DAM Select Ch.Cobert's Ernestine C.D.
	DAM Ch. Cobert's Windsong R.O.M.	**SIRE** Grand Victor Ch. Scorpio of Shiloh Gardens R.O.M.	**SIRE** Grand Victor Ch.Mannix of Fran-Jo R.O.M.
			DAM Waldesruh's Pud of Shiloh Gardens
		DAM Select Ch. Cobert's Golly Gee of Lakeside R.O.M. O.F.A.	**SIRE** G.V.Ch. Lance of Fran-Jo R.O.M.
			DAM Cobert's Melissa R.O.M.

THIS PEDIGREE IS CERTIFIED TO BE CORRECT TO THE BEST OF MY KNOWLEDGE AND BELIEF.

Signed _____ Date _____

407

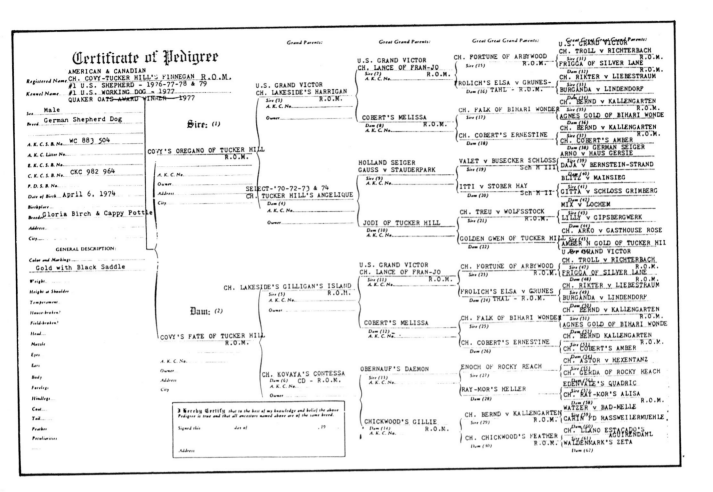

Certificate of Pedigree — American & Canadian — CH. COVY-TUCKER HILL'S FINNEGAN R.O.M.

Am. & Can. Ch. Cobert's Reno of Lakeside ROM
    Am. & Can. GV Ch. Lance of Fran-Jo ROM
    Cobert's Melissa ROM

Cobert's Sirocco of Windigail ROM

Ch. Cobert's Windsong ROM
    GV Ch. Scorpio of Shiloh Gardens ROM
    Ch. Cobert's Golly Gee of Lakeside ROM

Covy-Tucker Hill's Zinfandel ROM
    GV Ch. Lakeside's Harrigan ROM
    7 times Select Tucker Hill's Angelique CD ROM

Ch. Covy's Rosita of Tucker Hill

Ch. Covy's Felita of Tucker Hill ROM
    Ch. Lakeside's Gilligan's Island ROM
    Ch. Kovaya's Contessa CD ROM

Am. & Can., U.S. Select, Covy-Tucker Hill's Monte Alban, U.D., Am. & Can. C.D.X.

CH. COVY'S CARAWAY OF TUCKER HILL

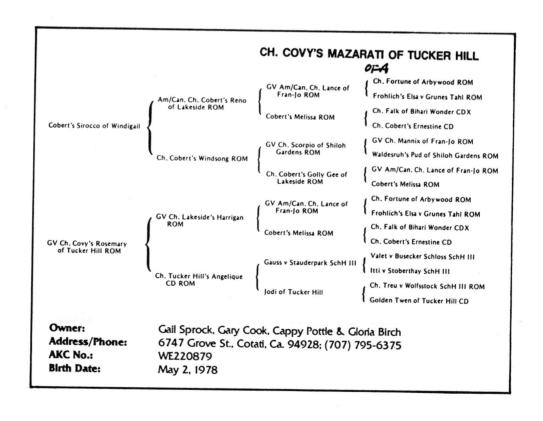

GV Ch. Lakeside's Harrigan ROM
- GV Ch. Lance of Fran-Jo ROM
  - Ch. Fortune of Arbywood ROM
    - GV Ch. Troll v. Richterbach ROM SchH III FH
    - Frigga of Silver Lane ROM
  - Frohlich's Elsa v. Grunes Tahl ROM
    - Ch. Rikter v. Liebestraum
    - Burgunda v. Lindendorf
- Cobert's Melissa ROM
  - Ch. Falk of Bihari Wonder CDX
    - Ch. Bernd v. Kallengarten SchH II ROM
    - Agnes Gold of Bihari Wonder
  - Ch. Cobert's Ernestine CD
    - Ch. Bernd v. Kallengarten SchH II ROM
    - Ch. Cobert's Amber

Ch. Tucker Hill's Angelique CD ROM
- Gauss v. Stauderpark SchH III
  - Valet v. Busecker Schloss SchH III
    - Arno v. Haus Gersie SchH III
    - Daja v. Bernstein-Strand SchH II
  - Itti v. Stoberthay SchH II
    - Elite v. Mainsieg SchH III
    - Gitta v. Schloss Grimberg SchH III
- Jodi of Tucker Hill
  - Ch. Treu v. Wolfsstock SchH III ROM
    - Mix v. Lochem SchH II
    - Lilly v. Gipsbergwerk SchH II
  - Golden Gwen of Tucker Hil CD
    - Ch. Arko v. Gasthaus Rose
    - Amber N Gold of Tucker Hill CD

1979

CH. COVY'S MAZARATI OF TUCKER HILL
OFA

Cobert's Sirocco of Windigail
- Am/Can. Ch. Cobert's Reno of Lakeside ROM
  - GV Am/Can. Ch. Lance of Fran-Jo ROM
    - Ch. Fortune of Arbywood ROM
    - Frohlich's Elsa v Grunes Tahl ROM
  - Cobert's Melissa ROM
    - Ch. Falk of Bihari Wonder CDX
    - Ch. Cobert's Ernestine CD
- Ch. Cobert's Windsong ROM
  - GV Ch. Scorpio of Shiloh Gardens ROM
    - GV Ch. Mannix of Fran-Jo ROM
    - Waldesruh's Pud of Shiloh Gardens ROM
  - Ch. Cobert's Golly Gee of Lakeside ROM
    - GV Am/Can. Ch. Lance of Fran-Jo ROM
    - Cobert's Melissa ROM

GV Ch. Covy's Rosemary of Tucker Hill ROM
- GV Ch. Lakeside's Harrigan ROM
  - GV Am/Can. Ch. Lance of Fran-Jo ROM
    - Ch. Fortune of Arbywood ROM
    - Frohlich's Elsa v Grunes Tahl ROM
  - Cobert's Melissa ROM
    - Ch. Falk of Bihari Wonder CDX
    - Ch. Cobert's Ernestine CD
- Ch. Tucker Hill's Angelique CD ROM
  - Gauss v Stauderpark SchH III
    - Valet v Busecker Schloss SchH III
    - Itti v Stoberthay SchH III
  - Jodi of Tucker Hill
    - Ch. Treu v Wolfsstock SchH III ROM
    - Golden Twen of Tucker Hill CD

Owner: Gail Sprock, Gary Cook, Cappy Pottle & Gloria Birch
Address/Phone: 6747 Grove St., Cotati, Ca. 94928; (707) 795-6375
AKC No.: WE220879
Birth Date: May 2, 1978

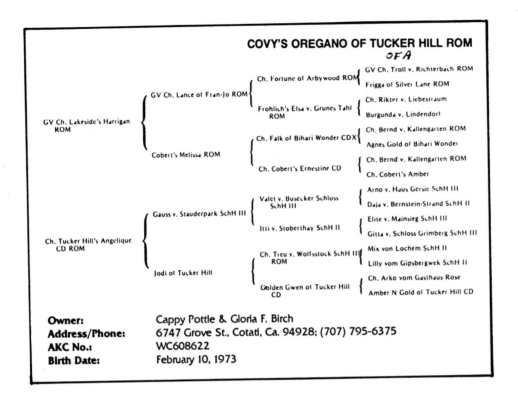

COVY'S OREGANO OF TUCKER HILL ROM
OFA

- GV Ch. Lakeside's Harrigan ROM
  - GV Ch. Lance of Fran-Jo ROM
    - Ch. Fortune of Arbywood ROM
      - GV Ch. Troll v. Richterbach ROM
      - Frigga of Silver Lane ROM
    - Frohlich's Elsa v. Grunes Tahl ROM
      - Ch. Rikter v. Liebestraum
      - Burgunda v. Lindendorl
  - Cobert's Melissa ROM
    - Ch. Falk of Bihari Wonder CDX
      - Ch. Bernd v. Kallengarten ROM
      - Agnes Gold of Bihari Wonder
    - Ch. Cobert's Ernestine CD
      - Ch. Bernd v. Kallengarten ROM
      - Ch. Cobert's Amber
- Ch. Tucker Hill's Angelique CD ROM
  - Gauss v. Stauderpark SchH III
    - Valet v. Busecker Schloss SchH III
      - Arno v. Haus Gersie SchH III
      - Daja v. Bernstein-Strand SchH II
    - Itti v. Stoberthay SchH II
      - Elite v. Mainsieg SchH III
      - Gitta v. Schloss Grimberg SchH III
  - Jodi of Tucker Hill
    - Ch. Treu v. Wolfsstock SchH III ROM
      - Mix von Lochem SchH II
      - Lilly vom Gipsbergwek SchH II
    - Golden Gwen of Tucker Hill CD
      - Ch. Arko vom Gasthaus Rose
      - Amber N Gold of Tucker Hill CD

Owner: Cappy Pottle & Gloria F. Birch
Address/Phone: 6747 Grove St., Cotati, Ca. 94928; (707) 795-6375
AKC No.: WC608622
Birth Date: February 10, 1973

PEDIGREE

Ch. Cuno von der Teufelslache
W - 341679 Black - Tan
4 November 1948

Inzucht auf:
Ingo Piastendamm (3-4)
Ferdl Secretainerie (4-4)
Claus Ueberfunder (5-5)

ELTERN	GROS-ELTERN	URGROS-ELTERN	URURGROS-ELTERN
VATER:	Harras vom Piastendamm SchH 111 FH	Ingo vom Piastendamm SchH 1 1	Gockel von Bern SchH Illa v. Oppeln-Ost SchH
Bingo		Birke vom Haus Mehner SchH1	Ferdl v. d. Secretainerie SchH Asta v. d. Badener-Hohe SchH
von der	Dolly vom Tharandter Forst SchH 1	Alf vom Piastendamm SchH 1 1	Amor v. Haus Ultra SchH 111 Lunte v. Piastendamm SchH1
Stellerburg SchH111		Gisa aus der Kressenhohle	Sigi v. d. Tatkraft PH SuchH Ilka v. Tharandter Forst ZPr
MUTTER:	Arry von der Gassenquelle SchH 1 1	Baldur vom Befreiungsplatz SchH 111 MHI	Sigbert Heidegrund ZPr. MHI Berna zur Saarkante SchH 1
Ulme		Claudia vom Marquardstein MHI	Ferdl v. d. Secretainerie SchH Ansa Landeszucht Wurttemberg SchI
vom	Poldila vom Haus Schutting SchH 1 1	Quell von Durmersheim SchH 111	Sigbert Heidegrund ZPr MHI Gisa v. Durmersheim ZPr
Maschtor SchH1		Cuna vom Hais Schutting SchH 1	Ingo v. Piastendamm SchH 1 1 Uxa v. Haus Schutting ZPr

410

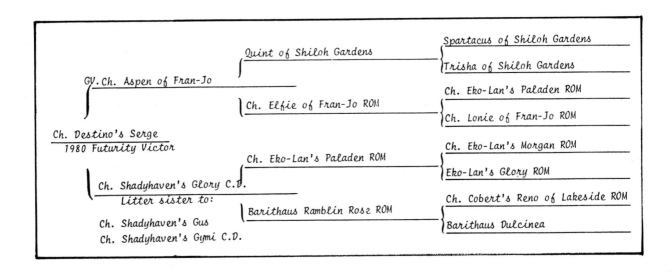

			Spartacus of Shiloh Gardens
		Quint of Shiloh Gardens	
			Trisha of Shiloh Gardens
GV.Ch. Aspen of Fran-Jo			Ch. Eko-Lan's Paladen ROM
		Ch. Elfie of Fran-Jo ROM	
			Ch. Lonie of Fran-Jo ROM

Ch. Destino's Serge
1980 Futurity Victor

			Ch. Eko-Lan's Morgan ROM
		Ch. Eko-Lan's Paladen ROM	
Ch. Shadyhaven's Glory C.D.			Eko-Lan's Glory ROM
Litter sister to:			Ch. Cobert's Reno of Lakeside ROM
Ch. Shadyhaven's Gus		Barithaus Ramblin Rose ROM	
Ch. Shadyhaven's Gymi C.D.			Barithaus Dulcinea

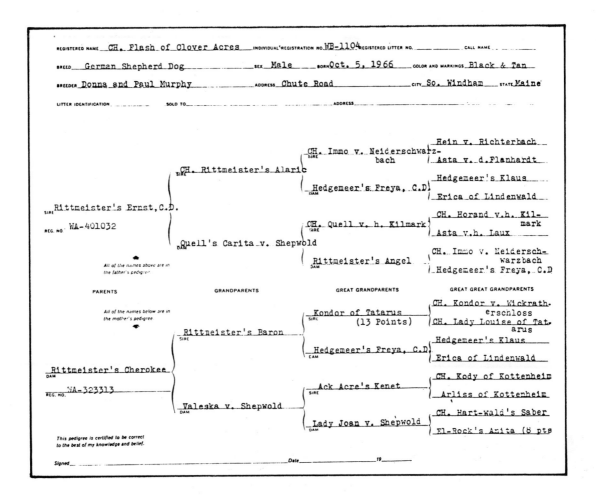

REGISTERED NAME **CH. Flash of Clover Acres** INDIVIDUAL REGISTRATION NO. **WB-1104** REGISTERED LITTER NO. _____ CALL NAME _____

BREED **German Shepherd Dog** SEX **Male** BORN **Oct. 5, 1966** COLOR AND MARKINGS **Black & Tan**

BREEDER **Donna and Paul Murphy** ADDRESS **Chute Road** CITY **So. Windham** STATE **Maine**

LITTER IDENTIFICATION _____ SOLD TO _____ ADDRESS _____

PARENTS	GRANDPARENTS	GREAT GRANDPARENTS	GREAT GREAT GRANDPARENTS
		CH. Immo v. Neiderschwarz-bach	Hein v. Richterbach
	CH. Rittmeister's Alaric		Asta v. d.Flanhardt
		Hedgemeer's Freya, C.D.	Hedgemeer's Klaus
Rittmeister's Ernst,C.D.			Erica of Lindenwald
REG. NO. WA-401032		CH. Quell v. h. Kilmark	CH. Horand v.h. Kilmark
	Quell's Carita v. Shepwold		Asta v.h. Laux
		Rittmeister's Angel	CH. Immo v. Neidersch-warzbach
			Hedgemeer's Freya, C.D
		Kondor of Tatarus (13 Points)	CH. Kondor v. Wickrath-erschloss
	Rittmeister's Baron		CH. Lady Louise of Tatarus
		Hedgemeer's Freya, C.D.	Hedgemeer's Klaus
Rittmeister's Cherokee			Erica of Lindenwald
WA-323313		Ack Acre's Kenet	CH. Kody of Kottenheim
	Valeska v. Shepwold		Arliss of Kottenheim
		Lady Joan v. Shepwold	CH. Hart-wald's Saber
			El-Rock's Anita (8 pts

All of the names above are in the father's pedigree

All of the names below are in the mother's pedigree

This pedigree is certified to be correct to the best of my knowledge and belief.

Signed _____ Date _____ 19___

HOHELUFT KENNELS

STATEN ISLAND, N. Y.

—

GERMAN SHEPHERD DOGS

PEDIGREE OF ___FRIGGA VON HOHELUFT___

A. K. C. No. __A 530480__

DATE OF BIRTH	May 21, 1941
SEX	Female
PLACE OF BIRTH	Staten Island
COLOR	Black and gray
BREEDER	John Gans
ADDRESS	Staten Island, N.Y.

SIRE: Champion Nox of Ruthland
U.S. Grand Victor 1941

- Champion Pfeffer von Bern
  German Sieger 1937
  U.S. Grand Victor 1937/38
  - Dachs von Bern
    - Alex von Ebersnacken
    - Vicki von Bern
  - Clara von Bern
    - Edo vom Pagensgrueb
    - Freude von Richrath
- Champion Carol of Ruthland
  - Ferdl von der Secretainerie
    - Odin von Stolzenfels German Sieger 1933
    - Tilde von der Secretainerie
  - Devise vom Haus Schuetting
    - Dachs von Bern
    - Dolly von Rehkolk

DAM: Champion Lady of Ruthland
U.S. Grand Victrix 1940

- Champion Pfeffer von Bern
  German Sieger 1937
  U.S. Grand Victor 1937/38
  - Dachs von Bern
    - Alex von Ebersnacken
    - Vicki von Bern
  - Clara von Bern
    - Edo vom Pagensgrueb
    - Freude von Richrath
- Champion Frigga von Kannenbaeckerland U.S. Grand Victrix 1936
  - Odinulf vom Haus Schuetting
    - Hussan vom Haus Schuetting
    - Mascha vom Haus Schuetting
  - Tilla vom Hallerwald
    - Utz von Fuessen
    - Cilberta vom Winnfeld

THIS PEDIGREE IS CERTIFIED TO BE CORRECT TO THE BEST OF OUR KNOWLEDGE AND BELIEF

DATED __January 24, 1942__

OWNER OF KENNEL

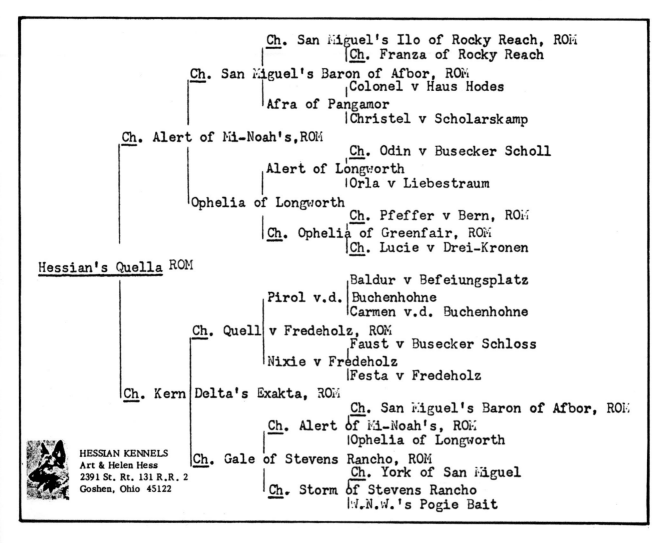

Ch. San Miguel's Ilo of Rocky Reach, ROM
Ch. Franza of Rocky Reach
Ch. San Miguel's Baron of Afbor, ROM
Colonel v Haus Hodes
Afra of Pangamor
Christel v Scholarskamp
Ch. Alert of Mi-Noah's, ROM
Ch. Odin v Busecker Scholl
Alert of Longworth
Orla v Liebestraum
Ophelia of Longworth
Ch. Pfeffer v Bern, ROM
Ch. Ophelia of Greenfair, ROM
Ch. Lucie v Drei-Kronen

Hessian's Quella ROM

Baldur v Befeiungsplatz
Pirol v.d. Buchenhohne
Carmen v.d. Buchenhohne
Ch. Quell v Fredeholz, ROM
Faust v Busecker Schloss
Nixie v Fredeholz
Festa v Fredeholz
Ch. Kern Delta's Exakta, ROM
Ch. San Miguel's Baron of Afbor, ROM
Ch. Alert of Mi-Noah's, ROM
Ophelia of Longworth
Ch. Gale of Stevens Rancho, ROM
Ch. York of San Miguel
Ch. Storm of Stevens Rancho
W.N.W.'s Pogie Bait

HESSIAN KENNELS
Art & Helen Hess
2391 St. Rt. 131 R.R. 2
Goshen, Ohio 45122

Immo v. Hassenfang

Axel v. d. Deininghauserheide

Helma v. Vogtlandshof

GR. VICTOR CH. Troll v. Richterbach, ROM

Fels v. Vogtlandshof

Lende v. Richterbach

Rosel v. Osnabrueckerland

CH. Kurt vom Bid-Scono

Utz v. d. Schwbenheimat

Arno v. Beerbach

Katja v. Leihenfeld

Bella v. d. Wagnersgruben

Hussan v. Sanriterstift

Cita v. Tauenwalde

Tilla v. d. Katenburg

1963 GRAND VICTRIX OF U. S.
CH. HESSIAN'S VOGUE ROM

CH. San Miguel's Ilo of RR, ROM

CH. Baron of Afbor, ROM

Afra of Pangamor

GR. VICTOR CH. Alert of Mi-Noah's, ROM

Alert of Longworth

Ophelia of Longworth

Ophelia of Greenfair, ROM

Hessian's Quella ROM

Pirol v. d. Buchenhohne

CH. Quell v. Fredeholz ROM

Nixie v. Fredeholz

CH. Kern Delta's Exakta, ROM

GV CH. Alert of Mi-Noah's ROM

CH. Gale of Stevens Rancho, ROM

CH. Storm of Stevens Rancho

CH Job of Gan Edan

CH Ozark of Gan Edan	CH Gabriel of Gan Edan	CH Beau of Fran-Jo-ROM	GV CH Lance of Fran-Jo ROM
			Fran-Jo's Kelly of Waldesruh
		Bee-Jay's Holiday of Gan Edan ROM	CH Britmere's Timothy of Lahngold
			Trulander's Crimson of Marsa
	Andoro's Aria	CH Zar-Zal's Ilko	GV CH Lance of Fran-Jo ROM
			CH Amber's Valiant Robin ROM
		Ellyn Hill's Diamond Flush ROM	CH Eko-Lan's Paladen ROM
			Ronette of Ellyn Hill
Fran-Jo's Dawn of Gan Edan ROM	CH Zeto of Fran-Jo ROM	GV CH Lance of Fran-Jo ROM	CH Fortune of Arbywood ROM
			Frohlich's Elsa V Grunestahl ROM
		CH Mirheim's Abby, ROM	GV CH Lance of Fran-Jo ROM
			CAN CH Kingsdown Amber
	Lonnie of Jo-Mar	CH Eko-Lan's Paladen ROM	CH Eko-Lan's Morgan ROM
			Eko-Lan's Glory ROM
		Elfie of Jo-Mar	GV CH Lance of Fran-Jo ROM
			Anka of Jo-Mar

Leistungszucht

Klodo aus der Eremitenklause

Rüde   stockhaarig

schwarz, gelbe Abzeichen

Wurftag: 15. Februar 1959   **Wurfjahr:** Neunzehnhundertneunundfünfzig

Züchter: Jean W.Klob,Staffelstein

Inzucht: Illa Haunstetten (3-3)   **Geschwister:**   Karlo sgbA/Karry sggrA/Kay
sggrA/Kim sggrA/King sggrA
Kirk sggrA/Kosak sggrA
Karin sgA/Kascha sgA

Wurfstärke   8,?   **Ammenaufzucht 4,o**

Eingetragen in das Zuchtbuch   Für die Richtigkeit vor-
für deutsche Schäferhunde (SZ)   stehender Angaben:
Bd.:   58
Nr.   97o94o   der Züchter   (Zuchtbuchamt)
                               (Jean W.Klob)

Ausgefertigt am 8.April 1959   Goethestr. 37
Staffelstein

                          Eintragungs-und Prüfungsbestätigung:

                          der oben bezeichnete deutsche Schäferhund
ist am 8. April 1959 in das Zuchtbuch für
deutsche Schäferhunde (SZ) unter
Nr. 97o94o eingetragen worden.

Diese Eintragung wird als der Richtigkeit entsprechend bestätigt.

Augsburg, den 23. August 1966   Das Zuchtbuchamt des SV
                                 I.A.:

I. Eltern	II. Groß-Eltern	III. Urgroß-Eltern	IV. Ururgroß-Eltern	
1 **Vater:** Arras vom Adam-Riesezwinger 899377 SchHIII FH +1957-62 **Farbe u. Abz.** sgrgA **Körbericht:** Knapp mittelgroß, gute Allgemeinerscheinung und Winkelungen, gut geschlossen, guter Gesamtgebäudeaufbau, schon reichlich schwer,Rücken fest, gute Winkelungen und raumschaffende Gänge, ruhiges sicheres Wesen, guter Kampftrieb. **ZB:** V **Geschwister:** Afra grgew,M/Asta sb	**3** Cito vom Coburger Land 751567 SchHII +1954-58 sgA **Körbericht:** Knapp mittelgroß, gute Kraft, guter Rücken, gute Brustverhältnisse, leicht flachrippig, abfallende Kruppe, gute Winkelungen, gut in Verfassung und Ausdruck, sicheres Wesen. **ZB:** V **Geschwister:** Carlo sgA SchHIII SG/Claus sgA/Cuno sgA/Cora sgA	**7** +Arno von der Bildhauergilde 628892 SchHII **8** +Ossy vom Schäfergruß 644079 SchHII	**15** +Cuno v. Alt Bebenberg 525204 SchHII **16** +Cilly v. Haus Theby 578933 **17** +Kosak v. Holzheimer Eichwald 565552 SchHI **18** +Centa v. Schäfergruß 572630 SchHII	
	4 Ella aus der Eremitenklause 833923 SchHI grgewgbA **Körbericht:** **ZB:** SG **Geschwister:** Edo grgbA/Eggo grgewgbA SchHIII SG/Edda sgbA,SG/+Eska sgbA SchHI SG/Esta sigrdgew SchHI SG	**9** +Ulf im Strudel 6o6631 SchHII **10** +Illa von Haunstetten 7o135o SchHIII FH	**19** +Super v. d. Buchenhöhe 561269 SchHI **20** +Xira im Strudel 555373 SchHI **21** +Cralo von Haunstetten 574473 SchHII **22** +Liesl v. Haunstetten 614796 SchHII	
2 **Mutter:** Halla aus der Eremitenklause 932021 SchHIII FH +1959-60 -65 **Farbe u. Abz.** sgbA **Körbericht:** Mittelgroß, und kräftig,bestens angelegt, mit sehr guten Brustverhältnissen und Winkelungen gut geschlossen und frei in den Gängen. Gut in Verfassung, Ausdruck und Wesen, ausgeprägter Kampftrieb. **ZB:** V-A **Geschwister:** Hanso sgbA SchHI/Hektor grgbA,ü/+Heike grgbA SchHII V/+Hella ngbA SchHI V/Hexe sgbA	**5** Iwo vom Johanneshauch 82o945 SchHI +1954-59 grgM **Körbericht:** Mittelgroß, knochenkräftig, gehaltvoll, gute Brustbildung und Festigkeit,normale Winkelungen und ausgreifende Gänge.Gut in Verfassung, Ausdruck und Wesen. **ZB:** V **Geschwister:** Illo sgrgA SchHI/Immo sgrgA SG/+Illa grgM SchHI V Ilse grgM/+Inge sgA SchHIII FH SG	**11** +Benno vom Herbeder Schloß 7o1662 SchHIII **12** +Ilse von Sieghaus 635893 SchHII	**23** +Claudius vom Hain 58667o SchHII **24** Bärbel v. d. Grengeldansburg 635578 SchHII **25** +Lord v. Zenntal 591767 SchHII **26** +Burga v. d. Marienbrücke 519633 SchHII	
	6 Freia aus der Eremitenklause 858489 SchHII +1957 sgbA **Körbericht:** Groß, kräftig, zeigt gute Allgemeinerscheinung und Verfassung, bei gutem Gesamtgebäudeaufbau ist der Oberarm leicht steil gelagert, gute Hinterhandwinkelung, gute kraftvolle Gänge. **ZB:** SG **Geschwister:** Falk grgbA/Falko sgbA/Fauna sgbA/+Flunk grgbA SchHII SG	**13** +Arno von der Pfaffenau 73309o SchHIII **14** +Illa von Haunstetten 7o135o SchHIII FH	**27** +Siggo v. Corneliunhof 6o64oo SchHIII FH **28** +Dora v. Haus Stephan 648578 SchHIII **29** +Cralo v. Haunstetten 574473 SchHII **30** +Liesl v. Haunstetten 614796 SchHII Schn

Certified Pedigree

WD 056587
INDIVIDUAL REG NO

Kane
CALL NAME

WM 198761
LITTER REG NO

AKC
REGISTERED WITH

Ch. Kubistraums Kane, ROM
REGISTERED NAME OF DOG

BREED **German Shepherd Dog** DATE WHELPED **March 11, 1975** SEX **Male**

BREEDER **Verna M. Kubik & Linda R. Dries** ADDRESS **Rt. 1 Box 145A Stillwater, Mn. 55082**

OWNER **Verna M. Kubik** Phone: 715-549-6365 after 6 p.m.

GENERAL DESCRIPTION **Black with Tan Markings**

SIRE

G.V. Ch. Lance of Fran-Jo, ROM

- Ch. Fortune of Arbywood, ROM
  - G.V. Ch. Troll V. Richterbach, ROM
    - Axel V. Deiningshauserheide
    - Lende V. Richterbach
  - Frigga of Silver Lane, ROM
    - Ch. Cito V. Hermannschleuse
    - Ch. Jewel of Judex
- Frohlich's Elsa V. Grunestal, ROM
  - Ch. Rikter V. Liebestraum
    - G.V. Ch. Bill V. Kleistweg, ROM
    - Sigga V. Liebestraum
  - Bergunda V. Lindendorf
    - Harold V. Schlehenbusche
    - Ch. Ylerta V. Liebestraum

Ch. Coberts Reno of Lakeside ROM
REG. NO. OFA #2270

- Ch. Falk of Bihari Wonder, C.D.
  - Ch. Bernd V. Kallengarten, ROM
    - Watzer V. Bad Melle
    - Carin V/D Rassweilermuhle
  - Agnes Gold of Bihari Wonder
    - Ch. Wotan V. Richterbach, CDX, ROM
    - Kobedl's Jetta
- Cobert's Melissa, ROM
  - Ch. Cobert's Ernestine, C.D.
    - Ch. Bernd V. Kallengarten, ROM
      - Watzer V. Bad Melle
      - Carin V/D Rassweilermuhle
    - Ch. Cobert's Amber
      - Ch. Marko V. Gurkenland
      - Hobby House Katja of the Hills

Kubistraum

DAM

G.V. Ch. Hollamor's Judd, ROM

- G.V. Ch. Yoncalla's Mike, ROM
  - Yoncalla's Mr. America
    - Ch. Bernd V Kallengarten, ROM
    - Yoncalla's Jola
  - Yoncalla's Collette
    - Ch. Fritz of Maryden, C.D.
    - DeLoma's Priscilla
- Panchon of Edgetowne
  - Ch. Bernd V. Kallengarten, ROM
    - Watzer V. Bad Melle
    - Carin V/D Rassweilermuhle
  - Ch. Ona of Edgetowne
    - Ch. Grendamar's Jose of Longworth
    - Ina of Edgetowne

Falkora's Catalina, C.D., ROM
REG. NO. WB 670790
OFA GS 2528

- Ch. Falko V. Celler Schloss, ROM
  - Ch. Bismarok V. Graustein, ROM
    - Ch. Nordraak of Matterhorn, ROM
    - Ch. Ulla of Rocky Reach, ROM
  - Holly V. Celler Schloss
    - Enoch of Rocky Reach
    - Leyva of Rocky Reach
- Jubilee V. Celler Schloss
  - Ch. Fant Wikingerblut
    - Ch. Ulk Wikingerblut, ROM
    - Sasha Wikingerblut, ROM
  - Robin of Nikral, ROM
    - Von Darian's Royal Talle
      - Ch. Von Darian's Cuno
      - Ch. Lark of Kingscroft

SEL. CH. LINNLOCH SUNDOWN VON FREYA

OFA #GS 9075-T

BEST IN SHOW WINNER

SELECT 1979 NATIONAL SPECIALTY • BEST MATURITY 1979 - NORTHWESTERN

Am & Can GV Ch Lance of Fran-Jo ROM OFA GS-401
Am & Can GV Ch Lakeside's Harrigan ROM OFA GS-2441
Cobert's Melissa ROM
Covy-Tucker Hill's Zinfandel ROM OFA GS-6054
Gaus v Stauderpark OFA GS-269
Sel Ch Tucker Hill's Angelique CD ROM OFA GS-1935
Jodi of Tucker Hill

Am & Can GV Ch Lance of Fran-Jo ROM OFA GS-401
Ch Salanchar Brinn v Liebestraum CD OFA GS-2310
Mira v Paradies der Vierfussler
Linnloch Klassie v Vel-Bren
Sel Ch Lakeside's Gilligan's Island ROM OFA GS-2409
Komot's Linnloch Glorianna OFA GS-2971
Tucker Hill's Quesa, CD

Owner: JAMES L. HALFERTY • 3615 Yorkshire Road • Pasadena, California 91107 • (213) 449-6520
Co-owner: MARY C. ROBERTS

BERGLUFT, reg.

P. O. BOX 148, SEWICKLEY, PA. 15143

PEDIGREE

NAME _____ LONG HAVEN'S FRIENDSHIP C.D.X. _____

A.K.C. REG. NO. WA-585468 _____ SEX F _____ DATE WHELPED September 7, 1962

BREEDER _____

SIRE			
	Eng. & Can. Ch. Vikkas Chieftan of Deanthorpe	Eng. Ch. Moonraker of Monteray	Juggernaut of Jonquest
			June of Eveley
		Jolna of Jonquest	Czar of Frairsbush
Ch. Chief Master of Tatarus			Janice of Jonques.
WA-141238	Ballerina of Tatarus	Utz of Tatarus	Ch. Uncus of Long-Worth
			Damsel of Tatarus
		Damsel of Tatarus	Prince Amor of Tatarus
			Playgirl of Tatarus
DAM			
	Ch. Bernd v. Kallengarten	Watzer v. Bad Melle	Axel von der Deininghauserheide SchH III
			Immo von Bad Melle
		Carin von der Rassweilermuhle	Kuno von Jungfernsprung
Valrich's Berna of Long's Haven			Cara von der Silberweide
WA-170833	Ch. Relita's Lucinda	Ch. Immo von Niederschwarzbach	Ch. Hein von Richterbach
			Asta von der Flanhardt
		Elexis of Relita	Ch. Grasslands Klodo
			Rhoda von Markath

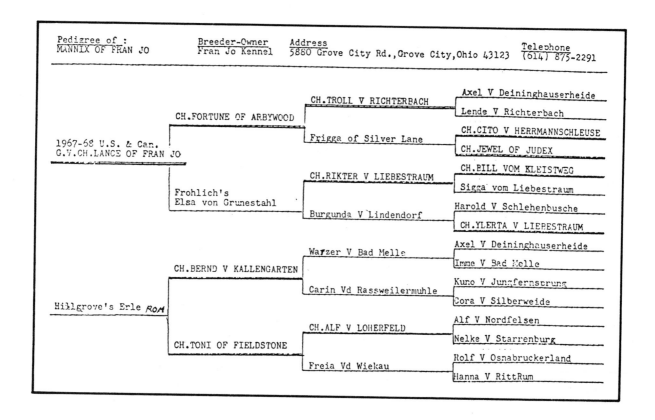

Pedigree of:
MANNIX OF FRAN JO

Breeder-Owner
Fran Jo Kennel

Address
5880 Grove City Rd., Grove City, Ohio 43123

Telephone
(614) 875-2291

		CH.TROLL V RICHTERBACH	Axel V Deininghauserheide
	CH.FORTUNE OF ARBYWOOD		Lende V Richterbach
1967-68 U.S. & Can.		Frigga of Silver Lane	CH.CITO V HERRMANNSCHLEUSE
G.V.CH.LANCE OF FRAN JO			CH.JEWEL OF JUDEX
		CH.RIKTER V LIEBESTRAUM	CH.BILL VOM KLEISTWEG
	Frohlich's Elsa von Grunestahl		Sigga vom Liebestraum
		Burgunda V Lindendorf	Harold V Schlehenbusche
			CH.YLERTA V LIEBESTRAUM
		Warzer V Bad Melle	Axel V Deininghauserheide
	CH.BERND V KALLENGARTEN		Imme V Bad Melle
		Carin Vd Rassweilermuhle	Kuno V Jungfernsprung
Hillgrove's Erle ROM			Cora V Silberweide
		CH.ALF V LOHERFELD	Alf V Nordfelsen
	CH.TONI OF FIELDSTONE		Nelke V Starrenburg
		Freia Vd Wiekau	Rolf V Osnabruckerland
			Hanna V RittRum

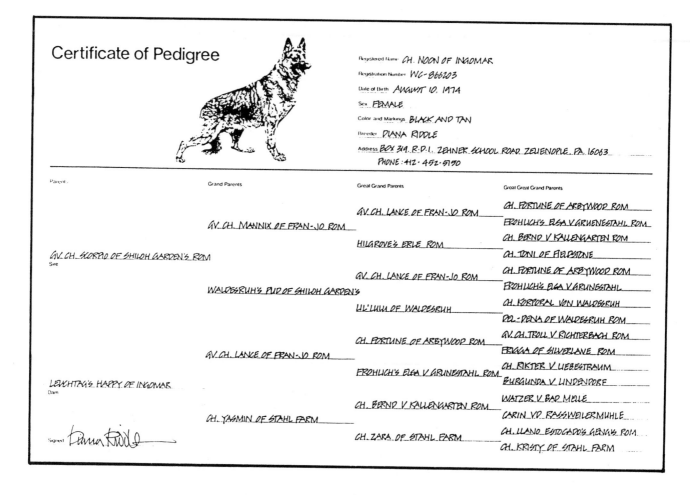

Certificate of Pedigree

Registered Name: CH. NOON OF INGOMAR
Registration Number: WC-866203
Date of Birth: AUGUST 10, 1974
Sex: FEMALE
Color and Markings: BLACK AND TAN
Breeder: DIANA RIDDLE
Address: BOX 34, R.D.I. ZEHNER SCHOOL ROAD, ZELIENOPLE, PA. 16063
PHONE: 412-452-5170

Parent	Grand Parents	Great Grand Parents	Great Great Grand Parents
		GV. CH. LANCE OF FRAN-JO ROM	CH. FORTUNE OF ARBYWOOD ROM
	GV. CH. MANNIX OF FRAN-JO ROM		FROHLICH'S ELSA V GRUENESTAHL ROM
		HILGROVE'S ERLE ROM	CH. BERND V KALLENGARTEN ROM
GV. CH. SCORPIO OF SHILOH GARDEN'S ROM (Sire)			CH. TONI OF FIELDSTONE
		GV. CH. LANCE OF FRAN-JO ROM	CH. FORTUNE OF ARBYWOOD ROM
	WALDESRUH'S PUD OF SHILOH GARDEN'S		FROHLICH'S ELSA V GRUNESTAHL
		LIL'LULU OF WALDESRUH	CH. KORPORAL VON WALDESRUH
			DEL-PENA OF WALDESRUH ROM
		CH. FORTUNE OF ARBYWOOD ROM	GV. CH. TROLL V RICHTERBACH ROM
	GV. CH. LANCE OF FRAN-JO ROM		FRIGGA OF SILVERLANE ROM
		FROHLICH'S ELSA V GRUNESTAHL ROM	CH. RIKTER V LIEBESTRAUM
LEUCHTAG'S HAPPY OF INGOMAR (Dam)			BURGUNDA V LINDENDORF
		CH. BERND V KALLENGARTEN ROM	WATZER V BAD MELLE
	CH. YASMIN OF STAHL FARM		CARIN VD. RASSWEILERMUHLE
		CH. ZARA OF STAHL FARM	CH. LLANO ESTOGADO'S GENJA'S ROM
			CH. KRISTY OF STAHL FARM

Signed: Diana Riddle

FEDERACION CANINA DE VENEZUELA

Certificado de Registro Genealogico

CAMPEON VENEZOLANO

NOMBRE: +++++++++++++++++ OLGA DE ONDARRETA ++++++++++++++++++

SEXO: Hembra.

RAZA: Pastor Alemán.

PAIS DE NACIMIENTO: VENEZUELA.

FECHA DE NACIMIENTO: +++Ocho de febrero de mil novecientos setenta y cinco+++

COLOR PREDOMINANTE Y MARCAS: Negro y marrón.

CRIADOR: María I. de Urquijo.

PADRES	ABUELOS	BISABUELOS
Ch. WINAKI'S HOMBRE OF LAKESIDE FCV 316-4270	Ch. Lance of Fran-Jo AKC WA466021 (9-65)	Ch. Fortune of Arbywood AKC W862973 (4-63)
		Frohlich's Elsa v Grunes Tahl AKC W960831 (6-60)
	Cobert's Melissa AKC WA912988 (3-69)	Ch. Falk of Bihari Wonder CD AKC WA469830 (7-67)
		Ch. Cobert's Ernestine CD AKC WA161142 (11-62)
Ch. LUR DE ONDARRETA FCV 316-3810	Oleg von der Doeheimerhöhe FCV 316-3771	Marko vom Cellerland SchHIII SZ 1169323
		Ira von der Goldlache SchHI SZ 1158445
	Cora vom Alten Kloster FCV 316-2379	Bernd vom Lierberg SchHIII FH SZ 1026193
		Kyra von der Bimsgrube SchHI SZ 1036336

PROPIETARIO

María I. de URQUIJO
6ª Transversal,
Quinta "María Luisa",
Altamira, Caracas 106.

CEDULA DE IDENTIDAD: 937735

ESTE CERTIFICADO ES NULO Y SIN VALOR SI NO ESTA SELLADO Y FIRMADO.

Asentado en el Registro Genealógico, Libro 3 *Tomo* XII
el día 17 *de* febrero *de* 1975.

PARTO No. U3162444

FUNCIONARIO AUTORIZADO

NO. DE REGISTRO: 316-4611

Kör- und Leistungszucht!   Körklasse Ia

Hüftdysplasie-Untersuchung = Kein Hinweis (H 168)

P O L L U X   vom   B u s e c k e r - S c h l o ß
==

SZ-Nr. 106 7301 - Wurftag: 18. März 1964 - AusbKz: SchH III FH
Schaubewertung "V"

Züchter: Alfred Hahn, Großen Buseck/Hessen
Besitzer: Walter Endeward, 3123 Bodenteich Kr. Uelzen/Han., Waldweg 49

Auszug aus dem Körbericht siehe Rückseite:

Tel. 05824/638

+ Valet vom Busecker Schloß SchH III ZB: "V" (hoher Vererber) Groß, gehaltvoll, mit sehr guten Ausdruck, festem Rücken, guter Brustbildung und guten Winkelungen der Vor- u. Hinterhand, ausgreifende Gänge, sicheres Wesen und ausgeprägter Kampftrieb	+ Arno v. Haus Gersie SchH III FH ZB: "V-A" (Sieger und hoher Vererber)	+ Edo vom Gehrdener Berg SchH III	+ Claudius vom Hain SchH II
			Haga vom Haus Schütting SchH I
		+ Delia vom Walburgitor SchH II	+ Lesko aus Kattenstroth SchH III FH
			+ Bera von Walburgitor SchH III
	+ Daja vom Bernstein-Strand SchH II ZB: "V"	+ Tao vom Friedlichenheim SchH III FH	+ Fred vom Haus Brenner SchH II
			+ Sonja von der Gnadentalermühle SchH I
		+ Asta von der Wallenstein-Eiche SchH III FH	+ Armin von der Trillke SchH III
			+ Isa aus den Twietbergen SchH III FH
+ Uri vom Busecker Schloß SchH I ZB: "SG" Klein, gehaltvoll, gestreckt mit guter Brustbildung u. ebensolchen Winkelungen, sehr gute Gänge; Sicheres Wesen, ausgeprägter Kampftrieb	+ Harras vom Busecker Schloß SchH II FH ZB: "V"	+ Armin vom Salon SchH III	+ Tyras vom Holzheimer Eichwald SchH III FH
			+ Cilly vom Haus Roll SchH II
		+ Ossie vom Gambacher Tal SchH I	+ Säntis von der Buchenhöhe SchH II
			+ Irla vom Gambacher Tal SchH I
	+ Daja vom Bernstein-Strand SchH II ZB: "V"	+ Tao vom Friedlichenheim SchH III FH	+ Fred vom Haus Brenner SchH II
			+ Sonja von der Gnadentalermühle SchH I
		+ Asta von der Wallenstein-Eiche SchH III FH	+ Armin von der Trillke SchH III
			+ Isa aus den Twietbergen SchH III FH

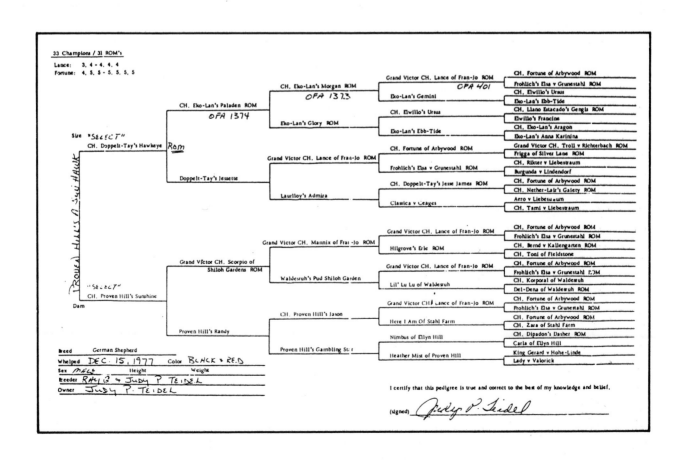

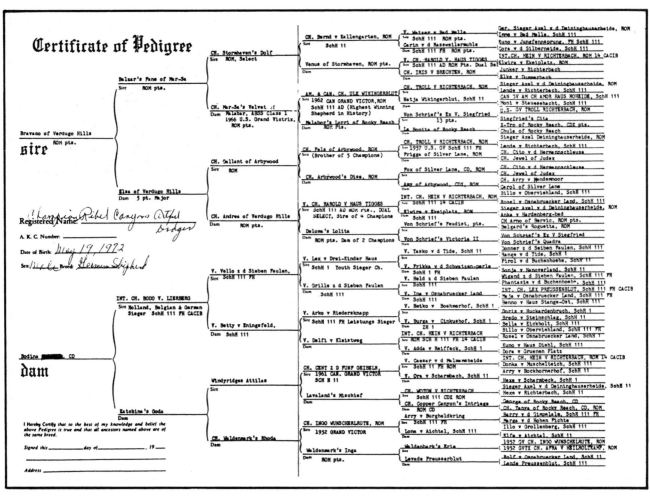

CERTIFIED PEDIGREE

BREED GERMAN SHEPHERD DOG COLOR AND/OR MARKINGS SABLE SEX MALE DATE WHELPED MAY 27, 1965

CALL NAME IGOR BREEDER G. HOPPE & A. CONSIDINE ADDRESS RTE 538, BOX 355, MONROEVILLE, N. J.

REG. NAME CH. TANNENWALD's IGOR A.K.C. REG. No. WA 599064 SELLER

| | | Sire FALK V.D. EMSSCHLEUSE |
| CH. HARRY V. DONAUKAI (Sire) | | Dam FREIA V. DONAUKAI |

VOLKER V. ZOLLGRENZSCHUTZHAUS (Sire)

| PERLE V. ZOLLGRENZSCHUTZHAUS (Dam) | Sire IGOR V. TEMPELBLICK |
| | Dam KRAFTA V. ZOLLGRENZSCHUTZHAUS |

JARDO's KURT OF COSALTA (Sire)

| CH. SERVIE V. ALEXYRVO HOF (Sire) | Sire CH. TROLL V. RICHTERBACH |
| | Dam BIANCA V. ALEXYRVO HOF |

JARDO's GRETA (Dam)

| JOARREN's DREAMY JEANETTE (Dam) | Sire WERRO ZU DEN SIEBEN FAULEN |
| | Dam JOLA V. D. GRAFSCHAFT HOYA |

| GRIMM V. D. FAHRMUEHLE (Sire) | Sire ARRY V. D. GASSENQUELLE |
| | Dam FELLA V. D. FAHRMUEHLE |

CH. ATLAS V. ELFENHAIN (Sire)

| LEXA V. OSNABRUCKERLAND (Dam) | Sire ROLF V. OSNABRUCKERLAND |
| | Dam VENA V. OSNABRUCKERLAND |

BRUNI OF TANNENWALD (Dam)

| WERRO ZU DEN SIEBEN FAULEN (Sire) | Sire FALKO ZU DEN SIEBEN FAULEN |
| | Dam LONA ZU DEN SIEBEN FAULEN |

ABADEE's JAN V. HAUS VISTA (Dam)

| HANNA V. EQUORD (Dam) | Sire PIROL V. D. BUCHENHOHE |
| | Dam UDA V. MASCHTOR |

I hereby certify that this Pedigree is true to the best of my knowledge _____

Signed

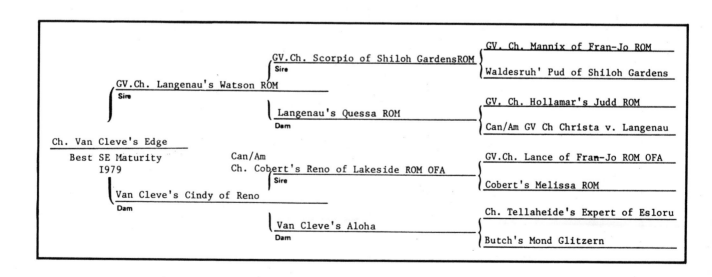

GV.Ch. Scorpio of Shiloh Gardens ROM (Sire)
- GV. Ch. Mannix of Fran-Jo ROM
- Waldesruh' Pud of Shiloh Gardens

GV.Ch. Langenau's Watson ROM (Sire)

Langenau's Quessa ROM (Dam)
- GV. Ch. Hollamar's Judd ROM
- Can/Am GV Ch Christa v. Langenau

Ch. Van Cleve's Edge
Best SE Maturity 1979

Can/Am Ch. Cobert's Reno of Lakeside ROM OFA (Sire)
- GV.Ch. Lance of Fran-Jo ROM OFA
- Cobert's Melissa ROM

Van Cleve's Cindy of Reno (Dam)

Van Cleve's Aloha (Dam)
- Ch. Tellaheide's Expert of Esloru
- Butch's Mond Glitzern

421

AMERICAN AND CANADIAN CHAMPION ULK WIKINGERBLUT, SCH H III A.D. CACIB

INBREEDING:
Lex Preussenblut (4-4,5) Maja Osnabruckerland (4-4,5)
Osnabruckerland Rosel-Rolf (3-3,4)

SIRE:
U.S. Grand Victor - 1957
Holland Sieger - 1956
*Int. Ch. Troll vom Richterbach
Sch H III FH
*1956 - 57

German Sieger - 1949
*Axel von der Deininghauseheide
Sch H III DFH FH

*Immo vom Hasenfang
Sch H III

*Nestor vom Wiegerfelsen
Sch H III Sch H FH
*Dorte v. Hasenfang
Sch H I

*Helma vom Hildergardsheim
Sch H III

*Gnom v. Kalsmunttor
Sch H III
*Tita v. d. Starrenburg
Sch H II

*Lende vom Richterbach
Sch H III

*Fels vom Vogtlandshof
Sch H III

*Cladius vom Hain
Sch H II
*Barbel v. Haus Trippe
Sch H I

*Rosel vom Osnabruckerland
Sch H I

*Lex Preussenblut
Sch H III FH
*Maja v. Osnabruckerland
Sch H III FH

DAM:
*Natja Wikingerblut
Sch H II
*1957 - 62

International Champion
*Ch Amor vom Haus Hoheide
Sch H III

*Drusus zu den Sieben-Faulen
Sch H III

German Sieger - 1951
*Rolf v. Osnabruckerland
Sch H III FH
*Wally z.d. Sieben-Faulen
Sch H III FH

*Christel vom Fredeholz
Sch H II

*Pitzo v. Fliederschlob
Sch H III
*Amsel v. Menkenmoor
Sch H III

*Moni vom Stuveschacht
Sch H I

German Sieger - 1951
*Rolf vom Osnabruckerland
Sch H III FH

*Lex Preussenblut
Sch H III FH
*Maja v. Osnabruckerland
Sch H III FH

*Quote vom Stuveschacht
Sch H I

*Liebo v. Stuveschacht
Sch H III FH
*Ute Preussenblut
Sch H I

*Angekort

CHAMPION VOX WIKINGERBLUT

INBREEDING:
Rolf Osnabrucker Land (5-3, 5, 5,)
(Osnabruckerland, Rosel-Racker, 5-5)

SIRE:
*Dick vom Backerkamp
Sch H III
*1961-66

*Argant von Detlefs Ruh
Sch H III, FH
*1957-62

*Yasko von der Tide
Sch H II

*Donner zu den Sieben-Faulen
Sch H III
*Ranga von der Tide
Sch H I

*Elfi vom Drei-Kinder-Haus
Sch H I

*Lars vom Equord
Sch H III, FH
*Frikka von der schwarzen Perle
Sch H I, FH

*Centa Backerkamp
Sch H I
*1960-61

*Bolte vom Steinbruckerteich
Sch H I, FH

*Sigbert vom Haus Arnold
Sch H III
*Kea vom Tiefenkreut
Sch H II

*Blanka vom Backerkamp
Sch H II

*Hein vom Richterbach
Sch H III
*Quuni vom Walburgitor
Sch H III

DAM:
*Quora Preussenblut
Sch H I
*1961-66

*Harry vom Eggetal
Sch H I

*Arko vom Sprekenhorst
Sch H II

*Dux vom Handweberdorf
Sch H I
*Asta vom Eggetal
Sch H I

*Elfi vom Eggetal
Sch H I

*Erlkonig vom Bruningswaldchen
Sch H II
*Asta von der Swistmuhle
Sch H I

*Moni vom Stuveschacht
Sch H I
*1954-59

German Sieger - 1951
*Rolf vom Osnabruckerland
Sch H III, FH

*Lex Preussenblut
Sch H III, FH
*Maja vom Osnabruckerland
Sch H III, FH

*Quote vom Stuveschacht
Sch H I

*Liebo vom Stuveschacht
Sch H III, FH
*Ute Preussenblut
Sch H I

*Angekort

CERTIFIED PEDIGREE

To be used in conjunction with litter nominations for The German Shepherd Dog Club of America, Inc., National Futurity Shows

WELLSPRING KENNELS

Breeder Franklyn & Rosalind Schaefer

Date Whelped Nov. 14 1976

I hereby certify that this Pedigree is to the best of my knowledge

Sig(ned) *Franklyn Schaefer* *Rosalind Schaefer*

Litter No. **H**

			G.V.Ch. Lance Of Fran-Jo ROM
		Ch. Eko-Lan's Morgan ROM (Sire)	EKo-Lan's Gemini
	Ch. Eko-Lan's Paladen ROM (Sire)		Ch. Elwillo's Ursus
		Eko-Lan's Glory ROM (Dam)	Eko-Lan's Ebb Tide
Ch. Doppelt-Tay's Hawkeye ROM (Sire)			Ch. Fortune Of Arbywood ROM
		G.V. Ch. Lance Of Fran-Jo ROM (Sire)	Elsa V. Grunestahl ROM
	Doppelt-Tay's Jessette (Dam)		Ch. Doppelt-Tay's Jesse James RO
		Laurlloy's Admira (Dam)	Classica V. Cenges

► **CH. WELLSPRING'S HOWARD JOHNSON** OFA #GS-8853

			Ch. Fortune Of Arbywood ROM
		G.V. CH. Lance Of Fran-jo ROM (Sire)	Frohlich's Elsa V Grunes Tahl RO
	Zeus Of Fran-JO ROM (Sire)		G.V. Ch. Lance Of Fran-Jo ROM
		Ch. Mirheim's Abbey ROM (Dam)	Ch. Kingsdown Amber
Ch. Amber's Flair ROM			Ch. Fortune Of Arbywood ROM
		G.V. CH. Lance Of Fran-Jo ROM (Sire)	Frohlich's Elsa V Grunes Tahl RO
	Amber's Dina (Dam)		Ch. Fels Of Arbywood
		Amber's DeCloudt's Cristl ROM (Dam)	Von Nassau's Ophelia ROM

FEDERACION CANINA DE VENEZUELA

Certificado de Registro Genealógico

CAMPEON VENEZOLANO

AKC WD768355 (Ch.)

NOMBRE		SEXO
WELLSPRING'S IROQUOIS ++++++++++++++++++++		Macho.

RAZA	PAIS DE NACIMIENTO
Pastor Alemán.	Estados Unidos de América.

FECHA DE NACIMIENTO
+++Dieciocho de Junio de mil novecientos setenta y siete+++

COLOR PREDOMINANTE Y MARCAS	CRIADOR
Marrón y negro.	Franklyn Schaefer y Rosalind Schaefer.

PADRES	ABUELOS	BISABUELOS
Ch. DOPPELT TAYS HAWKEYE AKC WC978054	Ch. Eko-Lan's Paladen AKC WD424558	Ch. Eko-Lan's Morgan AKC WB105335
		Eko-Lan's Glory AKC WD003637
	Doppelt-Tay's Jessette AKC WC450370	Ch. Lance of Fran-Jo AKC WA466021
		Laurlloy's Admira AKC WA971254
Ch. AMBER'S FLAIR AKC WC923298	Zeus of Fran-Jo AKC WC170280	Ch. Lance of Fran-Jo AKC WA466021
		Ch. Mirheims Abbey AKC WB104102
	Amber's Dina AKC WB325949	Ch. Lance of Fran-Jo AKC WA466021
		Amber's de Cloudt's Cristl AKC WA493208

PROPIETARIO	CEDULA DE IDENTIDAD 950886
María de PETER Avenida La Salle Quinta "Alpina" Sebucán, Caracas 1071.-	

Asentado en el Registro Genealógico, Libro 3 Tomo XXVI el día 29 de Abril de 1981

PARTE Nº ++++

FUNCIONARIO AUTORIZADO

Nº DE REGISTRO **316-9835**

423

Certificate of Pedigree

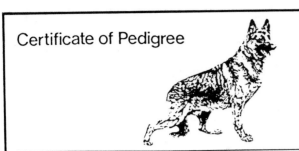

Registered Name: **CH. WINOBSKA OF INGOMAR**

Registration Number: **WP-961579**

Date of Birth: **NOVEMBER 24, 1977**

Sex: **FEMALE**

Color and Markings: **BLACK AND TAN**

Breeder: **DIANA RIDDLE AND JEROME W. ROZANSKI**

Address: **BOX 319, R.D.1, ZEHNER SCHOOL ROAD, ZELIENOPLE, PA. 16063**

PHONE: **412-452-5150**

Parents	Grand Parents	Great Grand Parents	Great Great Grand Parents
			CH. FORTUNE OF ARBYWOOD R.O.M.
		GV. CH. LANCE OF FRAN-JO R.O.M.	FROHLICH'S ELSA V GRUNESTAHL R.O.M.
	GV. CH. MANNIX OF FRAN-JO R.O.M.		CH. BERND V KALLENGARTEN R.O.M.
		HILGROVE'S ERLE R.O.M.	CH. TONI OF FIELDSTONE
GV. CH. CEASAR VON CARAHAUS R.O.M. Sire			JABDO'S KURT OF COSALTA
		SEL. CH. TANNENWALD'S VADR R.O.M.	BRUNI OF TANNENWALD
	ARETHA OF GLENTANNER		GV. CH. AXEL V POLDIHAUS R.O.M.
		WEBERHAUS WAR EMBER OF FRIES	HOFJE'S DARK VICTORY
			GV. CH. LANCE OF FRAN-JO R.O.M.
		GV. CH. MANNIX OF FRAN-JO R.O.M.	HILGROVE'S ERLE R.O.M.
	GV. CH. SCORPO OF SHILOH GARDEN'S R.O.M.		GV. CH. LANCE OF FRAN-JO R.O.M.
		WALDESRUH'S PUP OF SHILOH GARDENS	LIL LULU OF WALDESRUH
SEL. CH. NOOTKA OF INGOMAR Dam			CH. FORTUNE OF ARBYWOOD R.O.M.
		GV. CH. LANCE OF FRAN-JO R.O.M.	FROHLICH'S ELSA V GRUNESTAHL R.O.M.
	LEUCHTAG'S HAPPY OF INGOMAR		CH. BERND V KALLENGARTEN R.O.M.
		CH. YASMIN OF STAHL FARM	CH. ZARA OF STAHL FARM

Signed: *Diana Riddle*

Certificate of Pedigree

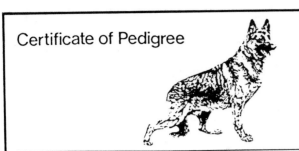

Registered Name: **CH. YASMIN OF STAHL FARM**

Registration Number: **WA-668501**

Date of Birth: **MAY 16, 1965**

Sex: **FEMALE**

Color and Markings: **BLACK AND TAN**

Breeder: **BERNICE D. STAHL AND SARAH LAYER KLING**

Address: **BOX 319, R.D.1, ZEHNER SCHOOL ROAD, ZELIENOPLE, PA. 16063**

PHONE: **412-452-5150**

	Grand Parents	Great Grand Parents	Great Great Grand Parents
		AXEL VD DENINGHAUSERHEIDE SCHH III P.P.H. F.H.	IMMO VOM HASSENFANG SCHH III
			HELMA VOM HILDEGARDSHEIM SCHH III
	WATZER V BAD MELLE		ROLF V OSNABRUCKERLAND SCHH III F.H.
		IMME V BAD MELLE	BETTY VOM HAUS HERBERHOLD
CH. BERND V KALLENGARTEN SCHH III Sire ANGEKOERT CLASS I. R.O.M.			IRAN VON DER BUCHENHOHE
		KUNO V JUNGFERNSPRUNG	BELLA VON HAUS WEINBERG
	CARIN VD RASSWEILERMUHLE		LESKO AUS KATTENSTROTH
		CORA VD SILBERWEIDE	BIOKA VON DER SILBERWEIDE
			AXEL VD DENINGHAUSERHEIDE SCHH III
		GV. CH. AXEL VOM POLDIHAUS R.O.M.	CH. PETRA V RICHTERBACH
	CH. LLANO ESTOCADO'S GENGIS R.O.M.		CH. NOTHER OF LONGWORTH
		CH. LLANO ESTOCADO'S CELE	CH. LLANO ESTOCADO'S ARROGANTE
CH. ZARA OF STAHL FARM Dam			CH. VOL OF LONGWORTH R.O.M.
		CH. GUSTO OF MACLAN	CH. LIESE V LIEBESTRAUM
	CH. KRISTY OF STAHL FARM		CH. POLVIC V. LIEBESTRAUM
		TILLIE OF MACLAN	MINPY OF MACLAN

Signed: *Diana Riddle*

Gestation, Whelping, and the Litter

When your bitch has been bred and is back at home, remain ever watchful that no other male gets to her until at least the twenty-second day of her season has passed. Prior to that time, it will still be possible for an undesired breeding to take place, which, at this point, would be catastrophic. Remember, she actually can have two separate litters by two different dogs, so *be alert and take care.*

In all other ways, the bitch should be treated quite normally. It is not necessary for her to have any additives to her diet until she is at least four to five weeks pregnant. It is also unnecessary for her to have additional food. It is better to underfeed the bitch this early in her pregnancy than to overfeed her. A fat bitch is not an easy whelper, so by "feeding her up" during the first few weeks, you may be creating problems for her.

Controlled exercise is good, and necessary, for your pregnant bitch. She should not be permitted to just lie around. At about seven weeks, the exercise should be slowed down to several sedate walks daily, not too long and preferably on the leash.

In the fourth or fifth week of pregnancy, calcium may be added to the diet; and at seven weeks, the one meal a day may be increased to two meals with some nutritional additives in each. Canned milk may be added to her meals at this time.

A week before she is due to whelp, your Shepherd bitch should be introduced to her whelping box, so that she will have accustomed herself to it and feel at home there by the time the puppies arrive. She should be encouraged to sleep there and be permitted to come and go as she pleases. The box should be roomy enough for her to lie down and stretch out in it; but it should not be too large or the pups will have too much room in which to roam, and they may get chilled if they move too far away from the warmth of their mother. Be sure that there is a "pig rail" for the box, which will prevent the puppies from being crushed against the side of the box. The box should be lined with newspapers, which can easily be changed as they become soiled.

The room where the whelping box is placed, either in the home or in the kennel, should be free from drafts and should be kept at about eighty degrees Fahrenheit. It may be necessary

Antje of Lone Birch at six years of age (she lived to be fifteen) winning under judge Henry Stoecker for owner-handler Gerlinde Hockla. Antje was the dam of Blanka and Biene v. Finsternwald.

H. A. STROHMEYER

A calendar from March 1924 featuring German Shepherds owned by Mr. J. C. Brady, Hamilton Farms Kennels.

Ch. Senta of Grafmar with her Grand Victor Ch. Pfeffer von Bern litter at Grafmar Kennels. Photo courtesy of Janet Churchill.

during the cold months to install an infrared lamp in order to maintain sufficient warmth, in which case guard against the lamp being placed too low or too close to the puppies.

Keep a big pile of newspapers near the box. You'll find that you never have enough of these when there is a litter, so start accumulating them ahead of time. A pile of clean towels, a pair of scissors, and a bottle of alcohol should also be close at hand. Have all of these things ready at least a week before the bitch is due to whelp, as you never know exactly when she may start.

The day or night before she is due, the bitch will become restless; she'll be in and out of her box and in and out of the door. She may refuse food, and at this point her temperature will start to drop. She will start to dig and tear up the newspapers in her box, shiver, and generally look uncomfortable. You alone should be with her at this time (or one other person who is an experienced breeder, to give you confidence if this is one of your first litters). The bitch does not need an audience or any extra people

around. This is not a sideshow, and several people hovering over the bitch may upset her to the point where she may hurt the puppies. Stay nearby, but do not fuss too much over her. Keep a calm attitude; this will give her confidence. Eventually she will settle down in her box and begin to pant; shortly thereafter she will start to have contractions and soon a puppy will begin to emerge, <u>sliding</u> out with one of the contractions. The mother immediately should open the sac and bite the cord and clean up the puppy. She will also eat the placenta, which you should permit. Once the puppy is cleaned, it should be placed next to the bitch, unless she is showing signs of having another one immediately. The puppy should start looking for a nipple on which to nurse, and you should make certain that it is able to latch on and start doing so at once.

If a puppy is a breech birth (*i.e.*, born feet first), then you must watch carefully that it is delivered as quickly as possible and the sac removed very quickly, so that the puppy does not drown. Sometimes even a normally positioned

427

birth will seem extremely slow in coming. Should either of these events occur, you might take a clean towel and, as the bitch contracts, pull the puppy out, doing so gently and with utmost care. If the bitch does not open the sac and cut the cord, you will have to do so. If the puppy shows little sign of life, make sure the mouth is free of liquid and then, using a Turkish towel or terry cloth, massage the puppy's chest, rubbing back and forth quite briskly. Continue this for about fifteen minutes. It may be necessary to try mouth-to-mouth breathing. Open the puppy's jaws and, using a finger, depress the tongue which may be stuck to the roof of the puppy's mouth. Then blow hard down the puppy's throat. Bubbles may pop out of its nose, but keep on blowing. Rub with the towel again across the chest, and try artificial respiration, pressing the sides of the chest together, slowly and rhythmically, in and out, in and out. Keep trying one method or the other for at least fifteen minutes (actual time—not how long it seems to you) before giving up. You may be rewarded with a live puppy who otherwise would not have made it.

German Shepherd Dog puppies owned by the famous Hamilton Farm Kennels of J.C. Brady during the 1920's.

Edith H. Overly, Halstor Kennels, with a litter of German Shepherd puppies.

If you are able to revive the puppy, it should not be put with the mother immediately, as it should be kept extra warm for a while. Put it in a cardboard box near a stove, on an electric heating pad, or, if it is the time of year when your heat is running, near a radiator until the rest of the litter has been born. Then it can be put in with the others.

The bitch may go for an hour or more between puppies, which is fine as long as she seems comfortable and is not straining or contracting. She should not be allowed to remain unassisted for more than an hour if she does continue to contract. This is when you should call your veterinarian, whom you should have alerted ahead of time of the possibility so that he will be somewhere within easy reach. He may want the bitch brought in so that he can examine her and perhaps give her a shot of Pituitrin. In some cases, the veterinarian may find that a Caesarean operation is necessary, because a puppy may be lodged in some manner that makes normal delivery impossible. This can occur due to the size of a puppy or may be due to the fact that the puppy is turned wrong. If any of the foregoing occurs, the puppies already born must be kept

A typical litter of six-month-old Ingomar Kennels German Shepherd puppies. Owned by Diana Riddle, Ingomar Kennels, Zelienople, Pennsylvania.

warm in their cardboard box, which should have been lined with shredded newspapers in advance and which should have a heating pad beneath it.

Assuming that there have been no problems, and the bitch has whelped normally, you should insist that she go outside to exercise, staying just long enough to make herself comfortable. She can be offered a bowl of milk and a biscuit, but then she should settle down with her family. Be sure to clean out the whelping box and change the newspapers so that she will have a fresh bed.

If the mother lacks milk at this point, the puppies will need to be fed by hand, kept very warm, and held against the mother's teats several times a day in order to stimulate and encourage the secretion of her milk, which will probably start shortly.

Unless some problem arises, there is little you need do about the puppies until they become three to four weeks old. Keep the box clean with fresh papers. When the puppies are a couple of days old, the papers should be removed and Turkish towels should be tacked down to the bottom of the box so that the puppies will have traction when they move. This is important.

If the bitch has difficulties with her milk supply, or if you should be so unfortunate as to lose the bitch, then you must be prepared to either hand-feed or tube-feed the puppies if they are to survive. We prefer the tube method as it is so much faster and easier. If the bitch is available, it is better that she continue to clean and care for the puppies in the normal manner, except for the food supplements you will provide. If she is unable to do this, then after every feeding, you must gently rub each puppy's abdomen with wet cotton to induce urination, and the rectum should be gently rubbed to open the bowels.

Newborn puppies must be fed every three or four hours around the clock. The puppies must be kept warm during that time. Have your veterinarian show you how to tube-feed. Once learned it is really quite simple, fast, and efficient.

After a normal whelping, the bitch will require additional food to enable her to produce sufficient milk. She should be fed twice daily now, and some canned milk should be available to her several times during the day.

When the puppies are two weeks old, you should clip their nails, as they are needle-sharp

Ch. Nanhalls Taurus, by Ch. Nanhalls Malachi ex Ch. Gail of Waldesruh, ROM, bred and owned by Nanhall Kennels, Dr. Wade Sanders and Gordon Pirie.

at this point and can hurt or damage the mother's teats and stomach as the pups hold on to nurse.

Between three and four weeks of age, the puppies should begin to be weaned. Scraped beef (prepared by scraping it off slices of raw beef with a spoon, so that none of the muscle or gristle is included) may be offered in very small quantities a couple of times daily for the first few days. If the puppy is reluctant to try it, put a little on your finger and rub it on the puppy's lips; this should get things going. By the third day, you can mix in ground puppy chow with warm water as directed on the package, offering it four times daily. By now the mother should be kept out of the box and away from the puppies for several hours at a time. After the puppies reach five weeks of age, she should be left in with them only overnight. By the time they are six weeks old, the puppies should be entirely weaned and the mother should only check on them with occasional visits.

Most veterinarians recommend a temporary DHL (distemper, hepatitis, leptospirosis) shot

Mexican Ch. Avenger of Ingomar, by Ch. Doppelt-Tay's Jentlemin Jim ex Weberhaus War Witch of Ember, bred by Diana Riddle and owned by Dr. Roberto Yslas.

The handsome winning Den-Lea's Really Raven, by Den-Lea's Jet Pilot, C.D.X., T.D., ex Jeff-Lynne's Emilie. Owned by Denise Kodner, Den-Lea Kennels, Highland Park, Illinois.

Ch. Hartwald's Harmony, a super show girl by Hartwald's Flint ex Hartwald Witchcraft. Handled by Ken Rayner.

when the puppies are six weeks old. This remains effective for about two weeks. Then, at eight weeks, the series of permanent shots begins for the DHL protection. It is a good idea to discuss with your vet the advisability of having your puppies inoculated against the dreaded parvovirus at the same time. Each time the pups go to the vet for shots, you should bring stool samples so that they can be examined for worms. Worms go through various stages of development and may be present in a stool sample even though the sample does not test positive. So do not neglect to keep careful watch on this.

The puppies should be fed four times daily until they are three months old. Then you can cut back to three feedings daily. By the time the puppies are six months old, two meals daily are sufficient. Some people feed their dogs twice daily throughout their lifetime, while others cut back to one meal daily when the puppy reaches one year of age.

The ideal time for Shepherd puppies to go to their new homes is when they are between eight and twelve weeks old, although some puppies successfully adjust to a new home when they are six weeks of age. Be certain that they go to their future owners accompanied by a description of the diet you've been feeding them and a schedule of the shots they have received and those they still need. These should be included with a registration application and a copy of the pedigree.

Am. and Can. Ch. Echowoods Valance of Louron, or "Smokey," filling his favorite job. This handsome Shepherd belongs to Mary Roberts and Tina Woodworth and is a son of Am. and Can. Ch. Covy-Tucker Hill's Finnegan, ROM, ex Echowoods Raquel of Louron, ROM.

CHAPTER SEVENTEEN

You and Your German Shepherd Dog

Zelda and Pierrot in 1960. Owned by Janet Churchill.

The popularity of German Shepherd Dogs is great all over the world, and in the United States the number of yearly A.K.C. registrations of the breed indicates that the German Shepherd Dog continues to remain near the top of the list of the most popular dog breeds—a tribute to the versatility, talents, and intelligence of these very worthy dogs. Sadly, many of them are not well cared for; and through neglect, lack of understanding, and sometimes downright disinterest on the part of their owners, the dogs become less than satisfactory as companions or pets. This is a pity, because there is no breed with more potential for outstanding loyalty and service than a properly managed Shepherd.

Versatility of Shepherds

It should be remembered that the German Shepherd is a true *working* dog, happiest when serving mankind, as he has done from his earliest sheep-herding days right up to the far more sophisticated duties he now performs. Such a dog deserves an understanding owner, one who appreciates him and his potential, one who is in-

terested in developing the dog's intelligence. No German Shepherd Dog should ever be left without at least basic obedience training. No German Shepherd Dog, no matter what your reasons for owning him, should be ignored and treated as a machine rather than as a living creature. No German Shepherd Dog should be turned loose to fend for himself by an owner who likes to have him "enjoy his freedom."

Because of the German Shepherd's superior intelligence, working with this breed can be exceedingly rewarding. The police have found this to be true, as has the military. All sorts of specialized tasks are now being performed by members of this breed, from bomb and drug detection and scenting out criminals to locating and rescuing lost persons and working as true Police Dogs, accompanying human "partners" in squad cars as they make their rounds (particularly in what are known as "high risk" areas), adding considerably to the safety of these men by their presence, courage, and alertness. If German Shepherds have ever received adverse publicity in the press, the tables are surely turned now. With consistent regularity New York and Connecticut newspapers, and I am certain those in other areas of the United States as well, carry accounts of incidents of heroism on the part of German Shepherds as they assist in law enforcement and in the apprehension of criminals. The German Shepherd is proving himself to have the keen nose of a scent hound, plus the size, strength, stamina, courage, and keen intelligence to make his results outstanding.

Although several other breeds share success in this field, somehow German Shepherds and "dogs for the blind" are synonymous in the minds of the general public. This is probably due to Morris Frank's famous "Buddy," the first widely publicized Seeing Eye Dog. Now that organization, Guiding Eyes for the Blind, Leader Dogs, and all organizations dedicated to this work consider Shepherds to be one of the satisfactory breeds of dog for this type of career.

Countless German Shepherds serve their masters as guard dogs on commercial property or at home. Somehow just the appearance of one of these impressive canines gives a would-be burglar, or any other person with less than honorable intentions, pause. And I am certain that many times a crime is averted by the protective presence of such a dog.

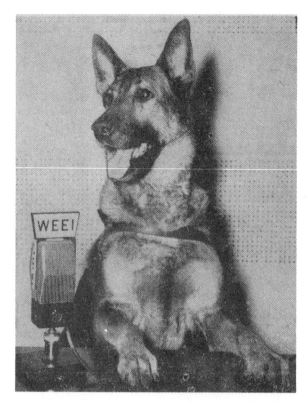

Bozo, a famous German Shepherd radio star who with his pals, Jerry and Sky, was a member of the cast of *The Lonesome Trailers* program some years back. This picture was published in response to many letters from listeners who could not believe that it was a real dog playing the part—but here he is, both real and handsome. Courtesy of Janet Churchill.

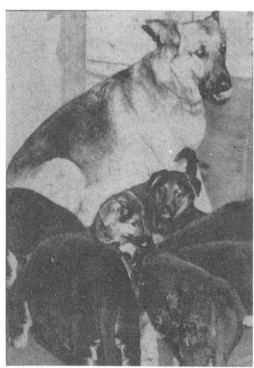

This is Beau, a hero-dog from Brooklyn, New York, who, locked in the cellar for the night by owner Lou Hollwitz, crashed through a glass door to give the alarm when the oil burner exploded. Among those saved from the smoke and gas-filled cellar were Beau's puppies, alive thanks to their sire's bravery. Courtesy of Janet Churchill, whose mother, purchased one of these puppies.

This German Shepherd Dog, Wolf, was a canine hero of World War I. In his mouth he is holding the Croix de Guerre presented to him by Marshal Foch. Wolf attended the American Legion Convention in San Francisco soon after the armistice. Photo courtesy of Janet Churchill.

Sentry duty, World War II, for which German Shepherds were widely used. Photo courtesy of Janet Churchill.

I do not believe in guard dog training for an animal who will live as a family member, and I am particularly against this being done by an amateur or uninformed owner. Should you determine that you wish such training for your dog, carefully investigate until you find a competent and reliable trainer who, through experience, really knows what he is doing. In the hands of an amateur, a partially or badly trained guard dog can become a real menace—a risk which should not be taken with a dog who will be part of your family, coming into contact with children, strangers, or people unaware of how to handle such a situation. The German Shepherd is instinctively protective of his home and people. That natural instinct, plus normal obedience training, should be all that is necessary to equip your dog for general family living and for watchdog duty.

While it is possible for them to manage in a limited area, German Shepherds really need more space in which to exercise than is generally supplied by apartment living. However, if it is

The famous "Bear" dog, Ch. Bar vom Weiherturchen, poses with his handler and friend Denise Kodner for a MONY insurance ad some years ago. This magnificent dog, with his fabulous show record, takes time off to do a stint for the advertising cameras.

Gerlinde Hockla with Ch. Jonvires Curt.

Chips Rayner winning with the Murphys' Ch. Paprika of Clover Acres.

the only breed for you and you are willing to provide the time and energy required for walking your dog a decent distance daily, it can be worked out. And certainly nothing could give a greater feeling of safety on city streets than a German Shepherd at one's side.

As a dog for companionship, nothing quite matches a German Shepherd. Their intelligence makes them almost seem to know what you are thinking. They are clean dogs in the house, are easily trained, and bask in personal attention. They are splendid dogs with children if both are raised together, strong enough to withstand the long hours of play which a youngster enjoys with his dog; and they are alert companions for a child, quick to sense danger should it arise and intelligent in their reaction.

A German Shepherd Dog is at his best when treated as a family member, permitted to share the daily routine, to live in the house, and to be a true companion to his owner. His brains and trainability make him fill this role admirably, which is one of the prime reasons why the breed has earned such enormous popularity with people wishing a dog for this purpose.

436

This is another famous movie dog, Lightning, the grandson of Strongheart who at only two years of age was already a star. Among his popular movies were *Case of the Howling Dog, Born to Fight, A Dog of Flanders,* and *Wings In The Dark.* For the latter, Lightning studied at The Seeing Eye, for dogs who learn to lead the blind, for which he showed outstanding aptitude having completed what is normally a five-month course of training in a mere three weeks. He is pictured here with co-stars from one of his movies, Frankie Thomas, Jr., and Helen Parrish. Lightning belonged to Earl Johnston. Photo from Janet Churchill's collection.

Ch. Lakeside's Chico on guard. Photo courtesy of Sharon Dwier.

Margie Brown snapped this delightful photo for the 1981 German Shepherd Dog Club of America calendar. We are grateful to her and to Mary Schuetzler for sharing it with our readers.

Opposite, above: Jan Churchill, famous lady of the Labrador Retriever Fancy, owned some lovely German Shepherds. Here she is with her daughter, Jenny, and three of her favorite Shepherds: left to right, Grayarlin's Pierrot, sire; Spenrock's Rebel Spy, pup; and Grayarlin's X-Elda, dam. This photograph courtesy of Miss Betty Dumaine. This dog sled met the school bus daily to bring Jenny home. **Below:** Movie star, Max the Bionic Dog. Logan Von Burgerland, by Am. and Canadian Ch. Lakeland's Harrigan, ROM, ex Dolly Von Burgerland. Dr. and Mrs. Zoltan Puskas, owners.

Responsibilities of Breeders and Owners

Whether you are a one-dog owner, the owner of a show kennel, one involved in obedience, or a breeder, there are definite responsibilities—to your dog or dogs, to your breed, and to the general public—involved which should never be overlooked or taken lightly.

It is inexcusable for anyone to breed dogs promiscuously, producing unneeded litters. The only time a responsible breeder plans a litter is when it is *needed* to carry on a bloodline or to provide dogs for which this breeder has very definite plans, including orders for at least half the number of puppies which will probably be born. Every healthy puppy deserves a good and loving home, assuring its future well-being. No puppy should be born to an uncertain future on someone's assumption that there will be no problem selling or otherwise finding a home for it, as very definitely this is not always easy. Overpopulation is the dog world's most heartbreaking tragedy. Those of us who love dogs should not add to it by carelessly producing more. If you have any reason to feel that the puppies may not be assured of homes, don't breed the bitch; wait for a more propitious time. Certainly no Shepherd breeder likes the thought of running around frantically trying to find someone who will take puppies off his hands, even if they must be given away. The latter usually is not a good idea anyway, as many people cannot resist saying "yes" to something which costs nothing, regardless of whether or

Gero von Finsternwald, owner-handled by Gerlinde Hockla, winning first in Bred-by-Exhibitor under Dr. Christopher Rummel.

Ch. Claiburne's Miss Marple, whelped January 26th 1980, sired by Ch. Covy-Tucker Hill's Finnegan, ROM. Owned by Mary Roberts and Dalene McIntire.

Ch. Von Tschudi's Adonis, born November 1977, sired by Ch. Covy-Tucker Hill's Finnegan, ROM. Owners, Mary C. Roberts and Marilyn Judy; Ralph S. Roberts handling.

not they really want it. As the Shepherd grows larger and demands more care, their enthusiasm wanes to the point that the dog soon is left to roam the streets where he is subject to all sorts of dangers, and the owner simply could not care less. If one pays for something, one seems to respect it more.

One litter at a time is all that any breeder should produce, making sure that all those puppies are well provided for prior to breeding for another litter. Breeders should do all in their power to ascertain that the home to which each of his puppies goes is a *good* home, one that offers proper care, a fenced in area, and a really enthusiastic owner. I have tremendous respect for those breeders who make it a point to check carefully the credentials of prospective purchasers, and I firmly believe that all breeders should do likewise on this important point. I am certain that no breeder wants any Shepherd puppy to wind up in an animal shelter, in an experimental laboratory, or as a victim of a speeding car. While complete control of such situations may not be possible, it is at least our responsibility to make every effort to turn our puppies over to people who have the same outlook as our own where love of dogs and responsibility

Ch. Hessians Glory handled by Art Hess, with judge Mrs. Evers, going Best of Breed over Specials at Blenner-hassett Kennel Club. This lovely bitch had been sold as a youngster to a new owner who was not pleased with her as a show prospect, so the Hesses bought her back, in poor condition, nursed her to her former good health, and made her a champion in ten shows at two of which she went on to Best of Breed. Helen and Art Hess owners, Hessian Kennels.

toward them are concerned and who realize that the ownership of a dog involves care, not neglect.

It is the breeder's responsibility to sell every puppy with the understanding that should the new owner find it necessary to place the dog elsewhere, you, the breeder, must be contacted immediately and given the opportunity to take back the dog or to help in finding it a new home. Many a dog starting out in what has seemed a good home has, under unforeseen circumstances, been passed along to others, only to wind up in exactly the sort of situation we most want to avoid. Keep in touch with what is happening to your dogs after they are sold.

The final obligation every dog owner shares, be there just one dog or many, is that of leaving detailed and up-to-date instructions in our wills about what is to become of our animals in the event of our death. Far too many of us are apt to procrastinate and leave this matter unattended to, feeling that everything will work out all right or that "someone will see to them." The latter is not too likely to happen, at least not to the benefit of the dogs, unless the owner makes absolutely certain that all will be well for them in the future.

If you have not already done so, please get together with your lawyer and set up a clause in your will specifying what is to be done with each and every dog you own and to whom each will be entrusted (after first ascertaining that this person is willing and able to assume the responsibility); also include details about the location of all registration papers, pedigrees, and kennel records, along with ways of identifying each dog. Just think of the possibilities of what might happen otherwise!

It is not wise to count on family members, unless they share your involvement with the dogs. In many cases our relatives are not the least bit "dog-oriented," perhaps they think we're a trifle crazy for being such enthusiasts, and they might absolutely panic at the thought of suddenly having even *one* dog thrust upon them. They might mean well, and they might try; but it is unfair to them and to the dogs to leave the one stuck with the other!

If you travel a great deal with your dogs, another wise idea is to post prominently in your vehicle and carry in your wallet the name, address, and telephone number of someone to be called to take charge of them in case of an accident. Of course, this should be done by pre-arrangement with the person named. We have such a friend, and she has a signed check of ours to be used in case of an emergency or accident when we are travelling with our dogs; this check

Ch. Quell of Valrech, owned by Val Wells.

443

will be used to cover her expenses to come and take over the care of our dogs should anything happen to make it impossible for us to do so.

The registration certificates of all our dogs are enclosed in an envelope with our wills, and the person who will be in charge knows each of them, and one from the other, so there will be no identification problem. These are all points to be considered, for which provision should be made.

We also owe an obligation to our older dogs who too often are disregarded. It disgusts me that so many supposedly great dog lovers think nothing of getting an older dog, even though well, happy, and enjoying life, out of the way to make room for younger show prospects or additional puppies. The people I consider to be genuine dog lovers are the ones who permit their dogs to live out their lives in comfort as loved, respected members of the household or kennel.

Ch. Tannenwald's Igor, ROM, pictured with his friend and handler Ken Rayner, retiring from the ring at eleven years of age. Igor lived in the best of health to be fourteen years old. Bred by Gert Hoppe and Agnes Considine; owned by Malvern Considine.

Spenrock's Maximilian, by Grayarlin's Pierrot ex Halstor's Lola of Rock Maple, C.D., was bred by Jan Churchill and is owned by Betty Dumaine of Pinehurst, North Carolina, who is holding the lead. Photo courtesy of Janet Churchill.

How quickly some of us seem to forget the pleasures these dogs have brought us with exciting wins and the devotion they have shown to us and our families!

So much for our responsibility to our dogs, but we also owe a responsibility to our breed: to keep up its quality and to protect its image. Every Shepherd breeder should breed only from and for high-grade stock and should guard against the market being flooded with excess puppies. We should display good sportsmanship and concern for the dogs at all times, and we should involve ourselves whenever possible in activities beneficial to the breed.

To the general public we owe the consideration of good dog ownership. Our dogs should not be permitted to run at large and annoy others. Dogs should not be left barking endlessly, tied outside or closed in the house. We should pick up after our dogs, as required in most cities, when we exercise them where people must walk. We should, in other words, enjoy our dogs without allowing them to infringe on those who may be less enthusiastic.

Shepherds make willing bedfellows. Here is Spenrock Maximilian, relaxing with his owner, Betty Dumaine, who is ex-M.F.H. of the Island Hunt (Ireland) and the Groton Hunt. For her devoted loyalty to and work on behalf of Thailand, Miss Dumaine has been made a member of that country's royal family.

Travelling With Your Shepherd

When you travel with a dog, you must always remember that everyone does not necessarily share your love of dogs and that those who do not, strange creatures though they may seem, have their rights too. These rights, on which we should not encroach, include not being disturbed, annoyed, or made uncomfortable by the presence and behavior of other people's pets. Shepherd owners, since theirs is an intelligent and easily trained breed, should have the dog well schooled in proper canine behavior by the time maturity is reached. Your dog should not jump enthusiastically on strangers, no matter how playful or friendly the dog's intentions. We may love having them do this to us, but it is unlikely that someone else will share our enthusiasm, especially in the case of muddy paws on delicate or light-colored clothes which may be soiled or damaged. A sharp "Down" from you should be promptly obeyed, as should be "Sit," "Stay," and "Come."

If you expect to take your Shepherd on many trips, he should have, for your sake and for his, a crate of appropriate size for him to relax in comfortably. In cases of emergency or accident, a crated dog is far more likely to escape injury. Left in a parked car, a crated dog should have the car windows fully open in hot weather, thus being assured sufficient ventilation. For your own comfort, a dog in a crate does not hang from the car window, climb over you and your passengers, and shed hair on the upholstery. Dogs quickly become accustomed to their crates, especially when started with one, as they should be, from puppyhood. Both you and the dog will have a more enjoyable trip when you provide him with this safeguard.

If you do permit your dog to ride loose in the car, see to it that he does not hang from the windows. He could become overly excited by something he sees and jump out; he could lose his balance and fall out should you stop short or swerve unexpectedly; he could suffer an eye injury induced by the strong wind generated by the moving car. All of these unnecessary risks can so easily be avoided by crating!

Never, ever, under any circumstances, should a dog be permitted to ride uncrated in the back end of an open pick-up truck. I have noted, with disgust and horror, that some people do trans-

Ch. Harry Luftigen Hoe He, owned by Edward Legee and Alfred Espinosa, taking Best of Breed under judge Mrs. Eleanor Cole at Hartford in 1970. Gerlinde Hockla handling.

Hilgrove's Grimm, owned by Virginia Engstrom, winning in 1966 with Gerlinde Hockla handling.

port their dogs in this manner, and I think it cruel and shocking. How easily such a dog can be thrown out of the car by sudden jolts or an impact! And I am sure that many dogs have jumped out at the sight of something exciting along the way, quite possibly into the path of an oncoming car. Some unthinking individuals tie the dog, probably not realizing that if he were to jump under those circumstances, his neck could be broken, he could be dragged alongside the vehicle or get under its wheels, or he could be hit by another vehicle. If you are for any reason taking your dog *anywhere* in an open back truck, *please* have sufficient regard for that dog to provide a crate to protect him. Also please remember that with or without a crate, a dog riding exposed to the sun in hot weather can really suffer and have his life endangered by the heat.

If you are staying in a hotel or motel with your dog, please exercise him somewhere other than in the parking lot, along the walkways, or in the flower beds of the property. People walking to and from their rooms or cars really are not thrilled at "stepping in something" left by your dog and should not be subjected to the annoyance. Should an accident occur, pick it up with tissues or a paper towel and deposit it in a proper receptacle; don't just let it remain there. Usually there are grassy areas on the sides or behind motels where dogs can be exercised with no bother to anyone. Use those places rather than the busy, more conspicuous, carefully tended areas. If you are becoming a dog show enthusiast, you will eventually need an exercise pen to take with you to the show. They are ideal to use when staying at motels, too, as they permit you to limit the dog's roaming space and to pick up after him easily. Should you have two or more dogs, such a convenience is truly a "must!"

Never leave your dog unattended in a room at a motel unless you are absolutely, positively, sure that he will stay quiet and not destroy anything. You do not want a long list of complaints from irate fellow-guests, caused by the annoying barking or whining of a lonesome dog in strange surroundings or an overzealous watch dog barking furiously each time a footstep passes the door. And you certainly do not want to return to torn curtains or bedspreads, soiled rugs, or other embarrassing (and sometimes expensive) evidence of the fact that your dog is not really house-reliable.

If yours is a dog accustomed to travelling with you and you are positive that his behavior will be acceptable when left alone, that is fine. But if the slightest uncertainty exists, the wise course is to leave him in the car while you go to dinner or elsewhere and then bring him into the room when you are ready to retire for the night.

When you travel with a dog, it is sometimes simpler to take along his food and water from home rather than to buy food and to look for water while you travel. In this way he will have the rations to which he is accustomed and which you know agree with him, and there will be no problems due to different drinking water. Feeding on the road is quite easy now, at least for short trips, with all the splendid dry prepared foods and high quality canned meats available, not to mention the "just remove it from the packet" convenience foods. And many types of lightweight, refillable water containers can be bought at many types of stores.

Wendy of Clover Acres. Owned by Don Matz; handled by Ken Rayner.

If you are going to another country, you will need a health certificate from your veterinarian for each dog you are taking with you, certifying that each has had rabies shots within the required length of time preceding your visit.

Remember that during the summer, the sun's rays can make an inferno of a closed-up car in a matter of minutes, so always leave windows open enough that there is sufficient ventilation for the dog. Again, if your dog is in a crate, this can be done easily and with safety. Remember, too, that leaving the car in a shady spot does not mean that it will remain shaded. The position of the sun changes quickly, and the car you left nicely shaded half an hour earlier may be in the full glare of the sun upon your return. Be alert and be cautious.

When you travel with your dog, be sure to take a lead and use it, unless he is completely and thoroughly obedience trained. Even if the dog is trained, however, using a lead is a wise precaution against his getting lost in strange territory. I am sure that all of us have seen in the "Lost and Found" columns the sad little messages about dogs who have gotten away or been lost during a trip, so why take chances?

Pfeffer of Clover Acres at Sussex Hills in November 1972. Owned by D. Panison; handled by Ken Rayner.

A magnificent head-study of a superb German Shepherd of the 1960's, Ch. Bar vom Weiherturchen, ROM. Owned by Barbara and John Schermerhorn and handled by Denise Kodner. Photo courtesy of Mrs. Kodner.

CHAPTER EIGHTEEN

Veterinarian's Corner

by Joseph P. Sayres, D.V.M.

Ch. Proven Hill's Jason taking Best of Opposite Sex at the German Shepherd Dog Club of Northern Indiana Specialty Show. Judge, Dr. Walter Frost. Handler, Arnold "Sonny" Moreno. Owners, Judy and Ray Teidel, Jr.

Until recent years, there has been a lot of misunderstanding and even animosity between veterinarians and breeders. Some distrust arose on the breeder's part because most veterinarians were not familiar with, or even interested in learning about, purebred dogs. Some of the problems encountered were peculiar to certain breeds and some would crop up at inconvenient times. Veterinarians were then beset by breeders who thought that they knew more about the medical problems of their dogs than the vets did. The veterinarians very often were called only for emergencies or when it was too late to save a sick dog that had been treated too long by people in the kennel. Another problem was that many breeders had never included veterinary fees in their budgets and were slow to pay their bills, if indeed they paid them at all.

Fortunately, these problems, to a large extent, have been solved. Education and better communication between breeders and veterinarians have eliminated most areas of friction.

Today, veterinary education and training have advanced to a point paralleling that of human standards. This resulted from advances in the field of Veterinary Science in the last two decades. Sophisticated diagnostic procedures, new and advanced surgical techniques, and modern well-equipped hospitals all make for improved medical care for our dogs.

Educated breeders now realize that, while they may know more about the general husbandry of their dogs and the unique traits of the German Shepherd, they should not attempt to diagnose and treat their ailments.

In choosing your veterinarian, be selective. He or she should be friendly, should be interested in your dogs, and, in the case of breeders, should be interested in your breeding programs. Veterinarians should be willing to talk freely with you. Such things as fees, availability for emergencies, and what services are and are not available should be discussed and understood before a lasting relationship with your veterinarian can be established.

You can expect your veterinarian's office, clinic, or hospital to be clean, free of undesirable odors, well equipped, and staffed by sincere, friendly personnel who willingly serve you at all times. All employees should be clean, neat in appearance, and conversant with whatever services you require. You may also expect your dog to be treated carefully and kindly at all times by the doctor and his staff.

Your veterinarian should participate in continuing education programs in order to keep up with changes and improvements in his field. He should also be aware of his limitations. If he doesn't feel confident in doing certain procedures, he should say so and refer you to qualified individuals to take care of the problem. Seeking second opinions and consultation with specialists on difficult cases is more the rule than the exception nowadays. That is as it should be.

You will know that if your veterinarian is a member of the American Animal Hospital Association, he and his facility have had to measure up to high standards of quality and are subjected to inspections every two years.

Many excellent veterinarians and veterinary hospitals by choice do not belong to the American Animal Hospital Association. You can satisfy your curiosity about these places by taking guided tours of the facilities and learning by word of mouth about the quality of medicine practiced at these hospitals.

So far, we have discussed only what you should expect from your veterinarian. Now, let's discuss what the veterinarian expects from his clients.

Most of all, he expects his clients to be open and frank in their relations with him. He doesn't like to be double-checked and second-guessed behind his back. He also wants you to handle your pet so that he, in turn, can examine him. He also expects you to leash your dog, to control him, and to keep him from bothering other pets in the room. He expects to be paid a fair fee and to be paid promptly for services rendered. Fees in a given area tend to be consistent, and variations are due only to complications or unforeseen problems. Medicine is not an exact science; therefore, things unpredictable can happen.

Sarego's Usyles, by Ch. Tannenwald's Igor, pictured with Ken Rayner.

Champagne of Bow Creek, by Ch. Tannenwald's Igor, with Ken Rayner.

If you are dissatisfied with the services or fees, then ask to discuss these things in a friendly manner with the doctor. If his explanations are not satisfactory or he refuses to talk to you about the problem, then you are justified in seeking another doctor.

The veterinarian expects to provide his services for your animals during regular hours whenever possible. But he also realizes that in a kennel or breeding operation, emergencies can occur at any time, and his services will be needed at off hours. You should find out how these emergencies will be handled and be satisfied with the procedures.

No veterinarian can be on duty twenty-four hours of every day. Today, cooperative veterinarians group together to take turns covering each other's emergency calls. Some cities have emergency clinics that operate solely to take care of those catastrophes that seem usually to happen in the middle of the night or on weekends.

My conclusion, after thirty years of practice, is that most disagreements and hard feelings between clients and veterinarians are a result of a breakdown in communication. Find a veterinarian that you can talk to and can be comfortable with, and you'll make a valuable friend.

In using veterinary services to their best advantage, I believe that you will find that prevention of diseases and problems is more important than trying to cure these things after they occur. In other words, an ounce of prevention is worth a pound of cure.

Congenital Defects

German Shepherd Dogs have their share of congenital defects. From the publication *Congenital Defects in Dogs* published by Ralston Purina Company, as well as other reliable sources, the following conditions are listed as congenital defects in German Shepherd Dogs:

a. Cataracts, Bilateral—Opaque lenses.

b. Clefts of lip and palate.

c. Conjunctival Dermoid Cyst.

d. Cryptorchidism—Non-descent of testicles.

e. Cystinuria—Predisposition to bladder stones.

f. Ectasia Syndrome—Defective retinal development.

g. Elbow Dysplasia—Ununited anconeal process.

h. Enostosis—Eosinophilic panostitis; bone inflammation.

i. Epilepsy.

j. Esophageal Dilatation.

k. Eversion of third eyelid (nictitating membrane).

l. Hemophilia A—Factor VIII deficiency, prolonged bleeding episodes.

m. Hip Dysplasia—See section on this subject near the end of this chapter.

n. Lupus Erythematosis.

o. Osteochondrosis Dessicans—Defective bone development.

p. Pancreatic Insufficiency.

q. Persistent Right Aortic Arch—Aorta develops from right fourth aortic arch instead of left.

r. Pituitary Dwarfism.

s. Renal Cortical Hypoplasia—Bilateral underdevelopment of kidneys.

t. Subaortic Stenosis—Narrow aorta below its valve.

u. Von Willebrandt's Disease—Prolonged bleeding episodes.

Vaccines

By proper and vigilant vaccination programs, the following contagious diseases can be eliminated: distemper, hepatitis, parainfluenza, leptospirosis, rabies, and parvovirus enteritis.

The vaccination schedule described below should be set up and strictly followed to prevent infectious diseases.

Distemper: Vaccinate when six to eight weeks old, with the second inoculation to be given at twelve to sixteen weeks of age. Revaccinate annually.

Hepatitis (Adenovirus): Follow the same schedule as for distemper.

Parainfluenza (Kennel cough): Follow the same schedule as for distemper.

Leptospirosis: Give first vaccine at nine weeks of age. Revaccinate with second DHLP (distemper, hepatitis, leptospirosis, parainfluenza) at twelve to sixteen weeks of age. Revaccinate annually.

Rabies: Give first inoculation at three to four months of age; then revaccinate when one year old, and at least every three years thereafter. If dog is over four months old at the time of the first vaccination, then revaccinate in one year and then once every three years thereafter.

Parvovirus: Give first vaccine at seven to eight weeks of age, second vaccine four weeks later, and third vaccine four weeks later. Duration of immunity from three injections established at one year at the time of this writing. See explanation below. Revaccinate annually.

Vaccines used are all modified live virus vaccines except for leptospirosis, which is a killed bacterium. New and improved vaccines to immunize against parvovirus have appeared recently. The long-awaited modified live virus vaccine of canine origin was made available recently. It is safe and will produce immunity lasting one year.

Other communicable diseases for which no vaccine has been perfected as yet are: canine coronavirus, canine rotavirus, and canine brucellosis.

Infectious and Contagious Diseases

Distemper

Distemper is caused by a highly contagious, airborne virus. The symptoms are varied and may involve all of the dog's systems. A pneumonic form is common, with heavy eye and nose discharges, coughing, and lung congestion. The digestive system may be involved as evidenced by vomiting, diarrhea, and weight loss. The skin may show a pustular type rash on the abdomen. Nervous system involvement is common, with convulsions, chorea, and paralysis as persistent symptoms. This virus may have an affinity for nerve tissue and cause encephalitis and degeneration of the spinal cord. These changes, for the most part, are irreversible and death or severe crippling ensues.

We have no specific remedy or cure for distemper; and recoveries, when they occur, can only be attributed to the natural resistance of the patient, good nursing care, and control of secondary infections with antibiotics.

That's the bad news about distemper. The good news is that we rarely see a case of distemper in most areas today because of the efficiency of the vaccination program. This is proof that prevention by vaccination has been effective in almost eradicating this dreaded disease.

Hepatitis

Hepatitis is another contagious viral disease affecting the liver. This is not an airborne virus and can only be spread by contact. Although rarely seen today because of good prevention by vaccination programs, this virus is capable of producing a very acute, fulminating, severe infection and can cause death in a very short time. Symptoms of high temperature, lethargy, anorexia, and vomiting are the same as for other diseases. Careful evaluation by a veterinarian is necessary to confirm the diagnosis of this disease.

The old canine infectious hepatitis vaccine has been replaced by a canine adenovirus type 2 strain vaccine which is safer and superior. The new vaccine seems to be free of post-vaccination complications such as blue eyes, shedding of the virus in the urine, and some kidney problems.

Parainfluenza

This is commonly called kennel cough. It is caused by a throat-inhabiting virus that causes an inflammation of the trachea (windpipe) and larynx (voice box). Coughing is the main symptom and fortunately it rarely causes any other systemic problems. The virus is airborne and highly contagious, and it is the scourge of boarding kennels. A vaccine is available that will protect against this contagious respiratory disease and should be given as part of your vaccination program, along with the distemper, hepatitis, leptospirosis, and parvovirus shots. Pregnant bitches should not be vaccinated against parainfluenza because of the possibility of infecting the unborn puppies. As there may be more than one infectious agent involved in contagious upper respiratory diseases of dogs, vaccination against parainfluenza is not a complete guarantee to protect against all of them.

Leptospirosis

This is a disease that seriously affects the kidneys of dogs, most domestic animals, and man. For this reason, it can become a public health hazard. In urban and slum areas, the disease is carried by rats and mice in their urine. It is caused by a spirochete organism which is very resistant to treatment. Symptoms include fever, depression, dehydration, excess thirst, persistent vomiting, occasional diarrhea, and jaundice in the latter stages. Again, it is not always easy to diagnose so your veterinarian will have to do some laboratory work to confirm it.

We see very few cases of leptospirosis in dogs and then only in the unvaccinated ones. The vaccine is generally given concurrently with the distemper and hepatitis vaccinations. Preventive inoculations have resulted in the almost complete eradication of this dreaded disease.

Rabies

This is a well-known virus-caused disease that is almost always fatal and is transmissible to man and other warm-blooded animals. The virus causes very severe brain damage. Sources of the infection include foxes, skunks, and raccoons, as well as domesticated dogs and cats. Transmission is by introduction of the virus by saliva into bite wounds. Incubation in certain animals may be from three to eight weeks. In a dog, clinical signs will appear within five days. Symptoms fall into two categories, depending on what stage the disease is in when seen. We have the dumb form and the furious form. There is a change of personality in the furious form; individuals become hypersensitive and overreact to noise and stimuli. They will bite any object that moves. In dumb rabies, the typical picture of the loosely hanging jaw and tongue presents itself. Diagnosis is confirmed only by a laboratory finding the virus and characteristic lesions in the brain. All tissues and fluids from rabid animals should be considered infectious and you should be careful not to come in contact with them. Prevention by vaccination is a must because there is no treatment for rabid dogs.

Canine Parvovirus (CPV)

This is the newest and most highly publicized member of the intestinal virus family. Cat distemper virus is a member of the same family but differs from canine parvovirus biologically, and it has been impossible to produce this disease in dogs using cat virus as the inducing agent; and conversely canine parvovirus will not produce the disease in a cat. However, vaccines for both species will produce immunity in the dog. The origin of CPV is still unknown.

Canine parvovirus is very contagious and acts rapidly. The main source of infection is contaminated bowel movements. Direct contact between dogs is not necessary, and carriers such as people, fleas, and medical instruments may carry and transmit the virus.

The incubation period is five to fourteen days. The symptoms are fever, severe vomiting and diarrhea, often with blood, depression, and dehydration. Feces may appear yellowish gray streaked with blood. Young animals are more severely affected, and a shock-like death may occur in two days. In animals less than six weeks old, the virus will cause an inflammation of the heart muscle, causing heart failure and death. These pups may not have diarrhea. A reduction in the number of white blood cells is a common finding early in the disease.

The virus is passed in the feces for one to two weeks and may possibly be shed in the saliva and urine also. This virus has also been found in the coats of dogs. The mortality rate is unknown.

Dogs that recover from the disease develop an immunity to it. Again, the duration of this immunity is unknown.

Control measures include disinfection of the kennels, animals, and equipment with a 1 to 30 dilution of Clorox and isolation of sick individuals.

Treatment is very similar to that for coronavirus, namely: intravenous fluid therapy, administration of broad spectrum antibiotics, intestinal protectants, and good nursing care.

Transmission to humans has not been proven.

Clinical studies have proven that vaccination with three injections of the new modified live virus vaccine of canine origin, with four weeks between injections, will be over ninety percent effective. Recent work at the James A. Baker Institute for Animal Health at Cornell University has shown that maternally derived antibodies can interfere with the immunizing properties of our vaccines for as long as fifteen to sixteen weeks. This means that some of our puppies, especially those from dams with good immunity, will not become susceptible to successful vaccination until they are sixteen weeks old. It is

Gloria Taylor's Ch. Hilgrove's Iris, Best of Breed at Eastern Dog Club, handled by Gerlinde Hockla.

also known that the maternal protection afforded these puppies, while enough to prevent successful vaccination, may not be enough to protect them from an exposure to the virus. The best advice is to give our puppies three inoculations of a canine origin modified live virus vaccine four weeks apart, starting when they are eight weeks old. Then, hope for the best and revaccinate annually.

Canine Coronavirus (CCV)

This is a highly contagious virus that spreads rapidly to susceptible dogs. The source of infection is through infectious bowel movements. The incubation period is one to four days, and the virus will be found in feces for as long as two weeks. It is hard to tell the difference sometimes between cases of diarrhea caused by coronavirus and parvovirus. Coronavirus generally is less severe or causes a more chronic or sporadic type of diarrhea. The fecal material may be orange in color and have a very bad odor; occasionally, it will also contain blood. Vomiting sometimes precedes the diarrhea, but loss of appetite and listlessness are consistent signs of the disease. Fever may or may not be present. Recovery is the rule after eight to ten days, but treatment with fluids, antibiotics, intestinal protectants, and good nursing care are necessary in the more severe watery diarrhea cases. Dogs that survive these infections become immune but for an unknown length of time.

To control an outbreak of this virus in a kennel, very stringent hygienic measures must be taken. Proper and quick disposal of feces, isolation of affected animals, and disinfection with a 1 to 30 dilution of Clorox are all effective means of controlling an outbreak in the kennel.

There is no vaccine yet available for prevention of canine coronavirus. Human infections by this virus have not been reported.

Canine Rotavirus (CRV)

This virus has been demonstrated in dogs with a mild diarrhea but again with more severe cases in very young puppies. Very little is known about this virus.

A milder type of diarrhea is present for eight to ten days. The puppies do not run a temperature and continue to eat. Dogs usually recover naturally from this infection. There is no vaccine available for this virus.

Canine Brucellosis

This is a disease of dogs that causes both abortions and sterility. It is caused by a small bacterium closely related to the agent that causes undulant fever in man and abortion in cows. It occurs worldwide.

Symptoms of brucellosis sometimes are difficult to determine, and some individuals with the disease may appear healthy. Vague symptoms such as lethargy, swollen glands, poor hair coat, and stiffness in the back legs may be present. This organism does not cause death and may stay in the dog's system for months and even years. The latter animals, of course, have breeding problems and infect other dogs.

Poor results in your breeding program may be the only indication that brucellosis is in your kennel. Apparently, normal bitches abort without warning. This usually occurs forty-five to fifty-five days after mating. Successive litters will also be aborted. In males, signs of the disease are inflammation of the skin of the scrotum, shrunken testicles, and swollen tender testicles. Fertility declines and chronically infected males become sterile.

The disease is transmitted to both sexes at the time of mating.

Other sources of infection are aborted puppies and birth membrane and discharge from the womb at the time of abortions.

Humans can be infected, but such infections are rare and mild. Unlike in the dog, the disease in humans responds readily to antibiotics.

Diagnosis is done by blood testing, which should be done carefully. None of the present tests are infallible and false positives may occur. The only certain way that canine brucellosis can be diagnosed is by isolating the *B. canis* organism from blood or aborted material and for this, special techniques are required.

Treatment of infected individuals has proven ineffective in most cases. Sterility in males is permanent. Spaying or castrating infected pets should be considered as this will halt the spread of the disease and is an alternative to euthanasia.

At present, there is no vaccine against this important disease.

Our best hope in dealing with canine brucellosis is prevention. The following suggestions are made in order to prevent the occurrence of this malady in your dogs.

Am. and Can. Ch. Covy's Babar of Tucker Hill, a 1981 champion by Covy-Tucker Hill's Zinfandel, ROM (Ch. Lakeside's Harrigan, ROM, ex seven times Select Ch. Tucker Hill's Angelique, C.D., ROM) ex Ch. Covy's Felita of Tucker Hill, ROM (Ch. Lakeside's Gilligan's Island, ROM, ex Ch. Kovaya's Contessa, C.D., ROM). Owned by Freeman and Theresa Spencer of Richmond, Virginia, and Gloria F. Birch and Cappy Pottle who bred him. Handled by Ken Rayner.

a. Test breeding stock annually and by all means breed only uninfected animals.

b. Test bitches several weeks before their heat periods.

c. Do not bring any new dogs into your kennel unless they have had two negative tests taken a month apart.

d. If a bitch aborts, isolate her, wear gloves when handling soiled bedding, and disinfect the premises with Roccal.

e. If a male loses interest in breeding or fails to produce after several matings, have him checked.

f. Consult your veterinarian for further information about this disease; alert other breeders and support the research that is going on at the James A. Baker Institute for Animal Health at Cornell University.

External Parasites

The control and eradication of external parasites depends on the repeated use of good quality insecticide sprays or powders during the warm months. Make a routine practice of using these products at seven-day intervals throughout the season. It is also imperative that sleeping quarters and wherever the animal habitates be treated also.

Fleas

These are brown, wingless insects with laterally compressed bodies and strong legs, and they are bloodsuckers. Their life cycle comprises eighteen to twenty-one days from egg to adult flea. They can live without food for one year in high humidity but die in a few days in low humidity. They multiply rapidly and are more prevalent in the warm months. They can cause a severe skin inflammation in those individuals that are allergic or sensitive to the flea bite or saliva of the flea. They can act as a vector for many diseases and do carry tapeworms. Control measures must include persistent, continual use of flea collars or flea medallions, or sprays or powders. The dog's bedding and premises must also be treated because the eggs are there. Foggers, vacuuming, or professional exterminators may have to be used. All dogs and cats in the same household must be treated at the same time.

Ticks

There are hard and soft species of ticks. Both species are bloodsuckers and at times cause severe skin inflammations on their host. They act as a vector for Rocky Mountain Spotted Fever, as well as other diseases. Hibernation through an entire winter is not uncommon. The female tick lays as many as one thousand to five thousand eggs in crevices and cracks in walls. These eggs will hatch in about three weeks and then a month later become adult ticks. Ticks generally locate around the host's neck and ears and between the toes. They can cause anemia and serious blood loss if allowed to grow and multiply. It is not a good idea to pick ticks off the dogs because of the danger of a reaction in the skin. Just apply the tick spray directly on the ticks which then die and fall off eventually. Heavily affected dogs should be dipped every two weeks in an anti-parasitic bath. The premises, kennels, and yards should be treated every two weeks during the summer months, being sure to apply the insecticide to walls and in all cracks and crevices. Frequent or daily grooming is effective in finding and removing ticks.

Lice

There are two kinds of lice, namely the sucking louse and the biting louse. They spend their entire life on their host but can be spread by direct contact or through contaminated combs and brushes. Their life cycle is twenty-one days, and their eggs, known as nits, attach to the hairs of the dog. The neck and shoulder region, as well as the ear flaps, are the most common areas to be inhabited by these pesky parasites. They cause itchiness, some blood loss, and inflammation of the skin. Eradication will result from dipping or dusting with methyl carbonate or Thuron once a week for three to four weeks. It is a good idea to fine-comb the dogs after each dip to remove the dead lice and nits. Ask your veterinarian to provide the insecticides and advice or control measures for all of these external parasites.

Mites

Less commonly occurring parasitic diseases such as demodectic and sarcoptic mange, caused by mites, should be diagnosed and treated only by your veterinarian. You are wise to consult your doctor whenever any unusual condition oc-

Ch. Grandee of Dornwald with Gerlinde Hockla in June 1971.

curs and persists in your dog's coat and skin. These conditions are difficult to diagnose and treat at best, so that the earlier a diagnosis is obtained, the better the chances are for successful treatment. Other skin conditions such as ringworm, flea bite allergy, bacterial infections, eczemas, and hormonal problems, among others, all have to be considered.

Internal Parasites

The eradication and control of internal parasites in dogs will occupy a good deal of your time and energy.

Puppies should be tested for worms at four weeks of age and then six weeks later. It is also wise to test them again six weeks following their last worm treatment to be sure the treatments have been successful. Annual fecal tests are advisable throughout your dog's life. All worming procedures should be done carefully and only with the advice and supervision of your veterinarian. The medicants used to kill the parasites are, to a certain extent, toxic, so they should be used with care.

Ascarids

These include roundworms, puppy worms, stomach worms, and milk worms. Puppies become infested shortly after birth and occasionally even before birth. Ascarids can be difficult to eradicate. When passed in the stool or thrown up, they look somewhat like cooked spaghetti when fresh or like rubber bands when they are dried up. Two treatments at least two weeks apart will eliminate ascarids from most puppies. An occasional individual may need more wormings according to the status in its system of the life cycle of the worm at the time of worming. Good sanitary conditions must prevail and immediate disposal of feces is necessary to keep down the worm population.

Hookworms

Hookworms are bloodsuckers and also cause bleeding from the site of their attachment to the lining of the intestine when they move from one site to another. They can cause a blood-loss type of anemia and serious consequences, particularly in young puppies. Their life cycle is direct and their eggs may be ingested or pass through the skin of its host. Treatment of yards and runs where the dogs defecate with 5% sodium borate solution is said to kill the eggs in the soil. Two or three worm treatments three to four weeks apart may be necessary to get rid of hookworms. New injectable products administered by your veterinarian have proven more effective than remedies used in the past. Repeated fecal examinations may be necessary to detect the eggs in the feces. These eggs pass out of the body only sporadically or in showers, so that it is easy to miss finding them unless repeated stool testing is done. As is true with any parasite, good sanitary conditions in the kennel and outside runs will help eradicate this worm.

Whipworms

These are a prevalent parasite in some kennels and in some individual dogs. They cause an intermittent mucousy type diarrhea. As they live only in the dog's appendix, it is extremely difficult to reach them with any worm medicine given by mouth. Injections seem to be the most effective treatment, and these have to be repeated several times over a long period of time to be effective. Here again, repeated fresh stool samples must be examined by your veterinarian to be sure that this pest has been eradicated. Appendectomies are indicated in only the most severe chronic cases. The fact that cleanliness is next to Godliness cannot be emphasized too often; it is most important in getting rid of this parasite.

Tapeworms

They are another common internal parasite of dogs. They differ in the mode of their transmission as they have an indirect life cycle. This means that part of their cycle must be spent in an intermediate host. Fleas, fish, rabbits, and field mice all may act as an intermediate host for the tapeworm. Fleas are the most common source of tapeworms in dogs, although dogs that live near water and may eat raw fish and hunting dogs that eat the entrails of rabbits may get them from those sources. Another distinguishing feature of the tapeworm is the suction apparatus which is the part of the head which enables the tapeworm to attach itself to the lining of the intestine. If, after worming, just the head remains, it has the capability of regenerating into another worm. This is one reason why tapeworms are so difficult to get rid of. It will require several treatments to get the entire parasite out of a dog's system. These worms are easily recognized by the appearance of their segments which break off and appear on top of a dog's feces or stuck to the hair around the rectal area. These segments may appear alive and mobile at times, but most often they are dead and dried up when found. They look like flat pieces of rice and may be white or brown when detected. Elimination of the intermediate host is an integral part of any plan to rid our dogs of this worm. Repeated wormings may be necessary to kill all the adult tapeworms in the intestine.

Heartworms

Heartworm disease is caused by an actual worm that goes through its life cycle in the blood stream of its victims. It ultimately makes its home in the right chambers of the heart and in the large vessels that transport the blood to the lungs. They vary in size from 2.3 inches to 16 inches. Adult worms can survive up to five years in the heart.

By its nature, this is a very serious disease and can cause irreversible damage to the lungs and heart of its host. Heart defect and lung pathology soon result in serious problems for the dog.

The disease is transmitted and carried by female mosquitoes that have infected themselves after biting an infected dog; they then pass it on to the next dog with which they come in contact.

The disease has been reported wherever mosquitoes are found, and cases have been reported in most of the United States. Rare cases have been reported in man and cats. It is most prevalent in warmer climates where the mosquito population is the greatest, but hotbeds of infection exist in the more temperate parts of the United States and Canada also.

Concerted effort and vigorous measures must be taken to control and prevent this serious threat to our dog population. The most effective means of eradication I believe will come through annual blood testing for early detection, by the use of preventive medicine during mosquito exposure times, and also by ridding our dogs' environment of mosquitoes.

Annual blood testing is necessary to detect cases that haven't started to show symptoms yet and thus can be treated effectively. It also enables your veterinarian to prescribe safely the preventive medicine to those individuals that test negative. There is a ten to fifteen percent margin of error in the test, which may lead to some false negative tests. Individuals that test negative but are showing classical symptoms of

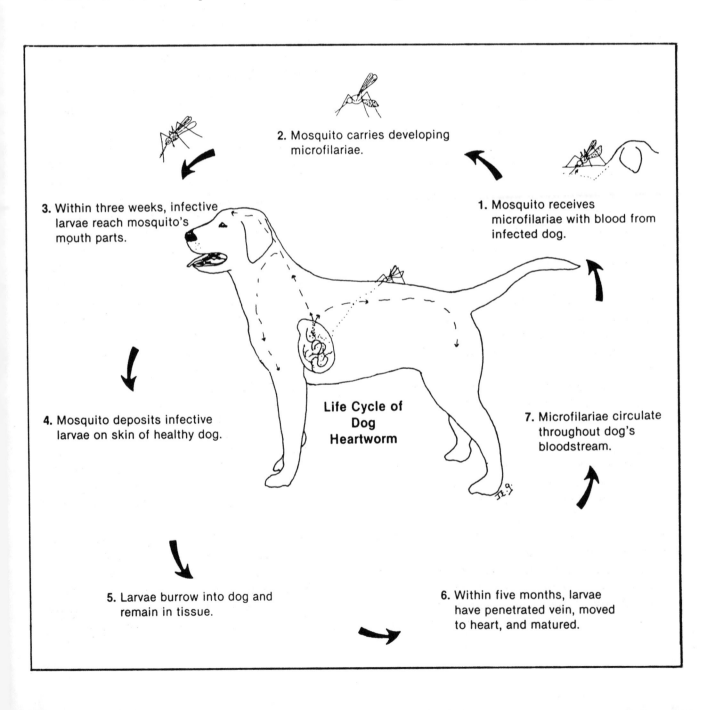

2. Mosquito carries developing microfilariae.

3. Within three weeks, infective larvae reach mosquito's mouth parts.

1. Mosquito receives microfilariae with blood from infected dog.

4. Mosquito deposits infective larvae on skin of healthy dog.

Life Cycle of Dog Heartworm

7. Microfilariae circulate throughout dog's bloodstream.

5. Larvae burrow into dog and remain in tissue.

6. Within five months, larvae have penetrated vein, moved to heart, and matured.

the disease such as loss of stamina, coughing, loss of weight, and heart disease should be further evaluated with chest X-rays, blood tests, and electrocardiograms.

Serious consequences may result when the preventive medication is given to a dog that already has heartworm in his system. That is why it is so important to have your dog tested annually before starting the preventive medicine.

In order to be most effective, the preventive drug diethylcarbamazine should be given in daily doses of 2.5 mg. to 3 mg. per pound of body weight or 5 mg. per kilogram of body weight of your dog. This routine should be started fifteen days prior to exposure to mosquitoes and be continued until sixty days after exposure. Common and trade names for this drug are Caricide, Styrid-Caricide, and D.E.C. It comes in liquid and tablet forms.

This drug has come under criticism by some breeders and individuals who claim that it affects fertility and causes some serious reactions. Controlled studies have shown no evidence that the drug produces sterility or abnormal sperm count or quality. Long-term studies on reproduction, when the drug was given at the rate of 4.9 mg. per pound of body weight (two times the preventive dose level) for two years, showed no signs of toxic effects on body weight maintenance, growth rate of pups, feed consumption, conception rate, numbers of healthy pups whelped, ratio of male to female pups, blood counts, and liver function tests. It is reported to be a well-tolerated medication, and many thousands of dogs have benefitted from its use. From personal experience, I find only an occasional dog who will vomit the medicine or get an upset stomach from it. The new enteric coated pills have eliminated this small problem.

However, if you still don't want to give the preventive, especially to your breeding stock, an alternative procedure would be to test your dogs every six months for early detection of the disease, so that it can be treated as soon as possible.

Heartworm infestation can be treated successfully. There is a one to five percent mortality rate from the treatment. It can be expected that treatment may be completed without side effects if the disease hasn't already caused irreversible problems in the heart, lungs, liver, kidneys, or

Ch. Breauhausens Appeal, or "Carla," pictured with her handler, Ken Rayner.

other organs. Careful testing, monitoring, and supervision is essential to success in treatment. Treatment is far from hopeless these days and if the disease is detected early enough, a successful outcome is more the rule than the exception.

In conclusion, remember that one case of heartworm disease in your area is one too many, especially if that one case is your dog. By following the steps mentioned here, we can go a long way in ridding ourselves of this serious threat to our dogs.

Home Remedies and First Aid

You have repeatedly read here of my instructions to call your veterinarian when your animals are sick. This is the best advice I can give you. There are a few home remedies, however, that may get you over some rough spots while trying to get professional help.

I think it is a good idea to keep on hand some medical supplies in a first aid kit. The kit should contain the following items: a roll of cotton, gauze bandages, hydrogen peroxide, tincture of metaphen, cotton applicator swabs, BFI powder, rectal thermometer, adhesive tape, boric acid crystals, tweezers, and a jar of petroleum jelly.

A word here on how to take a dog's temperature may be in order. Always lubricate the thermometer with petroleum jelly and carefully insert it well into the rectum. Hold it in place for two to three minutes and then read it. The thermometer should be held firmly so that it doesn't get sucked up into the rectum.

To administer liquid medicines to dogs, simply pull the lips away from the side of the mouth, making a pocket for depositing the liquid. Slightly tilt the dog's head upward and he will be able to swallow the liquid properly. Giving liquids by opening the mouth and pouring them directly on the tongue is an invitation to disaster because inhalation pneumonia can result. Putting it in the side of the mouth gives the dog time to hold it in his mouth and then swallow it properly.

Tablets are best administered by forcing the dog's mouth open, and pushing the pill down over the middle of the tongue into the back of his mouth. If put in the right place, a reflex tongue reaction will force the pill down the throat and thus be swallowed. There is no objection to giving the pills in favorite foods as long as you carefully determine that the medicine is surely swallowed with the food.

Vomiting

To stop vomiting, mix one tablespoon of table salt to one pint of water and dissolve the salt thoroughly; then give one tablespoonful of the mixture to the patient. After waiting one hour, repeat the procedure and skip the next meal. The dog may vomit a little after the first dose, but the second dose works to settle the stomach. This mixture not only provides chlorides but also acts as a mild astringent and many times in mild digestive upsets will work to stop the vomiting.

Diarrhea

In the case of adult Shepherds, give three or four tablespoons of Kaopectate or Milk of Bismuth every four hours. Use one-fourth of this dosage for puppies. Skip the next meal, and if diarrhea persists, then start a bland diet of boiled ground lean beef and boiled rice in the proportions of half and half. Three or four doses of this medicine should suffice. If the diarrhea persists and, particularly, if accompanied by depression, lethargy, and loss of appetite, your veterinarian should be consulted immediately. With all these new viral-caused diarrheas floating around, time is of the essence in securing treatment.

Mild Stimulant

Dilute brandy half and half with water, add a little sugar, and give a tablespoonful of the mixture every four to five hours. For puppies over three months old, reduce the dosage to a teaspoonful of the mixture every four to five hours.

Mild Sedative

Dilute brandy half and half with water, add a little sugar, and give a tablespoon of the mixture every twenty to thirty minutes until the desired effect is attained. For puppies over three months old, reduce the dosage to a teaspoonful of the mixture every twenty to thirty minutes.

Using brandy for both sedation and stimulation is possible by varying the time interval between doses. Given every four to five hours, it's a stimulant; but given every twenty to thirty minutes it acts as a sedative.

Minor Cuts and Wounds

Cleanse them first with soap and water, preferably Tincture of Green Soap. Apply a mild antiseptic such as Bactine or Tincture of Metaphen two or three times daily until healed. If the cut is deep, and fairly long and bleeding, then a bandage should be applied until professional help can be obtained.

Whenever attempting to bandage wounds, first apply a layer or two of gauze over the cleaned and treated wound. Then apply a layer of cotton and then another layer or two of gauze. The bandage must be snug enough to stay on but not so tight as

Ch. Exxon von Brone in 1976, winning a Best of Breed with Ken Rayner handling.

to impair the circulation to the body part. Adhesive tape should be applied over the second layer of gauze to keep the bandage as clean and dry as possible until you can get your dog to the doctor.

Tourniquets should be applied only in cases of profusely bleeding wounds. They are applied tightly between the wound and the heart, in addition to the pressure bandage that should be applied directly to the wound. The tourniquet must be released and reapplied at fifteen-minute intervals.

Burns

Application of ice or very cold water and compresses is the way to treat a skin burn. Apply cold packs as soon as possible and take the dog immediately to your vet.

Frostbite

Frostbite is a rarely occurring problem. The secret in treating this condition is to restore normal body temperature gradually to the affected parts. In other words, use cold water, then tepid water, to thaw out the area slowly and restore circulation. In cases of severe freezing or shock due to bitter cold temperature, take the animal to the veterinarian as soon as possible.

Abscesses and Infected Cysts

Obvious abscesses and infected cysts that occur between the toes may be encouraged to drain by using hot boric acid packs and saturated dressings every few hours until professional aid can be secured. The boric acid solution is made by dissolving one tablespoon of crystals to one pint of hot water. Apply frequently to the swollen area. Further treatment by a veterinarian may involve lancing and thoroughly draining and cleaning out the abscess cavity. As most abscesses are badly infected, systemic antibiotics are generally indicated.

Heatstroke or Heat Exhaustion

A word about the serious effects of heat on a dog is timely. It never ceases to amaze me how many people at dog shows have to be warned and advised not to leave their dogs in cars or vans on a warm day.

A dog's heat-regulating mechanism is not nearly as efficient as ours. Consequently, dogs feel the heat more that we do. Keep them as cool and as well ventilated as possible in hot weather. Another inducement for shock is taking your dog out of a cool air-conditioned vehicle and exposing him immediately to the hot outdoors. Make that change as gradual as you can because a rapid change can cause a shock-like reaction.

In cases of suspected heatstroke, which manifests itself with very high body temperatures (as high as 106° to 108°F. sometimes), severe panting, weakness, shaking, and collapse, act quickly to get him into a cold bath or shower or put ice-cold compresses on his head. Then, again without delay, rush him to the nearest veterinarian for further treatment. Prevention is the key here and with a little common sense, heatstroke and exhaustion can be avoided.

Poisons

Many dogs are poisoned annually by unscrupulous people who hate dogs. Many others are victims of poisoning due simply to the careless use of rat and ant poisons, insecticides, herbicides, anti-freeze solutions, drugs, and so forth. Dogs also frequently eat poisonous plants, either in the house or outdoors, which can lead to serious consequences. Common sources of these toxic products are named below.

Plants that can be a source of poison for dogs include the following (this list contains only the most common ones): daffodils, oleanders, poinsettias, mistletoe, philodendron, delphiniums, monkshood, foxglove, iris, lilies of the valley, rhubarb, spinach, tomato vines, sunburned potatoes, rhododendron, cherry, peach, oak, elderberry, black locust, jack-in-the-pulpit, Dutchman's-breeches, water hemlock, mushrooms, buttercups, poison hemlock, nightshade, jimson weed, marijuana, locoweed, and lupine.

Poisonous animals include such snakes as vipers, rattlesnakes, copperheads, water moccasins, and the coral snake. Lizards like the Gila monster and Mexican beaded lizard are bad. Some toads, spiders, insects, and fish also are potential sources of trouble.

Chemicals comprise perhaps the largest and most common source of poisoning in our environment. These are hazards that our dogs may be exposed to every day. Careful handling and awareness of these products are essential.

Toxic materials are found in arts and crafts supplies, photographic supplies, and automotive and machinery products and include such things as antifreeze and de-icers, rust inhibitors, brake fluids, engine and carburetor cleaners, lubricants, gasoline, kerosene, radiator cleaners, and windshield washers. Cleaners, bleaches and polishes, disinfectants, and sanitizers all contain products that potentially are dangerous.

Even health and beauty aids may contain toxic materials if ingested in large enough quantities: some bath oils, perfumes, corn removers, deodorants, anti-perspirants, athlete's foot remedies, eye makeup, hair dyes and preparations, diet pills, headache remedies, laxatives, liniments, fingernail polish removers, sleeping pills, suntan lotions, amphetamines, shaving lotions, colognes, shampoos, and certain ointments.

Paints and related products also can be dangerous. Caulking compounds, driers, thinners, paints, paint brush cleaners, paint and varnish removers, preservatives, and floor and wood cleaners all fit into the category.

Pest poisons for the control of birds, fungi, rats, mice, ants, and snails all can be toxic and sometimes fatal to dogs.

Miscellaneous items like fire extinguishers and non-skid products for slippery floors can be unsafe. Almost all solvents like carbon tetrachloride, benzene, toluene, acetone, mineral spirits, kerosene, and turpentine are bad.

The previous paragraphs serve only to illustrate how many products in our everyday environment exist which can be hazardous or fatal to our dogs.

In cases of suspected poisoning, be aware of what to do until professional help can be obtained:

a. Keep the animal protected, quiet, and warm.

b. If a contact is on the skin, eye, or body surface, cleanse and flush the area with copious amounts of water. Do this also if the dog gets something in his eye. Protect him from further exposure.

c. Inducing vomiting may be dangerous and should be done only on the advice of a veterinarian. Giving peroxide may induce vomiting in some cases. It is better to allow the animal to drink as much water as he wants. This will dilute the poison. Giving milk or raw egg whites is helpful many times to delay absorption of the toxic products.

Do not attempt to give anything by mouth if the patient is convulsing, depressed, or unconscious.

Do not waste time getting veterinary service. Take any vomited material and suspected causative agents, and their containers with you to the vet. When the suspected product is known, valuable time can be saved in administering specific treatment.

A word to the wise should be sufficient. Keep away from your dog all products that can harm him in any way.

Bloat

One of the most serious and difficult problems and real emergency situations that can occur is that of bloat. Other names for this condition are torsion and acute indigestion. This condition generally occurs in larger breeds after the consumption of a large meal (usually dry feed) and then the drinking of a lot of water immediately after eating. If this is followed by a vigorous exercise period, the stage is set for bloat. The stomach, being pendulous and overloaded at this point, can become twisted or rotated. This, of course, cuts off the circulation to the stomach and spleen and may also interfere with the large blood vessels coming to and from the liver. A shock-like syndrome follows and death may ensue shortly if heroic measures are not undertaken to save the stricken animal. If ever there was an emergency, this is truly one. Dry heaves, painful loud crying, and abdominal enlargement, take place in a very short time. Relief of the torsion requires immediate surgery to right the stomach to its normal position and to keep it there. Circulation may then return to normal.

In cases of acute indigestion without torsion, the distress and bloat may be relieved by passing a stomach tube to allow the gas to escape. At the risk of being redundant, it must be said that this condition is very acute and requires immediate and heroic action to save the victim.

Preventive measures for bloat include dividing the normal diet of these dogs into three or four meals a day. Water should not be given for one hour before and one hour after each meal, and no exercise is advisable for an hour or two after eating.

With breeders and veterinarians becoming more aware of the bloat syndrome, I feel that more of these cases will be saved than were in the past.

Whelping

We cannot leave the subject of emergencies without considering the subject of whelping. Most bitches whelp without any problems. It is wise, however, to watch them closely during this time. I feel that no bitch should go more than two hours in actual labor without producing a puppy. This includes the time before the first one as well as between puppies. If more than two hours elapse, then the dam should be examined by a veterinarian. It will then be determined if she is indeed in trouble or is just a slow whelper. This rule of thumb gives us time to find out if there is a problem, what it may be, and have time to save both dam and puppies in most cases.

It is good practice to have your bitches examined for pregnancy three and a half to four weeks after mating, as well as at term around the fifty-eighth to fifty-ninth day. These procedures will enable the veterinarian to discover any troubles that may occur during pregnancy, as well as alert him as to when the whelping is going to take place. Knowing this, he can plan to provide service, if needed during off hours.

Bitches that are difficult to breed, miss pregnancies, or have irregular reproductive cycles should have physical exams including laboratory tests to determine the cause of the trouble. These tests may be expensive, but a lot of breeding and sterility problems due to sub-par physical condition, hormonal imbalances, or hypo-thyroidism can be corrected. If a valuable bitch is restored to her normal reproductive capacity, the reward more than offsets the medical costs.

Another important thing to remember about whelping and raising puppies is to keep them warm enough. This means a room temperature

Still another Best in Show for the consistent winner Ch. Beech Hills Benji von Masco, this one at Laurel Highlands in April 1982 judged by Dr. Gerda Kennedy. Ken Rayner handling for Mary Ellen Thomas.

Chantilli of Bow Creek, by Ch. Tannenwald's Igor, with Ken Rayner.

of 80° to 85°F. for the first ten days to two weeks until the puppies are able to generate their own body heat. Be sure the dam keeps them close; leave a light burning at night for the first week so she won't lose track of any of them or accidentally lie on one of them. Chilling remains the biggest cause of death of newborn puppies. Other causes are malnutrition, toxic milk, hemorrhage, and viral and bacterial infections. Blood type incompatibilities have been understood lately as causes of trouble.

Consultation with your veterinarian concerning these and any other breeding problems you've had in the past may result in the solution of these problems. This may result in larger litters with a higher survival rate.

Care of the Older Dog

Providing medical services from cradle to grave is the slogan of many veterinarians, and rightly so. The average life expectancy for our dogs these days is about thirteen years. Sad to say, this is a short time compared to our life span. Larger breeds historically do not live as long as the medium-sized or smaller breeds. However, I think that with proper care your Shepherds should be expected to reach this expectancy.

Probably the most common ailments in older dogs are arthritis, kidney disease, heart prob-

lems, and cataracts; hip dysplasia may also become evident as the dog ages.

Arthritis

When your pet has trouble getting up in the morning, jumping up, or going upstairs, you can bet that some form of a joint problem is starting. Giving two enteric coated aspirin tablets three times a day for five days very often will help these individuals. This dosage is for adult dogs. It is relatively free of side effects and as long as nothing else is wrong, your dog will get a bit of relief.

Kidney Disease

Signs of kidney weakness are excessive drinking, inability to hold urine through the night, loss of weight, lack of appetite, and more than occasional bouts of vomiting and diarrhea. If any of these signs present themselves, it would be worthwhile to have a checkup. Very often corrective measures in diet and administering some medicine will prolong your dog's life.

Heart Problems

Some form and degree of heart problems exist in a lot of older animals. Symptoms of chronic congestive heart failure consist of a chronic cough, especially after exercise, lack of stamina, lethargy, abdominal enlargement, and labored breathing at times. If diagnosed and treated early in the disease, many heart patients live to a ripe old age.

Cataracts

Cataracts form in the lenses of most, if not all, old dogs. They are a part of the normal aging process. Total blindness from cataracts generally does not result for a long time. Distant and peripheral vision remain satisfactory for the expected life span of the dog. Rarely is total blindness produced by these aging cataracts before the dog's life expectancy is reached. There is no effective treatment for cataracts other than their surgical removal which is not recommended in the older patient that has any vision at all left.

Hip Dysplasia

It is becoming more evident that most of the arthritis in older dogs in large breeds is the result of problems in bone growth and development when the individual was very young. Problems such as panosteitis, hip dysplasia, elbow dysplasia, and osteochondrosis dessicans all are often precursors of arthritis. In Shepherds, according to information from the Orthopedic Foundation for Animals, circa 1974, hip dysplasia is found in 25.1% of the cases presented to them.

At any rate, hip dysplasia seems to be a developmental condition and not a congenital anomaly. It is thought to be an inherited defect, with many genes being responsible for its development. Environmental factors also enter into the severity of the pathology in the hip joints. Nutrition during the growth period has been an important factor. Overfeeding and over-supplementation of diets have caused an abnormal growth rate with overweight puppies. These individuals, if they were susceptible to hip dysplasia in the first place, show more severe lesions of hip dysplasia. Restricted feeding of growing dogs is necessary for normal bone growth and development.

Signs of hip dysplasia vary from one dog to another, but some of the more common ones are difficulty in getting up after lying for awhile, rabbit-like gait with both rear legs moving forward at the same time when running, lethargy, and walking with a swaying gait in the rear legs. In many cases, a period of pain and discomfort at nine months to one year of age will resolve itself; and even though the dysplasia is still there, most of the symptoms may disappear.

It is recommended that dysplastic individuals not be bred, that they not be allowed to become overweight, and that they have moderate exercise.

The selection of dysplastic-free individuals for breeding stock eventually will result in the production of sounder hip joints in affected breeds. This factor, of course, is only one consideration in the breeding and production of an overall better German Shepherd.

Canine Nutrition

After mentioning the problem of overfeeding and oversupplementation of puppies' diets with vitamins and minerals in the discussion of hip dysplasia, a few words about canine nutrition are in order.

It is generally agreed that great strides have been made in canine nutrition in the past few years and that most of our well-known commercial dog foods provide all the essential ingredients of a well-balanced diet for our dogs. Prob-ably the greatest problem is providing good quality protein in proper proportions. It behooves us to read dog food labels and to know what we are feeding and how much is necessary to provide the requirements for a lean healthy individual. The tendencies in our society today are to overfeed and under exercise both our dogs and ourselves.

We must know the energy content or caloric value of the foods we are feeding. Then we must determine the energy requirements of our dogs. These will vary with time and circumstances. Your adult Shepherd requires about twenty-five calories per pound of body weight daily for maintenance.

Generally speaking for the average adult German Shepherd house dog, a diet consisting of 16% high quality protein, 10% fat, and 44% carbohydrates is a good mix. For the working dogs, dogs being shown, or pregnant bitches, increase the protein and fat percentages by about 25% and decrease the carbohydrate proportion by 25%. To meet the needs of the increased stress of growth in young puppies and nursing bitches, the protein and fat components should be increased yet another 10 to 15% and the percentage of carbohydrates should be decreased by the same amount. Any stress situation means a rise in caloric requirement. For example, in the case of pregnancy, it is advisable to increase the amount of food intake by 20% after four weeks of gestation and by 75% after six weeks of gestation, and so forth.

We are assuming that the vitamins and minerals in the foods used are complete and balanced.

You may have to combine, mix, and juggle various types and brands of food to attain the desired diet, but don't despair; it can be done. Prescription and special diet foods are available through your veterinarian. These probably cost more initially but may pay off in the long run.

As to exactly how much to feed each individual dog, no one can give you a magic formula that works in all cases. My best advice is to use common sense and a scale. The guidelines on dog food containers have a tendency to be over-inflated. It is better to err on the low side than to overfeed. Remember, keep your dog slim and fit with a proper diet and plenty of exercise. That's not a bad idea for your own well-being also.

Glossary

To the uninitiated, it must seem that fanciers of purebred dogs speak a special language all their own, which in a way we do. The following is a list of terms, abbreviations, and titles which you will run across through our pages which may be unfamiliar to you. We hope that this list will lead to fuller understanding and that it will additionally assist you as you meet and converse with others of similar interests in the world of purebred dogs.

A.K.C. The commonly used abbreviation of American Kennel Club.

Albino. A deficiency of pigmentation causing the nose leather, eyerims, and lips to be pink.

Almond eye. The shape of the tissue surrounding the eye, which creates the almond-shaped appearance required by some breed standards.

American Kennel Club. The official registry for purebred dogs in the United States. Publishes and maintains the Stud Book and handles all litter and individual registrations, transfers of ownership, and so on. Keeps all United States dog show, field trial, and obedience trial records; issues championships and other titles in these areas as they are earned; approves and licenses dog show, obedience trial, and field trial judges; licenses or issues approval to all championship shows, obedience trials, and recognized match shows. Creates and enforces the rules, regulations, and policies by which the breeding, raising, exhibiting, handling, and judging of purebred dogs in the United States are governed. Clubs, not individuals, are members of the American Kennel Club, each of which is represented by a delegate selected from the club's own membership for the purpose of attending the quarterly American Kennel Club meetings as the representative of the member club, to vote on matters discussed at each meeting and to bring back a report to the individual club of any decisions or developments which took place there.

Angulation. The angles formed by the meeting of the bones, generally referring to the shoulder and upper arm in the forequarters and the stifle and hock in the hindquarters.

Apple head. An exaggerated roundness of the top-skull.

Apron. Frill, or longer hair, below the neck.

Bad bite. Can refer to a wryness or malformation of the jaw, or to incorrect dentition.

Bad mouth. One in which the teeth do not meet correctly according to the specifications of the breed standard.

Balance. Symmetry and proportion. A well-balanced dog is one in which all of the parts appear in correct ratio to one another: height to length, head to body, skull to foreface, and neck to head and body.

Beefy. Overmusculation or overdevelopment of the shoulders or hindquarters or both.

Benched Show. Dog show at which the dogs are kept on benches while not being shown in competition.

Best in Show. The dog or bitch chosen as the most representative of any dog in any breed from among the group winners at an all-breed dog show. (The dog or bitch that has won Best of Breed next competes in the group of which its breed is a part. Then the first-prize winner of each group meets in an additional competition from which one is selected the Best in Show.)

Best of Breed. The dog that is adjudged best of any competing in its breed at a dog show.

Best of Opposite Sex. The dog or bitch that is selected as the best of the opposite sex to the Best of Breed when the latter award has been made.

Best of Winners. The dog or bitch selected as the better of the two between Winners Dog and Winners Bitch.

Bitch. A female dog.

Bite. The manner in which the upper and lower jaws meet.

Bloom. The sheen of a coat in healthy, lustrous condition.

Blue-ribbon winner. A dog that has won

first prize in the class for which it is entered at a dog show.

Bone. Refers to the girth of a dog's leg bones. A dog called "good in bone" has legs that are correct in girth for its breed and for its own general conformation. Well-rounded bone is round in appearance, flat bone rather flattish. Light bone is very fine and small in diameter, almost spindle-like in appearance; legs are extremely slender. Heavy bone refers to legs that are thick and sturdy.

Brace. Two dogs, or a dog and a bitch, closely similar in size, markings, color, and general appearance, moving together in unison.

Breed. Purebred dogs descended from mutual ancestors refined and developed by man.

Breeder. A person who breeds dogs.

Breeding particulars. Name of the sire and dam, date of breeding, date of birth, number of puppies in the litter, their sex, and name of the breeder and of the owner of the sire.

Brisket. The forepart of the body between the forelegs and beneath the chest.

Brood bitch. A female dog used primarily for breeding.

CACIB. A Challenge Certificate offered by the Federation Cynologique Internationale towards a dog's championship.

Canines. Dogs, jackals, wolves, and foxes as a group.

Canine teeth. The four sharp pointed teeth at the front of the jaws, two upper and two lower, flanking the incisors; often referred to as fangs.

Carpals. Pastern joint bones.

Castrate. To neuter a dog by removal of the testicles.

Cat foot. The short-toed, round tight foot similar to that of a cat.

C.D. An abbreviation of Companion Dog.

C.D.X. An abbreviation of Companion Dog Excellent.

Ch. Commonly used abbreviation of champion.

Challenge certificate. A card awarded at dog shows in Great Britain by which championship there is gained. Comparable to our Winners Dog and Winners Bitch awards. To become a British champion a dog must win three of these Challenge Certificates at designated championship dog shows.

Champion. A dog or bitch that has won a total of fifteen points, including two majors, the total number under not less than three judges, two of which must have awarded the majors at A.K.C. point shows.

Character. Appearance, behavior, and temperament considered correct in an individual breed of dog.

Cheeky. Cheeks which bulge out or are rounded in appearance.

Chest. The part of the body enclosed by the ribs.

Chiseled. Clean-cut below the eyes.

Choke collar. A chain or leather collar that gives maximum control over the dog. Tightened or relaxed by the pressure on the lead caused by either pulling of the dog or tautness with which it is held by the handler.

Chops. Pendulous, loose skin creating jowls.

Cloddy. Thickset or overly heavy or low in build.

Close-coupled. Compact in appearance. Short in the loin.

Coarse. Lacking in refinement or elegance.

Coat. The hair which covers the dog.

Companion Dog. The first obedience degree obtainable.

Companion Dog Excellent. The second obedience degree obtainable.

Condition. General health. A dog said to be in good condition is one carrying exactly the right amount of weight, whose coat looks alive and glossy, and that exhibits a general appearance and demeanor of well-being.

Conformation. The framework of the dog, its form and structure.

Coupling. The section of the body known as the loin. A short-coupled dog is one in which the loin is short.

Cow-hocked. Hocks turned inward at the joint, causing the hock joints to approach one another with the result that the feet toe outward instead of straight ahead.

Crabbing. A dog moving with its body at an angle rather than coming straight at you; otherwise referred to as side-wheeling or side-winding.

Crest. The arched portion of the back of the neck.

Crop. Cut the ear leather, usually to cause the ear to stand erect.

Crossing action. A fault in the forequarters caused by loose or poorly knit shoulders.

Croup. The portion of the back directly above the hind legs.

Cryptorchid. An adult dog with testicles not normally descended. A dog with this condition cannot be shown and is subject to disqualification by the judge.

Cynology. A study of canines.

Dam. Female parent of a dog or bitch.

Dentition. Arrangement of the teeth.

Dewclaws. Extra claws on the inside of the legs. Should generally be removed several days following the puppy's birth. Required in some breeds, unimportant in others, and sometimes a disqualification—all according to the individual breed standard.

Dewlap. Excess loose and pendulous skin at the throat.

Diagonals. The right front and left rear leg make up the right diagonal; the left front and right rear leg the left diagonal. The diagonals correctly move in unison as the dog trots.

Dish-faced. The tip of the nose is placed higher than the stop.

Disqualification. A fault or condition which renders a dog ineligible to compete in organized shows, designated by the breed standard or by the American Kennel Club. Judges must withhold all awards at dog shows from dogs having disqualifying faults, noting in the Judges Book the reason for having done so. The owner may appeal this decision, but a disqualified dog cannot again be shown until it has officially been examined and reinstated by the American Kennel Club.

Distemper teeth. Discolored, badly stained, or pitted teeth. A condition so-called due to its early association with dogs having suffered from this disease.

Divergent hocks. Hock joints turn outward, creating the condition directly opposite to cow-hocks. Frequently referred to as bandy legs or barrel hocks.

Dock. Shorten the tail by cutting it.

Dog. A male of the species. Also used to describe collectively male and female canines.

Dog show. A competition in which dogs have been entered for the purpose of evaluation and to receive the opinion of a judge.

Dog show, all-breeds. A dog show in which classification may be provided, and usually is, for every breed of dog recognized by the American Kennel Club.

Dog show, specialty. A dog show featuring only one breed. Specialty shows are generally considered to be the showcases of a breed, and to win at one is a particularly valued honor and achievement, owing to the high type of competition usually encountered at these events.

Domed. A top-skull that is rounded rather than flat.

Double coat. A coat consisting of a hard, weather-resistant, protective outer covering over soft, short, close underlayer which provides warmth.

Down-faced. A downward inclination of the muzzle toward the tip of the nose.

Down in pastern. A softness or weakness of the pastern causing a pronounced deviation from the vertical.

Drag. A trail having been prepared by dragging a bag, generally bearing the strong scent of an animal, along the ground.

Drive. The powerful action of the hindquarters which should equal the degree of reach of the forequarters.

Drop ear. Ears carried drooping or folded forward.

Dry head. One exhibiting no excess wrinkle.

Dry neck. A clean, firm neckline free of throatiness or excess skin.

Dual champion. A dog having gained both bench show and field trial championships.

Dudley nose. Flesh-colored nose.

Elbow. The joint of the forearm and upper arm.

Elbow, out at. Elbow pointing away from the body rather than being held close.

Even bite. Exact meeting of the front teeth, tip to tip with no overlap of the uppers or lowers. Generally considered to be less serviceable than the scissors bite, although equally permissible or preferred in some breeds.

Ewe neck. An unattractive, concave curvature of the top area of the neckline.

Expression. The typical expression of the breed as one studies the head. Determined largely by the shape of the eye and its placement.

Eyeteeth. The upper canine teeth.

Faking. The altering of the natural appearance of a dog. A highly frowned upon and unethical practice which must lead, upon recognition by the judge, to instant dismissal from the show ring with a notation in the Judges Book stating the reason.

Fancier. A person actively involved in the sport of purebred dogs.

Fancy. The enthusiasts of a sport or hobby. Dog breeders, exhibitors, judges, and others actively involved with purebred dogs as a group comprise the dog fancy.

Fangs. The canine teeth.

F.C.I. Abbreviation of the Federation Cynologique Internationale.

Feathering. The longer fringes of hair that appear on the ears, tail, chest, and legs.

Federation Cynologique Internationale. A canine authority representing numerous countries, principally European, all of which consent to and agree on certain practices and breed identification.

Feet east and west. An expression used to describe toes on the forefeet turning outward rather than directly forward.

Fetch. Retrieving of game by a dog, or the command for the dog to do so.

Fiddle front. Caused by elbows protruding from the desired closeness to the body, with the result that the pasterns approach one another too closely and the feet toe outward. Thus, resembling the shape of a violin.

Field champion. A dog that has gained the title field champion has defeated a specified number of dogs in specified competition at a series of American Kennel Club licensed or member field trials.

Field trial. A competition for specified Hound or Sporting breeds where dogs are judged according to their ability and style on following a game trail or on finding and retrieving game.

Finishing a dog. Refers to completing a dog's championship, obedience title, or field trial title.

Flank. The side of the body through the loin area.

Flat bone. Bones of the leg which are not round.

Flat-sided. Ribs that are flat down the side rather than slightly rounded.

Fld. Ch. Abbreviation of field champion, used as a prefix before the dog's name.

Flews. A pendulous condition of the inner corners of the mouth.

Flyer. An especially exciting or promising young dog.

Flying ears. Ears correctly carried dropped or folded that stand up or tend to "fly" upon occasion.

Flying trot. The speed at which you should *never* move your dog in the show ring. All four feet actually briefly leave the ground during each half stride, making correct evaluation of the dog's normal gait virtually impossible.

Forearm. The front leg from elbow to pastern.

Foreface. The muzzle of the dog.

Front. The forepart of the body viewed head-on. Includes the head, forelegs, shoulders, chest, and feet.

Futurity Stakes. A competition at shows or field trials for dogs who are less than twelve months of age for which puppies are nominated, at or prior to birth. Highly competitive among breeders, usually with a fairly good purse for the winners.

Gait. The manner in which a dog walks or trots.

Gallop. The fastest gait. Never to be used in the show ring.

Game. The animals or wild birds which are hunted.

Gay tail. Tail carried high.

Get. Puppies.

Goose rump. Too sloping (steep) in croup.

Groom. To bathe, brush, comb, and trim your dog.

Groups. Refers to the variety groups in which all breeds of dogs are divided.

Gun dog. One that has been specifically trained to work with man in the field for retrieving game that has been shot and for locating live game.

Guns. The persons who do the shooting during field trials.

Gun-shy. Describes a dog that cringes or shows other signs of fear at the sound or sight of a gun.

Hackney action. High lifting of the forefeet in the manner of a hackney pony.

Ham. Muscular development of the upper

hind leg. Also used to describe a dog that loves applause while being shown, really going all out when it occurs.

Handler. A person who shows dogs in competition, either as an amateur (without pay) or as a professional (receiving a fee in payment for the service).

Hard-mouthed. A dog that grasps the game too firmly in retrieving, causing bites and tooth marks.

Hare foot. An elongated paw, like the foot of a hare.

Haw. A third eyelid or excess membrane at the corner of the eye.

Heat. The period during which a bitch can be bred. Also referred to as being "in season."

Heel. A command ordering the dog to follow close to the handler.

Hindquarters. Rear assemblage of the dog.

Hock. The joint between the second thigh and the metatarsus.

Hocks well let down. Expression denoting that the hock joint should be placed quite low to the ground.

Honorable scars. Those incurred as a result of working injuries.

In season. *See* **Heat.**

Incisors. The front teeth between the canines.

Int. Ch. An abbreviation of international champion.

International champion. A dog awarded four CACIB cards at F.C.I. dog shows.

Jowls. Flesh of lips and jaws.

Judge. Person making the decisions at a dog show, obedience trial, or field trial. Judges residing in the United States must be approved and licensed by the A.K.C. in order to officiate at events where points toward championship titles are awarded; residents of another country whose governing body is recognized by the A.K.C. may be granted special permits to officiate in the United States.

Kennel. The building in which dogs are housed. Also used when referring to a person's collective dogs.

Knee joint. Stifle joint.

Knitting and purling. Crossing and throwing of forefeet as dog moves.

Knuckling over. A double-jointed wrist, or pastern, sometimes accompanied by enlarged bone development in the area, causing the joints to double over under the dog's weight.

Layback. 1) Describes correctly angulated shoulders. 2) Describes a short-faced dog whose pushed-in nose placement is accompanied by undershot jaw.

Leather. The ear flap. Also the skin of the actual nose.

Level bite. Another way of describing an even bite, as teeth of both jaws meet exactly.

Level gait. A dog moving smoothly, topline carried level as he does so, is said to be moving in this manner.

Lippy. Lips that are pendulous or do not fit tightly.

Loaded shoulders. Those overburdened with excessive muscular development.

Loin. Area of the sides between the lower ribs and hindquarters.

Lumber. Superfluous flesh.

Lumbering. A clumsy, awkward gait.

Major. A win of either Winners Dog or Winners Bitch carrying with it three, four, or five points toward championship.

Mane. The long hair growing on the top and upper sides of the neck.

Match show. An informal dog show where no championship points are awarded and entries can usually be made upon arrival, although some require pre-entry. Excellent practice area for future show dogs and for novice exhibitors as the entire atmosphere is relaxed and congenial.

Mate. To breed a dog and a bitch to one another. Littermates are dogs which are born in the same litter.

Maturity Stakes. For members of the breed who the previous year had been entered in the Futurity Stakes.

Milk teeth. The first baby teeth.

Miscellaneous class. A class provided at A.K.C. point shows in which specified breeds may compete in the absence of their own breed classification. Dogs of breeds in the process of becoming recognized by A.K.C. may compete in this class prior to the eventual provision of their own individual breed classification.

Molars. Four premolars are located at either side of the upper and lower jaws. Two molars exist on either side of the upper jaw, three on either side below. Lower molars have two roots; upper molars have three roots.

Monorchid. A dog with only one properly descended testicle. This condition disqualifies from competition at A.K.C. dog shows.

Muzzle. 1) The part of the head in front of the eyes. 2) To fasten something over the mouth, usually to prevent biting.

Nick. A successful breeding that results in puppies of excellent quality.

Nose. Describes the dog's organ of smell, but also refers to his talent at scenting. A dog with a "good nose" is one adept at picking up and following a scent trail.

Obedience trial. A licensed obedience trial is one held under A.K.C. rules at which it is possible to gain a "leg" towards a dog's obedience title or titles.

Obedience trial champion. Denotes that a dog has attained obedience trial championship under A.K.C. regulations by having gained a specified number of points and first place awards.

Oblique shoulders. Shoulders angulated so as to be well laid back.

Occiput. Upper back point of skull.

Occipital protuberance. A prominent occiput noted in some of the Sporting breeds.

O.F.A. Commonly used abbreviation for Orthopedic Foundation for Animals.

Orthopedic Foundation for Animals. This organization is ready to read the hip radiographs of dogs and certify the existence of or freedom from hip dysplasia. Board-certified radiologists read vast numbers of these files each year.

O.T. Ch. An abbreviation of obedience trial champion.

Out at elbow. Elbows are held away from the body rather than in close.

Out at shoulder. Shoulder blades set in such a manner that joints are too wide and jut out from body.

Oval chest. Deep with only moderate width.

Overshot. Upper incisors overlap the lower incisors.

Pacing. A gait in which both right legs and both left legs move concurrently, causing a rolling action.

Paddling. Faulty gait in which the front legs swing forward in a stiff upward motion.

Pad. Thick protective covering of the bottom of the foot. Serves as a shock absorber.

Paper foot. Thin pads accompanying a flat foot.

Pastern. The area of the foreleg between the wrist and the foot.

Pedigree. Written record of dog's lineage.

Pigeon chest. A protruding, short breastbone.

Pigeon-toed. Toes point inward, as those of a pigeon.

Pile. Soft hair making a dense undercoat.

Plume. A long fringe of hair on the tail.

Poach. To trespass on private property when hunting.

Pointed. A dog that has won points toward its championship is referred to as "pointed."

Police dog. Any dog that has been trained to do police work.

Put down. To groom and otherwise prepare a dog for the show ring.

Quality. Excellence of type and conformation.

Racy. Lightly built, appearing overly long in leg and lacking substance.

Rangy. Excessive length of body combined with shallowness through the ribs and chest.

Reach. The distance to which the forelegs reach out in gaiting, which should correspond with the strength and drive of the hindquarters.

Register. To record your dog with the American Kennel Club.

Registration Certificate. The paper you receive denoting that your dog's registration has been recorded with the A.K.C., giving the breed, assigned names, names of sire and dam, date of birth, breeder and owner, along with the assigned Stud Book number of the dog.

Reserve Winners Bitch or **Reserve Winners Dog.** After the judging of Winners Bitch and Winners Dog, the remaining first prize dogs (bitches or dogs) remain in the ring where they are joined by the bitch or dog that placed second in the class to the one awarded Winners Bitch or Winners Dog, provided she or he was defeated only by that one bitch or dog. From these a Reserve Winner is selected. Should the Winners Bitch or Winners Dog subsequently be disallowed due to any error or technicality, the Reserve Winner is then moved up automatically to Winners in the A.K.C. records, and the points awarded to the Winners Bitch or Winners Dog then transfer to the one which placed Reserve. This is a safeguard award, for although it seldom happens, should the winner of the championship points be found to have been ineligible to receive them, the Reserve dog keeps the Winners' points.

Roach back. A convex curvature of the topline of the dog.

Rocking horse. An expression used to describe a dog that has been overly extended in forequarters and hindquarters by the handler, *i.e.*, forefeet placed too far forward, hind feet pulled overly far behind, making the dog resemble a child's rocking horse. To be avoided in presenting your dog for judging.

Rolling gait. An aimless, ambling type of action correct in some breeds but to be faulted in others.

Saddle back. Of excessive length with a dip behind the withers.

Scissors bite. The outer tips of the lower incisors touch the inner tips of the upper incisors. Generally considered to be the most serviceable type of jaw formation.

Second thigh. The area of the hindquarters between the hock and the stifle.

Septum. The vertical line between the nostrils.

Set up. To pose your dog in position for examination by the judge. Same as "stack."

Shelly. A body lacking in substance.

Shoulder height. The height of the dog from the ground to the highest point of the withers.

Sire. The male parent.

Skully. An expression used to describe a coarse or overly massive skull.

Slab sides. Flat sides with little spring of rib.

Soundness. Mental and physical stability. Sometimes used as well to denote the manner in which the dog gaits.

Spay. To neuter a bitch by surgery. Once this operation has been performed, the bitch is no longer eligible for entry in regular classes or in Veterans Class at A.K.C. shows.

Special. A dog or bitch entered only for Best of Breed competition at a dog show.

Specialty club. An organization devoted to sponsoring an individual breed of dog.

Specialty dog show. *See* **Dog show, specialty.**

Stack. *See* **Set up.**

Stake. A class in field trial competition.

Stance. The natural position a dog assumes in standing.

Standard. The official description of the ideal specimen of a breed. The Standard of Perfection is drawn up by the parent specialty club, usually by a special committee to whom the task is assigned, approved by the membership and by the American Kennel Club, and then serves as a guide to breeders and to judges in decisions regarding the merit, or lack of it, in evaluating individual dogs.

Stifle. The joint of the hind leg corresponding to a person's knee.

Stilted. The somewhat choppy gait of a dog lacking correct angulation.

Stop. The step-up from nose to skull; the indentation at the juncture of the skull and foreface.

Straight behind. Lacking angulation in the hindquarters.

Straight-shouldered. Lacking angulation of the shoulder blades.

Stud. A male dog that is used for breeding.

Stud book. The official record kept on the breeding particulars of recognized breeds of dogs.

Substance. Degree of bone size.

Swayback. Weakness, or downward curvature, in the topline between the withers and the hipbones.

Sweepstakes. Competition at shows for young dogs, usually up to twelve or eighteen months of age; unlike Futurity, no advance nomination is required.

Tailset. Manner in which the tail is placed on the rump.

T.D. An abbreviation of Tracking Dog.

T.D.X. An abbreviation of Tracking Dog Excellent.

Team. Generally consists of four dogs.

Thigh. Hindquarters from the stifle to the hip.

Throatiness. Excessive loose skin at the throat.

Topline. The dog's back from withers to tailset.

Tracking Dog. A title awarded dogs who have fulfilled the A.K.C. requirements at licensed or member club tracking tests.

Tracking Dog Excellent. An advanced tracking degree.

Trail. Hunt by following a trail scent.

Trot. The gait at which the dog moves in a rhythmic two-beat action, right front and left hind foot and left front and right hind foot each striking the ground together.

Tuck-up. A natural shallowness of the body at the loin creating a small-waisted appearance.

Type. The combination of features which makes a breed unique, distinguishing it from all others.

U.D. An abbreviation of Utility Dog.

U.D.T. An abbreviation of Utility Dog Tracker

Unbenched show. Dog show at which dogs must arrive in time for judging and may leave anytime thereafter.

U.D.T.X. An abbreviation of Utility Dog and Tracker Excellent.

Undershot. The front teeth of the lower jaw reach beyond the front teeth of the upper jaw.

Upper arm. The foreleg between the forearm and the shoulder blade.

Utility Dog. Another level of obedience degree.

Utility Dog and Tracker. A double title indicating a dog that has gained both utility and tracking degrees. Also known as Utility Dog Tracking.

Utility Dog and Tracker Excellent. A double title indicating a dog that has gained both utility and advanced tracking degrees.

Walk. The gait in which three feet support the body, each lifting in regular sequence one at a time off the ground.

Walleye. A blue eye, fish eye, or pearl eye caused by a whitish appearance of the iris.

W.C. An abbreviation of Working Certificate.

Weedy. Lacking in sufficient bone and substance.

Well let down. Short hocks, hock joint placed low to the ground.

Wet neck. Dewlap, or superfluous skin.

Wheel back. Roached back with topline considerably arched over the loin.

Winners Bitch or Winners Dog. The awards which are accompanied by championship points, based on the number of dogs defeated, at A.K.C. member or licensed dog shows.

Withers. The highest point of the shoulders, right behind the neck.

Working Certificate. An award earned by dogs who have proven their hunting ability and are not gun-shy.

Wry mouth. Lower jaw is twisted and does not correctly align with the upper jaw.

Index

This index is composed of three separate parts: a general index, an index of kennels, and an index of names of people.

Kennels

(Page references in **bold** face indicate location of kennel story.)

People